Foundation of Supply Management

JOSEPH R. CARTER, DBA, C.P.M.
THOMAS Y. CHOI, PH.D.

This publication is designed to provide accurate and authoritative information in regard to the subject matter covered. It is sold with the understanding that the publisher is not engaged in rendering legal, accounting or other professional service. If legal advice or other expert assistance is required, the services of a competent professional person should be sought.

Published by: Institute for Supply Management, Inc.™
Paul Novak, C.P.M., A.P.P., Chief Executive Officer

©2008 Institute for Supply Management, Inc.
P.O. Box 22160, Tempe, AZ 85285 USA
www.ism.ws

ISBN: 978-0-9815770-2-9

Introduction

Institute for Supply Management™ became the name for our association on January 1, 2001. The name was changed in recognition of the shifting role that you play in your profession. That role is not just about purchasing any more and has not been for many years.

The knowledge required to be a successful supply management professional has broadened more quickly than any of us might have predicted. Many factors caused this change, but none were more important than your willingness and ability to take on an expanded role.

ISM's new qualification, which will be launched in 2008, recognizes the expanded body of knowledge that you are expected to master. The Certified Professional in Supply Management (CPSM) is a qualification through which you demonstrate your mastery of the body of knowledge and commitment to the profession.

This three-book series represents a compendium of the broad knowledge of our profession. While these books don't represent all there is to know about our profession, they serve to open the door to the complete body of knowledge.

ISM is committed to the development and communication of this body of knowledge. These books, along with the resources that membership in ISM offers, will help you expand your knowledge and skills throughout your career.

Paul Novak, C.P.M., A.P.P.
CEO
Institute for Supply Management™

ISM — Your Source for Supply Management Resources

Institute for Supply Management, Inc.™ (ISM) has served the supply management profession since 1915. As the first and largest supply management institute in the world, ISM works with affiliated associations to continually keep its members well informed and trained on the latest trends and developments in the field. ISM's membership base includes more than 40,000 individual supply management professionals. A not-for-profit institute, ISM provides opportunities for the promotion of the profession and the expansion of professional skills and knowledge.

The information available from ISM is extensive. One of the greatest resources is the ISM Web site, www.ism.ws. In addition to general information, this expansive site features a vast database of supply management information, including a list of general supply management references as well as an extensive article database, listings of available products and seminars, periodicals, contact information for ISM affiliate organizations worldwide and links to other related Web sites. The *members only* online Career Center is a valuable resource for both individuals seeking jobs and organizations recruiting prospective employees.

The monthly Manufacturing and Non-Manufacturing *Report On Business*®, including the PMI for the manufacturing survey and the NMI for the non-manufacturing survey, continues to be one of the key economic indicators available today. ISM members receive this valuable report in the pages of *Inside Supply Management*® magazine. *Inside Supply Management*®, a monthly magazine (available to members only), is the authoritative resource for supply management executives, focusing on leadership strategies and trends.

The A.T. Kearney Center for Strategic Supply Leadership at ISM (CSSL) is an exclusive organization where today's and tomorrow's forward-thinking senior supply executives convene for thought leadership and a view into solutions and opportunities for the next two to four years.

Founded in 2004, the Center emerged because of a gap identified by today's senior leaders. The Center is committed to exploring the future two-year to four-year supply management horizon and translating it into robust, strategic development programs designed for executives.

The Center serves as a catalyst for new thought in the field of supply management. It is dedicated to closing the gap between the growing expectations of CEOs and the results delivered by their organizations' supply partners.

ISM also publishes the *Journal of Supply Chain Management,* a one-of-a-kind publication for supply management scholars. Authored exclusively by highly recognized scholars in supply-chain management, this quarterly subscription publication offers up-to-date research and thought-provoking studies.

Members also enjoy discounts on a wide variety of educational products and services, along with reduced enrollment fees for educational seminars and conferences.

For supply management professionals interested in a professional qualification, ISM administers the Certified Professional in Supply Management (CPSM) program. ISM members receive discounts on test preparation materials, study books and materials and examination fees.

To provide a forum for educational enhancement and networking, ISM sponsors the Annual International Supply Management Conference. The annual conference, which attracts more than 2,000 participants worldwide, provides a unique opportunity for members and nonmembers alike to learn from each other and share success strategies.

To learn more about ISM and the many ways it can help you advance your career or to join online, visit ISM at www.ism.ws. To apply for membership by telephone, call ISM customer service at 800/888-6276 (United States and Canada only) or +1 480/752-6276, extension 401.

Foundation of Supply Management

Joseph R. Carter, DBA, C.P.M.

Thomas Y. Choi, Ph.D.

Effective Supply Management Performance

Darin L. Matthews, CPPO, C.P.M.

Linda L. Stanley, Ph.D.

Leadership in Supply Management

Anna E. Flynn, Ph.D.

Series Overview

In recent years, the supply management profession has begun to mature. No longer looked at as just "purchasing" or "procurement," supply management is viewed today as an integrative process that spans many disciplines and activities, providing both internal and external linkages across the supply chain. Today, ISM defines supply management as:

> *The identification, acquisition, access, positioning and management of resources and related capabilities that an organization needs or potentially needs in the attainment of its strategic objectives.*
>
> *Supply management includes the following components: disposition/ investment recovery, distribution, inventory control, logistics, manufacturing supervision, materials management, packaging, product/service development, strategic sourcing, procurement/purchasing, quality, receiving, transportation/traffic/shipping and warehousing.*

This definition cuts across industry sectors, global economies, private and public organizations and types of purchases. It covers both the day-to-day issues faced by supply management professionals and the strategic issues that shape supply management's structure and its influence in the organization.

In keeping with the spirit of the new, broader definition of supply management, Institute for Supply Management™ has broadened the scope of its new qualification to fit the latest demands on supply management professionals. This three-book series was designed to specifically address the issues of concern to supply management professionals today. These books help professionals better understand the potential scope and concerns within supply management. These books also are designed to support the new Certified Professional in Supply Management (CPSM) examination and professional credentials.

The three books are organized around the three examinations of the CPSM as follows:

1. *Foundation of Supply Management*

2. *Effective Supply Management Performance*

3. *Leadership in Supply Management*

These three books all support the strategic supply management process across various industries, cultures and types of purchases. The strategic supply management process is illustrated in the following Figure I-1:

Figure I-1   Strategic Supply Management Process

On the far left of the figure is the vertical box, "Supply Management Strategy and Philosophy." This is the way that supply management is viewed by the organization and the way that supply management views itself. It embodies the culture of the supply management organization as it works to support the objectives of the larger organization.

At the top of the figure, the small vertical box "Overarching Concerns" deals with five major issues that supply management professionals face today: Risk Management, Social Responsibility, Strategic Outsourcing, Globalization Issues and Supplier Relationship Management. Supply management professionals must consider all five major issues in their strategic decision-making. While supplier relationship management has long been recognized as important by most progressive organizations, the other four issues have taken on a new importance in recent years. Because of their overarching nature, these issues are touched on in each of the three books in a variety of ways. More specifically, supply management professionals must ask the following questions:

1. What risks might we face and how can we plan for these risks?

2. How does the decision we are making fit with the organization's social responsibility objectives?

3. Is outsourcing an option for this particular decision? How would this affect the answers to these other questions?

4. Are there global solutions available, and how does the source of supply fit with the market in which we are selling? This may be particularly relevant for purchased services.

5. What type of relationship do we want to have with our supplier(s) for this item and why?

Within supply management, some basic "Process Steps" must occur, as illustrated in the middle of the figure. Virtually all organizations have a model for the execution of the supply management process that includes all these activities, although they may be divided into a different number of steps. The process begins with a thorough analysis of internal and external data to better understand the threats and opportunities in the internal and external environment. Next, specific strategies are developed for the particular purchase category and tactics for developing those strategies are identified. Closely related to this, the organization engages in a cost analysis of the item, looking for ways to better manage and reduce costs. It then narrows down the choice of suppliers through data analysis and bidding, negotiates and develops the contract. Finally, ongoing supplier measurement and management occurs, and may include supplier development efforts to improve supplier performance.

To support these activities, a supply management professional must work closely with other supply management professionals responsible for operations and logistics, as well as have an excellent system in place for managing and developing the organization's most valuable resource, its people. These are the "Supporting Structures" for supply management.

Volume 1, *Foundation of Supply Management,* deals with several of the more traditional areas of concern for supply management, yet looks at these issues from a leading-edge perspective. This volume covers data analysis, budgeting, cost management, including cost-price analysis and total cost of ownership analysis, and leasing arrangements. This book also provides an in-depth view of sourcing, negotiating and contracting with suppliers. Taken as a whole, these chapters provide an excellent perspective on the process steps associated with strategic sourcing. The final third of the book focuses on three of the overarching concerns of supply management: supplier relationship management, social and legal responsibility and international issues, including global sourcing, logistics and exchange rate and countertrade issues. This book is a critical read for those who might be relatively new to supply management, those who have not had a formal education in supply management and anyone who wants to stay abreast of the latest practices in supply management.

Volume 2, *Effective Supply Management Performance,* focuses on many of the operational issues that are part of a successful supply management performance. The latest surveys show that supply management professionals are responsible for a majority of the components of supply management; many of these are detailed in the definition of supply management provided previously. These are new areas of interaction for many supply management professionals. Volume 2 provides coverage of many operational issues such as project management, new product and service development, forecasting, warehousing, materials handling, logistics and international transportation, asset and inventory management and quality. These all provide supporting structures for supply management. The book closes with an in-depth discussion of supplier performance management and metrics and information systems as key ways to integrate knowledge within and across organizations. This book is a must-read for anyone newly assigned to operations-oriented issues or who supervises or manages transportation, logistics or inventory management personnel as part of his or her supply management responsibilities.

Volume 3, *Leadership in Supply Management,* focuses on many of the human resources issues that supply management professionals face. The first half of the book, "Creating a Shared Vision," explores management issues within the supply organization, such as managing and leading, developing shared values and setting direction, creating alignment and creating commitment for the supply organization's shared vision. These chapters deal with issues such as various leadership styles, developing strategies, aligning with internal and external stakeholders, team building and managing conflict. These are critical supporting structures for supply management. The second half of the book, "Managing Complexity," focuses on risk management and mitigation, developing business plans and linking these to the strategic sourcing process, including outsourcing, developing and staffing the supply management organization, providing rewards and professional development for supply management and executing the strategic sourcing process. This section includes a look at issues related to the overarching concerns of supply management, the process steps of supply management and the supporting structures. Taken as a whole, it deals with human resources and strategic issues of management that all supply management functions face. This book should be read by anyone who manages the supply management function or who is involved in the supply management strategy setting and planning process.

It has been a privilege to be involved in this important project, supporting the continued growth and recognition of the supply management profession. It has been challenging for all of those involved to capture the vast amount of material represented in these three volumes. The extensive practical and theoretical knowledge and expertise of the excellent group of authors will provide the reader with both a broad and deep perspective of the topics covered here. I hope you find these books both interesting and valuable as you study for the new CPSM examination or simply work on enhancing your own knowledge of supply management.

Lisa Ellram, Ph.D.
C.P.M., A.P.P., CMA
Series Editor

Lisa M. Ellram, Ph.D., C.P.M., is chair of the department of management at Colorado State University's College of Business. Ellram joined the CSU College of Business as Allen Professor of Business in 2006. Prior to that, she was the John and Barbara Bebbling Professor of Business at Arizona State University's W.P. Carey School of Business. Dr. Ellram earned her undergraduate degree and her MBA from the University of Minnesota. She earned her master's and doctorate from The Ohio State University. She is a certified management accountant.

Dr. Ellram is an award-winning educator and prolific publisher, and has spoken to audiences throughout the world. She has garnered sizeable grants for research in areas including strategic cost management, outsourcing, total cost modeling and supply chain sustainability. Dr. Ellram is a member of the Institute for Supply Management™ (ISM) and a member of the editorial review board for *Inside Supply Management*®. She is currently Editor-in-Chief of the *Journal of Supply Chain Management*.

Preface

The topics presented in this book were deliberately selected to prepare the supply management professional to be successful given the profound changes that lie ahead for the profession. Consequently, this book is about the fundamentals of supply management at its core. The book begins with data collection, analysis and management to provide the foundations for data-driven decisions (Chapter 2). An appropriate information system or e-procurement system plays an integral role. Cost management (Chapter 3) then emerges as an important strategic consideration. Once the data, information and strategic cost issues are considered, we then proceed to the mechanics of the sourcing process itself (Chapter 4). Here, such strategic issues as spend consolidation are treated. After that, an organization needs to address contracting issues (Chapter 5), negotiation (Chapter 6) and ongoing supplier management and development issues (Chapter 7).

Supplier relationship management (Chapter 8) and social responsibility (Chapter 9) need to be considered as overarching issues. A final chapter on international sourcing issues (Chapter 10) closes the book.

Figure P-1 presents a detailed process map linking chapters to the content flow of the book. A more detailed description of each chapter follows and is linked to the detailed process steps provided in the figure.

Process Steps

Supply management represents a service function in every organization. As such, collecting pertinent data to aid in decision-making and then analyzing them for application to service management situations are critical in what supply management professionals do. Chapter 2, "Data Collection, Analysis and Management," addresses how data management can be done through various procurement systems and can facilitate supply management activities. Chapter 2 will help the reader understand what data management entails, its potential benefits, and an execution process that will increase the likelihood of success for supply management applications. Data applications include forecasting, budgeting and understanding the major types of financial information, including profitability and solvency ratios. The basic data management system provides the backbone for setting up consistent and overarching supply strategies.

Chapter 3, "Strategic Cost Management," covers cost-related issues ranging from price/cost analysis to total cost of ownership. From Chapter 3, the reader will learn how to develop a basic framework for understanding price, profit and cost; understand how the different types of cost may affect supply decisions; develop an understanding of the fundamentals of cost analysis and a cost management program development; and get an overview of leasing.

Figure P-1   Strategic Supply Management Process

Supply Management Strategy and Philosophy	**Overarching Concerns**	Risk Management/Market Intelligence			
		Social Responsibility/Sustainability (Chapter **9**)			
		Strategic Outsourcing/Insourcing (Chapter **4**)			
		Globalization Issues (Chapter 10)			
		Supplier Relationship Management (Chapter **8**)			
	Process Steps	Data Management & Analysis (Chapter 2)	Category Strategy Development	Cost Analysis & Management (Chapter 3)	Select, Negotiate & Contract (Chapters **5, 6**)	Supplier Development & Performance Management (Chapter 7)
	Supporting Structures	Operations and Logistic Issues			
		Human Resource Management, Development and Measurement (**All** Chapters)			

(Note: Heavy topic coverage in a chapter is denoted in bold)

Supply management professionals are constantly encouraged by senior management to expand cost management efforts. Cost management has always been a primary tenet of supply management's mission. It will be no different in the future. Performance expectations are, however, being raised considerably as international competition forces organizations to squeeze unnecessary costs out of every part of their business. For supply management, this means widening the breadth of spend areas covered, managing costs more holistically and delivering cost savings faster.

Any organization, service, government, or manufacturing operation has the choice of buying or making the many factors of production used in the organization's daily business operations. This decision can cover a wide range of goods and services. Components, subassemblies, finished goods, plant and equipment, services, skills and knowledge may be purchased. The managerial choice between organizing for the internal provision of these items versus the external management of these factors of production is commonly known as the sourcing decision. Chapter 4, "The Sourcing

Decision," examines the process of identifying sources that could provide needed products or services for the acquiring organization.

Once the relationship with a supplier makes economic sense through strategic cost analysis and viable sources are identified, contracting and negotiation need to occur. In Chapter 5, "Contracting," and Chapter 6, "Negotiating," various forms of contracts and contracting processes are discussed. Also discussed are bidding and negotiation processes and the role of competition. Under fact-based negotiation, the discussion begins with key contents of the negotiation plan and objectives, and then moves into doing preparatory groundwork. It ends with the position analysis of both purchaser and supplier and actual conducting of negotiation.

Chapter 7 addresses the issue of ongoing supplier management and development. The supplier's performance needs to be evaluated. Depending on performance, a supplier may need to be developed in the performance areas where it is lagging. Supplier certification may be an important area of consideration when managing suppliers, as it brings structure to supplier management. As an organization contemplates new products or services, suppliers can be engaged in early supplier involvement. New ideas for improvement from suppliers can be harnessed into new products or services through value engineering and value analysis efforts.

Supplier relationship management is key to lowering transaction and overall administrative costs associated with operating in uncertain relationships. Chapter 8 considers various types of supply management relationships and their associated advantages and disadvantages. How to administer contracts with suppliers as part of an ongoing business relationship management is covered, as is supplier selection as it relates to supplier relationship management and how it is affected by diversity concerns and possible reverse marketing opportunities. Lastly, the concept of supply base management and its affect on supplier relationship management is introduced.

Institute for Supply Management™ (ISM) emphasizes the importance of social responsibility and sustainability to all of its members and the organizations the members represent. Chapter 9 covers a wide spectrum of issues surrounding the overarching implications of being socially responsible. Legal and ethical issues of supply management are covered. The foundational issues of agency, authority, and liability are introduced and their implications for supply management professionals are discussed. Finally, the chapter frames the supply management professional as a socially responsible agent that is entrusted by the organization and society at large.

It has been a foregone conclusion that an organization may not meet all its supply needs just by working with domestic suppliers. Thus, it is imperative that supply management professionals understand the fundamental managerial concerns involved in procuring from international sources. Chapter 10 takes us from preparing the organization for international sourcing to qualifying international sources, as well as additional managerial issues such as internal transportation and logistics. Specifically, Chapter 10 discusses the strategic importance of international supply management, describes procedural and managerial issues of concern in international procurement, examines the transportation/distribution implications of international markets, delineates the differences between buying from international versus domestic sources, examines the impact of international currency exchange rate fluctuations on international sourcing and discusses the implications of nonmonetary trade between two parties.

About the Authors

Joseph R. Carter is Professor of Supply Chain Management, the Avnet Professor in the W. P. Carey School of Business, founding Chair of the Supply Chain Management Department at Arizona State University and Senior Research Associate at CAPS Research.

Dr. Carter holds a DBA degree in Operations Management from the Boston University Graduate School of Management and is recognized as a Certified Purchasing Manager by the Institute for Supply Management™. He has been designated the Institute for Supply Management™ Professor Emeritus at Arizona State University.

Dr. Carter's research efforts have been oriented toward purchasing and supply management issues. Dr. Carter's research contributions encompass three major content areas: buyer and supplier communication processes and information exchange systems; international sourcing and supply chain management issues; and strategic procurement. Dr. Carter was a principle investigator on a major project examining the role of corporate procurement in the strategic outsourcing process and the outsourcing of procurement activities. He was a principal investigator on a multiphase study that examined the linkages between future economic trends, corporate objectives and business models, and procurement strategies and tactics. Dr. Carter's current research interests have placed him on a research team assessing ways to accelerate supplier innovations into the buying firm.

Dr. Carter is highly regarded for his contributions to graduate curriculum, the W. P. Carey MBA program, doctoral student mentoring and executive education. Several of Dr. Carter's case studies have been published in various textbooks; other cases have been used as teaching instruments by prominent business schools around the world, including Harvard in the United States, IESE in Spain and IMD in Switzerland.

Dr. Carter has received many academic and professional awards and has been involved in several research projects sponsored by the Institute for Supply Management™, the U.S. government, and CAPS Research. He is a much sought after speaker and consultant for both corporate and professional practitioner organizations worldwide.

Thomas Y. Choi is a Professor of Supply Chain Management at Arizona State University and the John G. & Barbara A. Bebbling Professor in Business. He is also the Outstanding Operations Management Professor at Yonsei University in Seoul, Korea. Dr. Choi is Doctoral Program Coordinator for the Supply Chain Management Department and is Faculty Director of the Global Supply Chain Management Certificate Program for the Executive Education. He received his Ph.D. from the University of Michigan and his AB degree from the University of California at Berkeley.

Dr. Choi is currently studying the supply base rationalization, second- and third-tier suppliers, supplier-supplier relationships, supply chain disintermediation and triadic relationships within supply networks. His articles have been published in the *Academy of Management Executive, Business Horizons, Harvard Business Review*, the *Journal of Operations Management*, the *Journal of Supply Chain Management, Production and Operations Management* and others. Dr. Choi has worked with Toyota, Honda, Chrysler, LG Electronics, Samsung, and other multinational organizations.

Contents

Chapter 3: Strategic Cost Management

Chapter 4: The Sourcing Decision

Chapter 5: Contracting

Chapter 6: Negotiating

Chapter 7: Supplier Management and Development

Chapter 8: Supplier Relationship Management

Chapter 9: Social and Legal Responsibilities of Supply Management Professionals

Chapter 10: International Sourcing Issues

1

An Introduction to Supply Management

The concept of a domestic market and economy has given way to the more practical realization that all markets are now part of a global economy. All organizations are linked and must compete as participants in the global marketplace. Consequently, it is widely acknowledged by industry leaders that becoming globally competitive requires an effective management of the productive material and service resources both within an organization and within an organization's supply chain. Cost, quality, delivery and customer satisfaction have become the watchwords in managing global operations. In their relentless pursuit to match and exceed the competition, industries are increasingly viewing supply management not just as a necessary function, but as a weapon in their strategic arsenal.

In many organizations, the movement toward an integrated supply management strategy has led to pervasive changes in organizational structure. Some of the leading organizations, such as Toyota Motor Co. and IBM Corp., have created much closer links between engineering, accounting and supply management. Procurement practices, transportation operations and locations of capital-intensive facilities are closely integrated. Clearly, a need exists to bring this important area to the attention of both practitioners and academicians.

This book deals with supply management and the increasingly important role that it plays in today's competitive environment. As industry struggles to compete effectively in the international market and gain a global prominence, the restructuring and renewal of operations is touted as the principal means to industrial resurgence. This has prompted global industries to examine their organizational structures and those aspects of their operations that have the potential to increase competitiveness — for example, strategic outsourcing options.

There is no commonly accepted definition of industrial competitiveness. It is generally agreed that *competitiveness* refers to an organization's ability to maintain and enhance its market share and profitability. Several generic strategies that an organization can employ to compete successfully in the market are:

- Function as a low-cost producer (i.e., concentrate on cost reduction);

- Produce a high-quality product (i.e., concentrate on quality);

- Serve as a technology leader;

- Compete through operational flexibility; or

- Combine these generic strategies.

The view of supply management in this book is somewhat different from that commonly encountered in textbooks on operations management. The Institute for Supply Management™ (ISM) defines supply management as the identification, acquisition, access, positioning and management of resources and related capabilities the organization needs or potentially needs to attain its strategic objectives. The various components of supply management include disposition/investment recovery, distribution, inventory control, logistics, manufacturing supervision, materials management, packaging, product/service development, purchasing/procurement, quality, receiving, strategic sourcing, transportation/traffic/shipping and warehousing.

The field now known as supply management has come a long way. During the days when large organizations had vertically integrated organizational structures, purchasing entailed primarily buying activities that required strict adherence to mechanical procedures. The purchasers would take orders from the operation or engineering department and then follow the well-delineated guidelines for buying goods or services. This type of purchasing required basic skills and certainly did not require a professional degree.

However, much began to change in the late 1980s and early 1990s. The field of procurement, which underwent a massive transformation from being reactive and mechanical to being more proactive and strategic and involved in a much broader spectrum of responsibilities, has now become supply management. In the past 10 years or so, the landscape of supply networks changed to a point where many suppliers are now considered long-term partners rather than short-term, easily expendable and replaceable sources of goods and services. Suppliers now contribute a large portion to the sourcing organization's competitive success. Toyota pioneered the approach toward supplier relationship management that most other organizations now subscribe to.[1]

Organizations have adopted titles such as chief procurement officer (CPO) or chief supply management officer, and many of these CPOs hold a vice president–level title. For instance, the head of supply management at Honda of America Mfg. Inc. carries the title of senior executive vice president. In the past, CEOs and presidents of large organizations moved up through the ranks of accounting or engineering. Recently, however, upper management has come out of the ranks of supply management. For instance, a former president of Chrysler LLC moved up through the ranks of procurement. What follows is a discussion of how this transformation has taken place from a historic perspective and its strategic significance.

This book is built on the body of knowledge that makes up the ISM specifications for the Certified Professional in Supply Management (CPSM) qualification. The goal of this book is to provide consistency in promoting the ISM body of knowledge and also to incorporate the most recent developments in the supply management field into the existing body of knowledge. To provide consistency, this book uses the definitions of key terms as reflected in the *ISM Glossary of Key Supply Management Terms* (2006).

CHAPTER OBJECTIVES

• Set a historical foundation to the study of supply management.

• Describe the evolution of our field from purchasing to supply management.

• Provide a brief perspective on the future of supply management.

Foundations of Supply Management

During the early 1980s, the world became aware of the quality concepts of W. Edwards Deming and Joseph Moses Juran largely through the success of the Japanese organizations. Subsequently, many organizations around the world also came to realize the importance of supplier quality. Several leading organizations came up with supplier quality programs and supplier certification programs such as Ford's Q1 or GM's Spear 1. We even saw the emergence of international certification agencies such as the ISO 9000 series of quality process certifications.

After this quality movement occurred, the race to bring goods and services to the market faster began. Time became the next competitive advantage during the late 1980s and early 1990s. Lexus and Acura first emerged in the market, challenging the luxury brands of Mercedes, BMW and Cadillac. They found a foothold in that competitive market niche by introducing very high-quality products, two or three years before Mercedes, BMW or Cadillac. Managers became aware of new product development strategies such as concurrent engineering, simultaneous engineering and platform engineering. These new approaches involved many different functions that merged into new product development activities in parallel rather than in series by tossing the designs over the walls that surrounded different functions within an organization such as design, manufacturing and procurement. The importance of involving suppliers in this process became apparent through initiatives such as early supplier involvement and value engineering/value analysis. The managerial approaches toward cross-functional sourcing teams were developed.

One of the major lessons organizations learned while they were competing on time to market was the potential competitive advantages gained by relying on suppliers. It was much more expedient when introducing a new product or service to turn to the supply market than to try to develop and coordinate their internal operations. As reliance on suppliers increased, organization size decreased through downsizing efforts. Furthermore, as the level of outsourcing increased, organizations simultaneously reduced or rationalized their supply base: the level of supplier reliance increased, while the overall number of suppliers decreased. Consequently, each remaining supplier generally received more work. In the automotive industry during the late 1980s and early 1990s, some parts suppliers were told by their major buying organizations (e.g., Ford) to merge and expand their capacity and capability. This effort gave birth to many new large integrated first-tier suppliers such as Johnson Controls Inc. and Tower Automotive. Many parts suppliers that did not become part of a top-tier supplier then became second-tier or third-tier suppliers. As the turbulent shakeout of the early 1990s settled down and organizations moved toward the 21st century, top managers come to realize two things:

1. Outsourcing permitted them to operate with fewer assets, which, in turn, increased their return on investment (ROI). Motorola Inc. refers to this approach as operating in an "asset-light" environment.

2. Top managers discovered that a dollar saved on the incoming parts and services generally impacted the bottom line much more significantly than a dollar increase on the sales side. In fact, as the percentage of outsourcing increased with respect to overall cost of goods sold (COGS), this impact of a dollar saved from the upstream side on the bottom line increased even more. Strategic sourcing became the mantra for many top supply management professionals by helping them build close relationships with suppliers and maintain competitive advantage, and offering them more efficient processes and capabilities. Beyond strategic significance, supply management also had more immediate, operational significance.

The Operational Importance of Supply Management

As stated previously, supply management encompasses a wide variety of responsibilities internal and external to the organization. This broader statement of the overall responsibilities of supply management includes the following seven items:[2]

1. *Provide an uninterrupted flow of materials and services to the operating system.* Many people assume that the basic tenet of supply management is to obtain the proper materials and services in the right quality, quantity, price and source. This is not the case. Without an assurance of supply, these other "rights" are meaningless. The authors once asked a supply management professional at General Motors what percentage of items that he purchased were custom-designed to meet specific GM needs. His surprising answer was "over 90 percent." If this supply management professional cannot assure supply, the other factors of quality, price, source, etc., will not come into play.

2. *Keep inventory investment at a minimum.*[3] The supply management function "spends" the vast majority of most organizations' sales revenues. An easy way to buy is to order in large quantities to secure a discounted price and efficiencies of transportation. This creates large inventories of expensive materials, and is unacceptable in today's business environment. Supply management professionals today continually strive to minimize inventories without loss of price or service quality. To this end, the supply management professional will do whatever is necessary to reduce uncertainty, such as improving his or her relationship with the supplier and becoming more familiar with the supply market. For global organizations such as Black & Decker, inventory management is a key to financial success.

3. *Maximize quality.* For years, supply management professionals have been involved in working with suppliers to improve the quality of incoming materials and services. But what can supply management professionals do to maximize a finished product's perceived quality and customer service? Because supply management is the link between the internal customer and the external supplier, the supply management professional is responsible for total quality management (TQM) with suppliers while assuring customer satisfaction. Supply management's role of being the gatekeeper of quality is accentuated when considering how organizations now rely more on suppliers for their competitive success. Organizations such as the General Electric Co. practice programs like Six Sigma to ensure quality remains paramount throughout the organization.

4. *Find and develop competent sources of supply internationally.*
The success of any supply management function can depend on its ability to locate preferred sources wherever they may exist, analyze their capabilities and select a supplier partner for a longer-term relationship. This may require a supply management professional to look beyond domestic suppliers to find the right supplier. The goal of supply management should be to find sources of supply that will give the organization a competitive advantage with its products and services and market position. For example, many organizations have discovered India as a competitive source of software engineering services.

5. *Standardize requirements for products and services.* For years, many organizations believed that custom-designed finished goods required custom-designed services and materials. The Japanese disproved this theory long ago — customized products and services come not from custom designing everything for every customer but instead from modularizing products and services and by offering a list of choices to the customer. A major task of supply management is to gather and disseminate information concerning how present and potential suppliers can help standardize the modularization process. This information should be made available during the design stage of product and service development. Standardization includes everything from requirements to contract terms and conditions. Intel Corp. and Intuit Inc. are examples of organizations that have worked diligently to standardize their services contracts.[4]

6. *Purchase materials and services at the lowest total cost of ownership (TCO).*[5] The profit leverage effect of supply management throughout the entire management cycle can be significant. Price, if measured broadly as the total cost of ownership, should always be supply management's primary service or material selection criterion. Price should not be the sole criterion for selecting a supplier, but it should be kept in mind that after all, price is the manifestation of underlying costs. It is up to the supply management professional to understand a supplier's price and its reasonableness, and to regard all transactions with suppliers from the perspective of TCO. American Express has effectively tied TCO to the purchase of service resources.

7. *Foster cross-functional relationships.* Supply management buys little for its own use since it is a staff, not line, function. The function exists solely to meet the needs of other functional areas and internal users. In that role, supply management frequently spans the boundaries that separate various functions into departments. This is consistent with present management philosophy that dictates a cross-functional

team approach toward problem-solving and process management. Supply management professionals have proven themselves to be valuable and productive leaders and members of these teams. As discussed previously, supply management has evolved from being viewed as little more than a clerical function to its present status as an integral part of strategic management that requires working with other functions and integrating their needs and meeting them.

The Future of Supply Management

Powerful external forces such as globalization, scarcity of raw materials and ascendency of China as an economic power will affect all businesses. A multitude of external forces will reshape markets, products and industries over the course of the next decade. To survive, organizations will have to rethink and revamp their business strategies to anticipate, react to and even to take advantage of these forces.

Recent research[6] indicates that supply management professionals are concerned about a variety of forces that will impact organization and supply management strategies. Foremost among these is the impact of China, India and other developing countries on the competitive landscape. The impact is expected to be felt on both the demand and the supply sides, and will create opportunities as well as challenges.

To meet this onslaught of new competition, organizations headquartered in developed countries will need improved economies of scale and market power on both the supply and sell sides to survive. To successfully compete, many organizations will be forced to merge and consolidate.

Government legislation and regulation of business has increased and will continue to increase on a global scale, requiring organizations to dedicate significant resources to ensure compliance. For example, both China and India have been strengthening legislation intended to protect the environment and promote the quality of exported products.[7] Government actions to support economic development, such as tax incentives and trade restrictions, will have a large impact on supply strategies. Political instability could require a rapid change in supply strategies.

Technology breakthroughs also will cause major changes in how products and services are provided. These changes may require capital investment, but will lower the customer's total cost of ownership and increase productivity. In many industries, core technologies will eventually be commoditized, forcing geographic consolidation and concentration of the supply base and fundamentally affecting supply-chain structure and relationships.

In some industries, the downstream supply chain will change rapidly because of economics and government policies. Within other industries, supply-chain dynamics will be influenced by the poor financial condition of major trading partners in the chain. This performance will reverberate up and down the chain, altering relationships and causing suppliers to seek other customers and/or sources of revenue.

The impact of private equity organizations also will be significant. Many organizations and suppliers have already been bought and taken private by these organizations. In looking to recoup their investments, the private equity organizations tend to slash costs, raise prices and change business relationships with their trading partners, affecting supply management and supply-chain strategies.

Organizations in developed economies will be held to high standards wherever they do business in the world. Supply management will be tasked with working with the supply base to ensure that the suppliers meet environmental standards. Customers, consumers, shareholders, nongovernment organizations and governments all will increase their scrutiny of corporate environmental practices in all regions of the world. They will demand that organizations take environmentally friendly actions such as using less packaging material, reducing carbon emissions and making products that can be readily recycled.

Tomorrow's business models and strategies will raise the bar for supply management. In response to these forces, organizations will shift their business models, adopt different strategies, pursue new revenue streams, squeeze costs further, make asset bases as lean as possible and reshape capital structures. The mission and role of supply management will be changed in a variety of ways.

The need for innovation will accelerate as organizations continue to aggressively pursue new geographic and demographic markets. With the demand and supply for innovation in a state of flux over the coming decade, and the limited resources within any one organization, supply management professionals must overcome the usual "not invented here" barriers and tap into all available sources, regardless of their origin.

Relationships between organizations and their external innovation sources may need to be structured differently in the future. This will be especially true where past adversarial approaches have deterred suppliers from sharing their best and brightest ideas. Financial support, equitable sharing of risks and benefits and two-way protection of intellectual property rights will need to be a part of the mix.

Supply management has always helped contribute to revenue generation. Close attention to costs for goods and services leads to more competitively priced products. A focus on quality and service reduces failure rates, improves availability and leads to higher customer satisfaction and loyalty. Innovations from the supply market lead to revenue increases from new products and services.

Already, there is widespread acknowledgment among supply executives of heightened top-down attention to supply-risk management. Extended global supply chains that include geographically distant, unproven (or even unknown) suppliers pose supply continuity, liability, reputational and intellectual property risks.

Supply management must more aggressively manage liability and safety risks as well. To ensure compliance with Sarbanes-Oxley legislation in the United States and similar laws being considered worldwide, supply management professionals must address internal controls as well as a range of possible risk-exposure areas that includes supply chain disruption, outsourcing, long-term contracting, leasing and supplier-managed inventories.

Performance expectations will be raised considerably as global competition and customer expectations force organizations to squeeze unnecessary costs out of every part of their business. For supply management, this means widening the breadth of spend areas covered, managing costs more holistically and delivering cost savings faster. Many of the issues presented previously are discussed in greater detail throughout this book.

According to the *ISM Glossary* (2006), *supply management* is the identification, acquisition, access, positioning and management of resources and related capabilities the organization needs or potentially needs to attain its strategic objectives. It deals with the planning and control of materials and service flows, from earliest suppliers to both internal users and end users, including disposal and end-of-life issues. Supply management attempts to cooperatively manage interorganizational relationships for the benefit of all parties involved and to maximize the efficient use of resources in achieving the organization's customer-service goals.

Supply management allows managers to optimize their resources, including inventories, capacities, transportation and logistics. Transaction mechanisms across many organizations substantially reduce expenses resulting from normal business uncertainties. The sharing of accurate demand information across the chain is cited by many as critical to achieving the maximum benefits of supply management.

Summary

As a result of the quality movement of the 1980s, organizations around the world came to realize the importance of supplier quality. The race to bring goods and services to the market faster began, and continues to this day. Managers became aware of new product development strategies such as concurrent engineering, simultaneous engineering and platform engineering. The importance of involving suppliers in these processes became apparent through initiatives such as early supplier involvement and value engineering/

value analysis. Outsourcing and strategic sourcing have become important strategies for the supply management professional. As organizations continue to expand globally, it will be important for the supply management professional to ensure he or she understands the forces that will continue to reshape markets, products and industries. In order to effectively compete, organizations and supply management professionals will have to rethink and revamp their business strategies to anticipate, react to and even to take advantage of these forces.

Key Points

1. The Institute for Supply Management™ (ISM) defines supply management as the identification, acquisition, access, positioning and management of resources and related capabilities the organization needs or potentially needs to attain its strategic objectives. The various components of supply management include disposition/investment recovery, distribution, inventory control, logistics, manufacturing supervision, materials management, packaging, product/service development, purchasing/procurement, quality, receiving, strategic sourcing, transportation/traffic/shipping and warehousing.

2. Supply management has become an integral part of an organization's success. With the advent of the quality movement of the 1980s, the supply management professional moved from being focused primarily on purchasing to becoming an integral part of an organization's success. The importance of the supplier/buyer relationship has led to an increasingly vital role for the supply management professional.

3. Supply management professionals understand the role that outsourcing has in their organizations, including an increased ROI. They understand that a dollar saved on incoming parts and services can have a more significant impact than a dollar increase in sales. Strategic sourcing became a competitive advantage for many organizations and supply management professionals by helping them build close relationships and develop efficient processes and capabilities.

4. The overall responsibilities of the supply management professional include providing an uninterrupted flow of materials and services to the operating system; keeping inventory investments at a minimum; maximizing quality; finding and developing competent sources of supply; standardizing requirements for products and services; purchasing materials and services at the lowest total cost of ownership (TCO); and fostering cross-functional relationships.

5. Supply management professionals' performance expectations will be raised considerably as global competition and customer expectations force organizations to squeeze unnecessary costs out of every part of their businesses. For the supply management professional, this means widening the breadth of spend areas covered, managing costs more holistically and delivering cost savings faster.

6. Trends affecting the supply management professional include increased government legislation and regulation of business on a global scale, continued breakthroughs in technology and sustainable business practices that ensure suppliers meet environmental standards.

2

Data Collection, Analysis and Management

Improved data analysis and the growth of analytics in supply management have been greatly aided by improvements in information technology over the past several decades. E-procurement (also referred to as e-supply) systems are critical for the collection, analysis and dissemination of most sourcing data. Without these systems, the volume of data generated by the sourcing process would overwhelm the supply management professional. Data would not be turned into useful information and decisions would be difficult to make. In this chapter, the methods used to manage the data generated by these systems and the types of decisions that are made using these data are discussed.

E-procurement, as defined in the *ISM Glossary* (2006), occurs when the transactional activities of the purchasing process are conducted electronically, typically over the Internet, to shorten the cycle time and lower the transaction costs of the acquisition process. For example, purchase orders, advanced shipping notices, invoices, planning information, forecasts, collaborative designs and much more are transmitted between at least two parties. In the supply management environment, electronic communication often occurs between buying and selling organizations. The growth in e-procurement is largely because of the emergence of broadly accepted standards, the development of relatively inexpensive computer hardware, the growing proliferation of e-procurement software and an increasingly competitive supply management environment.

This chapter begins with a presentation of the supply management transaction process and the role of e-procurement in controlling transaction costs. Next, two very data–intensive processes are discussed: forecasting and budgeting. In the forecasting and budgeting processes, assumptions are made about future market conditions, needs and pricing. These sections are followed with information on implementing supply strategies and timing purchases in anticipation of meeting forecasts. The chapter closes with a discussion of evaluating supplier offers, including financial ratio analysis and an introduction to cost/price analysis, both of which are integral to evaluating offers. The chapter ends with a summary of a SWOT (strengths, weaknesses, opportunities and threats) analysis.

CHAPTER OBJECTIVES

- Explain the role e-procurement can play in managing transaction costs.

- Highlight the importance of effective and efficient data collection, analysis and management.

- Explain the fundamental concepts of forecasting.

- Describe the types of supply management budgets and their use.

- List various buying strategies available for supply management professionals.

- Provide the supply management professional with the basics of supplier financial analysis.

The Supply Management Transaction Process

A supply management department buys a variety of materials and services. For the majority of items, the supply procedure is a very routine activity. The information flow in the typical supply process is established to support this routine, day-to-day activity and also provide information to a multitude of different individuals located in several functional areas. This information flow has developed over time into a series of procedures that meet three basic concepts:

1. The flow of information assists in the efficient use of supply management resources when conducting routine activities of the function.

2. The standard flow of information is clearly defined. For example, if a purchase order contains nine "electronic designees," the distribution of each is specified. This standardization of procedures helps the multitude of personnel supporting the system to process the transaction data with minimum effort and certainty.

3. The flow of information allows for managerial discretion. When conditions arise that are not routine or normal, responsible supply management professionals are informed about the condition. These professionals can take corrective action before any problems arise. An example of such oversight and discretion might be the spending authorization limits placed on procurement card (p-card) transactions at various responsibility levels.

Controlling Transaction Costs

Much attention has been devoted to reducing direct costs in the manufacture of a product or delivery of a service. Quietly, however, there has been an increasing awareness and anxiety throughout global industry concerning the explosive growth in overhead costs. As organizations develop multiple supply chains to support global markets and operations, there has been a tendency to uniquely duplicate systems, transactions, roles and responsibilities. Synergies and efficiencies have been elusive. For the sake of discussion, following is a simple definition of overhead costs.

The *ISM Glossary* (2006) states overhead involves costs associated with the operation of the organization as a whole. *Overhead* includes all costs related to the manufacture, purchase and delivery of items and services other than direct labor and purchase costs. Overhead costs include indirect labor, general and administrative expenses, capital equipment costs, engineering costs and logistics costs. Logistics costs can include the movement and coordination of all materials within an organization. Logistics overhead costs include the salaries of all personnel who coordinate these movements and include salaries of supply management, production planning, receiving, transportation and other support-staff personnel. Enterprise resource planning (ERP) systems such as from SAP AG and Oracle can help reduce these overhead costs.

What are the real causes of overhead costs? The bulk of overhead costs result from the sheer volume of transactions that occur in support of the operating system. These transactions involve exchanges of data and information necessary to support operations but do not directly add value to the finished product or service. Some transactions order, execute and confirm the movement of materials from one location to another; e.g., all order releases, advanced shipping notices and receipt confirmations transmitted between a buying organization and a supplier. Certain transactions balance the supplies of materials, labor and capacity; e.g., the conversion of general requirements into purchase orders to specific suppliers. Quality-assurance transactions involve the development of specifications and their transmittal to suppliers. Change transactions alter and update preciously transmitted data; e.g., engineering change orders communicated to suppliers. All of these transactions cost money in terms of material, time and personnel resources expended in their support.

Before the advent of e-procurement, most of the supply transactions were handled inefficiently, with large paper flows and many duplicated efforts. E-procurement helps reduce the cost of processing these transactions in two ways:

1. E-procurement can reduce the cost to process an individual transaction by eliminating clerical input and automating the transmittal processes. This not only reduces the cost of a single transaction, but also increases its effectiveness.

The e-procurement system can be so well integrated with the operations planning and control system that data need only be entered once.

2. The movement toward a fully automated e-procurement system requires an audit of existing transactions and their appropriateness (i.e., process analysis). Such an audit frequently leads to a reduction in the total number of transactions necessary. For example, in an e-procurement environment with advanced shipping notices and real-time receiving reports, are invoices transmitted by suppliers really necessary? In any case, if an organization cannot greatly decrease the number of transactions, e-procurement can make each transaction cost less in resource commitment. Anticipating and controlling costs are key aspects of the budgeting process.

Forecasting

With all the supply and demand data generated by the various e-procurement systems within the organization, forecasts may be developed. Forecasting as defined in the *ISM Glossary* (2006) is a process of making a prediction or estimation. For example, managers may predict or estimate future environmental conditions and their impact on the organization in terms of sales revenue, market share, supply availability and so on. Prediction is a similar but more general term and usually refers to the estimation of time series, cross-sectional or longitudinal data. In more recent years, forecasting has evolved into the practice of *demand planning* in everyday business forecasting for many organizations. The discipline of demand planning, also sometimes referred to as *supply-chain forecasting,* embraces both statistical forecasting and a consensus process.

Forecasting problems can be posed as the following questions:

- Will a 3.5 percent price increase be likely for office supplies next year?

- How much inventory should we aim to purchase over the next few months for each of 532 items?

- Will the EU economy continue to grow at a rate of at least 2.5 percent per annum over the next three years?

- Taking account of technical matters and concern among some communities, how long will it take to complete the planned pipeline?

- Which supply management skill sets will be most prevalent in the United Kingdom 10 years from now? Can we create training programs based on these forecasts of skill needs?

If supply markets never changed, it would not be necessary for supply management professionals to forecast. But because markets do and because a primary responsibility of supply management is to protect organizations from supply constrictions, it becomes necessary to forecast by trying to predict future trends and events.

There are many different kinds of forecasts. Fact-based forecasts use historical information, such as price or production date, to project future trends. Opinion-based forecasts use expert judgment to estimate future events, such as the impact of technology on a particular industry in the next 10 years. Another type of forecast, called a *change index,* is finding increasing use, and is the format used by the Institute for Supply Management™'s *Report On Business*®.

Forecasting is concerned with how to collect and process data. Decisions about how to structure a forecasting problem can be important. For example, when should one decompose a problem and address each component separately? In predicting the future supply and demand for semiconductors, does this category need to be decomposed into subcategories because of real-market differences in supply and demand? Forecasting includes such tactical matters as obtaining relevant up-to-date data, checking for errors in the data and making adjustments for inflation, working days and seasonality. Forecast error sometimes depends more on how information is used than on getting more accurate information. The question of what data is needed and how it is best used is determined by the selection of forecasting methods.

To supply management professionals, the ability to forecast required quantities, category availability and prices represents a competitive and strategic advantage. With the realities of global markets comes the necessity to study and forecast category and industry changes, based on worldwide category or industry studies. Some standard applications of forecasts for the supply management professional are explained in the following sections. Forecasting techniques are presented in more depth in Volume 2 of the ISM Professional Series, *Effective Supply Management Performance.*

Quantity forecasts of requirements for purchased goods and services are based on sales or usage projections, including the cyclical and/or seasonal characteristics for each need. Any quantity forecast is influenced not only by the timing of the requirement but also by forecasts of availability, price and rate of technological change.

Industry capacity and availability forecasts, which determine short-term and long-term availability, are based on category studies that examine global supply and demand, including sources of supply, reserves and the impact of technological change on the manufacturing or service process, uses and demand.

Cost or price forecasts include many factors beyond simply supply and demand, including influences of governmental action and laws or perceptions of supply shortages, such as those that might be caused by the threat of war or strike. In any forecasting exercise, potential influences on supply or demand in the market and quantitative projections of their impact must be considered.

Technology forecasts are occurring at an increasing rate and will continue. The impact of changing technology, such as price reductions and product obsolescence, must be forecast to determine the best types of sourcing strategies for items likely to be affected. Primarily, a technological forecast deals with the characteristics of tech-nology, such as levels of technical performance, like speed of a military aircraft, the power in watts of a particular future engine, the accuracy or precision of a measuring instrument, the number of transistors in a chip in the year 2015. The forecast does not have to state how these characteristics will be achieved. Technological forecasting usually deals with only useful machines, procedures or techniques and those com-modities, services or techniques intended for luxury or amusement.

Planning forecasts depend a great deal on the flow of accurate information about the supply markets. Decisions to build or expand capacity, the ability to fulfill sales projections, investment choices between new or existing technology and whether or not to enter certain markets are just a few examples. An important example of a planning forecast is *collaborative planning, forecasting and replenishment (CPFR)*. CPFR, as explained in the *ISM Glossary* (2006), is an initiative developed by the Voluntary Interindustry Commerce Standards (VICS) Association that allows collaborative pro-cesses across the supply chain. Some of the first applications involved a final retailer sharing its consumer demand forecasts upstream in the supply chain to enable manu-facturers of branded goods to produce and distribute their products to the retailer at lower costs. The concept aims to enhance supply-chain integration by supporting and assisting joint practices. CPFR seeks cooperative management of inventory through joint visibility and replenishment of products throughout the supply chain. Informa-tion shared between suppliers and retailers aids in planning and satisfying customer demands through a supportive system of shared information. This allows for con-tinuous updating of inventory and upcoming requirements, making the end-to-end supply-chain process more efficient. Efficiency is created through the decrease in expenditures for merchandising, inventory, logistics and transportation across all trading partners.

Assuring Supply

Supply assurance is important to all organizations but becomes more critical when lean supply arrangements are made, and when supply bases are rationalized to one or a few suppliers for each significant product or service. For example, warehouse trans-portation forecasting is the process of estimating the number of vehicles that will use a specific warehouse facility in the future. A forecast estimates, for instance, the number of trucks using a planned facility. Traffic forecasting begins with the collection of data on current delivery routes. Traffic data are used to develop a traffic demand model and plan facility resource needs.

Factors That Can Affect Forecasts

The practical output of any forecasting tool is accurate only as long as the conditions remain unchanged. But when do all conditions ever remain the same over periods of time approaching a year or even longer? The goal of forecasting is to provide a prediction that is better than simply relying on random chance for the estimate. Factors that can affect the accuracy of forecasts include fluctuating lead times, changes in money markets, changing labor conditions, changes in global trade, technological shifts and political factors.

Implementing a Supply Strategy

Several common techniques for implementing supply strategies are based on hedging, spot buying, dollar cost averaging and contracting. *Hedging* typically involves the sale of a futures contract to offset the purchase of a commodity. It also can involve the purchase of a futures contract to offset the sale of a cash commodity (that is included as part of an end product sold by the organization). An organization simultaneously enters into two contracts of an opposite nature — one in a cash market and one in a futures market. For example, hedging is used to safeguard profit margins when a sales contract with fixed prices and extended delivery is negotiated, but the raw material purchase is postponed. If material prices were to rise between the time of the order and the actual purchase of raw material, the profitability of the entire contract could be jeopardized. Similarly, hedging also is used to protect inventory values in a declining market. If declining prices cause finished product prices to fall, the organization will lose money because of the relatively higher cost of raw materials. With a futures contract, the organization can protect itself against price fluctuations in raw materials. For example, consider an organization that contracts in April to supply generators to be delivered to a customer in December. The generators contain 25,000 pounds of copper, which were figured in the bid price at $3.47 per pound (April). Because of production lead time, the copper will not be needed until September. To guard against a possible increase in the price of copper, the supply management professional buys a September futures contract for 25,000 pounds of copper at $3.55 per pound, which is the April price of copper for delivery in October. If the spot (cash) price rises, typically the futures price will rise by a similar amount.

The second technique mentioned is called spot buying. *Spot buying* is the practice of buying a commodity on the "spot" or in the open market for immediate delivery. This technique frequently is used to allow for natural variability in demand or need at any period of time. For example, a supply management professional can forecast the need for temporary labor accurately but not perfectly. This difference between accuracy and perfection creates the need for a supply management professional to enter the spot market to handle the variance.

The third technique is called *dollar cost averaging*. When purchasing a commodity, component or service over a long period, the value of the items purchased, and in some cases stored, is an average, based on the mix of quantities and prices of items bought at different times. The averaging process dampens the departure of short-term price fluctuations from long-term averages.

The final and most popular technique for implementing a forecast in the supply environment is *contracting*. Rather than selecting a supplier and placing an order each time a requirement occurs, most organizations today select suppliers for longer-term relationships. Toyota Motor Co., of course, is noted for this approach.[1] These contracting activities typically involve products whose consumption represents a significant dollar value on a continuing basis. Contracts also may be written to cover families of products or classifications of products, such as office supplies, healthcare benefits or temporary labor services. Agreements such as these may take many different forms, including multiyear contracts, life-of-product contracts, future delivery agreements, contracts for a percentage of a supplier's capacity or options on products or capacity.

Long-term contracting is becoming more prevalent and contract terms are extending. For example, the authors' conversations with ExxonMobil uncovered a strategy to lengthen contract duration for many suppliers to as much as five years. If the selection of a group of world-class suppliers is required to provide the supply management professional's organization a competitive advantage, then those suppliers and the long-term relationships that are formed typically will be enhanced with long-term contracts or agreements. There are several types of these long-term agreements; various clauses to consider including in such an agreement are mentioned in the following sections.

In any contract of long duration, both parties are at risk from input cost changes. A buying organization would not want to agree to a fixed-price contract, only to watch the worldwide price of the basic materials fall significantly. Entering into a long-term agreement only to find labor or materials prices rising likewise would harm the supplier. The mechanism for sharing such risk is called a price-change clause (or an escalation clause). An escalation clause according to the *ISM Glossary* (2006) is a contract clause generally permitting a specified increase in the price of goods or services in the event of certain conditions, such as an increase in the supplier's raw materials or labor costs. Escalation clauses in a contract usually also provide for de-escalation or a price-adjustment clause. This is one focal point of the satisfaction that both parties derive from the agreement. It is an equitable method of ensuring that both parties share the risk of economic changes beyond their control. The fact that many price-change clauses do not share risk equally illustrates why this is an element of a long-term agreement that must be carefully crafted. One example for long-term contracting is to have the supplier agree to provide materials, components or services not for a specific period, but for the entire life span of the product. This is called a *service life contract*.

In today's business environment, the supply management and supplier organizations are entering into close, collaborative relationships based on mutual benefit. Supply management professionals are reducing supply bases to those suppliers that are judged to be superior. In such cases, it is likely that the organizations will enter into agreements that represent the extent of the commitment, and typically span several years. Such a close relationship between a buyer and a seller to attain some advantage from each other in a positive way is an alliance. After following careful supplier selection procedures, some supply management professionals are entering into five-year and longer contracts. The key factor in such long-term relationships is the selection process that often takes six to 12 months, but need not be repeated until the long-term contract expires. In the formulation of such long-term agreements, supply management professionals must be sure that provisions are made for specific, periodic performance and satisfaction reviews by both parties. Problems must be addressed in a timely and orderly fashion. As with any long-term agreement, provisions for dissolution should be agreed on before contract signing and the buying organization should have a written exit strategy.

A supply management professional's organization may have only sporadic requirements that, nevertheless, are of major importance. In such cases, a supply management professional may want to ensure that the goods will be available from a particular supplier. If this is the case, a future delivery contract can be negotiated to ensure that productive capacity is reserved. Sole-source suppliers of such items as capital equipment may fall into this category. Price-change clauses, as discussed previously, are clearly critical to these contracts.

A purchase option is the right to purchase something under agreed terms for a specified period. When the specified period expires, so does the right. Such rights are granted for a negotiable fee, which is forfeited if the right expires without the right having been exercised. If an organization is considering a project that has not been finalized, but which has an element with a time constraint, the organization may try to acquire an option on the time-critical element. For example, if the construction of a new factory is being considered, a suitable piece of land might be optioned. In exchange for a fee, the interested organization might be given an option to purchase that property until a specific date. Within that time, the buying organization may exercise its option to purchase the property at a specified price. If the organization decides not to proceed with the project, it is not obligated to purchase the land, but will forfeit the option fee.

In a fast-moving international environment, it may not be possible to precisely predict the specific number of products, services or components that a supplier will be required to produce or deliver. In cases where the volume can be estimated, but the exact product mix is unknown, organizations may reserve portions of suppliers' operating capacity. This practice ensures the availability of outside, subcontracted manufacturing capability, even though the precise mix of products to be produced will not be known until later. This reduces the uncertainty and risk associated with insufficient capacity and potential lost orders. The trade-off is the possibility that full reserved capacity, for which the organization must pay, may not be needed. The timing of purchases is thus an important consideration. Forecasting and budgeting go hand in hand. Many of the data used in developing budgets are derived from forecasts.

Budgeting for Supply Management

A *budget* is a financial plan that covers a specified period, usually one year. It identifies financial resources allocated to products, services, departments and/or divisions of an organization. Budgets are also tools for allocating funds to accomplish the objectives of the organization. In many ways, a budget is an information-transmittal device that bridges the planning and execution stages of management.[2]

A budget is a financial plan that indicates planned future actions and the funding levels required for their completion. Types of supply-related budgets include: direct materials budget, indirect materials (maintenance, repair and operating supplies, or MRO) budget, capital expenditures budget and the operating expense budget of each supply management function. (*ISM Glossary,* 2006) To be effective, budgets must contain some means by which management can determine whether planned operations are being accomplished. To be meaningful, a budget must support the organization's strategic plan.[3]

Two elements are common to all budgets:

1. *A set of specific goals that relate to future operations.* Establishing goals is equivalent to defining the standards by which the organization is to measure its performance.

2. *A periodic comparison of actual results and established goals.* This represents the control feature of budgeting activity and usually is accomplished through the development and use of budget performance reports.

With few exceptions, budgets are developed in terms of cost. In fact, one of the major duties of the supply management professional is the review, evaluation and understanding of a supplier's actual or anticipated cost data. The evaluation phase itself involves the judicious application of experience, knowledge and judgment to the cost data of the supplier. The purpose of this evaluation is to project reasonable estimates of contract costs. These estimates then become the basis for negotiations between the supply management professional and the supplier, and are used for arriving at contract prices that are satisfactory to both parties.

A primary function of budgets is to help anticipate and control expenditures through the allocation of financial resources. By using flexible budgeting techniques, the supply management professional can control expenses relative to the level of business activity. In addition, if expenditures vary significantly from month to month, it is important for the finance function to be made aware of this so that the organization can arrange the most economical means of financing the extra expenditures. For example, a brand such as Green Giant, a large supplier of vegetables, purchases harvested crops during certain times of the year. It must pay farmers for the crops when they are harvested, though the associated canned and frozen vegetables will be sold over a period of many months. Thus, Green Giant may have a cash flow issue because it pays for the materials long before it sells the finished goods. For example, Green Giant could use its cash reserves, a line of credit or a short-term loan. If the organization can plan in advance how it will finance the payment to farmers, it will have options and be able to choose the most favorable one.

In some organizations, a budget indicates preauthorization of expenditures for projects, products, services or other expenses. The purchaser is authorized to spend up to the budgeted amount without gaining additional approvals.

As expenditures are made, they can be compared against the planned expenditures shown in the budget. Consequently, budgets become a management tool useful for the evaluation of expected verses actual results. Budget variances must be analyzed in light of activities. Some budgeted items such as total material costs should vary with the actual volume produced.

Standard costs (discussed in Chapter 3) are used in estimating budgets for materials and labor. Given a forecast of sales, the standard costs are used to estimate material and labor requirements. These costs then can be allocated across budget centers, departments or subsidiaries, as appropriate.

Elements Subject to Budgetary Control

The primary purpose of a materials budget is to identify the quantity and cost of the materials necessary to produce the predetermined number of units of finished goods or to provide services, and to also serve as a means of control. A properly prepared direct materials budget provides management with a tool that:

- Permits the supply management function to set up a purchasing schedule that ensures delivery of materials when they are needed;

- Leads to the determination of minimum and maximum levels of raw materials and finished parts that must be on hand; and

- Establishes a basis from which the treasurer or finance department can determine or estimate the financial requirements of the supply management department.

Although generally based on estimated prices and planned schedules, direct materials budgets may provide information that:

- Permits planned maximum lead time,

- Leads to an enhanced selection of sources,

- Reduces transportation costs,

- Provides a basis for planning workloads, and

- Helps in identifying forward-buying opportunities.

In addition, the direct materials budget may improve negotiations for products or services by reducing the pressure of time constraints. Other budget line items may be established to account for inventory items that are consumed within the organization, but are not directly attributable to each product or service.

Wages and salaries include not only the direct costs of supply management personnel, but benefits such as retirement contributions, and health and insurance benefits. Travel budgets cover expenses related to visiting current and potential supplier facilities. Expenses include transportation, food and lodging. Travel budgets also may include travel for training and other activities of those in the supply management department. Occupancy and energy costs are the overhead costs associated with the space occupied by supply management. Communication expenses include telephone charges, fax costs, e-RFx[4] costs, Internet access and postage. This expense includes subscriptions to information services and databases such as offered by Dun & Bradstreet, as well as books and DVDs for the supply management library, and magazine and journal subscriptions. Funds for attendance at education activities, such as seminars and classes, and professional organization memberships also are budgeted.

Steps in Budgeting

The first step in the budget process is review and concurrence on the organization's goals and objectives. This is important, because the budget will demonstrate, in financial terms, how these goals and objectives are to be met.

The next step is defining the needed resources in the budget process, beginning with general forecasts in terms of economic trends, purchase prices, sales and profit. This will provide more realistic estimates for revenues and expenditures. While certain forecasts may be provided by top management, finance or marketing, it is generally agreed that the actual budget requests are best developed at the level where implementation takes place. This is usually at the department level or lower. This approach generally works best because those responsible for implementation are in the best position to identify their own needs and generally are more motivated because they have input in the decision-making process.

The major categories of resources used in supply management include personnel, equipment, furnishings and training. Personnel expenses include salaries and benefits for the existing staff as well as proposed additions to staff and recruiting expenses such as travel, advertisements and relocation expenses. Equipment expenses include purchase, replacement or maintenance of computer hardware and software. Furnishings include tables, desks, chairs and other office fixtures. Training expenses include travel to seminars, seminar expenses and other training materials, including books, magazines, journals and DVDs.

Clearly, the cost of needed resources must be estimated accurately for a budget to be valid. The best starting point for this step is by closely analyzing the previous year's actual expenditures. This information then can be used to extrapolate figures for the new budget year.

Standard material purchase costs can be developed from historical data and/or from an analysis of supply market conditions for the coming budget period. These costs serve as targets against which to buy for a forthcoming period.

Presenting the budget and obtaining the appropriation is handled differently by each organization. It is common for a committee to be set up to review and consolidate all budgets and make recommendations, but there are many other approaches. After the budget has been presented and any changes made, appropriations are set to cover the approved expenses during the budgetary period.

The final step in the budget process is the control of expenditures during the budgetary year. The budget is the most widely used tool in organizations to provide financial control. This control activity, called *variance analysis,* occurs through the matching of appropriations and expenditures, and also through tracking expenditure

trends against budget estimates. Variances are analyzed and reasons for the deviations from the budget are identified. Corrective actions then are taken as necessary.

Types of Budgets

An organization can choose from several types of budgeting processes: zero-based, cash-flow, line-item and flexible. In addition, an organization often budgets separately for major expenditures, such as key programs or projects and major capital expenditures.

Zero-based budgeting is a process that does not use past experience to determine future needs. As defined in the *ISM Glossary* (2006), zero-based budgeting is an operating, planning and budgeting process in which each manager must begin each budgeting period with no predetermined allocations and must justify all proposed expenditures. All budget items are fully justified in detail and are viewed as new requests, as opposed to continuations of current programs. The assumption is that the budget is prepared from scratch, or is zero-based. The zero-based budget is helpful in questioning the traditional way things have been done because all programs, including those that have been in effect for years, are justified, prioritized and subject to scrutiny and approval. In reality, few organizations use a "pure" zero-based budget. Those that do generally use this type of budget for selected segments of the organization, and use the traditional historical/extension concept for developing the budget for all other areas.

A *cash-flow budget* links budgeted expenditures to revenue in each budgetary period. What can be spent is a function of what revenue is received. (*ISM Glossary,* 2006) With this type of budget, cash outlays are forecast over periods of time such as weeks or months. This type of budget is useful when tight cash controls are necessary, and can be used in conjunction with any other type of budget.

A *line-item budget* is formatted to show individual expenses during the budgetary period without tying those expenses into broad programs or goals. A typical line-item budget would include such categories as salaries, office supplies, travel, equipment, telephone expenses and postage. Each of these categories contains details of what these expenses are. For example, the travel section would show exactly what travel is to be taken and the estimated cost of each trip. Line-item budgets generally are incremental, meaning that they are primarily based on the previous budget period.

Flexible budgets are those that change depending on changing conditions, such as an increase or decrease in output. One type of flexible budget is known as the variable budget, which is a set of budgets that account for different conditions. Often, a flexible budget follows a formula that is used to determine the needed budget amount

based on output. The obvious advantage of flexible budgets is that they allow quick responses to changing conditions.

Program or *project budgets* also are known as *program planning budgeting systems (PPBSs)*. This type of budget often is used by not-for-profit and governmental entities. Program budgets tie the organization's goals and objectives to the programs or sections responsible for meeting those goals or objectives. To further the relationship between goals and funds spent, this type of budget normally uses productivity measurements and cost-benefit analysis. Program budgets offer management the ability to evaluate and make decisions on the need for various programs.

A *capital budget* according to the *ISM Glossary* (2006) is the budget for buildings, equipment and other long-term assets that are used for the operation of the organization. The primary purpose of the capital budget is to provide a formal summary of future plans for acquiring facilities and/or equipment. This area of budgeting is particularly critical because of the magnitude of funds involved and the length of time required for capital recovery. In addition, the capital expenditures budget can be used as a basis from which supply management can determine the best possible source for a given addition. Capital expenditures budgeting involves both short-range and long-range expenditures. Short-range expenditures must be included in a budget for the current year, and must be evaluated in terms of their economic worth. Long-range expenditures usually will not be implemented during the current budget period; thus, their inclusions in the budget can be in somewhat general terms.

The *open-to-buy (OTB) budget,* often used in the retail sector, is similar to a cash-flow budget. Open-to-buy budgets link cash requirements and expenditures during a budgeting period with available funds during the budgeting period. In retail, marketing strategies often are divided into separate programs that are measured by return on investment. The open-to-buy budget allocates funds based on the planned investment by budgeting period. Those funds then are used for inventory replenishment. When a requisitioner makes a request to buy, it may be limited by the availability of funds for that program and budgeting period. Limited funds also may affect the supply management professional's ability to obtain volume discounts.

The interpretation of actual versus budgeted spending should be approached with caution. For example, purchasing price variance (PPV) is the difference between the standard price and the actual price paid during a budget period. If an organization experiences unfavorable price variance (pays more than standard), is that bad? It depends. The organization still may be paying less than the market, which could give it a competitive advantage.

Buying Strategies

Strategic plans are developed with suppliers to support the operational flow management process and development of new products and services. In organizations where operations extend globally, sourcing should be managed on a global basis. The desired outcome is a win–win relationship, where both parties benefit, and reduction times in the design cycle and product development are achieved. Also, the supply management function develops rapid data communication systems, such as electronic data interchange (EDI) and Internet linkages to transfer possible requirements more rapidly. Activities related to obtaining products and materials from outside suppliers require performing resource planning, supply sourcing, negotiation, order placement, inbound transportation, storage and handling, and quality assurance. These activities also include the responsibility of coordinating with suppliers in scheduling, supply continuity, hedging and research of new sources or programs.

Among the strategies available to supply management professionals is purchase timing. The judicious use of forecast data can assist in selecting several appropriate options as depicted in Figure 2-1.

Spot buying is a short-term strategy employed in falling markets where supply management professionals wish to take advantage of decreasing prices with each successive purchase. Cash-flow constraints, or goods that are perishable or subject to rapid technology change, are other factors that might make this approach appropriate.

Advance purchases for use to cover a period of forecasted need are classified as *buying to requirements.* This practice is probably the most common, because it ensures supply while avoiding excessive inventory carrying costs. Even in a just in time (JIT)

Figure 2-1   Timing of Purchases

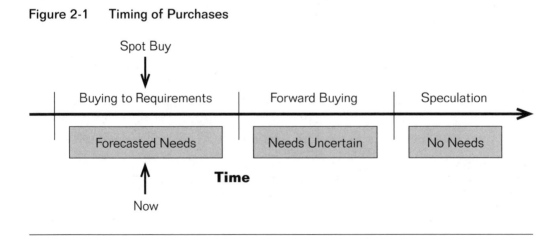

environment, the supply management professional needs to look at future requirements. Organizations often will guarantee a percentage of the forecasted requirements
to maintain flexibility. For example, the organization guarantees the next four weeks'
requirements. For weeks five through eight, the supply management professional
guaranties 90 percent of the forecasted requirements, and for weeks nine through 12,
75 percent.

Forward buying is sourcing goods or services beyond actual forecasted need.
Frequently, conditions such as potential supply constrictions or inflationary markets
cause supply management professionals to hedge price or supply by buying more of
a product than is forecasted. This practice protects the organization from shortages or
delays the impact of rising prices. The trade-off is increased inventory carrying costs.
The astute supply management professional will evaluate the trade-off between inventory carrying cost increases and the decreased risk of supply constriction or prices.

Speculative buying (volume purchase agreements) refers to purchasing material
in excess of current and future known requirements, with the intention of profiting
from price movement and resale. (*ISM Glossary,* 2006) These speculative goods may
be the same as those purchased for consumption, but quantities purchased will be in
excess of current or future needs. The intent is to take advantage of expected increases
in price to profit from the resale of the goods. When significant quantities of specific
products or commodities are needed, these requirements may be met through volume
purchase agreements. The primary objectives of these agreements are to ensure supply
and to consolidate requirements to maximize purchase leverage. Depending on the
duration of the demand, these agreements may be either short term or long term, and
may take many forms. These agreements range from specific descriptions of volumes
to be purchased to very nebulous descriptions.

Other Strategies That Affect Sourcing[5]

For several reasons it may be desirable to award contracts to suppliers of materials,
services or components for the life of the product. If duration of the need is limited,
it may not be cost-effective to rebid or renegotiate. Familiarity with need, use or
special supplier capabilities are other reasons for this type of supply strategy. Often
the agreement is developed between supply management professionals and suppliers
with a long, collaborative history. It may include activities such as joint engineering
of the components to be supplied. Many automobile companies, such as Ford, Honda
and General Motors, have traditionally awarded "life-of-product" agreements for a
particular model platform to suppliers who have expended significant resources on
engineering and development efforts.

Just in Time Manufacturing

Just in Time (JIT) manufacturing is more a philosophy of doing business than a specific technique. The JIT philosophy focuses on the identification and elimination of waste wherever it is found in the manufacturing system. The concept of continuous improvement becomes the central managerial focus. Several of the more highly publicized results of JIT implementation are the initiation of a pull system of manufacturing; significant reductions of raw material, work-in-progress and finished-goods inventories; significant reductions in throughput times; and large decreases in the amount of space required for the manufacturing process. The greatest improvements for an organization implementing JIT is usually in the area of quality. If there is little or no raw material inventory, then incoming raw material and components must be of impeccable quality, or manufacturing will cease. Similarly, each intermediate manufacturing step must yield high-quality output, or the process will stop.

The aim of JIT as stated previously is to reduce waste and cost throughout the entire supply chain. If a manufacturer decides that it no longer will carry raw material inventory and that its suppliers must carry the inventory, this does not reduce supply-chain costs. It only transfers those costs from one link in the supply chain to another. While those additional inventory carrying costs may be borne for the short term by the supplier, they eventually must be passed on in the form of higher prices.

One of the most-often-cited difficulties in the implementation of JIT is a lack of cooperation from suppliers because of the changes required in their systems. In addition to changing from traditional quality-control inspection practices to the implementation of statistical process control, the supplier is asked to manufacture in other than the usual lot sizes and to make frequent deliveries of small lots with precise timing. Additionally, the supplier normally is required to provide the supply management professional access to its master production schedule, shop floor schedule, materials requirements planning system, managerial system and financial statements. Clearly, supply management professionals must be cooperative and persuasive in converting supply chains to JIT operations.

Supplier selection, single sourcing, supplier management and supplier communication become critical issues for supply management professionals in implementing JIT. Critical issues in JIT supplier selection include quality-control methods, proximity, manufacturing, flexibility and reliability. JIT organizations and their suppliers develop close collaborative relationships supported by long-term, single-source contracts. The concept of alliances often is applied to the JIT purchaser-supplier relationship.

Following supplier selection, careful supplier performance measurement and management often lead to supplier certification — a designation reserved for those suppliers whose quality, on-time delivery and reliability have been proven over long periods of time. Close, frequent JIT purchaser-supplier communication is essential in both directions. Suppliers are given long-range insight into the supply management professional's production schedule. Often, this look ahead spans a dozen weeks or more, with the nearest several weeks' schedule frozen. This allows the supplier to acquire raw materials in a stockless production mode and to supply the supply management professional without inventory buildups. Suppliers provide daily updates of progress and production schedules and problems.

Consignment Inventory

Inventories that are owned by a supplier but are stored at the supply management organization's facility are said to be on consignment. These goods are billed to the organization only after they have been consumed. At first glance, this practice seems to be advantageous to both the supply management organization and supplier. The supplier has a guaranteed sale, while the supply management professional has the security of on-site inventory without inventory investment. However, there are potential problems with this procedure. For example, even though consignment inventory is stored at the purchasing organization's warehouse, it still is owned by the supplier. As such, the supplier may want to remove some items to sell to another customer, while the supply management professional whose facility stores the goods is counting on those items to cover its own requirements. The fact that the purchasing organization does not invest in consignment inventory, but only pays as it is used, does not relieve the purchasing organization of the responsibility for managing the inventory.

Commodity Exchanges

A large number of agricultural goods, metals, other natural resources and currencies are traded on dedicated exchanges, known as commodity exchanges.[6] The exchanges create a marketplace where buyers and sellers may freely trade their commodities. For example, General Mills and Cargill are active players on the grain exchange, as is expected given their products. BMW is an active player on the currency exchanges, given its global market segments. The movement of prices on a commodity exchange (market dynamics) may not be related to the supply or demand of an item. Often, most of the transactions that take place on a commodity exchange are not made by actual users or suppliers of the specific commodity. Additionally, the quality of goods being traded may not be adequate for actual use by the purchaser, or the commodity may not be traded on a spot or a futures market.[7]

Supplier-Managed Inventory

With supplier-managed inventories, the supplier is responsible for ensuring stock levels are maintained at appropriate levels in the supply management professional's facility, and for replenishing items when stock is low. Ownership of supplier-managed inventories depends on the arrangement between the supply management professional and the supplier. The supplier usually bills the buying organization for usage. The transactions take place electronically.

Evaluation of Supplier Offers

The evaluation of supplier quotations and proposals to determine the best overall competitive offering for a product or service is one of the primary responsibilities of supply management. Each situation should be handled in the manner best suited to the circumstances at hand, but a common process framework can be applied. For example, Toyota Motor Co. would evaluate a supplier offer to provide office supplies far differently than a supplier offer to provide design and engineering services. The latter is far less dependent on price and far more dependent on the value-based arrangement between Toyota and the supplier. Thus, a common strategic supply process can be used to manage both acquisitions. The following section will address some of the important issues to consider when evaluating supplier offers. Supplier financial information often is reviewed as a part of screening suppliers or early in the process of evaluating supplier's offers. This information is a key to understanding the supplier's financial viability, as well as opportunities for negotiating with the supplier.

Supplier Financial Information

The supplier's financial structure can provide valuable insights for the supply management professional and often is related to the discussion of cost and price information that follows and that is expanded on in Chapter 3, "Strategic Cost Management." Nokia does an extensive supplier financial analysis both during the supplier selection process and on an annual review basis.[8] Therefore, the next section first reviews financial information that may be obtained from an organization's income statement or balance sheet. Two major types of information that may be of interest to a supply management professional are *profitability* and *liquidity*.

Figures 2-2 and 2-3 present the basic ratios that measure profitability and liquidity and how this information may be used in negotiations. The figures used to make these calculations come from supplier financial statements. The *balance sheet* is an accounting of the organization's assets and liabilities at a specific point in time. The *profit and loss statement (P&L)* and *statement of earnings* show the organization's sales and the expenses incurred to generate its income. *The cash flow statement* shows the organization's sources and uses of funds, as well as the change in available cash over the reporting period. All these statements usually are generated quarterly and annually for publicly held organizations. *Margin analysis* reflects various measures of the organization's profitability in relation to its sales. Gross profit and operating profit calculations are in the following sections. Very poor ratios compared to the industry averages may indicate financial problems that should be discussed with the supplier before committing to a long-term agreement.

Figure 2-2   Profitability Ratio Analysis

RATIO	FORMULA	APPLICATION IN SUPPLY MANAGEMENT
Gross Profit Margin	(Sales − Cost of sales) / Sales	Provides insight on amount of income the supplier has left to cover nonproduction overheads and profit per dollar of sales. This figure may be compared to the industry average to determine the organization's production efficiency.
Operating Profit Margin	Profit before taxes / Sales	Shows the organization's profit before tax, which may be interesting to compare to industry averages; a high margin may create an opportunity to negotiate lower prices.
Return on Investment (ROI)	Net income / Total capital invested	Shows how well the organization is investing its money. Organizations with higher-than-industry-average ROIs may be using their assets well and may be in a strong financial position.
Return on Assets Employed (ROAE)	Net income + Interest expense after tax / Average capital employed	A measure of how the organization is using its assets, including the impact of borrowed funds.
Return on Total Assets (ROTA)	Net income / Total assets	Measures the organization's efficiency in generating income based on its assets invested.

Figure 2-3   Liquidity Analysis

RATIO	FORMULA	APPLICATION IN SUPPLY MANAGEMENT
Working Capital	Current assets − Current liabilities	An organization's day-to-day liquidity; should be greater than one if an organization is to cover current expenses. Not as useful as quick ratio because all current assets may not be perfectly liquid. If low, the supplier may be willing to negotiate better prices to obtain cash.
Current Ratio	Current assets / Current liabilities	Test of short-term debt-paying ability. Indicates the potential willingness of a supplier to make concessions to obtain cash.
Quick Ratio	(Cash + Marketable securities + Current receivables) / Current liabilities	This measure includes only the assets that can be converted quickly into cash, where one means it can cover current expenses. Indicates how desperate the supplier may be for early payments or to provide attractive quantity discounts to liquidate inventory. Major price concessions may be made for quick cash.

Cash flow or *liquidity analysis* is an organization's ability to meet short-term financial obligations. Key liquidity ratios are shown in Figure 2-3. Cash flow or liquidity can be a powerful force in a negotiation. For example, a petrochemical supplier that had abundant cash available represented a major customer to its supplier but had a cash shortage because of a recent expansion and debt obligations. The buying organization recognized this difference in cash needs and arranged a creative payment schedule, moving it from a net 30 to net 60 with no adjustment in price. Cash was not as important to the supplier as to the buyer, but this buyer represented an important customer. As a result, the supplier was willing to make this concession in payment terms.

In addition to profitability and liquidity, another valuable piece of information is the percentage of the buyer's sales in relationship to the supplier's total sales. This information determines the type of leverage the buyer might have with the supplier. Such information may be particularly beneficial when combined with the other ratios presented in the previous two figures.

Inventory levels also can be important information derived from the asset section of the balance sheet. If inventory is high, the organization might be more willing to make a quick sale than if inventory is low. Also, the level of inventory in combination with cash availability may provide insights to the supplier's incentive to reduce the price but receive early payments.

In addition to checking the balance sheet and income statements, reading the notes to the financial statements in the supplier's annual report also may be valuable. Explanations about acquisitions, damages, spin-offs, large expenditures and related activities can affect an organization's financial position. Other sources for suppliers in the United States may be found in the special notes in the 10-Ks issued by the Securities and Exchange Commission (www.sec.gov/) or by Dun & Bradstreet (www.dnb.com/). In addition, comparisons to industry ratios for U.S.- and non-U.S.-based organizations are readily available online at such sources as http://moneycentral.msn.com./[9]

The main point of this discussion is to research available information to determine what may be an incentive for the supplier to meet both the supplier's and the supply management professional's goals. Research may provide insights that previously went unnoticed. If the supplier is a private organization and does not make its financial statements public, two options are available: (1) if the supply management professional is an important customer, the supplier may be willing to provide the financial information on a confidential basis; or (2) supply management can generate industry averages and assume that the supplier of choice is close to the average. If the supplier passes the financial ratio analysis hurdle, supplier responsiveness is the next consideration.

Supplier Responsiveness to an RFx

Perhaps the most critical aspect in evaluating bids offered by suppliers is ensuring that the quotation or statement of work (SOW) within the bid response meets the specifications and requirements of the initial RFQ, RFP or RFI package. This is important because the supply management professional must ensure that the supplier will meet the specifications, requirements or statement of work defined in the solicitation. If not, the supply management professional must be aware of the implications in accepting the bid. Not meeting specifications or submitting an alternate statement of work can have either a positive or negative affect on the supply management professional's business. At best, it can result in an alternate design or service at a lower cost, which may be acceptable to the supply management professional's organization. At worst, it may cause quality concerns or it may not meet the minimum requirements defined by the buying organization. Supply management professionals have the responsibility to ensure that: (1) suppliers are quoting to specification or (2) the quoted exceptions are acceptable to the entire organization. To fairly evaluate all the quotes received, suppliers must quote based on a comparable set of specifications or a comparable statement of work. Otherwise it is extremely difficult to determine which supplier offers the most competitive package.

As with the base specifications and statement of work, suppliers must be aware of the quality requirements and all other terms and conditions for the goods or services as part of the initial solicitation package. In their responses, suppliers must acknowledge that they will meet these requirements. If suppliers quote exceptions, the supply management professional must ensure that the organization fully understands the effect of each exception, and the supply management professional must determine whether the alternative proposals are acceptable.

Most solicitations include a set of contract terms and conditions that the supply management professional has developed to match the risks and issues related to the product or service being considered. Suppliers typically respond with alternative language to reduce their own risks. Including these contract terms and conditions in the solicitation allows the supply management professional to consider contractual issues along with other aspects of the evaluation.

Supply management organizations often will not consider an alternative proposal unless the supplier also has quoted the specific item or service requested. In addition, presale technical service is offered by some organizations as a part of the quotation process, particularly when technical products or services are being purchased. Supply management must ensure that it does not take unfair advantage of suppliers offering presale technical assistance to which it is entitled prior to award. Acceptance of more presale service than is customary in the industry may obligate the organization to more than is anticipated.

Technical and Operational Analysis

Technical analysis involves determining if the supplier's proposal will satisfy the specifications or statement of work. Supply management should actively involve the engineering, manufacturing, materials control, operations, marketing and other using departments in the technical analysis of the bid. This is a natural extension of involving these departments in the initial definition of specifications or statement of work.

Operational analysis consists of evaluating the feasibility of the product or service being purchased. Though it might be technically capable of the work, organizations often conduct an operational analysis to verify the economics, ease of use and functioning feasibility of the product or service.

Cost and Price Analysis

Cost analysis is defined in the *ISM Glossary* (2006) as an evaluation of actual or anticipated cost data (material, labor, overhead, general and administrative and profit). Cost analysis is the application of experience, knowledge and judgment to data to project reasonable estimated contract costs. Estimated costs serve as the basis for buyer-seller negotiation to arrive at mutually agreeable contract prices. A comprehensive cost analysis begins with an understanding of the industry that the potential suppliers represent as well as an understanding of each supplier's supply chains. This analysis is completed prior to the solicitation and provides industrywide data on which the competitive proposals will be evaluated. This analysis includes:

- The structure of the industry, such as a monopoly or open competition,

- The market structure, such as international versus domestic,

- Cost drivers and price trends, and

- Technology trends and barriers to entry by new competitors.

Cost or price analysis is frequently the most important element of the bid evaluation process. Cost or price analysis often is performed by supply management, sometimes with the involvement of finance, using an engineering estimate, or with a cross-functional team. Several types of cost or price analysis can be applied, but generally only one method is used to evaluate a specific quotation. For an organization buying a service, a cost or price analysis would begin with a detailed examination of the statement of work.

Price analysis as defined in the *ISM Glossary* (2006) is the comparison of a supplier's price proposal (bid) against reasonable price benchmarks, without examining or evaluating the separate elements of the cost and profit making up the price. Some form of price analyzing is required for every purchase. Price analysis can be accomplished by analysis of competitive price proposals, comparison with catalog or market prices, comparison with historical prices or use of independent cost estimates.

To maintain good supplier relations, it is important to provide the supplier with a reasonable profit to pursue the business in the first place and to continuously deliver future products or services. Analysis of costs versus profits is important to assess the viability of the supplier and subsequently its quotation.

Price is just one element of total cost. Total cost of ownership of a product include pretransaction, transaction and post-transaction costs. It requires the identification and analysis of the cost drivers. Costs may include acquisition expenses, transportation, duty and brokerage fees, costs of quality programs, accounting costs, late delivery, warranty, service and transportation fees, and customer support, to name a few. Analysis of the total cost provides a clearer picture of the complete financial implications of a purchase. The use of total cost for evaluating quotations is an increasingly accepted supply management practice in both the public and private sectors.

One widely accepted application of cost analysis is activity-based costing. *Activity-based costing (ABC)* is a cost management method for attributing indirect costs to the activities that drive cost. This approach is in contrast to more traditional accounting methods that pool and allocate indirect costs on a formulaic basis that does not necessarily reflect the true cost structure. Activity-based costing recognizes that not all activities and processes use the same amount of indirect resources. Activity-based costing is an allocation approach that uses multiple indirect cost pools with different cost drivers rather than a single cost pool.

At the outset of manufacturing a new product, it is reasonable to assume that the supplier will use extra time or material while learning how to produce the product efficiently. As time progresses or volume increases, the supplier has the opportunity to capitalize on manufacturing efficiency to reduce overall manufacturing costs. This "learning curve" helps the supplier become better able to offer more attractive pricing once the product is in production. The learning curve concept also applies to purchased services. It will take time for the services supplier to gain the necessary experience and expertise.

A cost analysis is a tool that incorporates not only the purchase price of the piece of equipment, but also all operating and related costs over the life of the item, including maintenance, downtime, energy costs and salvage value. Prior to calculating costs in terms of net present value, the supply management professional must first define the key operating cycle for the equipment, as well as all the other factors that affect costs. Life-cycle costing assists in evaluating equipment purchases with different initial purchase prices and different operating costs over the useful life of the equipment.

Supplier Capability and Responsibility

Supply management should review the many aspects of a supplier's ability to meet the requirements of the contract and check the organization's references of both past and present customers. For example, many organizations not only ask for references from existing customers but also from any customers who have ceased doing business with the supplier in the past year. These organizations prefer to speak with customers who have decided to take their business elsewhere. Some important factors to consider include:

- *Past performance.* The past performance of a supplier on similar jobs and implications for performance on future contracts should be carefully evaluated.

- *Capacity.* The supplier's capacity to take on additional business.

- *Skills.* The skills the supplier has to manage the specific product or service in question.

- *Integrity.* The supplier's integrity and conduct in past business dealings.

- *Time in business and market.* Length of time in business as well as track record and evidence of sustainability.

- *Certification and licensing.* Verification that a supplier has the appropriately documented certifications and licenses. For example, these could include "right to use" for software or other intellectual property that is part of a proposal or ISO 9000 certification.

- *Financial factors.* Financial factors may influence the final selection of a supplier. When financial information will be required for analysis by the supply management professional, it is prudent to ask for the information in the RFP or RFQ.

Data Mining and Tools

Data mining (DM — also called "knowledge-discovery" in databases) is the process of automatically searching large volumes of purchasing data for patterns such as classification, association rule mining and clustering. Data mining is a complex topic and has links with multiple core fields such as computer science. A fairly recent topic in supply management, data mining adds value to rich seminal computational techniques from statistics, information retrieval, machine learning and pattern recognition. A simple example of data mining is its use for retail sales. If a clothing store records the purchases of customers, a data mining system could identify those customers who favor silk shirts over cotton ones. Another example is that of a supermarket chain, which, through analysis of transactions over a long period of time, found that beer and diapers often were bought together. Although explaining this relationship may be difficult, taking advantage of it is easier by placing the diapers close to the beer in a supermarket. A final example is the efficient use of a procurement data warehouse to aid in the effective spend analysis of items/services purchased across a large multinational organization.

Data mining has been defined as "the nontrivial extraction of implicit, previously unknown, and potentially useful information from data"[10] and "the science of extracting useful information from large data sets or databases."[11] The process involves sorting through large amounts of data and picking out relevant information.

SWOT Analysis

A SWOT analysis is a strategic planning tool used to evaluate the strengths, weaknesses, opportunities and threats involved in a project, business venture or in any situation requiring a decision. It involves monitoring both the internal and external environment of the organization. The required first step in SWOT analysis is a definition of the desired end state or objective. The objective must be explicit and approved by all participants in the SWOT analysis process. Failure to identify correctly an end state leads to wasted resources and possibly failure of the enterprise. A SWOT analysis is comprised of the following:

- *Strengths:* attributes of the organization that are helpful to achieving objectives,
- *Weaknesses:* attributes of the organization that are harmful to achieving objectives,
- *Opportunities:* *external* conditions that are helpful to achieving objectives, and
- *Threats:* *external* conditions that are harmful to achieving objectives.

SWOT analyses are used to develop possible strategies by asking and answering the following four questions:

1. How can the organization use each strength?

2. How can the organization eliminate its weaknesses?

3. How can the organization exploit each opportunity?

4. How can the organization defend itself against each threat?

Summary

Improved communication between supply management professionals and suppliers is imperative. The use of e-procurement should facilitate close interaction and rapid communication between supply management professionals and suppliers. In addition to the transmission of purchasing information, it enhances communication of production plans (to provide forward visibility to the supplier) and production schedules from the supply management professional to the supplier whether the organization produces a good or provides a service.

E-procurement allows the supplier to pass operational "economies of scale" to the supply management organization in the form of lower purchasing costs, and generates transportation "economies of scale" that increase the feasibility of more frequent lean deliveries.

Key Points

1. The importance of data collection, analysis and management through the use of e-procurement systems has grown dramatically. Supply management professionals must influence the design and development of e-procurement systems by understanding what they are and their potential benefits and following an implementation process that will increase the likelihood of success for e-procurement applications and resulting data management.

2. There has been an increasing awareness and anxiety throughout the world concerning the explosive growth in overhead costs. As organizations develop multiple supply chains to support international markets and operations, there has been a tendency to duplicate systems, transactions, roles and responsibilities.

3. The budgeting process helps the organization determine its funding needs. It is a control and monitoring mechanism for the organization.

4. Types of budgets include zero-based, cash-flow, line-item and flexible. Organizations also may use separate budgets for capital expenditures as well as specific projects.

5. Forecasting is the process of estimation in unknown situations. It has evolved into the practice of demand planning or management in everyday business forecasting for many organizations. The discipline of demand planning, also sometimes referred to as supply-chain forecasting, embraces both statistical forecasting and a consensus process.

6. Several common techniques for implementing supply strategies based on forecast data include hedging, spot buying, dollar cost averaging and contracting.

7. Evaluating supplier offers in a systematic way is critical and includes considering:

   - Key supplier financial ratios,

   - A supplier's responsiveness,

   - Information gained from technical and operational analyses of the supplier, and

   - Cost and price analysis.

8. Data mining is the process of electronically searching large volumes of data and picking out relevant information.

9. A SWOT analysis is a strategic planning tool used to evaluate the strengths, weaknesses, opportunities and threats involved in a project or in a business venture or in any other situation requiring a decision. It involves monitoring the internal and external environments.

3

Strategic Cost Management

Supply management professionals are constantly encouraged by senior management to expand cost management efforts. Cost management has and always will be a primary tenet of supply management's mission. Performance expectations, however, are being raised considerably as global competition forces organizations to squeeze unnecessary costs out of every part of their businesses. For supply management professionals, this means widening the breadth of spend areas covered, managing costs more holistically and delivering cost savings faster.

Wide differences exist between organizations in the breadth of external spend managed or influenced by their supply management professionals. At one end of the spectrum, some organizations are just beginning to address fragmented spending that limited the organization's leverage in expenditures for certain categories. Also, some supply management professionals have been unable to penetrate certain spend areas because of pushback from powerful users or lack of expertise on the supply team. Furthermore, despite attention over the past decade on capturing and understanding spend profiles, some organizations are still several years away from systems and tools to overcome the limitations of multiple ERP systems and lack of common supplier and item-coding schemes.

In contrast, supply management at other organizations have already overcome information and organizational barriers to extend their influence deeply into the full range of external expenditures. They leverage volumes across units globally and aggressively pursue opportunities jointly with users for traditional purchase categories as well as in nontraditional areas (e.g., facilities management, legal, advertising, contract manufacturing). Supply management also challenges assumptions about internal expenditures, examines organization competitiveness against marketplace alternatives and helps the executive team evaluate outsourcing options. These organizations, which will become the standards against which other organizations are measured, include a growing number of organizations such as Honda, Toyota Motor Co., Intel

Acknowledgement: A special thank you to Lisa Ellram for her contributions to this chapter.

Corp., Amerigroup Corp., LG Electronics, American Express, Bank of America and Ericsson.

Taking a more holistic view to understand the influence of the drivers of cost is required. Supply management professionals are expected to eliminate unnecessary expenditures and maximize value received from remaining expenditures. A range of tools and techniques can be used, including complexity reduction, greater standardization, tighter management of specifications and demand, compliance management, price benchmarking, should-cost analysis and total cost of ownership analysis.

CHAPTER OBJECTIVES

• Provide a brief discussion of price versus cost analysis.

• Explain how a more thorough knowledge of cost elements can be used to better understand supplier operations.

• Present total cost of ownership (TCO) as a viable way to understand costs.

• Describe various approaches to estimating costs.

• Provide an in-depth discussion of cost management programs.

• Present information to help understand lease arrangements.

A Framework for Understanding Costs

Price is the amount of money or its equivalent for which anything is bought, sold or offered for sale. In contrast, cost is an outlay or expenditure of money, time, labor, trouble, etc., paid to produce, accomplish or maintain any good or service. Price and cost are related: Price minus cost equates to profit margin.

Price analysis was presented in Chapter 2. It fits best in competitive situations in which the suppliers have comparable offerings and there are few hidden costs. Price analysis works with one-time buys or where the item purchased is not critical enough that the buyer needs to deeply understand its cost makeup. Some people may think that price research is simply a matter of comparing one supplier's price to other prices in the market; however, it is much more involved. It is necessary to understand the supplier's pricing structure and tactics to know how to prepare for price-reduction efforts.

Cost analysis is a method of identifying and comparing as many of the product/ service-related costs as possible to ensure that the price finally paid is reasonable in terms of the market, industry, supplier's cost structure, the organization's needs, and the end use of the product, service or material. The supply management professional, however, does not have to conduct a detailed cost study of every item purchased to ensure a fair price. Whether a detailed study is conducted or not, costs should be tested against logically established in-house targets. Cost analysis is appropriate when the supply management professional wants to better understand what makes up the costs of an item, improve the item's cost structure or modify it. It may be appropriate for unique or custom buys, where the supply management professional believes the supplier is overcharging or there may be room for improvement in the supplier's processes. It also may be appropriate before the supply professional enters into high-value long-term contracts or alliances, so the supply management professional has a better understanding of what he or she is committing to and where there may be potential opportunity. Cost analysis also is a means of identifying and eliminating unnecessary costs.

Proper application of price and cost analysis can result in a wide range of benefits — from the obvious reduction of outlay for purchased materials or services to improved supplier performance, revision of inventory policy and increased control of quality and delivery. Often, suggestions for design or operations process improvement also result from price/cost analysis. These and many other benefits arise primarily from knowledgeable supply management professionals properly applying these techniques. They require the supply management professionals to be objective and to keep broadening their perspectives as they review the requirements.

In some purchasing situations, cost may be more relevant, while at other times price is the primary concern. The critical decision is to determine when, what type and to what extent research should be conducted on price and cost factors. A U.S.-based retailer, for example, was buying high-end Italian purses. The purses were handmade by skilled craftsmen in a remote Italian city. The retailer attempted to reduce prices by promising an increased volume but the approach failed. Volume was not a relevant factor that would affect the Italian purse maker's costs or price because the main cost consideration was the high variable cost of labor. This was much higher than any fixed costs such as plant and equipment. In addition, the price was established on a cost-markup basis.

The retailer was much more successful when analyzing different variable costs: the processing costs of the invoices and the shipping costs. The retailer found a way to reduce both costs that resulted in decreased prices. For the retailer, attempting to manage administrative variable costs was successful while leveraging fixed costs had no impact. Figure 3-1 illustrates the key elements that make up a supplier's cost. The *product cost roll-up* includes direct materials, direct labor, other direct and overhead. This also is often called the *cost of goods* or *cost of sales.* As presented in Chapter 2 during the discussion of ratio analysis, the product's gross margin is its price less the

Figure 3-1   Major Elements in a Supplier Cost Breakdown

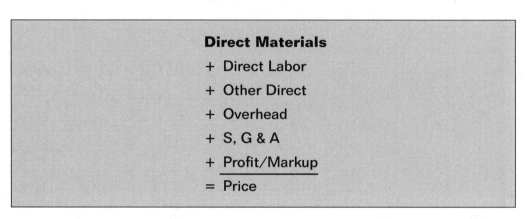

cost of goods. This represents what the organization has in profit to cover all its sales, general and administrative costs (S, G & A) and make a contribution to operating profit or margin. The organization still must pay taxes and interest before it accounts for its net profit after tax. From this, it should be clear that if price is reduced without a change in cost structure, the profit margin must be reduced. The supplier will not be happy about reducing its profit margin and cannot be expected to have profit reduced year after year. Unless profits are extremely large, the supplier will need to focus on some aspect of cost to reduce price, and may cut corners as a result. The ideal situation would be to reduce costs and prices so that both the supplier and the buyer benefit.

For both the supplier and the buyer to benefit, it is necessary to determine how best to manage pricing and cost factors. An attempt to identify and manage the wrong cost variables will lead to frustration and failure, as demonstrated in the Italian handbags example. The buyer must understand what costs can be most easily reduced and conduct research on these variables. The next section will discuss the elements of cost and several ways in which this information can be obtained and used.

Elements of Cost

The term *elements of cost* is frequently used to define the individual factors of cost that are involved in the development, manufacture and sale of a product or service. In addition to influencing the market as a whole, supplier cost is significant in price determination. To conduct a cost study and analyze its results properly, the supply management professional must have a basic knowledge of the accounting terminology and method used, and must be familiar with the techniques used to estimate materials, labor and overhead.

The following discussion reviews nine types of cost:

1. Standard

2. Relevant/irrelevant

3. Direct

4. Indirect

5. Fixed

6. Variable

7. Average total

8. Marginal

9. Opportunity cost

Standard Costs

Standard costs can be defined in terms of either manufactured products or services. For manufacturing, standard costs are predetermined costs of manufacturing a single unit or a number of product units during a specific period in the immediate future. For example, in the bakery business, standard costs often are developed "per dozen." These are the planned costs of a current product and/or future operating conditions the organization expects. For services, standard costs are the predetermined costs of providing a single unit of service or a number of service units during a specific period in the immediate future. One must keep in mind that standard costs are developed under a set of certain assumptions about operator efficiency, capacity utilization and labor and materials prices. As these change, the standards become less accurate. Standard costs generally are re-evaluated annually as part of the annual planning process.

Proper use of standard costs can be of great benefit to management. For the supply management professional, standard costs provide a basis for developing budgets, controlling costs and measuring efficiencies within the organization. Standard costs also are used to identify cost-reduction options, evaluating bids and negotiating contracts.

The standard cost of materials is the planned price for the materials based on the projected environment in a given time period, generally one year. Purchase price variance (PPV) is the difference between the standard costs and the actual price paid.

As mentioned in Chapter 2, purchase price variance generally is not a good measure of supply performance because it does not consider changes in the market or whether the original standard price set is realistic.

Relevant Versus Irrelevant Costs

Some costs change when a process is changed, while others remain the same. For decision-making or analysis purposes, *relevant costs* are those costs that will change for the organization if a particular decision is made. For example, the organization has outsourced processes that will free up 10,000 square feet of office space; there are no other immediate uses for that office space. The rent on the freed space is an irrelevant cost to the immediate decision, because the organization still leases the office building, must pay rent on the freed space and has no alternative uses for it. One problem that occurs when analyzing relevant versus irrelevant costs is the level of analysis. For instance, the function within the organization that freed up the 10,000 square feet of office space no longer may have the cost of that space allocated to them. However, the organization as a whole still must pay the entire lease. Thus, at a systemwide level, the cost is irrelevant to the analysis because the cost will not change whether the 10,000 square feet is used or not.

Direct Costs

In manufacturing, costs usually are accumulated and differentiated by categories called direct and indirect. Direct costs are defined as those that can be accurately attributed to a product or service — for example, material or labor. A subassembly may require three hours of production labor *(direct labor)* and $25 worth of material *(direct material)* per unit. As the number of units increases (barring learning curves and quantity breaks), the amount of labor and material per subassembly will increase directly; that is, two units will require six hours of labor (at the rate for labor established for the required skill level) and $50 for material, these are direct costs. Within the services industry, direct materials might be materials used on a job, such as copier parts for a copy machine repair, as well as the cost of the direct labor of the person performing the repairs. Other kinds of costs beyond labor and materials that are frequently considered direct appear in the category *other direct,* which includes such items as travel expenses to visit customers, inspection labor and electricity used by a smelter on a metered machine.

Indirect Costs

Indirect costs, although no less real than direct costs, are not immediately attributable to any given unit of production. At the very least, their identification with a unit is difficult. These costs are necessary for the operation of the plant, factory or process, or the delivery of a service. Examples of indirect costs for goods and services include building depreciation expenses, property taxes, building maintenance, general employee training and executive salaries. Indirect costs often are called manufacturing overhead, or, simply, overhead. Overhead often is charged to products or services at a predetermined rate based on historical expenses adjusted for known changes in costs and expenditures. In general, all plant labor that is not classified as direct labor ends up in this category. These costs traditionally are charged to the product or service based on a percentage of direct labor. If the level of indirect costs is not related to the level of direct labor, distortions in cost allocations can occur. Activity-based costing management attempts to improve overhead allocation, as shown in a later section of this chapter.[1]

Fixed and Variable Costs

Fixed and variable costs are important considerations and must be understood during price/cost analysis. Variable costs, such as direct labor, materials and commissions to salespeople, increase as output increases. Fixed costs, such as general and administrative expenses, plant, equipment and property taxes, remain constant. For example, a specialty retailer of perfumes and other high-end cosmetics would like to order 5,000 units (ounces) of perfume and promote it throughout its stores during the next year. This perfume comes in a highly decorative container, the retail price is $160 per ounce, and the wholesale price is $120 per ounce. In the past, the retailer never ordered more than 500 ounces per year. Because of the much larger order, the retailer attempted to secure a quantity discount. Should the wholesaler grant the buyer a quantity discount? The buyer needs to research the basic economic principles of fixed costs and variable costs to understand how to proceed.

The fixed costs for the perfume manufacturer include plant, equipment and labor. These costs will exist for the supplier whether the sale is completed or not. For this perfume, the fixed costs were determined to be approximately $1 million per year. This figure did not vary as a function of the quantity of a particular perfume produced within the plant. The plant usually operated at full capacity so no idle resources existed. The plant averaged 40,000 ounces per year, so the average fixed cost per ounce was $25.

The variable costs that increase with each unit of production include the rare fragrant ingredient used in the perfume and the packaging; these costs are about $70 per ounce. This can be broken down further as follows: $40 for the perfume materials and labor and $30 for the packaging including both a crystal bottle and velvet box. The fixed costs plus variable costs for the materials equal $95 ($25 + $70). Dedicated administrative costs, including purchase order transmission, accounts receivables and account managers, were allocated at $5 per ounce. The total cost to the perfume manufacturer is $100 per ounce ($25 + $70 + $5). The only cost that would be immediately reduced per unit with a larger order is the administrative cost of $5, a small percentage of the total cost. These costs are shown in Figure 3-2.

What should the target price be? The fixed costs are invariant. The administrative costs are small and the core ingredients of the perfume cannot be changed. Two possibilities exist. First, when purchasing ingredients in large volumes, the perfume manufacturer may be able to acquire some of its ingredients at a discount; however, the fragrance is extremely rare and a high worldwide demand exists for it. Second, the packaging could possibly be changed to a lower cost material that is not handcrafted. Or, possibly, the manufacturer could buy large quantities of packaging materials at lower prices. However, because the packaging is handcrafted, it is unlikely that costs will drop significantly as the quantity is increased.

In this case, the analysis must focus on variable material costs. The possibility of different packaging materials and the potential cost reductions would seem to be the best candidate for cost reductions. Research in the form of a value analysis could address this issue. However, it is clear that simply expecting a price reduction because of

Figure 3-2   Perfume Cost Breakdown at Different Volumes

COST FACTOR (PER UNIT)	500 OUNCES	WITH 4,500 ADDITIONAL UNITS	WITH 4,500 ADDITIONAL UNITS IF NOT AT CAPACITY
Price	$120	$120	$120
Variable	$ 70	$ 70	$ 70
Fixed	$ 25	$ 25*	$ 0–25 **
Administrative Costs	$ 5	$ 5	$ 5
Total Manufacturing Cost	$100	$100	$ 75–100
Total Profit per Unit to Perfume Manufacturer	$ 20	$ 20	$ 45–20

*Note that because the plant is operating at full capacity, there is no reduction in fixed costs. The manufacturer actually may have more demand than it can supply. As a result, it may have to divert capacity from another customer to meet this demand.

**Note that because the plant is not operating at full capacity, as long as the supplier continues to sell its other production at the current price, additional fixed cost should not be charged to any incremental production because that would just increase the supplier's profit.

a large volume would not be reasonable because of the low fixed costs and the high variable costs.

A very different approach would occur if a manufacturer were not operating at capacity, and a product had low variable costs. In this situation, the buyer should expect a nice price reduction with a high volume order. For example, if the 4,500 additional units created no added fixed costs, the buyer could try to negotiate up to a $25 per unit price reduction on the incremental units, based on the fact that the supplier has already "covered" its fixed costs of production, and all incremental units that share part of the fixed cost burden at a rate of $25/unit add $25 to the supplier's profit (see Figure 3-2).

An understanding of fixed and variable costs often is the starting point when preparing for price/cost analysis, participating on a new product development team or analyzing two suppliers with different levels of fixed and variable costs. The analysis should determine the general industries and specific suppliers' fixed and variable costs and available capacity. When supply management professionals have a poor understanding of these basic variables, they end up frustrated and do not achieve their goals. They believe that the failure was caused by poor execution skills, when in reality the failure was the result of poor planning and analysis.

Semivariable costs are also a consideration. Semivariable costs include both fixed and variable cost elements. Costs may increase in steps or increase relatively smoothly from a fixed base. Examples include supervision and utilities (such as electricity, gas and telephone). Supervision costs tend to increase in steps as a supervisor's span of control is reached. Utilities typically have a minimum service fee and costs increase relatively smoothly as more of the utility is used.

Average and Marginal Costs

The consideration of fixed costs and variable costs is extremely important when planning the cost/price analysis. The perfume example is obviously simplified compared to many situations. Two additional concepts are important during the cost/price analysis: average total cost (ATC) and marginal cost (MC).

Average cost = *total cost* divided by the *rate of output,* or
Average total cost = *total cost* divided by *total output*

At the simplest level, if the total cost for a restaurant to supply 10 steak dinners is $75, the average cost is $7.50. But total costs change as the rate of output increases. For instance, one person may be able to cook and serve 10 steak dinners but an additional server or cook may be required if 15 dinners were to be served simultaneously. The average cost would increase because of the extra server required for the five additional dinners.

Consider an organization that produces lightweight, denim jackets. Figure 3-3 shows how average costs change as the rate of output varies. Row M of the cost schedule indicates the fixed, variable and total costs of producing 15 jackets per day. Fixed costs are $120 (factory and machine rentals); variable costs are $125 (denim and labor). Thus, the total cost of producing 15 jackets per day is $245. The average cost for this rate of output is simply the total cost ($245) divided by the quantity (15) or $16.33 per day. The average total cost is indicated in column 5 of Figure 3-3 and by the points on the graph.

Figure 3-3   Average Costs Versus Rate of Output

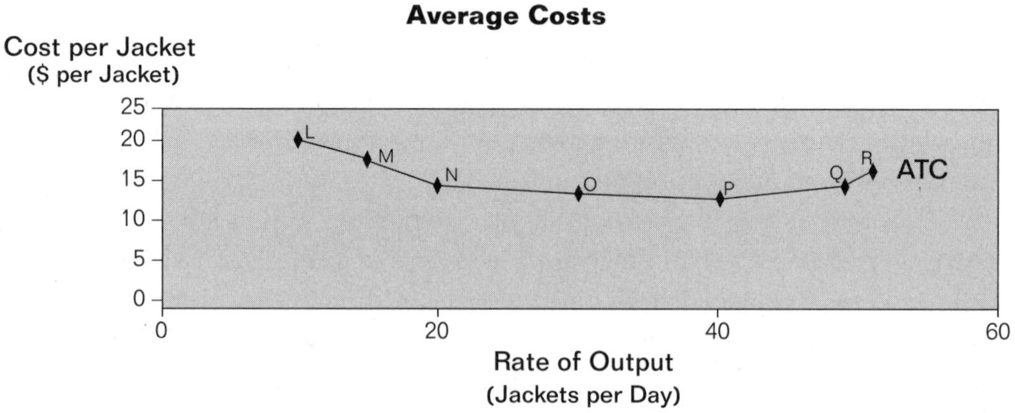

Average Costs

	(1) RATE OF OUTPUT	(2) FIXED COSTS	+	(3) VARIABLE COSTS	=	(4) TOTAL COSTS	(5) AVERAGE COSTS
K	0	120		0		120	—
L	10	120		85		205	$20.50
M	15	120		125		245	$16.33
N	20	120		150		270	$13.50
O	30	120		240		360	$12.00
P	40	120		350		470	$11.75
Q	50	120		550		670	$13.40
R	51	120		633		753	$14.76

In the price/cost analysis process, an important point of the ATC curve is its "U" shape. Average costs start high, fall and then rise once again giving the ATC curve a distinctive U shape. The goal is to find the low point in the U curve and order this amount because this would be the lowest average total cost (ATC).

The initial decline in ATC is largely because of fixed costs. At low rates of output, fixed costs are a high proportion of total costs. It is very expensive to lease or buy an entire factory to produce a few jackets. To reduce average costs, it is necessary to make full use of the plant and equipment. As output increases, the fixed costs of production are distributed over an increasing quantity of output. Fixed costs no longer dominate total costs as production increases (compare the second and third columns in Figure 3-3). As a result, average costs tend to decline. Average total costs do not fall forever; they bottom out (as illustrated by point P in Figure 3-3), then start rising again. What accounts for this turnaround?

The upturn of the ATC curve is caused by rising *marginal costs.* Marginal costs refer to the change in total costs when one more unit of output is produced. In practice, marginal cost is easy to measure; just observe how much total costs increase when one more unit of output is produced. Rising marginal costs imply that each additional unit of output becomes more expensive to produce. Why is this? Why does the third jacket cost more than the second jacket? The explanation lies in the production function. As the capacity is approached, output increases at an ever-slowing degree. It is a level of diminishing marginal product. The supply management professional should either know the most effective order volume for this is the point at which the best price can be obtained or be able to determine when to spread volume among suppliers versus leverage volume.

Many supply management professionals believe that increased volume should result in decreased prices and will act accordingly. This discussion on fixed, variable, average total, and marginal costs clearly indicates that it is not that easy. The production function must be analyzed. The supply management professional must understand the relationship between the four types of costs discussed here: fixed, variable, average total and marginal. Then the supply management professional can focus on the correct cost factor.

At this point, it is important to remember that a good supply management professional focuses on the interests of both parties to the transaction. Understanding the cost structure will assist in focusing on the supplier's best interests.

Opportunity Cost

Opportunity costs represent the "lost opportunity" for the organization by spending money or tying up money in one investment opportunity rather than the other. For example, if an organization has a great deal of money tied up in China, it loses the opportunity to invest that money elsewhere around the globe. This does not mean that the China investment is bad, just that it was undertaken and thus used some of the organization's resource portfolio. The next section discusses total cost of ownership, an analysis approach used by organizations to better understand their true cost of doing business.

Total Cost of Ownership

No matter what the supply management professional's sources of price/cost information, the supply management professional cannot adequately identify total cost until he or she has considered quality, delivery and many other relevant factors. The importance of these factors varies according to the requirement itself. Some organizations, whose need for high-quality or on-time delivery is critical, have developed indexes by which the supplier's performance in these areas can be measured.

Quality and delivery are, of course, more important in some businesses than they are in others. In buying a subelement for a missile, quality may well be the overriding concern. Delivery may be extremely critical in another area. For example, in ship supply purchasing, delivery is so important that special supplier delivery controls have been instituted. Two factors — limited dock space at major ports and the time that the ship is scheduled to sail — make delivery schedules very tight. Typically, supplier's deliveries are scheduled hourly. Because the delivery schedule is so demanding, the supply management professional and the supplier often negotiate a financial penalty for late deliveries.

Other factors that the supply management professional must consider in judging total cost are such variables as transportation, taxes, insurance, handling, special packaging, duties, brokerage fees and terms. Thus, *total cost of ownership (TCO)* is an assessment of all the direct and indirect costs involved with the acquisition, use and disposal of an item. For instance, purchase price is a direct cost, but other items, such as product training, warranties, maintenance, storage and transportation, are considered indirect costs. In other words, purchase price may be only a small part of TCO.

A straightforward application of TCO is the acquisition of an automobile fleet for the sales department of a large financial services organization. The price of each vehicle is one consideration, but many other factors, including the cost of insurance, gas mileage, maintenance and depreciation, must be considered. When sourcing for an automobile, most buyers will consider only the purchase price; however, the cost of a warranty is a major item that also should be considered. It is best to research the warranty coverage and price compared to other manufacturers' warranties. It may be easier to analyze the price of the warranty than the price of the automobile if the dealer is providing the warranty service. Why? The dealer may be able to provide the service at a relatively low cost but cannot change the cost of the automobiles.

Figure 3-4 presents a way to think about total cost. In that diagram, the top and the bottom parts are narrower than the middle. The reason for this is that the pre-acquisition and disposal aspects of total cost may be less obvious or even ignored in a negotiation.

To indicate the many possible costs, an aerospace organization listed more than 40 items that could be involved potentially in the total cost, a few of which follow:

1. *Unit price.* Purchase price quoted by the supplier.

2. *Cash discount.* Early payments of discounts offered if payment is made during a prescribed period.

3. *Delivery performance.* Cost incurred by the buyer as a result of early or late delivery.

4. *Payment period.* Number of days after shipment or delivery of supplies before payment is due.

5. *Progress payments.* Extent to which payment is required by the supplier prior to shipment or delivery.

Figure 3-4   Total Cost of Ownership for Fleet Automobiles

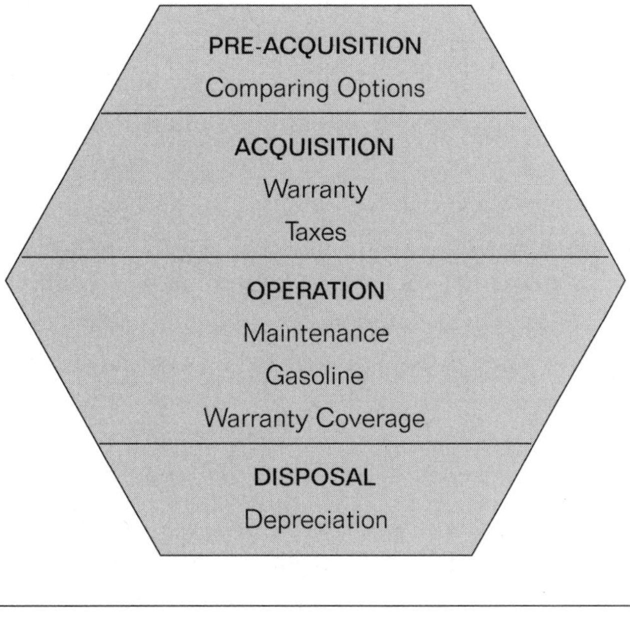

PRE-ACQUISITION
Comparing Options

ACQUISITION
Warranty
Taxes

OPERATION
Maintenance
Gasoline
Warranty Coverage

DISPOSAL
Depreciation

---

6. *Freight costs.* Additional costs associated with inventory in transit, where the buyer has taken title.

7. *Transit inventory.* Organization costs associated with inventory in transit, where the buyer has taken title.

8. *Run interruption costs.* Costs related to the supplier's acceptance of the buyer's orders that interrupt the production run or sequencing order.

9. *Tooling costs.* Tooling costs incurred by the supplier expressed as unit cost or lump sum.

10. *Packaging.* Special packaging costs based on the buyer's request.

11. *Escalation costs.* Additional costs above the purchase price because of the escalation of labor, materials and inventory costs.

12. *Cost of nonconforming material.* Costs incurred by the buyer in dealing with and tracking rejected or nonconforming products.

13. *Warranty.* Cost incurred by the supplier in providing warranty coverage as requested by the buyer.

Depending on the situation, each of the factors listed could possibly warrant attention during product development as well as during the price/cost analysis process. Research could indicate the most relevant costs and the extent to which they could be the focus of a cost-reduction effort. For instance, an organization was importing a rare, natural medicinal extract derived from the trees of the Amazon region in South America. The prices were extremely high, but the supply management professional believed that it was largely a matter of market supply and demand. The research, however, indicated differently. The supplier had no knowledge of transportation so it was paying an exorbitant price to a freight forwarder in Brazil. The cost-reduction focus turned to the freight forwarder on behalf of the supplier rather than on the price of the extract. This is also an example of *landed cost.* A common term in logistics, landed cost refers to the cost of the purchased item, plus freight, handling and any customs charges, duties, storage to a designated point and so on, associated with getting the product from the supplier to the buyer's dock.

Life-Cycle Costing

Life-cycle costing (LCC) is a type of total cost of ownership analysis that deals specifically with equipment purchases. Life-cycle costing considers the purchase price of the equipment, plus all operating and usage costs of the item over its useful life. These costs include maintenance, downtime, scrap or loss, energy, training, installation, as well as salvage and disposal costs minus investment cost recovery. For most capital equipment, these additional costs are greater than the price of the equipment. Think of a desk ink-jet printer, which may retail for $100 or less. The cost of replacement ink-jet cartridges may be around $40 each. It is easy to see where the money is being made by the supplier. Over a certain print volume, laser printing becomes much less expensive on a cost per page, even though the initial cost is significantly higher. While replacement ink is also higher for laser printers, it lasts substantially longer. LCC analysis should be conducted for all capital acquisitions. Thus, rather than looking at the total cost of one printer versus the other, the organization needs to look at a *unit total cost (UTC)*. UTC reflects the total cost of ownership of an item per relevant unit of output. For a printer, it might be cost per printed side. For raw materials, it might be the same as the landed cost per unit (explained previously). For hourly labor, it might be total cost per hour, assuming the output is the same. If not, it would be total cost to complete a given task.

The utility of LCC extends to other areas, such as long-term outsourced labor contracts. This often involves a consideration of *total cost for performance of services.* A large nuclear power generation facility outsourced all its security labor to a third party. Its selection was determined based primarily on price. The supplier attained a low price by paying the security guards lower-than-market wages. This resulted in a fairly high turnover of guards. In addition to the cost of training new guards, the buying organization paid between $2,000 and $3,000 for extensive background checks for each guard. Because of the high turnover, this expense was extensive. The buying organization performed a TCO analysis and concluded it would be cheaper to pay a more competitive wage, improve employee retention and reduce the cost of background checks. The organization renegotiated the contract with the supplier based on its findings, and both parties benefited under the new contract.

Activity-Based Costing Management

Activity-based costing management (ABCM) is an approach that recognizes that not all activities and processes use the same amount of indirect resources. Activity-based costing is an allocation approach that uses multiple indirect cost pools with different cost drivers rather than a single cost pool. All indirect costs are identified and costs that have similar drivers are pooled together. This creates more accurate cost allocation than most conventional cost accounting systems.[2] ABCM is very supportive of improved TCO analysis, because it creates a more accurate picture of how activities drive cost.[3]

Other Cost Considerations

Within the area of TCO analysis and cost management in general, a number of other cost concerns exist. For example, the cost of carrying inventory is a hidden cost that may vary significantly based on the choice of supply. For example, if the supply professional is purchasing from a supplier in China, and the supply management professional takes ownership of the inventory when it leaves the supplier's location, the supply management professional may own additional inventory for more than a month versus shorter ownership using a domestic supplier. This ties up funds that the organization must either pay interest on or use for inventory rather than for other options (opportunity cost). Some estimates gauge that the average organization's investment in inventory may represent between 25 percent to 40 percent of its invested capital.[4] This figure includes the cost of funds tied up in inventory, overhead, insurance and taxes, obsolescence, spoilage and shrinkage, space costs and any handling cost. To the extent that not all suppliers create the exact same inventory carrying costs, this is a relevant consideration in supplier selection and negotiation. To the extent that an organization can improve its inventory management, this is also a relevant consideration. The *cost of quality*[5] is similar in nature, for it is a hidden cost that may vary significantly by supplier. Poor quality may increase the buying organization's costs of carrying inventory, for it may need extra inventory to ensure it has enough good inventory. It may increase the cost of materials handling, inspections, returns, customer returns and replacement, plant performance and so on. When Intel Corp. discovered more than 20 years ago that one of its suppliers was providing significantly higher-quality materials that contributed to significantly higher production yields, it began to make the cost of quality an explicit consideration in its supplier selection and evaluation process.

Intangible costs also should be considered. These costs are very difficult to measure, but they still may affect the organization's profitability indirectly. These include issues such as loss of customer goodwill and tarnished image from shipping poor-quality product, or outsourcing customer service and call center operations to people who have not been properly trained or do not understand the culture or expectations of the clientele. While these are very difficult to quantify, they can be estimated, and certainly should be mentioned as part of a cost analysis or TCO analysis if they present a potential concern.

Cost Estimating

Cost estimating is a valuable part of any cost management program. If a supply management professional is familiar with the various concepts of cost, then logically he or she also should be able to estimate costs as a tool for comparison. Several large organizations, such as Deere & Co., Toyota Motor Co. and Honda, have recognized this by assigning estimating personnel directly to the supply management organization or making them available to supply management. Organization policy makes this a formal relationship.

There are three basic approaches to cost analysis:

1. *Roundtable approach.* Experts are brought together to develop cost estimates, usually without detailed drawings, statements of work or bills of materials, and with limited information on specifications.

2. *Comparison estimating.* Based on determining the historical cost of the same or similar item as the one being estimated and adjusting or projecting the historical cost for future production. This comparison may be performed at the cost element level or total price level.

3. *Detailed analysis estimating.* Characterized by a thorough review of all components, processes and assemblies. This method is the most accurate of the three methods for estimating the direct cost of production. It is also the most time-consuming and expensive. The level of detail can be varied to meet an organization's needs. Each of these methods is detailed in Figure 3-5.

Estimating a supplier's costs can be based on a *should-cost* philosophy — exploring what an item *should* cost, based on data gathering and analysis, rather than comparing prices quoted by suppliers. As a result of this cost analysis, the supply management organization often develops a *target cost*[6] for what it is willing to pay for an item. Often, this is based on a combination of the supplier's price, testing the market for pricing (i.e., what the organization can afford to pay and still be profitable), and what it estimated based on the should-cost analysis. While more organizations are estimating suppliers' costs as a basis for changing their requirements, improving processes or seeking price reductions, cost estimating for services purchases still is relatively rare in practice.[7]

Because there are several industrially accepted accounting procedures for cost accumulation and overhead allocation, the supply management professional must analyze the supplier's method in terms of product need and equity. However, the major elements of cost do not change from one system to the next, and supply management professionals should be familiar with them. In some cases, detailed cost estimates can be requested from the suppliers and used to make comparisons. In others, the suppliers' costs will not be available and the supply management professionals will have to rely solely on their own estimates.

Figure 3-5   Cost Analysis Methods

	ROUNDTABLE	COMPARISON	DETAILED
Relative Accuracy	Low Limited data used	Moderate/High Depending on data, technique & estimator	High Based on engineering principles
Relative Estimator Consistency	Low Different experts give different judgements	Moderate/High Depending on data, technique & estimator	High Based on uniform application of principles
Relative Speed of Development	Fast Little detailed analysis	Moderately Fast Especially with repetitive use	Slow Requires detailed design & analysis cost
Relative Development Cost	Low Fast & little data development cost	Moderate Depending on need for data collection & analysis	High Detailed design & analysis cost
Relative Data Required	Low Based on expert judgements	Moderate Only requires historical data	High Requires detailed design & analysis

Developing a Cost Management Program

Any effective cost management program must include both a short-term and long-term approach. Neither tactic will ultimately be successful without the other. Completion of a short-term strategy can be accomplished in a few weeks and involves two basic steps: (1) organizational analysis and (2) opportunity analysis.

Organizational Analysis

To be effective in developing and executing cost management programs, the supply management function needs to be effectively organized. The objective of an organizational analysis of the supply management function is to determine how the function can be streamlined and reorganized to not only cut costs, but also to increase effectiveness and productivity. Distribution of responsibility among supply management professionals may be imbalanced. Perhaps those supply management professionals responsible for committing the majority of the organization's expenditures are too isolated from the chief procurement officer (CPO) or lack a thorough understanding of the organization's strategy.

If the current supply management organization is ineffective, the supply management professional can approach the reorganization assignment in several ways:

- Raise the reporting level of key supply management professionals to as high a level as possible consistent with the importance of their respective assignments.

- Rearrange reporting linkages so that related supply management professionals report to the proper people.

- Eliminate underused positions and consolidate tactical functions where possible.

- Minimize the number of management reporting levels.

- Make final adjustments based on the strengths and weaknesses of the people involved in the function and organization.[8]

Opportunity Analysis

Opportunity analysis reviews whether an organization has effectively implemented some of the leading acquisitions practices followed by best-in-class organizations in various industries. The practices that can serve as the foundation of any cost management program in the longer term include:

- Contract rationalization and consolidation;

- Standardized, global processes;

- Productivity management, including work standards and comparative performance review;

- Segmentation of process components, center-led with dedicated staff (e.g., bidding, e-sourcing, negotiations, etc.);

- Extensive use of POs versus signed agreements;

- E-enablement modules integrated with enterprisewide ERP platforms;

- Use of strategic sourcing with dedicated resources for establishing strategies for key commodities (categories); and

- Use of low-cost business service centers, especially globally.

From a TCO perspective, other forms of cost management include improved form, fit and function; improved ease of use; administrative savings (such as streamlining department efficiency or benefiting from e-procurement); and improved quality.

These should all create real bottom-line savings for the organization. For example, an organization that institutes an online ordering system for office supplies may save money by eliminating stored supplies that are more subject to pilferage, damage and obsolescence. It no longer may need to dispose of print cartridges that are past their date or fit printers that have been retired.

Issues to Consider When Establishing a Cost Management Program

Cost management programs provide a systematic forum for reducing the total cost of acquiring and using a product or service. However, cost management should not be achieved at the expense of quality, or, as discussed previously, hidden costs will be incurred. Today, many organizations' cost management programs focus explicitly on value — either maintaining or increasing the value and service received by the purchase while reducing cost. The principal objective should be to leverage improvement opportunities, such as the changes in technology, environment and on-the-job experience, to control costs.

Cost reduction is an effort to trim the costs associated with acquiring and using a particular product or service. Cost reductions may be obtained by selecting alternative materials, processes, services, sources and purchasing methods. For example, as more organizations adopt lean inventory methods, they tend to work with little or no supply buffers, resulting in reduced inventory costs. However, if a supply or delivery problem occurs, the supplier will have to use a premium form of transportation to ensure the continuity of production (in a manufacturing environment) or service availability (in a nonmanufacturing environment), which will raise costs. As supply management professionals and internal customers gain experience with lean techniques, they will have to work together to identify why problems occur and develop solutions to reduce costs. Cost reduction or cost savings result in a lower price paid for a comparable purchase made in the past. It is measurable, and has direct spend reduction implications for the organization.

Cost avoidance is defined as an effort to prevent or reduce supplier price increases or ancillary charges, or to delay an expenditure. This may be accomplished through the use of value analysis, negotiation and a variety of other techniques. Because these savings are less tangible, there is continuing discussion over reporting cost-avoidance savings. Care should be taken to keep cost-avoidance savings separate from cost-reduction savings.

Cost containment is typically a detailed plan to hold costs and purchase prices within certain target limits over a specific period. For example, a service provider might work with a supplier to remove $1,000 in cost to produce and deliver the service over a period of time. This may be accomplished by using value analysis, negotiations and a variety of other techniques.

Calculating cost avoidance/reduction is key to the success of the organization's cost management program. At PraxairTechnology Inc., an air-products supplier, cost savings are kept strictly separate from cost avoidance. In addition, all the savings are calculated by a controller, explained to the business units and submitted for their approval. This ensures that cost savings do not simply evaporate. They are accounted for. If the business unit chooses to spend the savings or otherwise use it, rather than apply it directly to profit, that is a strategic decision that the business unit has to explain to top management. This enhances the credibility of reported cost savings immensely. The objectives of cost management methods include tangible cost savings and future cost avoidance. For example, by using freight consolidation, lower truckload rates can be obtained from a carrier — the amount of cost savings is clearly tangible. However, negotiating a smaller rate increase may mean cost avoidance that is less tangible. In evaluating the performance of any cost management program, it is important not to lose sight of cost-avoidance benefits, as well as direct cost savings.

The success of Praxair's programs, as well as cost savings programs at organizations such as Bank of America and Toyota, depend a great deal on top management support. Some cost management programs, such as value analysis, involve fundamental changes in the design of products and services. This requires willing participation and wholehearted cooperation from many departments or functions. A clear mandate and participation from top management help ensure the close coordination necessary in such programs. Lack of top management support is detrimental to morale, and effectiveness, and could result in the inability of the cost management program to reach its full potential.

Coordination with other departments and business units is essential to successful cost management programs. The supply management professional must understand the needs of internal customers and obtain their cooperation and support for the cost management initiatives. The supply management professional must be sensitive to areas the business wants to emphasize, and its areas of future growth and retrenchment, or time can be spent on areas of diminishing importance. Thus, consideration of *product/service longevity* and where the product or service is in its life cycle is important. The needs of the internal customers must be met, or they will reject supply management's cost management efforts.

Various cost management initiatives have different implementation *time requirements*. Supply management should simultaneously implement programs that take limited time and those that take more time so that savings are realized quickly, as well as in the long term. Consideration must be given to the cost benefit analysis of a particular cost management initiative. The time it takes to develop and implement the program versus the potential payback must show a positive return. For example, developing a *standardization program* is time-consuming and has organizationwide implications. Yet, such a program is essential in terms of reducing costs by eliminating unnecessary and costly variations in products and services. Standardization of equipment increases the use of that equipment, decreases spare parts inventories, and reduces maintenance downtime. This lowers the unit cost of the service.

Implementing a Cost Management Program

A cost management program aims to identify and eliminate unnecessary costs and obtain cost efficiency without affecting the quality of the raw material, component parts or systems involved. Any cost management program may contain some of the critical elements discussed in the following sections.

Centralized Buying. Various types of organizationwide buying agreements can be used for cost management. One common organizational type is *centralized buying*. With centralized buying, a specific department or supply management professional is given total authority and responsibility for purchasing for the organization. Centralized buying offers the following advantages:

- By consolidating purchases of all departments/divisions, the supply management function has greater clout and can obtain better prices.

- Standardization among operating units helps an organization obtain better prices by taking advantage of supplier economies of scale and reduced inventories.

- It reduces administrative expenditures for both the supplier and buying organizations.

- The supply management organization can develop specialization and greater expertise in source development.

Critics of centralized buying believe that it slows the acquisition process and increases lead times. They also argue that being away from the point of use makes it difficult to understand the internal customer's needs and can stifle innovation, especially when business units are geographically diverse.

Lead-Divisional Buying. *Lead-divisional buying* is a compromise between centralized and decentralized buying. Under this method, the division that consumes the largest quantities of a category is made responsible for the sourcing of that category for all internal customers in the organization. While this gives the organization clout in negotiations, it also ensures that the sourcing division is closer to the internal customer's needs.

Other Buying Methods. *Commodity councils* often are used to obtain the advantages of both centralized and decentralized buying. With this method, a committee composed of representatives from various user divisions is formed. Decisions made by commodity councils capture the needs of various internal customers, yet result in the clout achieved through centralized buying.

Pool buying involves the consolidation of requirements of multiple organizations into a single large order to obtain better pricing. At the same time, suppliers can use the economies of scale and pass on part of their savings to the purchaser. As a result, both parties win. The costs of administering a pool buying or cooperative purchasing program are shared by the participants, who in some cases may have been unable to afford the administration costs of purchasing individually. Consortia are another form of pool or cooperative purchasing.

Previous Japanese business success has led many business analysts and researchers to investigate Japanese business practices. One of the characteristics identified is a long-term association between buying and supplier organizations. Further research uncovered the Japanese understanding of the need for significant operating efficiency and dedication in all phases of the business' processes. A major requirement for achieving efficiency is sustained research and development and investment in technology by all members of the supply chain. In addition, close cooperation between all members of the supply chain is needed. At other times, the organization may make an *equity investment* in an important supplier. This gives the supplier extra cash to invest in its operations and the buying organization a greater stake in the supplier's success. Suppliers look for stability in exchange for increases in proactive participation with buying organizations, and the willingness to invest in technology and management processes. The buying organization is in a position to influence stability through the use of long-term returns from the business investments made by the supplier's and purchaser's organizations. However, the buying organization also must be able to resist the draw of short-term price cuts by competitors of the incumbent supplier, or this type of relationship will not work. The trend in various industries today is toward longer-term contracts as espoused by organizations such as ExxonMobil, Cargill and Toyota.

Another way of creating interest among suppliers in closer supplier-purchaser cooperation is to source total lifetime requirements of a certain part from a single supplier. This gives a much more accurate picture of the extent of the business a supplier is likely to have for a particular part or family of parts. Consequently, the supplier is better able to gauge the level of business and make judicious decisions about the extent of cooperation and business investment.

As the supply management professional and supplier work together to find ways to lower costs, they should share the productivity gains. The exact nature of the sharing will vary by supplier and category. This will encourage both parties to continue looking for improvements. There are several interesting ways to foster such shared concerns. For example, *target costing* is the determination of the cost of an item or service that both the buyer and the supplier believe will be the likely outcome, given normal business conditions and the application of learning curves to recognize efficiencies derived from experience. In the same vein, target pricing is the practice of identifying a selling price and working with suppliers to arrive at appropriate costs for achieving profitable sales for both organizations. This is also called *price-based costing*.

Identifying Savings Opportunities

Although the simple principle of purchasing a specified item or service at the least expensive price from qualified suppliers might seem like an obvious goal, the importance of meeting this goal is never truly realized or accomplished by supply management. A number of specific purchasing techniques can be leveraged and incorporated into any cost-reduction program:

1. *Use an ABC stratification system.* The single most important step in identifying savings opportunities within supply management is the implementation of an ABC stratification system for purchased products and services. Under an ABC system, all products and services purchased by an organization are classified into three groups. An A classification signals that the item/service is either in the most expensive category, is the most critical to the organization's operations, or both. Most supply management resources should be expended managing these A products and services both effectively and efficiently. B and C products/services, although important, do not justify the same scrutiny.

2. *Foster competition among suppliers.* Competition is a key element to effective sourcing. Competition between suppliers should result in a bidding war, but also should foster a creative challenge to improve the products and services being purchased.

3. *Design for reuse.* Organizations such as Intel use flexible designs that have multiple applications and that can be reused in different product generations. Sometimes these designs have a higher initial price tag, but the savings created by rationalizing inventories and delaying costly total redesigns create a lower TCO.

4. *Be selective in single sourcing.* Single sourcing is used for a limited number of direct materials parts where integrated supplier involvement is critical. Much of what Honda and Toyota purchases are not single-sourced. Even when Honda has

only one supplier for the headlights for an Accord, it has another supplier for the headlights for the Civic, creating indirect competition and the ability to test the market for price and technology changes, without violating a close supplier relationship. In most cases, a supply management department should avoid locking itself into a single-supplier situation unless there are extremely good reasons for doing so. Any smart, single-sourced supplier will do whatever it can to move itself from a single-sourced situation to one of sole sourcing by adding unique services, integrating uniquely into the organization's planning systems, etc.

5. *Standardize products/services.* Standardization and commoditization of products and services is an important, but often overlooked, cost savings opportunity in the supply management area. Whenever possible, using custom-designed products and services should be avoided. Standardized products and services are less expensive in both the short term and the long term. Often one standardized product or service can be substituted for a wide range of purchased ones with no degradation of quality, efficiency or effectiveness.

6. *Know when to negotiate with suppliers.* With the supply of many products and services now constrained, their prices probably will fluctuate and escalate in the years ahead. Proper supply management negotiation and bidding techniques are more vital than ever for the effective and efficient operation of the organization. The supply management professional's job is to combat these price increase trends by examining the supplier's pricing structure for opportunities for cost and price reduction. Negotiation should be used when intense examination and discussion of certain aspects of cost must be undertaken jointly with a key supplier or suppliers. In most cases, this is the exception to the rule. Bidding should be used when marketplace competition is the most effective way to maintain pricing integrity. In other cases, a little bit of both techniques can be used.

7. *Insist on a highly capable supply management staff.* Because most of an organization's sales dollars are expended through the supply management department, and because the best way to reduce purchasing costs is to allow supply management professionals to innovate, it is imperative that the supply management department is staffed with supremely competent and experienced professionals.

8. *Understand the impact of changes on operations.* Switching to a lower-cost supplier that creates more work for the organization may not be a cost savings at all. Similarly, a higher-price, full-service supplier may actually reduce the organization's TCO. Be sure to consider the big picture and get buy-in from those affected before making major changes.

9. *Consumption management also is important.* Supply management may negotiate significant reductions in travel costs, only to have people make more trips. Consumption management is the purview of top management. If top management is interested in really realizing bottom-line savings, it must require the businesses to manage consumption, regardless of prices paid. If getting good value or a set amount of expenditure is the real key, consumption management may not be an issue.

Types of Leasing Arrangements

A lease is essentially a type of financing arrangement that an organization makes when acquiring capital equipment. Supply management professionals may be called on to analyze and recommend various options for financing. Suppliers may include a variety of financing options in a proposal or quotation. Leases include terms related to the length of the payment, the number of payments and whether ownership of the leased assets transfers to the lessor. It is important for those involved in capital equipment purchases to understand some of the fundamental issues in leasing. It is sound practice to involve financial experts, preferably from within the organization, in the detailed analysis of leases options. More details on lease arrangements are included in the appendix at the end of this chapter.

Summary

Effective supply management will increasingly involve the use of price/cost analysis and the most effective application of data possible — requirements that demand enlightened, aggressive and strongly motivated supply management personnel. The supply management professional who effectively practices the techniques of price/cost analysis will be capable of handling an organization's material requirements authoritatively. The supply management professional's strength and confidence during negotiations will increase, ensuring more effective control of material costs.

Key Points

1. It is essential to develop a basic framework for understanding price, profit and cost. This includes understanding how different types of cost may affect cost identification, including fixed, variable, average, indirect and opportunity.

2. Supply management professionals need to develop an understanding of total cost of ownership (TCO) analysis, life-cycle costing and the application of this approach

to goods, services and capital expenditures. TCO is an assessment of all the direct and indirect costs involved with the acquisition, use and disposal of an item.

3. There are three different methods of cost estimating supply management professionals can use: (1) roundtable, (2) detailed and (3) comparison.

4. A successful cost management program includes both short-term and long-term strategies. A short-term strategy can be accomplished in a matter of weeks using organizational and opportunity analyses.

5. It is important for supply management professionals to have a basic understanding of leases. Leases include terms related to the length and number of payments, and whether ownership of leased assets transfers to the lessor.

Appendix: *Understanding Leasing Arrangements*

According to the Financial Accounting Standards Board (FASB), "If at its inception a lease meets one or more of the following four criteria, the lease shall be classified as a capital lease by the Lessee. Otherwise, it shall be classified as an operating lease."[9]

1. The lease transfers ownership of the property to the lessee by the end of the lease term.

2. The lease contains a bargain purchase or bargain lease renewal option.

3. The lease term is equal to 75 percent or more of the estimated economic life of the leased property.

4. The present value at the beginning of the lease term of the minimum lease payments equals or exceeds 90 percent of the fair market value (FMV) of the leased property at the inception of the lease. (The FMV of the property is to be reduced by any investment tax credit or energy credit retained by the lessor prior to determining the 90 percent base.)

The lessor's discount rate shall be the implicit rate in the lease. The lessee's discount rate shall be his or her incremental borrowing rate unless the implicit rate in the lease can be determined and that rate is lower. Criteria 3 and 4 are ignored when the beginning of the lease term is within the remaining 25 percent of an asset's economic life. This situation occurs when used assets are leased during the last 25 percent of their economic lives. If none of the aforementioned criteria are met, then the lease is considered a true lease and is referred to as an operating lease.

Types of Lease Arrangements

CAPITAL LEASE

The FASB divides all leases into two basic classifications, a capital lease or an operating lease.[10] A capital lease is not really considered a true lease at all, but rather is a sale of equipment from the lessor's viewpoint and a purchase from the lessee's viewpoint; whereas, an operating lease is a true lease from both the lessor's and lessee's viewpoints. Capital leases can be further subdivided into three types of leases: a sales-type lease, a direct finance lease, and a leveraged lease where the lessee wants to use as little of the organization's money as possible.

OPERATING LEASE

This type of lease is used by organizations to satisfy internal customer needs or help facilitate business operations. Most often, these types of leases satisfy short-term requirements and are used for a period of time considerably shorter than the asset's useful life. They are used when capital-intensive equipment is required for short periods or is subject to rapid obsolescence, and when the leasing organization is not interested in owning the equipment. Rental of an automobile for a week or rental of a copier to support short-term conference needs are examples of this type of lease.

FINANCIAL LEASE

This type of lease runs for the full life of the equipment and typically is entered into for financial considerations — when the lessee seeks to gain financial leverage and related long-term financial benefits. A financial lease is represented as an asset on the lessee's books. There are three major types of financial leases:

1. *Full payout.* With this type of lease, the lessee pays the full purchase price, plus interest charges, maintenance, insurance and administrative cost.

2. *Partial payout.* This type of lease gives the lessee credit for the residual value of the leased item after the lease period is completed. The lessee pays the difference between the original purchase price and the resale value, plus interest charges. A typical automobile lease is an example of this kind of lease.

3. *Lease/Purchase.* Under this type of contract, the lessee has the option to purchase the equipment at the end of the lease or at specific time intervals. Typically, this option is exercised at the end of the lease. The purchase price is representative of the residual value of the asset. It may be determined at the outset or may be based on market value at the time the asset is purchased. Purchasing an automobile at the end of a three-year lease is an example of this alternative.

OTHER TYPES OF LEASE ARRANGEMENTS

Leveraged Lease. A leveraged lease is one that involves a third-party lessor who buys the asset from an equipment producer and leases it to another organization. These leasing arrangements become available because of the unique tax arrangements and the borrowing power the lease provides the lessor. Typical lessors are large investors, such as insurance organizations, pension funds or investments groups. The lender's debt is primarily secured by an asset and to some extent by the financial capacity of the lessee.

Master Lease. A master lease is similar to a blanket order contract. It uses pre-determined and negotiated terms and conditions for various equipment leased over a given period. A master lease is more applicable for operating-type leases when needs are for shorter periods. It allows the purchaser to negotiate set terms and conditions, and when different short-term needs arise, to merely negotiate price and length of use. In addition, a purchaser could negotiate rates for a category of equipment and extend master lease terms to all the equipment. For example, if an organization agrees to lease forklift trucks from a local equipment dealer, the terms and conditions of the standard lease also might apply to pickups.

Dry Lease/Wet Lease. This type of lease, which originated in the aircraft industry, addresses the amount of service provided under the contract. A dry lease provides only for financing and often is called a straight lease. A wet lease includes not only financing but also fuel and maintenance for the piece of equipment.

Sale and Leaseback. In a sale and leaseback arrangement, the owner of the equipment or property sells the asset to a second party and then leases it back. The primary reason for this type of lease is to generate capital. Proceeds from the sale of the equipment or property can be put to alternate uses, while the asset continues to be used on a leased basis. This method provides a good way for an organization to obtain needed capital, while maintaining use of the asset.

Methods of leasing vary greatly and are limited only by the ability of the provider or other lessors' marketing creativity. Offers such as pretrading automobiles or leasing of land and buildings for long periods all carry the same fundamental principle. The lessor seeks to increase the sale of equipment and/or make a profit on the difference between the cost of the asset and the payments received, while the lessee seeks to minimize cash outlay. The lessee may be short of cash or may have more attractive options for available capital. Whatever conditions allow both parties to meet their needs can constitute a leasing arrangement.

Options on leases can include service additions for the equipment, maintenance and software, or upgrades to newer models. When reviewing these options, the lessee should be aware that the cost of these additions are being rolled into the equipment lease and will restrict future flexibility. Also, the equipment owner may restrict what type and brand of enhancements are allowed on, or used in conjunction with, the leased equipment.

Types of Lessors

THIRD-PARTY LESSORS

Third-party lessors produce no actual product. Instead, they purchase equipment from manufacturers and, in turn, lease the equipment. Third-party lessors sometimes are referred to as "full-service" lessors. These normally include organizations or individuals who find returns from this type of investment attractive, making a profit on the difference between lease payments received less the total cost of the asset.

MANUFACTURERS

Manufacturers who make high-technology or high-cost products often find that offering leasing options can increase sales. For example, the high cost and potential obsolescence of large computers make them more desirable to users as leased items. Thus, manufacturers often will become lessors of their products. At times, this can be a mechanism for managing demand for and moving a product, such as a new luxury automobile, into the marketplace. Because there is no choice of alternate products (the manufacturer only leases its own equipment), this type of lease normally is referred to as a *captive lease.*

BANKS

Banks operate as lessors in a similar fashion to that of third-party lessors. Typically, banks put up a portion of the capital, borrow the remainder and use the lessee's payments to cover the cost of borrowing plus profit.

INTERNAL LESSOR

Leasing arrangements also can be made within an organization, particularly in large multidivisional or multinational organizations. Investment decisions in one area of the organization might be maximized by purchasing and leasing equipment elsewhere within the organization. Also, equipment produced by one division might be offered for lease within the organization itself.

OTHER LESSORS

At times, institutional investors and/or wealthy individuals may form financial consortia to supply capital for leasing arrangements. These investors put up a portion of the purchase price and financing is obtained on the remainder. The debt is secured through lease payments. The lessee can benefit through receiving lower lease rates, because the individual lessors (who put up only a fraction of money) claim tax deductions on the entire cost of the equipment. Therefore, to get quality leases, the lessor is willing to provide favorable rates.

Financial Factors in a Lease Decision

A number of financial factors weigh for and against a decision to lease instead of purchase. These include:

INFLATION

As a general rule, leasing is a more costly way to obtain a piece of equipment than purchasing because, in addition to finance charges, the lessor bears all the risks associated with ownership, including inflation. This risk is consequently reflected as a cost component of rental payments.

CAPITAL/BUDGET CONSIDERATIONS

One of the chief advantages of leasing is that it makes capital available for other, more profitable purposes. A large outlay of capital is replaced by smaller regular payments, as the asset is used. However, the total leasing charges over the life of the equipment normally exceed the cost of the equipment. Although leasing usually is more costly than purchasing in the long run, this must be weighed against the need of the asset when funds are limited or when alternate opportunities for use of those funds are available.

REIMBURSEMENT FROM THIRD PARTIES

Many equipment manufacturers sell their leasing contracts. This typically results from a leveraged lease when the manufacturer or equipment provider is not interested in collection activities. Payments by the lessee then are made to a third party, who pays the manufacturer directly.

INTEREST RATES

If a supply management professional is considering purchasing instead of leasing, interest costs on financing must be considered. Rates and the burden of long-term debt may make the purchase less attractive.

BALANCE SHEET CONSIDERATIONS

Leasing can make an organization's balance sheet appear to be stronger than it would if the equipment was financed. Because leasing is shown as an expense on the income statement in the period it is incurred, no debt is shown on the balance sheet. When financing an asset, the amount financed is shown as a liability until it is paid off. The use of leased assets may allow the organization to show a greater return on assets than if the assets were owned (by understanding the assets used to create income). Given equal profits and the same assets, the organization that leases its assets will show the higher return on assets.

CASH-FLOW ANALYSIS

Purchase and lease options can have different effects on cash flow, depending on tax implications and the structure of the lease payments. Generally, leasing enhances the cash flow of an organization.

DEPRECIATION

Typically, the owner of the asset has the ability to depreciate the asset. When a decision is made to lease, the lessee forgoes the opportunity to depreciate the asset for the other benefits of leasing.

TAX CONSIDERATIONS

Classified as operating expenses, lease payments are completely deductible from taxable income, while owned equipment must be depreciated over the asset's useful life. The lessee may realize tax savings if lease payments exceed allowable depreciable amounts.

RESIDUAL VALUE

When a lease is over, the lessee does not own the equipment and is precluded from reaping any residual value that the asset may have in the marketplace. The purchaser should be aware of the type of equipment being leased and the relationship between allowable depreciation and residual value for that type of asset.

PAYMENT SCHEDULES

Payment schedules reflect the due dates for lease payments and are useful in preparing cash-flow analysis.

Operational Factors in a Lease Decision

A number of operational factors weigh for and against a decision to lease instead of purchase. These include:

OBSOLESCENCE

By leasing instead of buying a piece of capital equipment, the risk of obsolescence is reduced or eliminated for the lessee. Lessees can even negotiate a lease in which the leased equipment is replaced by new or updated models on a predetermined schedule.

MAINTENANCE SERVICES

The lessor bears the cost of maintenance in most leases. This frees the lessee from administration of service matters and provides properly trained labor to maintain the equipment. Maintenance becomes particularly important if the item is complex. Some lessors own and operate their own production and repair shops and usually will provide expert service. Often, as a provision of the lease, the lessor provides alternate equipment during any extended downtime.

ADMINISTRATIVE OVERHEAD

A lease may eliminate the need for extensive recordkeeping and management of labor, thus reducing the need for direct overhead expenses. As with other decisions to out-source, the cost is known and fixed. The cost structure is simple, freeing administrative time to concentrate on the organization's value-added activities.

OPERATING COST

Costs to be considered include utility, energy, air, environmental, water and labor required in putting the asset to use. The administrative cost of monitoring these activities can be minimized through various leasing arrangements.

LIFE OF THE ASSET

By purchasing instead of leasing an asset, the supply management professional has control over the asset throughout its entire life. An asset, when fully depreciated, still may provide value that exceeds its residual value. Some assets may even appreciate over time, such as land.

CUSTOMIZATION

Because a lessee does not own the piece of equipment, it cannot be modified or altered without the permission of the lessor. These restrictions also may extend to the addition of accessories that interact with the equipment.

TERM OF LEASE

The length of the lease is determined by the contract and reflects the time the asset will be needed. Some leases are open-ended and can be canceled following a formal notification period.

Other Factors in a Lease Decision

A number of other factors weigh for and against a decision to lease instead of purchase. These include:

OWNERSHIP BENEFITS

Lessees can be restricted regarding the use of the equipment they lease and may be required to provide lessors with access to the equipment on request. By owning instead of leasing equipment, the purchaser has the benefit of having complete control of the asset and the ability to use the equipment in any way the supply management professional wishes, including the ability to add components that are off-brand (e.g., external disk drives from another manufacturer). Although ownership carries the burden of disposing of the asset at the end of its useful life or when it is no longer needed, the owner enjoys the benefits of any residual value. In addition, the asset might provide value to the organization for years after it has been fully depreciated.

LIMITATION OF SOURCES OF SUPPLY

When suppliers are limited, leasing offers an alternative to purchasing. By considering leasing, a supply management professional may negotiate with a number of lessors and then consider the best option. Also, leasing may entice the supplier to provide a better offer than might otherwise have been presented; increasing competition might lead to a better procurement.

EARLY TERMINATION

When entering into a leasing agreement, a supply management professional should fully understand the implications of early termination, should that become desirable or necessary. The longer the life of the lease, the more important this becomes.

INSURANCE

When entering into a lease, insurance requirements should be fully understood. For example, which organization will be responsible for insurance and which one will benefit from any insurance payoff?

ORGANIZATION POLICY

Many organizations maintain formal or informal policies regarding leasing. For example, in high-tech industries, there is a tendency to lease because of the fast pace of technology changes. Organizations with a high rate of growth also may have leasing policies to minimize debt and increase working capital.

EMERGENCY SITUATIONS

Leasing can provide equipment for short-term requirements. If a particular piece of equipment is temporarily out of service, leased equipment can provide operating continuity. If funds are not approved, or if products do not justify short-term capital outlay, leased equipment may fill the need. Leasing also can provide access to equipment in short supply or with long lead times. Lessors may have focused on these market conditions or, through leverage with suppliers, have these assets available for lease.

Legal/Accounting Considerations

The financial, tax and legal implications for the organizations involved in leasing are generally covered by Uniform Commercial Code (UCC) Article 2A and FASB Statement Number 13. Major topics under each are discussed in the following sections.

UNIFORM COMMERCIAL CODE 2A — LEASING

Article 2A of the UCC covers leases and legal implications for merchants. The section contains five parts:

- Part 1: General Provisions

- Part 2: Formation and Construction of Lease Contract (includes offers, performance, warranties and casualties to identified goods)

- Part 3: Effect of Lease Contract (includes enforceability, title, sublease, liens on assets or equipment and creditor rights)

- Part 4: Performance of Lease Contract, Repudiated, Substituted and Excused (includes assurance of performance, anticipatory repudiation, excused or substituted performance and irrevocable promises)

- Part 5: Default (includes notices of default, lessor/lessee remedies, waiver of objections, liquidation of damages, cancellation and termination)

FASB 13

The FASB details proper methods for recording accounting transactions in business. Statement 13 deals with leases and lists appropriate transactions for lessors, lessees and third parties in various types of leasing arrangements. A lease is described as an agreement conveying the right to use plant, property or equipment for an agreed-on period.

The FASB differentiates between two basic kinds of leases. The first is a capital lease. Under this type of contract, the benefits and risks of ownership are transferred to the lessee. In this case, the property or equipment should be recorded as an acquisition by the lessee and a sale by the lessor. This is similar to a financial or leveraged lease. Under the second type of lease, an operating lease, neither an asset nor an obligation is recorded on the lessee's statement of financial position. Instead, rental payments are shown as an expense on the income statement in the period in which it occurred.

The FASB standards provide guidance for the various leasing alternatives and their implications in a financial environment. A supply management professional involved in leasing should be aware of these accounting standards and the various alternatives to acquisition that they represent.

SARBANES-OXLEY

The Sarbanes-Oxley Act of 2002 — also known as the Public Organization Accounting Reform and Investor Protection Act of 2002, and commonly called SOX or Sarbox — is a U.S. federal law passed in response to a number of major corporate and accounting scandals. Under Sarbanes-Oxley, two separate certification sections came into effect — one civil and the other criminal. Section 302 of the act mandates a set of internal procedures designed to ensure accurate financial disclosure. This impacts the financial control of leases. The signing officers (supply management professionals) must certify that they are "responsible for establishing and maintaining internal controls" and "have designed such internal controls to ensure that material information relating to the organization and its consolidated subsidiaries is made known to such officers by others within those entities, particularly during the period in which the periodic reports are being prepared."

Moreover, under Section 404 of the act, management is required to produce an "internal control report" as part of each annual Exchange Act report. The report must affirm "the responsibility of management for establishing and maintaining an adequate internal control structure and procedures for financial reporting." Under both Section 302 and Section 404, Congress directed the SEC to promulgate regulations enforcing these provisions. External auditors are required to issue an opinion on whether effective internal control over financial reporting was maintained in all material respects by management. This is in addition to the financial statement opinion regarding the accuracy of the financial statements. The requirement to issue a third opinion regarding management's assessment was removed in 2007.

4

The Sourcing Decision

Sourcing has been a key business strategy for organizations in many industries for more than a quarter of a century.[1] Organizations, on average, seem to be buying more and producing less internally. This trend has been driven by globalization and the desire to focus internal resources on core competencies while outsourcing the rest. Automotive companies have been sourcing manufacturing operations, business services and lines of business globally since the early 1980s. More recently, the contract manufacturing sector has grown as the result of considerable sourcing by electronic industry OEMs outside the United States. Business processes such as information technology, logistics, human resources management, payroll and certain elements of procurement also have been outsourced. For example, American Express is one organization that has outsourced much of its procure-to-pay (P2P) operations to India. LG Electronics and Samsung also have been active in sourcing much of their needs outside of Korea.

Across the globe, competitive pressures and the need for quarter-to-quarter financial performance improvement are driving an increase in the magnitude of sourcing across industries worldwide. Organizations are establishing and executing sourcing plans to match competitors in their sourcing endeavors; improve noncompetitive cost structures; focus on core competencies; reduce capital investment and overall fixed costs; achieve cost competitive growth in the supply base for goods, services and technologies in an organization's value chain; and establish a future sales footprint in a low-cost country by sourcing simple goods or business processes.

These factors are forcing organizations to fully evaluate their sourcing models to determine their viability in today's highly competitive world.

CHAPTER OBJECTIVES
• Explain ways to identify sources both domestically and internationally.

• Highlight how to narrow the number of sources available during supplier selection.

• Explain how to compare an existing versus a new source of supply.

• Describe the best method to use in agreeing on a competitive price, competitive bidding or negotiation.

• Discuss the myriad financial issues in sourcing decisions.

Sourcing Defined

A distinction must be made between two related terms: sourcing and the sourcing cycle. The Institute for Supply Management™ defines the two terms as follows: *sourcing* is the process of identifying sources that could provide needed products or services for the acquiring organization and the *sourcing cycle* is the seven-step process through which an organization acquires its goods and services: (1) recognition of need; (2) specification of need in terms of quality, quantity and timing; (3) search for potential sources; (4) analysis of suppliers and proposals; (5) negotiation with, and selection of, a supplier; (5) administering the contract; (6) evaluation of performance and feedback to supplier; and (7) disposal of excess, scrap or surplus. (*ISM Glossary,* 2006)

A significant shift came about in the early 1980s, when international manufacturing work began to migrate to areas that offered lower labor costs. Initially, this occurred on a regional basis, as happened within the United States when manufacturing moved from expensive urban areas to rural areas that offered cheaper land, tax incentives and employees willing to work for lower wages. More recently, organizations have sourced their internal needs in lower-cost countries. Large organizations such as General Electric and Dell have sourced select service functions (such as call centers and back-office functions) to lower-cost countries. This sourcing is not solely motivated by the pursuit of low-cost labor sources, but also by the desire to be closer to and gain improved access to markets, as evidenced by the fact that Japanese and German automakers have located "international" suppliers in North America, Asia and Europe.

Although the work being sourced to India-based and China-based suppliers has received the majority of the attention, countries such as the Philippines, Brazil, Russia, Ireland and the Czech Republic are also significant locations for supply. The recent trend is toward more international sourcing of services, such as call centers, accounts payable and medical transcription. During that same period, organizations started to source noncore activities to local or regional suppliers that provided specialized expertise and lower costs. The rise in global IT sourcing, contract manufacturing and worldwide third-party logistics industries characterizes this activity.[2]

Organizations must establish a viable and well-understood sourcing strategy up front, one that includes careful consideration of what goods and services, and possibly whole lines of business, are most suited to this activity. Supply management needs to establish current and future expectations for suppliers, and perform due diligence vis-à-vis the capability of the chosen supplier(s). The organization also must be able to execute the sourcing cycle. Finally, supplier performance must be closely tracked, accompanied by any necessary corrective actions occurring in tandem with ongoing management and development of the new supply base.

The Sourcing Decision

Any organization, service, government or manufacturing operation has the choice of buying or making the many factors of production or services used in the organization's daily business operations. This decision can cover a wide range of goods and services. Components, subassemblies, finished goods, plant and equipment, services, skills and knowledge may be purchased. The decision between keeping the provision of these items in-house versus contracting them to another organization is commonly known as the *sourcing decision.*

Over the past 20 years, many detailed investigations of the sourcing decision have been made worldwide, as evidenced by all the publications and research available on strategic sourcing. These studies suggest that of all the business decisions made, more errors are made concerning sourcing than any other supply management issue. Given the complexity and far-reaching impact of such decisions, this is not a surprising finding. Unfortunately, the total cost of incorrect sourcing decisions can run into millions of dollars a year. Before starting the sourcing cycle, supply management should evaluate the overall situation to determine which operational factors and methods of sourcing are the most appropriate.

The Strategic Nature of the Sourcing Decision

The sourcing decision, taken over a wide range of factors, can be critical to an organization because the decision sets an organization's economic boundary; that is, the competitive character of the enterprise.

An organization should consider which items it buys and which items it makes in terms of strategic and tactical considerations. Strategic considerations should focus on several issues, including:

1. The nature of market conditions impacting the buying organization,

2. The business the organization wants to be in, and

3. The organization's core competencies.

In one situation, a manufacturer of personal computers may decide that it does not want to be in the business of making hard drives. Rather, it may decide that it will purchase the hard drives instead. In another situation, the manufacturer of personal computers may decide that its core competency is in designing, integrating, assembling and marketing personal computer systems, rather than in manufacturing operating systems.

Conversely, the manufacturer of operating systems might decide that its core competency is in producing operating systems, not in the assembly and marketing of personal computers. The items that tend to be sourced internationally require proprietary design or manufacturing knowledge and must be within the financial and technical capabilities of the organization.

Tactical considerations focus on the operational efficiency of the organization. Tactical issues include direct and indirect costs, integration of plant operations, availability of internal capacity, the need for direct control over quality, confidentiality, reliability of available suppliers, volume requirements, fluctuations in the workforce and effect on labor relations.

Sourcing decisions are frequently assigned to midlevel supply management professionals. While this is justified given the routine nature of small dollar buy decisions, top management must consider the strategic implications of the few sourcing decisions that can impact the strategic direction of an organization. Many sourcing decisions have substantial strategic implications in the entire planning process that transcend functional orientations. Sourcing decisions can affect an organization's "competitive advantage" and impact the types of choices available in the planning process. For example, Intel's decisions as to where, why, how and from whom to source capital equipment, CAPEX, can prove crucial to its future competitive position in the marketplace.

Some sourcing decisions may be relatively unimportant in themselves, yet when considered as part of the entire business, they may have a considerable impact on the organization's strategy. Two primary factors frequently temper sourcing decisions:

1. Management must have a clear understanding of those activities in which the organization has particular competence and those that are best carried out by others; that is, core versus noncore competencies. There is much more to consider with respect to the sourcing decision than just internal technical capabilities such as capacity, expertise and cost. Many other strategic issues that affect an organization's competitive strengths and weaknesses must be considered as important inputs to the sourcing decision. Such issues reside primarily with top management and not with functional-level decision-makers.

2. Management must assess the relative cost advantage of sourcing from both a long-term and a short-term perspective. One early, yet still relevant study indicated

that very few organizations made any type of major structural changes because of sourcing-related decisions.[3] Even when major changes were made, they stemmed from solutions to sourcing problems and not from perceived opportunities for competitive advantage. Even today, most sourcing decisions use price as a primary determinate of change. Total cost analysis — clearly distinguishing between relevant and irrelevant costs — is essential to effective decision-making (see Chapter 3, "Strategic Cost Management").

Management must realize that sourcing decisions that impact strategic advantage often are complex and replete with qualitative factors. The sourcing decision is difficult to evaluate because a host of factors must be considered, many of which are highly subjective in nature.

Understanding Market Conditions

Market conditions can be categorized using several criteria, including stage of the product's or service's life cycle, whether it's a buyer's or seller's market, or a product risk/value matrix.

Product/Service Life Cycle. The product life cycle consists of five stages or phases: (1) precommercialization, (2) introduction, (3) growth, (4) maturity and (5) decline. In the precommercialization phase, supply management seeks flexibility because the project (e.g., whether to manufacture a product or provide a new service) still is uncertain. Supply management would be involved in supplier selection, product design or service specification development and early supplier involvement. Supply management would focus on the selection of components, prompt delivery of materials for research and development (R&D), standardization and product redesign (to reduce potential supply problems) or specific service provision metrics.

In the introduction phase, supply management seeks to balance the chances of product failure with the need for adequate materials to be available if the product succeeds in the marketplace. Supply management would likely favor subcontracting to avoid risking assets, developing preferred and standby suppliers, working with suppliers to correct quality or delivery problems, dealing with engineering changes or focusing on leasing equipment to reduce risk.

In the growth phase, supply management's main responsibility is to ensure continuity of supply. They would favor a *make* strategy to ensure continuity by exercising greater control over product or service inputs. Supply management also might look at developing additional sources of supply and negotiate for lower input prices. In the maturity phase, supply management's goal is to reduce lead times and costs, and to ensure continuity of supply. The supply strategy would include long-term contracts, use of aggressive price negotiation, and continuous improvement to drive down costs. In the decline stage, supply management continues to look for lower-cost sources, may have to deal with asset recovery of equipment and inventory, and may begin to use subcontractors, as assets are reassigned to new products or services. Rapid adaptability to changing conditions is more important than input prices at this stage. Some of the factors that affect market conditions and complexity are summarized in Figure 4-1.

Type of Market. Another classification system for market conditions is whether an organization is dealing with a buyer's or a seller's market. In a buyer's market, the supply management professional has greater leverage than the seller because supply is greater than demand and the economic forces of business cause prices to be close to the supply management professional's estimate of value. (*ISM Glossary,* 2006) The supply management professional may be able to obtain concessions, not only on price but also on payment terms, inventory stocking levels or delivery. In a seller's market, the supply management professional cultivates relationships with as many suppliers as possible to ensure continuity of supply and because demand is greater than supply and the economic forces of business give suppliers the upper hand in the marketplace. (*ISM Glossary,* 2006) If supply and demand are somewhat balanced, the supply management professional will pursue a mixed strategy, depending on the current market conditions.

Risk/Value Matrix. A market conditions dimension model uses a risk/value matrix in which the horizontal axis is the value of the item and the vertical axis is the risk of supply (see Figure 4-2). In the high-risk, high-value quadrant, the supply

Figure 4-1   Drivers of Market Complexity

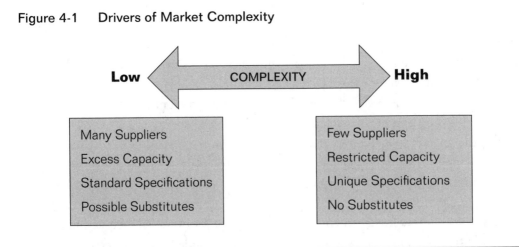

Figure 4-2   Supply Risk/Value Matrix

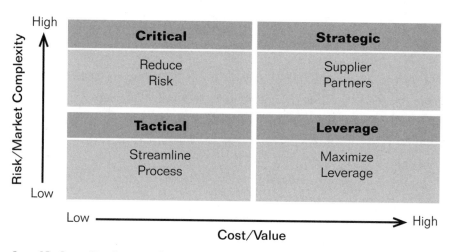

Source: J.R. Carter, "Development of Supply Strategies," *The Purchasing Handbook,* 7th Edition (McGraw-Hill, 2005).

management strategy would focus on strategic relationships in order to build competitive advantage. For high–risk, low-value items, the goal is to reduce risk. For low-risk, high-value items, the supply management professional should take a leverage strategy to maximize profits. For the low-risk, low-value quadrant, the goal is to acquire items at minimum cost. Figure 4-3 illustrates a possible application of the risk/value matrix

Figure 4-3   Supply Risk/Value Application: Restaurant Chain

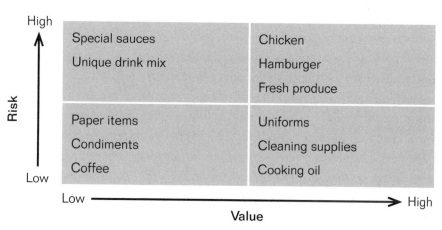

in the fast-food restaurant industry. This concept is discussed more fully in Volume 3 of the ISM Professional Series, *Leadership in Supply Management.*

Understanding Commodity Markets

In commodity markets, buyers and sellers can freely interact. The commodity must be able to be graded reasonably accurately and be large enough that no single buyer or seller can influence the market. When dealing with a commodity, the supply management professional needs to consider the organization's objectives and philosophy, the commodity's importance to profit or loss, and the price volatility of the commodity. When a volatile commodity is a major cost factor to an organization, the risk of a price change at the time of the raw material purchase and the sale of the finished product often is used as a measure of risk.

One method for evaluating risk is to ask management to rank the various kinds of risk, such as highly fluctuating material costs, product or service vulnerability to competition, the cost of expanding existing facilities, the cost of new product or service introduction and changes in economic conditions. For the supply management professional to manage the risks associated with commodities, good forecasting systems and good information databases are required. Control methods may include:

- Establishing coverage or commitment limits,

- Implementing an organizational safeguards-review committee,

- Having a formal upper-management oversight process,

- Having multiple supply management professionals in different parts of the organization work together, and

- Monitoring strategies and purchases paperwork by the finance department.

A possible performance measure for evaluating commodity purchasing is a comparison of weekly purchases to the actual buying price, including all costs of delivery.

An important part of managing a commodity is the forecast (see Chapter 2). In developing a commodity forecast, the supply management professional should include the use of supply factors, such as inventory levels of suppliers and internal customers, future production or service need outlook, transportation availability and government programs that may influence commodities. The supply management professional also should include demand factors, such as consumption trends, real verses artificial demand, and government actions. For example, as an organization plans the need for temporary labor, it must look at available supply matched with forecasted demand, including capability needs and projected growth.

A Decision-Making Approach to Identifying Sources

The task of identifying potential suppliers and evaluating them for eventual selection is an important supply management activity. Identifying potential suppliers starts with locating sources of supply and continues with the analysis of competition, evaluating various issues, certification of suppliers and often developing approved supplier lists. Many aspects of competition are important to purchasing decisions regarding source availability and selection. These include:

- Full and open competition

- Limited competition

- Technical competition

- Single sourcing

- Sole sourcing

- Multiple sources

Full and open competition exists when many suppliers are available to choose from and no collusion occurs among them. Competition in this setting typically promotes product and service improvements and places the buyer in a strong position regarding prices. Broadening the search to include international suppliers may increase the likelihood of finding full and open competition.

Limited competition exists when few suppliers exist, limiting supply management professionals' choices in selection and creating more difficult pricing experiences. Limited competition can exist regionally when only a few organizations sell items or services that are in demand. Limited competition also can exist locally when only two or three suppliers seem to copy each other in behavior and pricing.

Technical competition exists when, for special product, technology or patent reasons, only one or a few suppliers are available for selection. This was the case with flat panel displays some years ago when this equipment was available only from limited suppliers.

Single sourcing exists when a buying organization actively concentrates purchases of a particular product or service with one source in preference over others in a competitive marketplace. (*ISM Glossary,* 2006) This practice is common today in the formation of alliances and early supplier design involvement (ESDI) relationships. Some of the reasons for this are quality improvements, administrative simplification, joint-schedule planning, smooth logistics links, electronic data interchange, early supplier involvement in product or service design, and joint costing and pricing benefits.

This practice runs counter to the traditional approach of using several suppliers to maintain competition among them and to hedge the risk of one of them failing to meet the business needs of the supply management professional; that is, supply continuity. Supply management can guard against supply disruptions by having multiple suppliers provide similar, but not identical items. For example, LG Electronics could use one supplier for a certain size of LCD panel and another single-source supplier for a different size. This allows LG a backup plan to get one supplier up to speed on the other's products in the event of failure. It would not be as seamless as using multiple sources, but would be more effective than relying on one supplier for all LCD sizes.

In contrast, *sole sourcing* exists when only one source is available (such as an electrical utility in many cities and towns across the globe). Sole sourcing also exists when only one source provides a product or service that the organization wants to buy.

Multiple sourcing involves using two or more suppliers for the same or like products or services. By using multiple sources, supply management professionals can eliminate certain risks in the acquisition process and ensure continuity of supply. These include the disruption of supply because of problems at the supplier's site and leverage against price increases. Multiple sourcing is an appropriate option for those supply management professionals who do not wish to become the sole support for a supplier or overly depend on a supplier. While multiple sourcing tends to keep the chosen sources competitive, a frequent drawback is a short-term orientation and the absence of a strong, long-term relationship and commitment required for a true alliance. Recent author experiences involving many industry sectors worldwide suggest a movement away from multiple sourcing. Many organizations will continue to follow policies that call for a rationalization of the supplier base to leverage cross-unit purchases with fewer companies that meet high standards of quality, service and delivery at a competitive cost. In some instances, multiple sourcing involves a combination of insourcing[4] and outsourcing. Note that an inherent conflict may exist between the initiative for fewer sources and socially and economically disadvantaged supplier program goals of both public sector supply management professionals and government agencies around the world.

Nature of Sources

While considering potential supply sources for a product or service, a number of choices are open to the supply management professional. Each presents distinct advantages and disadvantages.

When buying in bulk, often it is preferable to buy from suppliers whose materials can be obtained at a cost that does not include a distributor's markup or profit. These suppliers also may have special designs available. However, if a supply management professional has limited warehouse space and capability and needs only small amounts of a particular product, or needs to purchase a wide range of products made by many different suppliers, using a distributor is preferable. For example, Avnet Inc. and Arrow Electronics are large distributors of electronic equipment and parts that also provide logistics-oriented value-added services to their clients.

Small suppliers may be more able and willing to specialize in certain goods than are large suppliers. On the other hand, large suppliers usually are better able to keep up with the demands of a buying organization if the volume of business grows or becomes international.

Buying from international sources creates greater competition, offering a wider range of products or services and usually better prices. International suppliers also may be better able to provide superior technical service. However, domestic sources offer distinct advantages as well. Domestic sources can provide faster delivery at lower costs, usually are more willing to tailor their businesses to the supply management professionals' needs, and may be interested in maintaining a higher level of service. Sourcing from domestic sources also creates goodwill toward the organization within the community. In many ways, giant energy companies such as Chevron Corp. are required to invest funds in using domestic sources of supply. Also, buying from a strategic business unit (SBU) of one's organization is an example of being required to do business with a mandatory supplier.

Because production downtime penalties and service provision disruptions can be extremely expensive and result in lost marketing opportunities, a contingency development program should be part of the overall managerial role of supply management. This program should include establishing backup or alternative suppliers. For example, consider the fire at the Philips Electronics major microchip manufacturing facility. Both Nokia and Ericsson depended a great deal on this plant for supplier production. Nokia responded quickly, moving production to other Phillips plants and to other suppliers. Ericsson did not, so that by the time Ericsson decided to do something proactive, Nokia had secured most of the free capacity in the industry. As a result, Ericsson lost $400 million in sales, with production disrupted for months. Nokia came out relatively unscathed, and with an enhanced reputation for supply-chain risk management.[5]

Special programs for minority, women-owned and disadvantaged (socially and economically) suppliers continue to grow and develop in the public, private and not-for-profit sectors. These supply management programs are undertaken for a number of reasons, including government legislation, social responsiveness, increased sales and alternative sources of supply.

Cooperative buying typically is used by supply management professionals to increase purchasing effectiveness. This involves joining two or more groups or organizations to prepare specifications and proposals, collectively receive bids and make awards to the lowest bidders. Then, each organization issues its own contract and is responsible for administering the remainder of the procurement function, including its own payments. This type of buying arrangement enables smaller users to secure the price and other advantages of large-volume purchasing. The national healthcare systems in many countries use this form of group purchasing.

A *joint venture* is an investment undertaken by two or more organizations. For example, NUMMI in Fremont, California, is a successful joint venture of General Motors and Toyota.[6] Joint ventures enable partners to share costs, technology and intellectual capital; reduce financial, technical and political risks; and achieve economies of scale that would not be possible individually. Risks of joint ventures include providing technical knowledge to partners that enable them to become competitors (loss of IP), less control over the project or conflicts among the partners. Many forays by multinational organizations into the Chinese marketplace have required using joint ventures.[7]

Finding Suppliers That Strategically Align

Theoretically, any organization could take the insource decision to its extreme and own or control most of its factors of operations. For example, at one time the Ford Motor organization was highly integrated vertically. Ford owned iron ore mines, shipping organizations, steel mills, rolling plants, parts-fabrication operations and assembly operations. If this integrating of functions were continually profitable, eventually every industry would merge itself into one giant industrial conglomerate. However, there are boundaries to the profitability of merging disparate functions under one business. Therefore, the sourcing decision must be made within the confines of the strategic capabilities of the organization and the resource base available to exploit that capability.

Existing Versus New Sources

The decision to continue using existing sources or to try new sources depends on a number of factors and situations that may increase both advantages and disadvantages for either alternative. The major considerations include:

- Market conditions
- Product complexity/technology changes

- Urgency of need
- Quality expectations
- Supplier processes
- Adequacy of competition
- Cost versus value of sources
- Long-term needs
- Long-term relationships
- Need for modification of the supplier base
- Change in the supplier's organization
- Supply continuity

If a supply management professional works with only one supplier (single source), he or she needs to maintain greater surveillance of market conditions to be sure that the supplier remains competitive. By seeking new sources for the product or service in demand, the supply management professional can guard against unreasonable increases in price or deterioration in quality by current suppliers.

An existing supplier may be the sole owner of a certain patent or process, precluding the possibility of using other sources. Also, if the product or service involves costly tool, die, mold, training or setup charges, the expense of duplicating this equipment or service also will discourage using new suppliers. However, remaining with existing suppliers may result in a supply management professional's loss in terms of new technology offered by a new supplier's product or service.

The establishment of a new supplier inevitably will involve time and expense for training that organization. If the product or service is needed quickly, using a new source may not be practical. At one time, the supply management function of a major high-tech manufacturer was so inundated with requests to review new suppliers that it did a total cost of ownership (TCO) analysis on the cost of qualifying suppliers. Between destructive testing of products, reviewing supplier financials, making site visits, verifying processes and more, the organization determined that depending on the type of materials/components, it could cost between $50,000 and $250,000 to qualify a source! The appropriate figure was used as part of the cost-benefit analysis before determining whether to seriously investigate new supply sources.

An existing supplier may provide such outstanding quality that buying elsewhere may not be a serious consideration. However, if a current supplier's quality has been marginal, a new supplier may be a prudent alternative. A new source may be eager to gain the business and may make special efforts to provide superior service.

How does the supplier produce and distribute the product or service, and to what extent does the supplier outsource? What are the supplier's processes for acquiring, producing and maintaining the goods and services? In some sense, the supply management professional needs to certify processes in the same way that the ISO 9000 series of process certifications ensures superior quality. However, a supplier process certification does not ensure that the process is the best, just that the supplier will be aware of the strong and weak points of the process.

New suppliers may represent opportunities for expanded supply options and competition. For example, a new supplier may be able to help the supply management professional out of a sole-source situation. A new supplier may offer technical or other support not available from current sources. However, the supply management professional must be prudent when considering new sources. Is the new supplier underbidding to get the business? How will this type of supplier behavior affect the buying organization at a later date? The more critical the product or service, the more carefully the potential new source should be evaluated. Use of thorough specifications and statements of work, appropriate contract clauses for future price negotiations, and careful evaluation of supplier cost data are just some of the tools available when a supply management professional is considering a new source.

The purchase price of a product may be as little as one-third of the total cost of ownership. Continuity of supply is the first concern of supply management professionals, while the purchase price may be a lesser issue. Quality, service and technical support, and supplier innovation all contribute to the TCO. Responsiveness and problem resolution, maintenance and operating costs, and salvage value also are factors that must be considered when determining total cost. (For a thorough discussion of TCO, see Chapter 3, "Strategic Cost Management.")

By seeking new sources of supply, a supply management professional works to protect the organization's supply lines in case one of the existing suppliers is unable to perform as promised. However, remaining with existing suppliers is advantageous if such organizations have proven they can and will meet standards of quality, service and delivery at competitive prices over the long term. Such a supplier may be a good candidate for some type of alliance arrangement.

A fundamental objective of supply management is the creation of competitive advantage through development of a world-class supply base. The close, collaborative buyer-supplier activities that characterize these relationships usually are developed in context of long-term involvement. Rapid changing of suppliers typifies a concentration on price to the exclusion of total cost. Changing suppliers is an expensive activity. Most supply management professionals indicate that total cost differentials must be significant to make changing worthwhile. The better a supplier knows the supply management organization, and the longer the focus of the relationship, the more willing a supplier will be to invest in cost-saving activities on behalf of the supply management organization.

The identification of potential suppliers and the development of new sources is important to maintaining an assurance of supply. Despite precautions in the supplier selection process, some sources always will perform less than satisfactorily. Usually, such suppliers should be put on notice and given the opportunity to correct poor performance before being dropped. At times, however, replacing suppliers who continue to perform below expectations with new suppliers may be the only feasible course of action.

If an existing supplier undergoes a major change, such as new key leadership, a merger, a purchase by private equity or a takeover, the likelihood of discontinuity in supply or quality may increase. When a single individual creates and manages an organization, the organization often grows too large for the individual to handle and smooth operations may be disrupted. These circumstances may warrant seeking new suppliers. This latter concern can be especially true when practicing *low cost country sourcing (LCCS)*. During LCCS, a new, smaller supplier can be selected. This supplier frequently can grow rapidly without a professional management structure evolving at the same pace.

The supply management professional's prime directive is the assurance of supply. Supply disruption is an important consideration when deciding whether to use existing sources or buy from a new source. Supply continuity with existing suppliers can be enhanced if realistic risk management and contingency plans through multiple production facilities, effective production and quality-control systems, and succession plans for management are in place. Supply disruption with new sources may result from an inability to provide promised price, quality and service because of a number of factors, including poor communication of requirements to the supplier, an inability of the supplier to meet requirements, capacity limitations and an unexpectedly quick phase-out of the previous supplier. In some instances, supply continuity problems with a current supplier may not be solved by seeking a new source. Working with the existing supplier may be the best alternative.

The Decision to Use Competitive Bidding and/or Negotiation

Bidding can be formal or informal. In formal bidding, specifications are written, requests for proposal are advertised and responses from all prequalified suppliers are evaluated. A contract is awarded to the lowest qualified bidder. In informal bidding, the supply management organization may preselect or limit the suppliers from whom it solicits proposals. The requirement may not be advertised or widely distributed. Bids are solicited informally from suppliers, typically electronically but also by telephone, fax and e-mail attachment. E-procurement software and systems have greatly automated this process.

The degree of competition and market conditions should determine the use of bidding versus negotiation. When the market consists of a large number of suppliers, competitive bidding often is the preferred course of action. If there are few suppliers of the needed product or service, competitive bidding can be less effective.

Industry norms and standards are other important considerations. Products that are manufactured to the same general specifications by all producers are commonly referred to as "industry standard products." Because of the competitive nature of the markets for these products, competitive bidding rather than negotiation is ordinarily used for acquisition. Custom-made products and especially services, by contrast, may not have sharply defined specifications or many capable suppliers. In these situations, negotiation may be the preferred tactic.

An electronic method for obtaining competitive bids in common use today is a *reverse auction*. A reverse auction (also called procurement auction, e-auction, sourcing event or e-sourcing) is a tool used in industrial business-to-business procurement. A reverse auction is a fixed-duration bidding event hosted by a single supply management organization, in which multiple prequalified and invited suppliers compete for business. Potential suppliers review the requirements, choose to bid and enter their selling prices. Suppliers' prices are visible to competitors, often resulting in successively lower prices. (*ISM Glossary,* 2006) In an ordinary auction (also known as a *forward auction*), buyers compete to obtain a good or service; e.g., eBay bidding. In a reverse auction, sellers compete to obtain business.

The prices that buyers obtain in a reverse auction reflect the narrow market that it creates at the time when the auction is held. Thus, it is possible that better value in the form of prices, as well as better quality, delivery performance, technical capabilities, etc., could be obtained from suppliers not engaged in the bidding or by other means such as collaborative cost management and joint process improvement.

The supply management professional may award contracts to the supplier who bid the lowest price. Or a supply professional could award contracts to suppliers who bid higher prices depending on the buyer's specific needs with regards to quality, lead time, capacity or other value-adding capabilities. However, supply management professionals frequently award contracts to incumbent suppliers, even if prices are higher than the lowest bids, because the switching costs to move work to a new supplier are higher than the potential savings realized by the switch. This outcome, while very attractive to the supply management organization, can be criticized by both new and incumbent suppliers. The time available to obtain the product or service must allow for competitive bidding. This includes time for supply management professionals to obtain information through an eRFI (electronic request for information) and evaluate bid invitations, as well as time for suppliers to respond to them. If adequate time is not available, the supply management professional usually will turn to negotiation. If the dollar value of the item is relatively low, the time and expense of competitive bidding is probably unjustified for both buyer and supplier. A product or service that is purchased frequently generally is a poor candidate for competitive bidding because of the time requirements of the blanket order, systems contract or procurement card.

If the specifications are clear to both the buyer and the supplier, competitive bidding may be used. However, when the supply management professional anticipates changes in the specifications or when the specifications are not clearly defined, negotiation becomes more useful for the procurement process.

The type of contract desired is another determinant of whether to solicit bids or negotiate. For example, fixed-price contracts are based on a price that will not differ from that agreed on at the time of the ordering. This type of contract is a good candidate for competitive bidding. Cost reimbursable and indefinite delivery quantity contracts, also called blanket contracts, are better candidates for negotiation as the costs are more uncertain and often the terms need to be changed after the contract is created.

International Supply Chains and Sources

International sourcing is now an automatic expectation to respond to competition. But the choice of where to obtain goods and services is not a static decision. It is subject to continual re-evaluation. In addition, there is strong evidence that the shift has been toward so-called "low cost country suppliers."[8] Yet, conditions in these countries often are not well known. At the same time, best practices in sourcing dictate a multi-attribute, weighted decision, rather than basing supplier location on a single factor, for example, on labor cost alone.

Effective sourcing decisions require good processes to evaluate the many factors related to where to source; that is, how to find the supplier locations internationally that align best with future plans. These processes often will include a screening step with respect to geography, for factors such as infrastructure, market attractiveness and cost levels are characteristics of regions or countries rather than of specific suppliers. All these screening factors frequently lead supply management professionals to consider low-cost countries and geographies for their supply needs. As mentioned earlier, the work being transferred to India-based and China-based suppliers has received the majority of the headlines, while countries such as the Brazil, Russia and the Czech Republic also are significant locations for outsourcing.[9]

Domestic sourcing is advantageous for many supply management professionals because the same culture, languages, laws, transportation links and communications apply for the supply management professional and the supplier. However, international sourcing can provide such benefits as greater quality, lower prices, a wider range of goods and services, and greater competition. The use of international sources presents a number of special considerations, including:

- Exchange rates

- Payment processes

- Duties

- Transportation costs and timing

- Applicable laws

When sourcing internationally, the supply management professional must consider the rate of exchange, the price at which one currency can be bought with another currency. The relative position of the exchange rate between two nations affects the price level of traded purchases and sales between them, creating either an advantage or a disadvantage for the buyer. The problem is that currency levels often are unpredictable and thus constitute a true risk in conducting global business. Chapter 10, "International Sourcing Issues," covers currency exchanges in-depth.

There are two major forms of payment for international purchases. The most frequent is a *letter of credit,* which is a document that assures the seller that payment will be made by the bank issuing the letter of credit on fulfillment of the terms of the sales agreement. (*ISM Glossary,* 2006) The second form is a *bill of exchange* or a *draft.* This is a document issued by the supplier instructing the supply management professional to make payment in full at a specified point in time or under specified circumstances, similar to a check that instructs a bank to pay on a depositor's behalf. This becomes a negotiable instrument if and when the buying organization acknowledges its obligations by signing, upon which it becomes a trade acceptance. In general, international sourcing can be expected to tie up capital for longer periods of time than will domestic purchase transactions.

Increasingly, trade occurs between affiliates or subsidiaries of the same organization. This simplifies the international sourcing process and reduces overhead costs. For example, rather than sourcing with a letter of credit, a Chinese supply management professional with a German subsidiary supplier would have its German subsidiary execute a domestic German purchase transaction. The subsidiary then would sell to the Chinese sister organization on open account. Subsidiary purchases are becoming more common.

Duties are taxes levied by governments on the importation, exportation or use of goods. Most goods entering into domestic markets anywhere in the world have duties assessed on them. The three major types of duties include:

1. *Specific.* Charged as a specified rate per unit (e.g., 15 ECU for each crate).

2. *Ad valorem.* Customs duty charged on the value of goods that are dutiable, irrespective of quality, weight or any other considerations. The ad valorem rates of duty are expressed in percentages of the value of the goods, usually ascertained from the invoice (e.g., 3 percent ad valorem). (*ISM Glossary,* 2006) This is the type of duty most often applied.

3. *Compound.* Combine specific and ad valorem rates (e.g., $2.15 per gallon plus 8 percent ad valorem).

The benefits of international sourcing must be weighed against the costs of longer transportation timeframes. Shipments into Canada from Mexico can be transported over land via truck and rail, but other international shipments may have to be made by air or ship. Air transport involves relatively high freight charges, yet is the preferred method for cross-border shipments of sensitive items such as electronic equipment and perishables (food, flowers, etc.). Today, almost any developed country can be reached by air within 24 hours from nearly any point in the world. Overseas shipping containerization services include lower costs for the transportation of goods, but at much slower speeds. Water transportation typically is used for large volume purchases and the transport of raw materials. In addition to the transportation charges, inventory carrying costs will increase because of the increased inventory in the supply line caused by longer lead times. One of the often-overlooked costs of international sourcing is the additional inventory necessary to support the extended logistics pipeline. For example, it may take up to five weeks for a shipment to move from an Asian supplier via sea to a supply management professional in Hamburg. Continuous use of an item requires an uninterrupted flow from the supplier to the supply management organization. Logistics inventory costs must be included when comparing total landed costs of international suppliers versus domestic suppliers.

In international sourcing, the governments of both the supply management professionals' and suppliers' countries have laws that will affect the transactions, which can complicate the flow of goods across borders. Governments, for example, place various types of restrictions on imports, including import licenses, customs duties and quotas. Governments also typically require complex sets of documents, including export licenses, import declarations, certificates of origin, commercial invoices, customs invoices, insurance policies and bills of lading. In addition, the United Nations Convention on Contracts for the International Sale of Goods (CISG) has produced a relatively new body of law that brings some uniformity to the rules governing international sales. The CISG has had a significant effect on international supply management professionals and suppliers.[10]

Import/Export Quotas

The supply management professional must be particularly aware of import quotas that may restrict supply, especially later in the year. It may be advantageous to purchase the year's requirements as quickly as possible to reduce the organization's chances of not being able to acquire material. If the quota is reached before year-end, the supply management organization may have to lobby with government regulators to relax the quota or consider an exception.

Financial Issues in Sourcing Decisions

Supply management professionals can add value to the organization by developing an understanding of financing strategies. Knowledge of these strategies is helpful to the supply management professional working on cross-functional teams, when such matters are raised by others on the team. Supply management professionals are in an excellent position to watch conditions in the marketplace and can be the eyes and ears of management. They can identify trends and watch for economic conditions that will favor or harm the organizations.

Depreciation and Appreciation

Depreciating is a process of cost allocation — not asset valuation. As defined in the *ISM Glossary* (2006), depreciation is an allocation of a portion of the value of an asset as an expense during the current period. It represents the declining value of the asset as a cost. As a noncash expense, it acts as a tax shield and reduces tax payments. The depreciation of assets is of concern to the supply management professional for it relates to the decision to buy, lease capital equipment or outsource processes. Failure to depreciate properly can lead to poor decisions. Normally, supply management's objectives do not include purchasing goods that will appreciate in value for the purposes of reselling them at a profit. Supply management's primary objective is to ensure that goods and services are available when needed.

Bond and Currency Markets

If an organization is sourcing internationally, supply management may be involved in deciding whether to purchase in the supplier's local currency or in the supply management professional's currency. If the contract is negotiated in the supplier's currency, supply management must be aware of the situation, understand the implications of exchange-rate fluctuations, and work with the appropriate department to manage the effects of exchange rates. Normally, supply management's objective is to maintain the profit margin if the exchange rate varies. This can be accomplished by hedging on the exchange rate or by negotiating the contract in the buyer's currency. Supply management has little, if any, direct interaction with bond markets, but can integrate a general understanding of these markets with other data collected for forecasting and strategy planning and development.

Tax Laws

Many supply management professionals are concerned with tax laws for a variety of reasons. If the organization is subject to a tax on inventory, the supply management professional may have to plan acquisitions to minimize taxes. It would not be desirable to receive a large order the day before the tax liability is determined. Countries charge very different duties among items and components, often based on the value added to the item prior to entering the country. Tax laws may affect decisions such as leasing versus purchasing and make versus buy through the treatment of depreciation. The supply management professional needs to keep accurate records of all transactions — including transactions via EDI and procurement cards — and work with accounting to determine sales tax liabilities.

Interest Rates

Interest rates are of concern to the supply management professional for a variety of reasons. For example, as interest rates rise, the supply management organization's cost of capital will increase. This will increase inventory carrying costs and lead the organization to purchase smaller quantities more frequently. Rising interest rates would cause the supplier to try to maintain smaller inventories, potentially increasing the risk of stockout, because the supplier would be less likely to be able to fill all orders.

The movement of interest rates may influence the financial viability of marginal suppliers, increase or decrease an organization's cash flow, affect prices paid for products or services or produce other consequences that impact buying and leasing decisions. Supply management professionals are responsible for developing the sophistication needed to understand how financial aspects of the economy may impact the decisions they make for their organizations (see Chapter 10, "International Sourcing Issues").

Payment Terms

Payment terms involve the discount rate and the amount of time the supply management organization is able to keep the money before paying. Typical payment terms include:

- *Net 30 days.* Payment of the entire invoiced amount is to be made within 30 days of the invoice date.

- *Net 10th prox.* Payment of the entire amount is to be made by the 10th of the month following the invoice date.

- *2 percent 10/net 30.* Payments received within 10 days from the date of invoice receive a 2 percent discount; otherwise the full amount is due in 30 days. This is equivalent to an annual interest rate of 36 percent.

A payment terms tool available to the organization is the negotiation of an extension of the terms of payment to 60 days, 80 days or even longer, depending on the needs of the supply management professional's organization.

Cash Flow

Cash flow is closely related to the payment term and is defined in the *ISM Glossary* (2006) as the movement of money through an organization. It is the measure of inbound revenues and outbound expenses by time period. Extended terms improve the buying organization's cash flow by allowing it to retain its cash longer. The supply management professional must plan acquisitions and negotiate payment terms within the context of the organization's cash flow. The supply management professional is responsible for not placing an order with a supplier knowing the funds are not available to pay for the good or service. Therefore, the supply manager may have to buy smaller quantities than might be economically desirable. Supply management also needs to consider how contract terms and conditions will affect the supplier's cash flow and liquidity.

Regulations

The supply management professional should be familiar with the numerous regulations that exist. Some general categories include the U.S. Uniform Commercial Code, antitrust and trade, federal procurement, international trade (CISG), intellectual property, health and safety and environmental. In many instances, supply professionals are in a position to track international and national regulatory trends and develop a sense of how potential and actual regulations may affect an organization. This information should be shared with internal clients and upper management, as appropriate, and used in the planning process. For example, not long ago many countries signed a pact designed to significantly reduce access to carbon-based levels called the Kyoto Accord.[11] Organizations need to plan for the phaseout of equipment emitting high levels of restricted gasses or find substitute equipment. Obviously, the forward-thinking supply management professional can use this information to help internal clients plan for the future.

Supplier Investment (Financing)

Sometimes it is advantageous to help suppliers acquire resources to improve their capacities or get them through tough financial situations. This can be accomplished in a number of ways: a direct loan to the supplier, an alliance arrangement, cosigning a loan or providing other financial backing. The supply management professional must avoid violating any country-specific regulations concerning local investing when working in this area.

Private Equity

Private equity is a broad term that commonly refers to any type of equity investment in an asset in which the equity is not freely tradable on a public stock market. More accurately, private equity refers to the manner in which the funds have been raised, namely on the private markets, as opposed to the public markets. Private equity organizations were commonly misunderstood to invest in assets that were not in the public market. However, this no longer is the case — larger private equity organizations, such as Kohlberg Kravis Roberts & Co. (KKR) and the Blackstone Group, invest in companies listed on public exchanges and take them private, which is what this happened in 2007 when the Chrysler Division of Daimler-Benz was taken private. Passive institutional investors may invest in private equity funds, which are, in turn, used by private equity organizations for investment in target companies. Categories of private equity investment include the leveraged buyout, venture capital, growth capital, angel investing and mezzanine capital. Private equity funds typically control management of the companies in which they invest, and often bring in new management teams that focus on making the organization more valuable to their investors.

Centralized Purchasing

As presented in Chapter 3, a centralized supply management department is a potentially effective way to reduce costs. Centralized supply management determines the needs of the various divisions or facilities, selects suppliers and negotiates the purchases for the entire organization. This strategy makes sense when there is commonality of materials across divisions or locations, and when consolidating the requirements gives the organization more leverage with suppliers. When one division of an organization is the primary user of a commodity or product, that division negotiates the contracts with the supplier and other divisions or locations purchase off that contract. The organization is able to obtain lower prices because of the higher total volume and because the supplier has to negotiate with only one entity.

Summary

Sourcing refers to a business or organization attempting to acquire goods or services to accomplish the goals of the enterprise. Though several organizations attempt to set standards in the sourcing process — ISM, for example — processes can vary greatly among organizations. Typically, the word *sourcing* is used interchangeably with the words *purchasing* and *procurement* and generally is considered a major part of the supply management process. Supply management professionals guide the organization's acquisition procedures and standards. Most organizations use a three-way check as the foundation of their sourcing programs that involves three departments in the organization completing separate parts of the acquisition process. The three departments do not all report to the same senior manager to prevent unethical practices and lend credibility to the process. These departments can be supply management, receiving and accounts payable; engineering, supply management and accounts payable; or a plant manager, supply management and accounts payable. Combinations can vary significantly, but supply management and accounts payable departments usually are two of the three departments involved.

As e-procurement has become the norm, the trend away from the daily procurement function (tactical purchasing) resulted in several changes in supply management. With the focus away from transaction management, the supply management professional has been able to focus on negotiating contracts and procurement of large capital equipment. Both of these functions permitted supply management departments to manage and make financial contributions to the organization. Supply management professionals not only focus on the bidding process and negotiating with suppliers, but on the entire supply function. In these roles, they are able to add value and maximize savings for organizations. This value is manifested in lower inventories, less personnel, and getting the end product or service to the organization's customers more efficiently and effectively. The supply management professional's success in these roles has resulted in new assignments outside of the traditional purchasing function including logistics, materials management, distribution, warehousing and outsourcing. More and more supply management professionals are becoming true professionals by handling additional functions of their organization's operation.

Key Points

1. Although related, there is a distinction between sourcing and the sourcing cycle. The Institute for Supply Management™ defines the two terms differently.

2. Numerous factors affect the decision to use competitive bidding and/or negotiations, including market conditions and the availability of multiple viable sources.

3. The sourcing decision, made considering a wide range of factors including market conditions, the organization's business focus, and its core competencies, can be critical to an organization for the decision sets an organization's economic boundary and impacts the competitive character of the enterprise.

4. When classifying an organization's competencies into core versus noncore competencies, the supply management professional also must consider the type of market (buyer or seller) and the risk/value matrix. There is a variation in an organization's capabilities and focus, depending partially on its strategies.

5. The task of identifying potential suppliers and evaluating them for eventual selection is an important supply management activity.

6. The decision to continue using existing sources or to try new sources depends on a number of factors and situations that may create both advantages and disadvantages for either alternative, including the cost of switching from an existing supplier to a new one.

7. Supply management professionals can add value to the organization by developing an understanding of financing and leveraging strategies that then can be used to make recommendations and decisions.

5

Contracting

In the course of procuring goods and services, supply management professionals naturally deal with contracts. From receiving proposals and quotations from suppliers to signing contracts, supply management professionals oversee the entire process. They play a major role by providing and taking the lead in framing the facts involved in the negotiation. For instance, at Eastman Kodak Co. supply management professionals play a central role in identifying a sourcing opportunity as well as working on the detailed requirements involved in outsourcing.[1] As a result, supply management professionals become the most informed group of people in the organization to lead and manage the contracting process with a supplier.

Both the buying organization and the supplier must agree on the facts presented to them. Only then can they stand a reasonable chance of reaching an agreement leading to a contract. A contract needs to be mutually beneficial and fruitful for long-term relationships. Negotiation is a critical part of the contracting process, especially when the work required has not been finalized at the purchaser's end or unresolved terms and conditions remain. Because of this, negotiation and contracting are discussed in separate chapters of this book. Figure 5-1 illustrates the contracting process and how negotiation and contract administration fit into the overall process. Negotiation is addressed in-depth in Chapter 6 ("Negotiating") and contract administration is discussed as part of the overall relationship-building process in Chapter 8 ("Supplier Relationship Management").

Supply management professionals are ultimately responsible for ensuring that the terms and conditions of the contract are honored and for resolving conflicts as they arise. Frequently, conflicts do arise during the course of a contract. In this regard, a contract serves an important purpose for both the buyer and the supplier — it explicitly delineates the roles and responsibilities of both parties and helps to reach an understanding and, thus, resolution. Contracting and negotiation affect all facets of procuring products and services.

Figure 5-1   Contracting and Negotiation Process

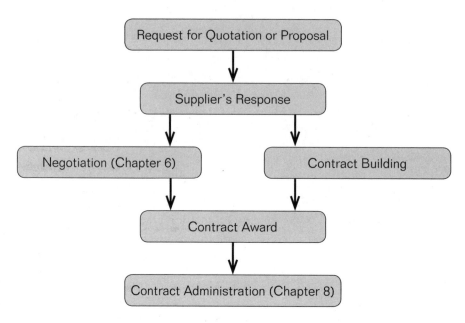

Source: Adapted from R.M. Monczka, R.J. Trent and R. B. Handfield, *Purchasing and Supply Chain Management,* 3rd ed. (Mason, OH: South-Western College Publishers, 2004).

CHAPTER OBJECTIVES

• Frame contracting in the context of the overall buying cycle.

• Study various types of solicitations and how to use the information from solicitation to arrive at the best possible contract.

• Consider various elements of a contract and other obligation documents.

• Obtain an overview of the different types of contracts.

The Basic Purchasing Process

When considering contracting, a supply management professional must have a qualitative understanding of how the contracting-related supply management activities (e.g., choosing the type of contract, preparing for solicitation, bidding, etc.) are embedded in the overall purchasing process. For instance, the specific characteristics of requested products or services must be clearly communicated and understood by the supply management professional. Only then can these requirements be correctly reflected in the contract. In addition, price requirements must be considered and contingencies planned for potential disputes.

When acquiring products and services, a basic sequence of steps must be followed to ascertain the robustness of the contracting process from the initiation of the transaction to its completion. Almost every large organization adheres to a clearly stated procedure when supply management receives a materials request. For instance, ABC Technologies (now part of SAS) follows a procedure regarding how the purchasing process should unfold if a specific supplier is stipulated by the user — the procedure delineates policies involved in contacting the supplier, identification of responsible parties and explicit steps to be taken.[2] Overall, purchasing policies typically delineate the objectives and guidelines for what needs to be accomplished and the procedures through which the needs are met. Different organizations may call the steps by different names or break down the steps differently, but the following activities are required:

1. Communicating need,

2. Understanding requirements,

3. Selecting suppliers,

4. Determining price,

5. Placing orders,

6. Following through,

7. Verifying charges and reconciling discrepancies, and

8. Completing orders and maintaining records.

Communicating Need

The buying process begins when the need is communicated from a user to the supply management department, either through a purchase requisition, through a bill of materials or through a supply management professional's discussions with a user group. A purchase requisition is a written or electronic request from an internal user/customer to supply management for the procurement of products or services from suppliers. The bill of materials is like a "recipe" that provides the list of quantities and descriptions of all materials required to produce one unit of a finished product.

A purchase requisition is issued either by the inventory control or a user department. The supply management component of inventory control places orders when the stock level goes down to the reorder point. Also, a user department (e.g., engineering department or marketing) may issue a purchase order if the item is needed for a specific and often immediate use, or if it is a nonstocked item.

Understanding Requirements

Once supply management receives the requisition, the supply management professional reviews it and determines what is being asked based on knowledge, past experience and discussions with the customer. If anything is unclear, supply management is responsible for asking the user to clarify the specifics of the requirements. Supply management must maintain a good relationship with the internal customers.

Without a clear understanding, whatever happens from this point on in the buying process will be fraught with problems. In particular, if the requisition involves a new item or service, the supply management professional must work closely with the internal customer to develop an understanding of all the requirements and present options to the customer. At the same time, the supply management professional typically has opportunities to shape the requirements from materials or services required to terms and conditions sought by the user. Finally, depending on the strategic importance of the item and the level of supply market risk, the decision must be made regarding the number of suppliers and the nature of the contracts.

Selecting Suppliers

The understanding of the internal customer requirements must be applied to supplier selection. The supply management professional has the knowledge of each supplier's strengths and weaknesses and is in the best position to match the requirements with supplier capabilities and their business aspirations. A small number of potential suppliers need to be identified from the market.

For items purchased regularly, supply management usually has developed a list of prequalified preferred suppliers. For new items, inquiries can be made to current suppliers or to the suppliers the internal customer suggests. When working with new and existing suppliers in a new capacity, supply management may request information from suppliers regarding their financial status, technology capability or any other issues that require clarification. As the search is further narrowed, it also may be necessary to visit prospective suppliers' facilities to validate the information received.

Determining Price

Generally, a price for the purchased items is determined in three ways: through requests for quotation, requests for proposal and suppliers' catalogs.

Request for Quotation (RFQ). The *ISM Glossary* (2006) defines a request for quotation (RFQ) as a solicitation document used to obtain price quotes for a specified product or service. This often is a follow-up to an earlier request for information. If the requirements for the item can be described objectively, an RFQ can be developed and issued to potential suppliers. When the specified time has passed, the bidding process is closed and the quotations are studied, compared and clarified. In many organizations, some negotiations may occur at this stage. The contract then is developed and the purchase order is issued to the chosen supplier. Depending on the country the supply management professional is working with, variations in cultural norms may require altering the way business is accomplished. For example, when dealing with Asian suppliers who value personal relationships, a visit to the supplier may be a prerequisite and the establishment of a relationship will need to occur before issuing an RFQ and obtaining a valid quotation. In fact, only when a common understanding has been reached with the supplier can specifications be accurately interpreted and integrated into the process.[3]

Request for Proposal (RFP). The *ISM Glossary* (2006) defines a request for proposal (RFP) as a solicitation document used to obtain offers of price and a proposed method of executing a project. When specifications cannot be described objectively because the product or service is not yet fully developed or specified, the supply management organization is interested in getting the supplier's ideas, and/or some uncertainties surrounding technology or materials used exist, an RFP can be issued. In this case, negotiation or bargaining between buyer and supplier typically takes place to determine the scope of the product or service purchased, as well as the price. In some situations, several suppliers may be brought together to develop a joint proposal — these suppliers work with the buying organization, with the understanding that their knowledge of the proposal will have an impact on how well they can respond to the bidding process that results.[4] In the end, one or more suppliers can be chosen for negotiation.

Suppliers' Catalogs. For low-volume commodity items, prices can be obtained from suppliers' catalogs. In these cases, preset trade discounts may be offered.

Placing Orders

The purchase order issued to the supplier is the legal document that binds both buyer and supplier organizations to the terms agreed on. Even if the order is placed over the telephone or via e-mail, the order must be confirmed by issuing an official purchase order.

Once the supply management professional records all the pertinent information on the requisition — name of the supplier, price and quantity — the purchase order can be prepared for signature. For complex and longer-term purchases, a separate contract is developed, including specifications, terms and conditions, with reference to the purchase order. Once the supplier receives the purchase order, it sends a confirmation to the supply management organization indicating receipt of the purchase order and the delivery date. Copies of the purchase order also are sent to the internal customer and to the accounting department, as well as to the receiving and inventory control functions of supply management. This can be accomplished electronically by most organizations, without generating paper copies.

Following Through

Supply management typically assigns a group that is responsible for making sure orders arrive on time. Computers list outstanding orders with scheduled delivery dates. Critical and overdue orders are followed through by direct communication and expedited if necessary. Ideally, this should never be necessary; in reality, however, unforeseen events occur and this step works as a risk-mitigation strategy. The extent to which follow-through is necessary varies from supplier to supplier and from order to order.

Verifying Charges and Reconciling Discrepancies

Once the order arrives, the receiving record is issued and the supplier sends the purchasing organization the invoice. This invoice then is checked against the original purchase order and the receiving record. The quantity is reviewed and terms and conditions are verified. Much of this reconciliation can be performed electronically.

When there is agreement, the invoice is approved and the supplier is paid. If discrepancies exist, a notification is sent to the buyer, generally by the accounts payable department. If the invoice from the supplier contains errors, the supply management professional sends it back to the supplier for correction, also generally electronically. When the materials received are rejected for poor quality, the purchaser contacts the supplier for return and replacement. Often, per agreement from the supplier, the rejected materials are charged back to the supplier. Reconciling discrepancies is more difficult with service businesses because the value creation occurs in real time between the service provider and the customer. When there are perceived discrepancies, they typically result in complaints, negative word of mouth and refusal to repurchase. The supply management professional must have a clear strategy about how to handle and recover from such discrepancies.

Completing Orders and Maintaining Records

The supply management department typically maintains an electronic file of active orders that have not been completely filled. When the delivery is completed and payment is made to the supplier, the order should be "closed" — recorded as having been completed. All three forms of the original purchase order, the invoice and the receiving record should be kept in the permanent file — most organizations now maintain these records electronically.

If partial shipments were made, the filing should occur only after the final shipment. In most cases, the file of completed orders is stored by purchase order number for future retrieval purposes. In many instances, the records of all transactions typically are kept in soft copy and maintained by the supply management department. Any notable events that may have occurred during the transaction are recorded there as well for future reference. The records can be retrieved by product, service or supplier organization name. The supply management department should work with the operations and legal departments and establish a policy regarding how long records are maintained, in what form or who should have access to them. Particular care should be taken with international suppliers and the rules of their countries.

Solicitations for Contracting

A major way to secure the best possible contract for all parties concerned is the solicitation step. For instance, the U.S. government posts solicitations for RFPs or *invitations for bid (IFBs)* on purchases ranging from domestic air travel for government workers to teaching workshops for state prisoners.[5] The wording used in these contract solicitations is specific yet covers a wide range of information in a comprehensive way. For instance, a solicitation lists the nature of the contract being advertised, published date, branch of government agency, estimated value of the contract, duration and locations. In that regard, careful planning is an absolute requirement. Preparation for solicitation typically takes place for bids, quotations and proposals with pertinent specifications, terms and conditions. Once a response is received from the supplier, the contract can be created, moving toward an eventual contract award and subsequent administration.

Not all contracts, however, stem from solicitation. Solicitation is an intensive approach to establishing a contract, which may elicit responses not only from the existing suppliers but also from new ones. If suppliers have been doing the work required and relationships with these suppliers are built on a long-term basis, contracting might not require a formal solicitation. Supplier management and relationship maintenance are discussed in Chapter 7, "Supplier Management and Development," and Chapter 8, "Supplier Relationship Management." For instance, some contracts, commonly referred to as *evergreen contracts,* include a contractual provision that the contract is automatically renewed unless a party gives notice to the contrary.[6] Many leading organizations, such as Caterpillar, Bose Corp., or Chrysler, employ evergreen contracts when a supplier has a long-term partnership with the buying organization. Both the buying organization and the supplier understand that the contract is continued unless serious performance problems occur. In this type of situation, work sometimes begins even before the detailed terms and conditions of contracts are worked out. Based on past practices and mutual trust, the supplier begins work knowing that the details can be worked out.

Methods of Communication

When soliciting, it first is necessary to communicate the acceptable product or service attributes. For tangible goods, acceptance criteria include the measurements taken from an incoming inspection and the allowable results. For services, these include the definition of the finished deliverables, which may be a look, a perceived state of well-being or a report.

There are primarily three types of communication methods — performance and design specifications, internal versus external specifications, and supplier samples. Descriptions of these methods are shown in Figure 5-2.

Figure 5-2   Types of Communication Methods

TYPES	DESCRIPTIONS
Performance and Design Specifications	Performance specifications define the characteristics of an acceptable product or service, and design specifications provide the details of how the product should be made or how the service needs to carried out.
Internal Versus External Specifications	Internal specifications are specifications that the organization has agreed to use internally within itself, and external specifications are specifications set by the industry or government.
Supplier Samples	A physical sample can be used to communicate specifications. When the sample meets the buying organization's requirements, the sample then is typically referenced as "specifications."

Generally, the details of how to arrive at the performance characteristics are left to the supplier. The buyer focuses on results as captured by the performance specifications. When performance specifications are used, the process is commonly referred to as *black box* sourcing and the supplier has maximum latitude to determine how to achieve the required performance. This leads to an *outcome-based* contract.[7] Design specifications give the buying organization maximum control over the process through which an outcome is achieved. This approach typically is referred to as *white box* sourcing and leads to a *behavior-based* contract in which what is being controlled is not the outcome but the behavior that is required to manifest the desired outcome. In this case, the buying organization assumes the risk for proper performance of the end product.

As for internal and external specifications, they should overlap as closely as possible. Both the buyer and supplier organizations should mutually understand what is wanted as well as how it will be measured.

When a physical sample can be used to communicate specifications, the terms will state that other products should be produced just like the sample. Often, service also can be sampled. Once the buying organization samples a service process such as a training class or a catering operation, it may document the key characteristics of the sample and request that subsequent services duplicate it.

Types of Solicitations/Bids

Solicitation of proposals can take many forms. Ten most frequently used types include:

1. Offer to buy versus offer to sell,

2. Informal bids/quotations,

3. Electronic solicitations,

4. Competitive proposals,

5. Sealed bids,

6. Restricted competition,

7. Noncompetitive negotiations,

8. Two-step bidding,

9. Alternate and innovative proposals, and

10. Online bidding.

To understand the concept of *offer to buy* versus *offer to sell,* one must keep in mind that a contract must have an offer and an acceptance. Commonly, it is advantageous for the buying organization to solicit suppliers' offers to sell. Thus the buyer retains the power of acceptance. Otherwise, an offer to buy must be sent to a supplier who may fail to respond. In this case, without the supplier's acceptance, there is no contract and no supply of products or services.

Informal bids or quotations refer to telephone, written or electronic quotations with dollar values that are less than a pre-established monetary limit between a buyer and a supplier. Informal quotations also may be used to solicit budgetary information from suppliers for estimating purposes. In this instance, it is critical that the supplier mark the quote as being informal. The buying organization must understand clearly that the submitted proposals are primarily for budgetary purposes and are subject to change.

Many buying organizations today *solicit bids or proposals electronically* via e-mail and EDI. They also may solicit bids through an extranet, an organization's Web site that provides a limited amount of accessibility to persons outside the organization. An extranet often is used to link with actual and potential suppliers. (*ISM Glossary,* 2006) Requests to bid or requests to sell also can be posted on online, open-market Web sites. For instance, Converge Global Trading Exchange is a distributor for high-tech parts, and its online trading Web site allows organizations to buy and sell high-tech parts in a secondary market.[8]

In a competitive world, all organizations strive to survive and meet market demand, and, in a theoretical state of "perfect" competition, they would make just enough to stay in business.[9] Understanding competition is fundamental to contracting. Even though the concept of perfect competition is merely theoretical, buying organizations attempt to simulate it to the best of their ability. This starts with the *practice of competitive proposals.* This practice is initiated by an RFP, a solicitation document used to obtain a price offer and a proposed method of executing a project. (*ISM Glossary,* 2006) An RFP delineates the buying organization's requirements and criteria for proposal evaluation. After the submission of timely proposals by the maximum number of possible suppliers, the buying organization concludes with the award of a contract to the one supplier, considering price, quality and the other factors or outcomes desired that are included in the solicitation.

A bid may be submitted in *a sealed envelope* to prevent its contents from being revealed or known before the deadline. This type of solicitation frequently is used for buying services such as building or maintenance contracts, construction and equipment, but it also may be appropriate for selling scrap and surplus.

In some instances, *restricted competition* may prohibit the buying organization from obtaining more than one proposal. Some of the reasons for restricted competition include specialization of the resources required to deliver the product or service, lack of competition in a specific geographic region, and regulatory restrictions.

In situations where specifications are not yet clear or complete, it probably is best to communicate with the supplier and negotiate the terms and understanding in a *nonconfrontational, noncompetitive* way. Even if a performance specification has been developed, negotiation may be appropriate if uncertainty exists about to the supplier's ability to meet quality and delivery requirements. In either of these situations or in other situations where one supplier is clearly superior in the areas of critical skills, capabilities and technologies, it may be advantageous to negotiate with only that supplier.

A *two-step bidding* technique is used when inadequate specifications preclude the initial use of competitive bidding. In the first step, bids are requested only for technical proposals without any prices. In the second step, bids are sent only to those suppliers that submitted acceptable technical proposals, and then these suppliers are asked to submit updated bids with pricing. (*ISM Glossary,* 2006)

Some suppliers, in order to win the contract, may choose to submit a proposal that takes it outside the format requested in the call for proposals. *Alternate proposals* generally are accepted and may, in fact, be encouraged when a supplier responds to the RFP. In some solicitations, such as IFBs, however, alternate proposals may not be allowed and may even disqualify the proposal — this should be specifically pointed out in the bid document. From the buying organization's perspective, there is no single way to write an RFQ, RFI, RFP or IFB. The structure, content and method of managing the information before, during and after submission of the bid by the supplier should be guided by the principles of ethical and fair supply management practice and organizational policy. The supply management professional also should understand the business culture in the applicable country or industry and that some forms of bidding may not be appropriate in all places.

An increasingly common method of bidding in electronic commerce is *online bidding,* where an organization invites or requires suppliers to submit their bids over the Internet. (*ISM Glossary,* 2006) Supply management organizations not only are posting RFQs and RFPs on their Web sites, but they also are encouraging or even requiring suppliers to submit their quotes electronically. Many organizations now have developed and implemented online bidding systems to increase buying efficiency. For instance, an international organization called Beta Products that manufactures engineered products for the transportation industry has moved through several implementation phases of an online bidding system.[10] Even with multiple divisions, the organization was able to consolidate the database and standardize the decision-making process.

Requests for Information

This stage of activity often is used to gather information about potential suppliers and gain marketplace intelligence; it is critical in conducting a *fact-based* negotiation. RFIs give the supply management professional the opportunity to obtain information about supplier capabilities and make decisions about potential future relationships.

The primary purpose of an RFI is to obtain general information about products, services or suppliers. It is an information request, not binding on either the supplier or the purchaser, and often is sent prior to specific requisitions for items. (*ISM Glossary*, 2006) Often, an RFI is used when there are uncertainties involved in product or service specifications.

Of course, potential benefits and problems exist with RFIs. An RFI is a quick survey and is intended for a ready response. The process may help the buyer in budgeting or selecting an alternate process or product of which it was not previously aware.

A drawback to an RFI is that if the method is used too often, potential suppliers may refuse to respond. At the same time, some buyers can abuse it — instead of conducting the research themselves, some buyers may habitually resort to RFIs as primary methods of gathering information. After RFI information is received, the organization may choose to negotiate with one of the suppliers, or it may develop an RFQ and solicit bids. Prior to negotiation or bid acceptance, the burden is on the supply management professional and his or her negotiation team to verify suppliers' submitted information and obtain information beyond what the suppliers provided.

In contrast, an IFB generally is used when all specifications are known in terms of the detailed description of the product or service needed, delivery schedule and quantities; the only deciding factor is price. An IFB is a request made to potential suppliers for a bid on goods or services to be purchased. In government purchasing it often is the solicitation document used in sealed bidding and in the second step of a two-step bidding process. (*ISM Glossary*, 2006)

Suppliers' Conferences

In certain situations, the supply management organization may want to meet with the suppliers prior to inviting them to bid on a job. These are called prebid or preproposal conferences. Their main purpose is to clarify specifications and answer questions from suppliers in an open and equitable manner. (*ISM Glossary*, 2006)

Some proposals are complex because of the specifications, the newness of the technology, the large number of suppliers involved in bidding, the amount of business to be awarded and the critical nature of the resulting contract. In these situations, a prebid or preproposal conference may be an appropriate way to communicate information to the supply base so when suppliers bid, they would do so fully informed.

At the prebid conference, the buying organization's team meets with all potential suppliers who attend. Topics generally covered at these meetings include blueprints and specifications, statement of work (SOW) of service, quotation due dates, terms and conditions of quotation, delivery schedules and materials, releasing procedures, invoicing procedures and documentation including incentives. Additional requirements may result once the business is awarded, such as reporting, insurance, background checks, security clearances and permits. If changes to the solicitation result from the conference, the supply management professional issues a written amendment to the solicitation to all suppliers.

All potential bidders should be invited to the prebid conference. Sometimes, when there are discrepancies in the number of participants from various suppliers, suppliers with only one or two representatives may feel slighted. Therefore, it is important to communicate in advance how many people from each supplier are allowed to attend the conference. Attendees from the buying organization should include supply management and affected internal-user departments.

Prebid meetings establish a forum for two-way communication between the buying organization and the supplier to discuss the details of the RFQ, RFI, RFP or IFB package at the beginning of the bid process. The buyer needs to ensure that bid packages are sent to suppliers well in advance of the meeting so that they have adequate time to review its contents. By meeting in an open forum, the buyer will quickly learn of any discrepancies or errors in the bid package. Any corrections should be made as a written addendum to the original bid package. This can expedite the bid process, as well as ensure that the information received complies with all requirements.

A potential disadvantage to the prebid meeting is the time it takes to meet with all the potential suppliers. In addition, overuse may discourage some suppliers from attending, especially in peak seasons for their trades or industries.

Solicitation Procedures and Concepts

The basic concepts underlying solicitation procedures involve openness and fairness. All suppliers need to be given a level playing field at the start of the process by providing them with comparable information. The subsequent evaluation process must be transparent and follow good business practices.

Comparable Information. To provide a common baseline for evaluating bids, all suppliers must receive the same information in the original quotation package. If additional information is provided to suppliers during the quotation process, all quoting suppliers should receive that information.

Good Business Practices. Fairness and business ethics is another important concept. The nature of the competitive bidding process assumes that the contract will be awarded to the supplier providing the best proposal that responds to the supply management organization's award criteria whether that is price, quality, delivery, customer service, technology or a combination of these factors or others required by the supply management organization. Therefore, it is critical to confirm before the bid requests are issued that all suppliers receiving a bid are qualified to receive the business. In those situations where business is not awarded to the lowest bidder, a written memo explaining the decision criteria should accompany the quote in the file. All suppliers who submit quotes should be notified whether or not they are the successful bidder. Information submitted by a supplier to a buyer as part of a quotation response should remain confidential except in the public sector where statutes may require that it become public information.

Generally, a solicitation should include the following information:

- A complete specification of the item or a statement of work (SOW) of the service to be quoted;

- The quantity to be quoted;

- Where and when the items are to be shipped or installed, or where and when the services are to be performed;

- The due date of the quotation; and

- Product, service due date or timeline.

An *expression of interest (EOI)* may be issued as a preliminary step to formal solicitation. An EOI should contain relevant and sufficient information to allow a supplier organization to decide whether or not it wants to be a prospective bidder. (*ISM Glossary,* 2006)

Response time required should be fair. When stipulating the response time, the buying organization needs to consider how long the supplier may take to complete the analysis and prepare the bid. Allowing a reasonable time ensures a more thorough response from the supplier and projects the image of fairness. The buying organization should not make this time unduly short as a way to eliminate potential suppliers.

The issue date is important for it affects the receipt date and the opening and closing dates; therefore, care must be taken when a solicitation package is issued. For instance, issuing a solicitation that will place the closing date on a holiday in whatever country the supplier is located should be avoided — offices at both the buying organization and the supplier may be closed. Also, if possible, it makes sense to avoid issuing solicitations during a supplier's peak season. This may reduce the number of responses and increase prices. Appropriate planning by internal customers and supply management staff can remedy these situations.

Opening and closing dates also are key. One of the fundamental pieces of information in the solicitation proposal is the due date of the quotation. RFQs and IFBs normally have opening dates, while RFPs have closing dates. The buyer needs to consider the complexity of the bid, the timing constraints within the buying organization and the number of bids concurrently issued to the same group of suppliers. Bid due dates should be realistic and enforceable.

Bonds and Other Types of Surety

A bond is a written instrument executed by a bidder or contractor (i.e., the principal) and a second party (i.e., the surety) to ensure fulfillment of the principal's obligation to a third party. Types of bonds include performance bonds, payment bonds. and bid bonds. (*ISM Glossary,* 2006) In general, bonds increase the cost of bidding and tend to reduce competition. At the same time, using bonds does not guarantee financial recovery. In such a case, failure of a supplier to meet the performance requirements of a contract generally can be handled by the buying organization's legal department. Figure 5-3 offers an overview of various types of bonds and other types of surety.

Figure 5-3   Overview of Bonds and Other Types of Surety

TYPE	DESCRIPTION
Bid Bonds	A bid bond provides financial assurance that the bidder will honor its obligations under the contract. (*ISM Glossary,* 2006) It guarantees that if the order is awarded to a specific bidder, it will accept the purchase contract. If the bidder refuses, the extra costs to the buying organization of going to an alternative source are borne by the insurer. Bid bonds sometimes are used by government agencies and in construction bidding, and bring a third party into the transaction.

(continued)

Figure 5-3   continued

TYPE	DESCRIPTION
Performance Bonds	The performance bond secures the performance and fulfillment of all the undertakings, covenants, terms, conditions and agreements contained in the contract. It normally is accompanied by a payment bond (particularly in a construction contract) and is provided after the submission of a bid bond. (*ISM Glossary*, 2006) Performance bonds often are used in international sourcing and construction bidding. The supply management professional can, as a condition of doing business, require the supplier to post a performance bond guaranteeing prompt delivery of goods that meet specifications. In the case of construction projects, a performance bond guarantees that the work will be completed according to specification and time requirements if the supplier fails.
Payment Bonds	The payment bond protects the buying organization against liens that may be filed by employees or subcontractors against the buying organization if the prime supplier does not pay its suppliers or employees. A payment bond usually accompanies a performance bond.
Deposits	Bid deposits may be requested as devices to discourage financially unstable suppliers. These usually are issued for substantial bids. Bid deposits generally cover the amount in liquidated damages to which the buying organization would be entitled should the supplier not perform according to the terms of the agreement.
Letters of Credit	A letter of credit is a document that ensures the seller that payment will be made by the bank issuing the letter of credit on fulfillment of the terms of the sales agreement. (*ISM Glossary*, 2006) It normally is used in international business transactions.
Real Estate	The purchaser could require the supplier to put other assets, such as real estate, into an escrow account as a form of surety that the supplier will meet its obligations or forfeit the asset.
Escrow	A temporary monetary deposit such as real estate or cash is placed with an independent third party by agreement between two parties. The escrow money or asset is released when certain agreed-on conditions have been met. (*ISM Glossary*, 2006) Cash may not be a good approach for it may affect the supplier's liquidity and its ability to perform because of lack of available cash to purchase the necessary materials and services.

Complexities in the Bidding Process

During the course of solicitation and receiving offers, problems may arise that require action on behalf of the supply management professional. This could result in a *time extension and amendments to the solicitation.* Here, a supplier might raise a concern if one supplier is granted a time extension to respond to a bid and others are not. If an extension is offered to one supplier, then all suppliers must be notified that they are granted the same extension. Changes to the original bid must be communicated to all suppliers bidding in a consistent and timely manner. Regarding *late bids without time extensions:,* the buying organization must make clear its policy on late bids before issuing a quotation. The practice of not accepting late bids and returning them unopened is common.

Offers may come with *errors, irregularities or omissions.* If a supplier identifies a mistake in a bid after submission, it is good practice to allow that supplier to withdraw its bid. Courts generally allow this under two circumstances: (1) The mistake was mechanical or clerical in nature, not an error in judgment; (2) the bidder was not negligent in making the error (it was an honest mistake) or in delaying notification to the supply management professional of the error. In addition, the buying organization may find discrepancies in the bid. If so, it should seek confirmation of the bid from the bidder before proceeding with the award. If a mistake is confirmed, the bidder should be allowed to withdraw its bid without penalty.

There also could be a *conflict of interest.* A conflict of interest is a situation in which an individual has a personal interest as well as a job responsibility, with the possibility of a conflict between the two. The individual's actions may be influenced by his or her personal interest to the detriment of performing his or her professional responsibility effectively. (*ISM Glossary,* 2006) Fundamental ethical practice requires that no employee of the buying organization who has any authority to purchase goods or services, or is in a position to influence decisions in any way with respect to purchases, should have a vested interest in the supplier of goods and services to the buying organization. The vested interest applies to employment, holding positions such as a director, financial interest or other business relationships with the supplier. As a result, *protests* might occur. Suppliers are entitled to a reasonable explanation if not selected. However, care should be taken to guard against disclosing the information contained in competitors' bids unless, as with a public purchase, such disclosures are required by law. Additional information provided to the supplier may assist its ability to better meet the needs of the buying organization during the next round of the quotation process. In the public sector, if a supplier or prospective supplier disagrees with an action or a decision of the supply management professional, it may file a protest and request an administrative review of the action or decision.

Other problems potentially entail *confidentiality/security* and *alternate proposals.* As with all purchasing documents, files containing proposals, whether electronic or print, should be secured to prevent unauthorized access. Confidential information about one supplier should not be shared with others. Also, suppliers often propose products or services that are different from those specified in the initial request to bid. Many of these proposals have merit; therefore, the buying organization should institute a policy of whether and how to consider these. Lastly, there is the *debriefing process.* When the award is made and the contract has been signed, some organizations have a policy of informing all suppliers of the name of the successful supplier. The debriefing process also should include internal customers. The internal users should be advised about the successful supplier. Possibly, some of the internal staff will be working with the supplier; if that is likely, necessary arrangements should be made to introduce the internal staff to the supplier's personnel. Any third-party organizations that will be involved in the contract also should be advised.

Contracts

After a successful process of solicitation, the supplier that best fulfills the requirements is identified. This supplier then is engaged in a negotiation to arrive at terms and conditions that include price, delivery, quality and other requirements. At this point, both parties must be willing to create a contract that legally binds them to fulfill their obligations. In general, a contract is viewed as being different from an agreement. A contract is a legally enforceable written or oral agreement between two or more competent parties that defines a job or service to be performed. The legal definitions of a contract and an agreement are different. In the United States, a contract is defined in Uniform Commercial Code (UCC) Section 1-201 (11) as "the total legal obligation which results from the parties' agreement as affected by this Act and any other applicable rules of law." (*ISM Glossary,* 2006) An agreement can build on both parties' spoken language or visible actions and may facilitate a contract, while a contract legally obligates them to meet the requirements in good faith and with due diligence. In the United States, UCC Section 1-201(3) defines an agreement as "the bargain of the parties in fact as found in their language or by implication from other circumstances including course of dealing or usage of trade or course of performance … Whether an agreement has legal consequences is determined by the provisions of the Act, if applicable; otherwise by the law of contracts." (*ISM Glossary,* 2006) Because of the growth of interstate and international commerce, the law of contracts has been shaped by a process of developing uniform statutes that are designed to codify certain legal principles in a consistent manner from state to state within the United States and even across national boundaries.[11]

Elements of a Contract

Four basic elements make up the foundation of a contract — offer and acceptance, consideration, competent parties and legality of purpose. Initial discussions of price, quality and delivery terms are all part of reaching a mutual understanding and agreement, but they are not considered a legally binding contract. However, a purchase order or price quotation submitted to the other party through a formal communication channel may, in fact, be legally biding. Figure 5-4 provides a summary of these four elements.

Subsequent to an offer, a counteroffer may be made. A counteroffer is an offer to enter into a transaction on terms different from those originally proposed. (*ISM Glossary,* 2006) Once a counteroffer is made, it negates the original offer and delineates a modified offer. If the buyer issues a purchase order, which constitutes an offer, the supplier may issue a communiqué to inform the buyer that it has been accepted. This acknowledgment or formal acceptance creates a *bilateral contract.* The element of consideration in contracting refers to the legal requirement for a contractual promise to be binding; something of value must be given up in exchange. Both parties must be viewed as competent as defined in Figure 5-4.

Figure 5-4   Overview of Contract Elements

ELEMENTS	DESCRIPTIONS
Offer and Acceptance	Proposal to make a contract and subsequent agreement: Both parties express interest and willingness to create a contractual relationship. An acceptance is the indication of an offeree to be bound by the terms of an offer; may be by communication or behavior.
Consideration	Legal requirements for creation of a valid contract involving an exchange of value for value.
Competent Parties	Legal requirements for the creation of a valid contract encompassing age, mental capacity (requisite understanding of the transaction) and authority (acting for oneself or on behalf of another).
Legality of Purpose	Legal requirement for creation of a valid contract that is consistent with federal, state or provincial constitutions and not in violation of legal status or public policy.

Source: ISM Glossary of Key Supply Management Terms (Tempe, AZ: Institute for Supply Management, 2006).

Terms and Conditions

Terms and conditions (Ts & Cs) is a generic phrase referring to various requirements imposed on contracting parties by the language of their contract. (*ISM Glossary,* 2006) A contract consists of both standard and custom terms and conditions. *Standard terms and conditions* are what the buying organization wants to apply to every contract. Several potential issues are involved with standard terms and conditions: changes to the contract, cancellation, subcontracting, confidentiality, delivery, shipping, indemnity, legal venue, applicable laws, inspection, payment terms, packaging and warranties.

Custom terms and conditions are unique to the specific contract or purchase order. Custom terms and conditions may address such things as acceptance testing, updating service information, emergency services, financing, installation, training, initial provisioning, maintenance, spare parts and contract renewal.

It is appropriate to include all terms and conditions on all solicitations to avoid surprises and disagreements later in the award process. As discussed earlier, during the follow-through, verifying charges and reconciling discrepancies stages of the purchasing process, disagreements may take place. Having well-articulated terms and conditions will assist in resolving those disagreements to the benefit of both parties.

Types of Obligation Documents

A contract may be rendered orally or in writing — both are legally binding for goods. However, only a written contract is binding for services. Services are not covered in the Uniform Commercial Code in the United States. A prudent supply management professional may use oral contracts when the convenience of an oral contract is high and the risk of contract violation is low. For instance, if a buyer is pressed for time (e.g., there is not enough time to issue a written contract) and the purchase involves a low-cost item, then the buyer may issue an oral contract. Also, when the buyer and supplier have maintained a long and fruitful relationship, the supplier may begin work based on an oral contract. In either case, the oral contract should be followed by a written one such as a purchase order.

Written Contracts. The Statute of Frauds, a provision from English law adopted in the United States to prevent fraud and perjury, requires certain contracts to be in writing to be enforceable for cautionary and evidentiary reasons. For instance, prior to 1677 in England, contracts involving real and personal property did not require writing. Then, in 1677, the law was changed to require writing under the English Statutes of Frauds.[12] Subsequently, most of the states in the United States enacted similar laws. Contracts covered by the requirement include sale of goods for $500 or more, lease of goods for $1,000 or more, contracts for services that cannot be performed within one year and real estate transactions. (*ISM Glossary,* 2006)

Acceptable Oral Contracts. In some circumstances, oral contracts are acceptable for goods worth $500 or more. The first circumstance arises if one party, in fact, documents in writing the content of the oral contract and sends a copy to the other party. The second circumstance applies if it is evident that specific actions have been taken. For instance, the goods are made specifically to the purchaser's order and are not readily salable to others (e.g., custom-made goods or purchaser-labeled goods). The third circumstance occurs if both parties behave as if a contract exists and actually perform their obligations under the oral contract. The last circumstance occurs if the party against whom the contract is to be enforced admits under oath that a contract existed.

Trading Partner Agreements. Because of the Statute of Frauds, supply management transactions conducted electronically without written contracts may pose problems similar to those with oral contracts. Before engaging in an electronic transaction, partners should agree on some general rules for conducting such business. A *trading partner agreement* is actually a contract establishing the electronic relationship and covers the basic contract requirements, including standard terms and conditions that will apply to any transactions completed under the agreement.

Letters of Intent. This is a precontractual document used to express expectation of contract formation in the future. When properly drafted, a letter of intent should create no binding obligation on either party. (*ISM Glossary,* 2006) When the letter of intent is issued, it is expected to be superseded by a legally binding contract.

The purpose is to gain time in a commitment to a supplier prior to issuing a more complete purchase order or contract. Often, letters of intent are issued when the buyer needs to reserve capacity at the supplier's facility, the total volume of business to the supplier is yet unclear, the buyer needs the supplier to maintain an inventory of certain parts or raw materials (e.g., what is needed for the provision of a service), or the supplier needs some evidence to secure bonding.

Purchase Orders. This is perhaps the most common type of obligation document prepared by a supply management professional to describe the terms and conditions of a purchase. In the contracting process, the purchase order may function as an offer, an acceptance, a confirmation of an oral agreement or a trigger for a periodic performance (release) under an established contract. (*ISM Glossary,* 2006) For instance, if a purchase order is issued in response to a supplier's quotation, then the purchase order may serve as an acceptance. However, if a purchase order is issued as an offer, it may not constitute a contract; it becomes a contract only when the supplier signs and returns an acknowledgment copy of the purchase order to the buyer. The purchase order is consider a unilateral contract when it is based on an offer by one party, with acceptance formed by the actions of another. In such a case, there is only one promise (the offer), but performance by the other party serves as acceptance and creates the contract.

There are exceptions to terms and conditions. For instance, when a written confirmation is sent in response to an oral agreement, the recipient of that confirmation has a certain amount of time — for example, 10 days — in which to object to the terms expressed in the confirmation. These objections may be reflected in either rejection of the offer or a counteroffer made by the recipient of the offer. As discussed previously, depending on the situation, it could be the supplier or the buyer that issues the objection. This type of exception to terms and conditions must be clearly communicated to the party that made the offer before the transaction is completed because once goods are shipped or services are rendered, the party receiving the goods or services may be deemed to have accepted the original terms on which they were offered.

Electronic Purchasing. Given the spirit of the Statute of Frauds, transactions accomplished electronically may face problems similar to those with oral contracts. To overcome such shortcomings, both parties enter an agreement regarding the general rules when engaging in electronic purchasing. This is called a *trading partner agreement*. This agreement is, in fact, a contract establishing the electronic relationship and covering the basic terms and conditions that apply under the agreement. For instance, an electronic signature is acceptable if the agreement includes explicit reference to this and contains the actual signature. In 1999, the United States adopted the Uniform Electronic Transactions Act (UETA). According to UETA, electronic records are the equivalent of written documents and electronic signatures are the equivalent of handwritten signatures for legal purposes. An electronic signature is defined by law as "an electronic sound, symbol or process that is attached to or logically associated with a record that is executed or adopted by an individual with the intent to sign the record."[13]

Types of Contracts

Contracts can be categorized by their characteristics and purposes. However, almost all contracts revolve around some type of pricing plan. For instance, fixed-price contracts begin with a previously agreed estimate for the price of the contracted work, while cost-based contracts arrive at the price based on the cost of the actual work performed.

Fixed-Price Contracts

This type of contract refers to a family of contracts whose common characteristic is a ceiling beyond which the buyer bears no responsibility for payment. (*ISM Glossary,*

2006) As contract terms lengthen or as the complexity of the development or performance increases, supplier risk generally rises with this type of contract.

Figure 5-5 offers an overview of fixed-price contracts, including a description of what each type means, how it can best be applied and managerial implications for both the supplier and the buyer.

Figure 5-5   Overview of Fixed-Price Contracts

TYPE	DESCRIPTION/ APPLICATION	IMPLICATIONS FOR SUPPLIER	IMPLICATIONS FOR PURCHASER
Firm Fixed Price	The buyer agrees to pay the supplier a set price for the specified goods or services. It is considered the simplest form of contract.	In an inflationary environment, the supplier would assume more risk.	Once the price is accepted by the buyer, it is firm. If the anticipated inflationary price increase does not occur, the buyer would have paid too much.
Fixed Price With Escalation	To hedge against the fluctuating future prices of raw materials and parts or services, escalation clauses are included in the basic fixed-price contract. This type of contract generally is applied when the product or service being procured is to be supplied over a long period of time.	The supplier is protected against cost increases.	The buyer is protected against losses should costs decrease.
Fixed Price With Redetermination	When there are many uncertain variables to contend with, the buyer and supplier may choose to revisit the price for the purpose of redetermining it at a later point in time.	The supplier is protected against future uncertainties, but will have to engage in negotiation again.	The buyer is protected against future uncertainties, but will have to engage in negotiation again.

(continued)

Figure 5-5   continued

TYPE	DESCRIPTION/ APPLICATION	IMPLICATIONS FOR SUPPLIER	IMPLICATIONS FOR PURCHASER
Fixed Price With Incentives	Offers incentives to both the supplier and the buyer to engage in cost reduction even after the contract is signed.	The supplier receives savings when costs are successfully reduced.	The buyer receives savings when costs are successfully reduced.
Fixed Price Level of Effort	Used when neither the work nor the results can be specifically defined before performance. Both parties agree on a specific level of effort after which they will assess the results and decide if additional work is required.	The supplier is guaranteed to be paid for the work it conducts. However, if the work conducted falls outside of the agreed-on terms, payment may be disputed.	The buyer only pays for the work conducted. This type of contract is most appropriate for research and development and laboratory work.
Fixed Price With Downward Price Protection	Similar to the fixed price with escalation, except that the price may be adjusted downward because of changes in costs.	If the price of raw materials and parts or services moves upward, the supplier assumes the loss.	The buyer is protected from losses when the price moves down.
Fixed Price With Remedies	Allows for adjusting the price when damages occur during the life of the contract.	The supplier is covered against potential damages.	The buyer is covered against potential damages.

Source: M. Leenders, H. Fearon, A. Flynn and P.F. Johnson, *Purchasing and Supply Management* (Burr Ridge, IL: McGraw Hill/ Irwin, 2002); R.M. Monczka, R.J. Trent and R.B. Handfield, *Purchasing and Supply Chain Management* (Mason, OH: South Western College Publishers, 2005).

Firm Fixed-Price Contracts. In *firm fixed-price contracts,* the price, once the contract is agreed on and signed, is not subject to change, regardless of what happens to economic conditions, industry competition and supply market. The agreed-on price is reached through price quotation, the bidding process or negotiation. Because the supplier may incur higher costs than what was used to fulfill the contract (due to increasing market prices for procured raw materials and parts), the supplier may try to work in a reasonable profit margin to account for any potential increases. At the same time, the opposite may be true. Therefore, the buyer needs to understand the supply market conditions that the supplier faces before agreeing to a firm fixed-price contract.

The actual cost of the raw materials, parts or services can be highly uncertain, and depending on how the prices of raw materials and parts behave in the market, there will always be a "winner" and "loser" under the basic firm fixed-price contract. In the case of the *fixed price with escalation contract* or the *fixed price with downward price protection,* the escalation clause allows the contracted price to go either up or down depending on the circumstances. Both parties should agree on how changes in cost are determined; for instance, in the United States, the Producer Price Index (PPI) for specific materials could be used for this purpose.

Many unknown factors can exist at the time of contracting, beyond just the raw materials cost or service process issues as in the case of the fixed price with escalation contract. Proposed technology may not be proved, labor cost might change significantly or the amount of raw materials and parts to be used could not be determined with confidence. Therefore, at the time of contracting, both the supplier and the supply management professional would agree on a fixed price based on their best cost estimates. In the *fixed price with redetermination* contract, the buyer and supplier would redetermine the cost and arrive at a more informed price, typically when the product or service volume has reached the agreed-on level. Both parties need to discuss and agree on whether the redetermined price would apply only for work still to be performed or would apply for all or a portion of the work performed prior to the redetermination.

In the case of redetermination of a contract, the buyer and the supplier agree on the target price based on their best estimates; however, in the case of an *incentives contract,* the contract includes a stipulation for potential cost reduction performed by the supplier. When the cost reduction is achieved by the supplier over time, the savings are shared by both the buyer and supplier. The percentage for sharing is typically 50/50 but can be negotiated. The *fixed price with incentives contract* occurs most frequently when the unit or service cost is high at the time of contracting and the contract spreads over a long period of time. This type of contract is also more common for projects based on work such as construction or for custom-made equipment. The fixed price with incentives contract also is known as the fixed price per unit level of effort. The level of effort can be measured by the number of clients the salesperson visits or the number of hours of testing at a fixed rate per hour.

As is evident from the description, the *fixed price with downward price protection* offers maximum protection for the buyer. If the price moves up, the contract is not negotiated and the buyer receives the gain. However, if the price moves down, the buyer renegotiates the price.

During the life of a contract, damages can occur so both parties may choose to include clauses for such potential damages by establishing a *fixed price with remedies* contract. Some examples of damages include general, special, incidental and consequential damages. A fixed price with remedies contract may make the remedies against these damages explicit or may include any other potential damages beyond what the law typically may allow. General damages are those that "can readily be proven to have occurred" from an identifiable breach.[14] General damages are contrasted with special damages. Special damages are those that are unique to a given situation. While the ability to foresee special damages must be proven before they can be recovered, no such proof is required for general damages. Incidental damages, a subcategory of general damages, are expenses reasonably incurred in the inspection, receipt, transportation and care of goods rightfully rejected. Consequential damages are a subcategory of special damages. Consequential damages are a result of damage, loss or injury that arises not directly from a party's act (such as breach of contract) but from some consequence or result of that act; e.g., lost profit, lost revenue, personal injury or property damage. (*ISM Glossary,* 2006) These normally include lost profits and other damages resulting as a consequence of a supplier's inability to perform.

Cost-Based Contracts

These contracts guarantee the supplier a price sufficient to cover allowable costs plus whatever additional amount is negotiated. Suppliers are allowed to incur reimbursable costs up to a predetermined level. See Figure 5-6 for an overview of these types of contracts.

In the case of the *cost plus fixed fee* contract, the supplier is paid for the cost expended or the ceiling, whichever is lower, plus a fixed fee that is agreed on at the time of contracting. The *cost plus percentage* form of contract gives little to no incentive to the supplier to be judicious about controlling costs. This contract offers the supplier the cost incurred as well as a percentage of that cost. Most public sector organizations do not permit this form of contract. It is commonly used by distributors of spares, operating supplies and similar items. The problem is that it provides little incentive for the distributor to try to control prices from its suppliers.

The *cost plus incentive fee* form of contract is similar to the fixed price with incentives contract in that both sides agree on a target. However, the base price depends on the cost incurred during the course of work and not on a fixed price agreed on at the time of contracting. The *cost without fee* contract often occurs between a funding agency and nonprofit organizations such as research groups or universities. It allows

Figure 5-6   Overview of Cost-Based Contracts

TYPE	DESCRIPTION/ APPLICATION	IMPLICATIONS FOR SUPPLIER	IMPLICATIONS FOR BUYER
Cost Plus Fixed Fee	This contract puts a ceiling on how much the supplier can spend; otherwise, the supplier bears the risk of having to pay for the cost incurred beyond that level.	The supplier is ensured of covering its costs plus a fee as long as it stays within the predetermined ceiling amount.	The buyer is protected from the potential risk of the supplier incurring too much cost.
Cost Plus Percentage of Cost	The buyer agrees to reimburse the supplier for the cost incurred plus a percentage markup for that cost.	In essence, the supplier is rewarded for spending money.	The buyer is liable for the cost incurred by the supplier.
Cost Plus Incentive Fee	The buyer agrees to pay the supplier for the target cost plus an additional fee as an incentive.	If the cost comes out above the target cost, the supplier loses that amount from the incentive fee.	If the cost comes out below the target cost, the buyer and supplier share the savings at the agreed-on proportions (generally, 50/50).
Cost Without Fee	Supplier receives payment for the costs it incurs but nothing else.	Supplier is allowed to cover the cost.	The buyer receives services from the supplier without paying a profit margin.
Cost-Sharing	Both the buyer and supplier agree to share costs.	The supplier shares the costs and benefits of work being conducted.	The buyer shares the costs and benefits of work being conducted.

the nonprofit organization to cover its costs such as overhead, labor and expenses incurred but it allows no profit. With the *cost-sharing* contract, both the supplier and buyer are responsible for what happens during the life of the contract. For this form of contract to work, it is imperative that both parties agree on a clearly understood set of operating guidelines, how the costs are going to be shared and in what proportion.

Indefinite Delivery Contracts

This form of contract is used when the exact times and quantities of future deliveries are not known at the time of contracting. (*ISM Glossary*, 2006) It is used to cope with uncertainties involved in the production schedule, timing of a service activity, quantity of materials or the frequency of the service required. Figure 5-7 offers a list of major types of indefinite delivery contracts and a brief description of each.

Figure 5-7   Overview of Indefinite Delivery Contracts

TYPE	DESCRIPTION
Indefinite Delivery/ Indefinite Quantity	Specifies minimum and maximum quantities, but not specific quantities and delivery dates. The buyer is obligated to place requirements with a specific supplier during a given period of time.
Delivery Order and Task Order	Provides a method of initiating a specific delivery order, either written or oral. The written order keeps the same format as the regular purchase order, except it does not have to contain all the terms and conditions for it is written against an existing contract; it just needs to reference the indefinite delivery contract. To initiate a delivery of service, a task order rather than delivery order is required.
Time and Material	Provides fixed hourly rates that include: (1) wages, overhead, general and administrative expenses and profit; and (2) materials, generally at cost, including, if appropriate, material handling costs. (*ISM Glossary*, 2006) Most automobile repairs, for example, are conducted under time and material contracts.
Blanket Agreement	Entails a term commitment (usually one year or more) to a supplier for certain goods or services over a predetermined period of time at predetermined prices, or at prices to be determined based on market or other conditions. This practice is aimed at reducing the number of small orders, using short-term releases to satisfy demand requirements.
Reimbursements	Represents a contract under which the buyer agrees to purchase 100 percent of its need for a particular product or service during a given period from a single supplier. No specific quantity is specified, although estimates based on past use may be provided to the supplier.

Letter Contracts

This is a preliminary written contractual instrument that authorizes the contractor to begin immediately performing the manufacturing or service requested. The letter contract typically is followed by a definitive contract. (*ISM Glossary,* 2006)

Dealer's Agreement

This can be an agreement or a contract, expressed or implied, and occurs between a supplier and a dealer or is issued by a supplier. With this agreement, the dealer is granted the right to purchase, sell or distribute or service the supplier's merchandise.

Service-Level Agreements

Supply management increasingly finds itself acquiring a broader range of services. Contrasted with materials, contracting services requires more diligent, day-to-day effort in developing specifications and in monitoring performance. To expedite services contracting, the supply management professional should establish a *master services agreement (MSA)* or a *professional services agreement (PSA)* with key service suppliers.[15] These agreements typically contain all contracting terms and conditions, the metrics and means of measurement, the consequences in the event of failure to perform and any longer-term aspects of the agreement so they do not have to be renegotiated each time a new contract is established with a particular supplier. A *statement of work (SOW)* can simply be attached to the master agreement for the particular portion of the service work the supplier is contracted to perform. More discussion on SOW appears in the appendix, "Key Considerations in Preparing Contracts," at the end of this chapter.

One type of service work that occurs for all organizations on an ongoing basis is maintenance work. For such work, performance expectations must be stated clearly and measurable specifications must be set up and communicated to the supplier. In particular, when monitoring during the process of service delivery becomes difficult, a performance-based agreement needs to be established with the supplier, so the buyer can assess the quality of the rendered services after they have been rendered. These issues typically are addressed in the SOW.

Licensing Agreements

A license issued by the owner of intellectual property grants the licensee the right to use the protected property, often in exchange for payment of a one-time fee or an ongoing royalty, usually a percentage of sales or a fixed amount per unit produced. Supply management professionals often have the responsibility of negotiating and administering license agreements with suppliers. Examples of licenses include software, patents, technology and copyrights. More on licensing and intellectual property appears in the appendix, "Key Considerations in Preparing Contracts," at the end of this chapter.

Master Purchase Agreements

Master purchase agreements refer to contractual arrangements with a supplier that define price and terms of business but do not contain specifics of release or delivery. Separate purchase orders are released later as goods or services (e.g., IT hardware, desktop, supplies and materials) are needed and reference the master purchase agreement, whose price and terms are incorporated by reference. (*ISM Glossary,* 2006)

Construction Contract

Construction contracting is different from purchasing for a manufacturing or service organization, because construction procurement involves both manufactured goods and services. It also exists in a project environment. Construction purchasing can be characterized as occurring infrequently but entails usually definable and precisely describable goods and services.[16] Supply management professionals should use contract documents that are based on industry standards; these can be obtained from the American Institute of Architects.[17]

Summary

Contracting is an integral part of the supply management responsibilities and process. The process of procurement offers supply management professionals necessary information to arrive at a contract — from understanding needs to translating those needs to a solicitation, and ultimately building and awarding a contract. Once the contract is established, supply management professionals are responsible for following through with the order and ultimately making sure that the user's needs are fulfilled while maintaining pertinent information for future purposes. Supply management professionals need to communicate with internal users and then communicate with the external suppliers through the solicitation process.

This chapter offers an overview of various types of communication methods and solicitations/bids. It covers solicitation procedures and terms and conditions of those solicitations. The essentials of contracts are covered, from understanding the basic elements of a contract to considering the different types of documents that bind buyers and suppliers into obligatory relationships. Two major types of contracts are introduced: fixed-price and cost-based. Fixed-price contracts begin with an agreed-on price estimated before the work is conducted, while cost-based contracts are developed based on the actual cost of the work performed. Some of the key considerations

in preparing contracts are covered in the appendix to this chapter, "Key Considerations in Preparing Contracts."

Key Points

1. Supply management professionals oversee everything from the process of product
   or service development, receiving proposals and quotations to the signing of a
   contract. Their knowledge of suppliers and the associated supply market plays an
   integral role in this process.

2. Supply management issues either performance specifications or design specifications. Performance specifications define the characteristics of the acceptable
   product or service, and the supplier engages in the design of the product or service
   to meet the specifications. Design specifications, in contrast, provide the details of
   how the product needs to be made or how the service needs to be carried out.

3. A contract at its core must have an offer and an acceptance. If the purchasing
   organization issues an offer to buy, the supplier must respond and agree to sell. If
   the supplier issues an offer to sell, the buyer must respond and agree to buy.

4. When all specifications are known in terms of the detailed descriptions of the
   product or service, competitive bidding is appropriate. However, when there are
   uncertainties about the specifications, proposals are typically sought from the
   suppliers.

5. When the content of a bid is complex and new to suppliers, a prebid or preproposal conference may be used. All potential suppliers must be invited to the
   conference.

6. All suppliers must receive the same quotation package and must be given an equal
   opportunity to bid by having access to comparable information and the subsequent evaluation process. All steps need to be transparent and fair.

7. A bond ensures fulfillment of the principal's obligation to the third party. However, bonds generally increase the cost of bidding and their use tends to reduce
   competition.

8. When procuring services, a statement of work (SOW) is used to define the exact
   contents of the service requested.

9. Intellectual property rights cover such issues as patents, copyrights and trademarks.
   With suppliers taking up more new product and service development and as more

new product and service ideas become embedded into another product or service, these issues become more salient when procuring goods and services from external suppliers (see the appendix, "Key Considerations in Preparing Contracts," at the end of this chapter).

Appendix: *Key Considerations in Preparing Contracts*

Given the various types of legally biding contracts, considerations now are given to the potential issues that may arise when preparing them. The most commonly addressed issues are statements of work, intellectual property rights and international laws governing sales transactions.

Statements of Work

The procurement of services requires a statement of work (SOW) to define exactly what work is being contracted.[18] All purchases of service work, no matter how simple, must have a clear definition stating what work is to be done, the boundaries of that work including the timeline, the expected end result and the criteria for evaluating performance and quality. As the service purchased gets more complex, the SOW also gets more complex. A well-conceived SOW provides the means to manage the service work throughout its duration.

WORK BREAKDOWN STRUCTURE.

For lengthy and complex services, the SOW may be broken into smaller segments with a detailed description of each segment. Each segment then is managed as a separate subproject, with the overall project broken down using a project management chart to sequence the activities.

HOLD POINTS/MILESTONES.

When a large service contract is broken down into smaller segments, the continuation of the overall contract may be contingent on the successful completions of each segment. At the completion of a segment, a quality assessment may take place to explicitly acknowledge that the SOW has been met to that point. When several dependent segments merge to one point in the progression of a service project, it is called a *hold point* or a *milestone*. Approval must be granted before the work proceeds. The hold points or milestones are put in place to control deviations that occur during the project.

PERFORMANCE EVALUATION FACTORS.

All SOWs should clearly explicate all performance and quality criteria and how they will be measured. Communication needs to take place on an ongoing basis.

When the supplier's performance is evaluated, the results should not be a surprise to either party.

Intellectual Property Rights

Intellectual property (IP) refers to various types of intangible personal property that have an inherent commercial value and are legally protected in different ways. They include copyrights, patents and trademarks or servicemarks. (*ISM Glossary,* 2006) When preparing contracts, supply management professionals must be aware of the IP rights that might potentially be involved in the transaction.

With the advent of technological advancement and increased outsourcing, the issue of IP rights has come to the forefront of supply management. For instance, when IP is involved, the typical buyer–supplier relationship takes on a new meaning where the knowledge itself becomes the element of transaction. Here, the buyer becomes the licensee and the supplier becomes the licensor. The compensation issues are discussed with the direct involvement of lawyers and engineers and generally have a long-term implication. Figure 5-8 frames the buyer–supplier relationship in a licensee–licensor context.

PATENTS.

A patent in essence signifies the right to exclude others. Sanctioned by a government, it creates a monopoly and gives the patent holder the sole right to make,

Figure 5-8   Buyer-Supplier Relationship Versus Licensee-Licensor Relationship

MANAGERIAL ISSUES	BUYER-SUPPLIER	LICENSEE-LICENSOR
Item Purchased	Materials and services	Knowledge
Sender of Item	Supplying organization	Licensing organization
Terms of Payment	Per delivery or PO	Per agreement
Major Players	Buyers and engineers	Lawyers and business managers
Length of Relationship	Short- and long-term	Generally long term

Source: T.Y. Choi, J. Budny and N. Wank, "Intellectual Property Management: A Knowledge Supply Chain Perspective," *Business Horizons* 47(1) (January 2004): 37–44.

use and/or sell the patented articles and to prevent others from doing so without the holder's permission (license). (*ISM Glossary,* 2006)

When technologies come together to create a cumulative system of technologies, the effort to exclude others from using IP can be difficult. In fact, it can cause a deadlock: When radio technology first emerged in the United States, many inventors that held IP in this area were reluctant to engage each other in a cross-licensing arrangement.[19] In the end, it took an act of the U.S. Navy to overcome this deadlock. The Navy brought together various U.S. organizations that owned complementary patents. Finally, in 1919, under pressure from the Navy, the Radio Corporation of America (RCA) was created and eventually succeeded in commercializing radio technology.

COPYRIGHTS.

A copyright represents protection by U.S. law, which grants the authors and creators of original literary, dramatic, musical, artistic and other intellectual property, published or unpublished, the exclusive right to publish, reproduce, display, sell, perform, transmit or prepare derivative works from the original work. *(ISM Glossary,* 2006) As with any IP procurement, the licensee must try to obtain rights to the work produced for its organization that are as broad as possible and include indemnification provisions to protect the organization in the event the material being acquired infringes on some other party's copyright.

To this end, it is critical for a supply management professional to understand the embedded nature of IP. In other words, one organization's IP might become embedded in another organization's IP; when this happens, the supply management professional does not want to be surprised by this occurrence. High-tech organizations work hard to get their IPs embedded in other technologies so they can collect licensing fees. A UK-based joint venture organization, called ARM, illustrates this. ARM's market base was very limited at first, but then it developed Reduced Instruction Set Computer (RISC) technology used in microprocessors. ARM began to license out this IP to various other organizations, including Texas Instruments Inc. and Intel Corp. Because this microprocessor technology is now used ubiquitously, ARM has presence in many different, multiple industries from automobiles to consumer entertainment.[20]

TRADEMARK OR SERVICEMARK.

A trademark is an identifying label, symbol or word(s) for exclusive use with a particular product (trademark) or service (servicemark). The licensee can obtain the rights to use the licensor's trademark in the promotion of the licensee's own organization. One key difference between trademarks and other IPs such as patents and copyrights is that trademark rights can last indefinitely as long as the holder of this IP continues to use it to identify its goods or services and renews its application periodically. For instance, IBM may license out its trademark. One often discovers IBM's trademark on a ream of white copy paper. In this case, the copy paper manufacturer licensed IBM's trademark from IBM because it most likely felt that the IBM trademark would associate its product with IBM and its quality reputation. Organizations often are willing to license trademarks from a successful organization, even if it's to a different industry, to elevate the perception of its own products.

Laws on International Transactions

The United Nations Convention on Contracts for the International Sale of Goods (CISG) is a treaty that governs international sales transactions.[21] This treaty was first signed in Vienna in 1980; thus, it often is referred to as the Vienna Convention. It came into force in 1988 when it was ratified by 10 countries — the U.S. Senate ratified it in 1986. It is designed to create consistency in rules that govern international sales transactions and now has been accepted by countries that account for two-thirds of the world trade.

Ultimately, the CISG affects all organizations from countries that have ratified it and included it in their own legislation (e.g., Mexico, Canada, European Union). However, the parties make an explicit agreement regarding the CISG and can opt out of the law's coverage.

CISG is not intended to cover the sale of services. It is possible that some contracts could encompass both goods and services. If so, the law does not apply to contracts in which the provision of labor or other services outweighs the supply of manufactured goods.

Further Considerations

Many other considerations must be addressed when preparing contracts, ranging from consenting to subcontracts to warranty issues.

RIGHT TO SUBCONTRACT.

Unless explicitly addressed, contracts permit the prime contractor to subcontract to meet requirements. Supply management professionals typically reserve the right to evaluate subcontractors retained by the prime contractor. Typically, the contractor's right to subcontract is enforced in all cost-plus contracts and also in fixed price with incentives contracts.

NOTICE OF AWARDS.

The supply management organization's policy determines whether to send the notice of award to all bidders. Sending the notice to all bidders is common practice for large dollar value contracts such as construction contracts but not for smaller, more routine types of contracts. The key for the supply management organization is to be consistent in its practice and to demonstrate good supply management practices.

PAYMENT TERMS.

Payment terms involve a trade-off between the time the buyer organization keeps the money before paying and the discount the supplier offers as an incentive for early payment. For instance, *net 30 days* means payment of the entire invoiced amount to be made within 30 days of the invoice date. The term *2 percent 10/net 30* generally means payments received within 10 days from the date of the invoice receive a two percent discount; otherwise, the full amount is due in 30 days (these terms are discussed in Chapter 4, "The Sourcing Decision").

ROYALTIES.

A royalty is a payment made in return for some privilege or right, often associated with intellectual property such as patented or copyrighted materials. The payment is made by agreement with the property owner. For example, a supply management organization may make payments to an author for publishing and selling his or her works, or to the holder of a patent for the privilege of using it.

CONSIDERATION OF DOMESTIC AND INTERNATIONAL LAWS.

In international sourcing and purchasing, the governments of both the buyer's and supplier's countries have laws that will affect the transactions and can complicate the flow of goods across borders. If a mine in Australia supplies iron ore to a steel organization in Japan or Korea, both organizations need to be aware of each other's laws. For example, governments place various types of restrictions on imports, including import licenses, customs duties and quotas. Governments also typically require complex sets of documents, including export licenses, import declarations, certificates of origin, commercial invoices, insurance policies and bills of lading. In addition, the CISG, which was discussed previously, brings uniformity to rules governing international sales.

INSURANCE AND INDEMNIFICATION.

In some situations, the supplier should carry a certain amount of insurance and indemnify the buying organization against injuries. Most supply management organizations specify in the contract the type and amount of insurance required. The clause might include statements about property damage, public liability, builder's risk, errors and omissions, workers' compensation, etc.

TERMINATION OF CONTRACT.

Termination means the action of one party pursuant to specific contract language to end a contract for some reason other than breach by the other party. Upon termination, all obligations are discharged, except breach of rights and obligations based on prior performance. Cancellation differs from termination in that it implies cause and does not excuse the causing party from damages resulting from its failure to perform.

CONFIDENTIALITY POLICIES.

Most of the information that surfaces during a purchasing transaction about suppliers and competitors is confidential. Also confidential are such information sources as bids, supplier proposals, pricing, drawings, designs, strategies, wage and salary information, software programs or scientific formulas.

FORCE MAJEURE.

This term translates as "a superior or irresistible force" and refers to a contract provision under which major and usually uncontrollable events (e.g., severe weather, fire, or war) may excuse a party, in whole or in part, from the performance of its contractual obligations. This provision is commonly referred to as an "act of God" and normally is included in standard purchase order forms to protect both the buyer and the supplier.

RESTRAINT OF TRADE.

Restraint of trade is defined as the effect of an act, contract, combination or conspiracy that eliminates or stifles competition, effects a monopoly, artificially maintains prices or otherwise hampers or obstructs the course of business as it would be carried out if left to the flow of natural and economic forces. (*ISM Glossary,* 2006) Supply management professionals need to keep in mind that the purpose behind all antitrust legislation is to protect the free enterprise system. The four primary laws regarding the restraint of trade in the United States are the Sherman Antitrust Act, Clayton Act, Federal Trade Commission Act and Robinson-Patman Act.

HOMELAND SECURITY.

Following the September 11, 2001, attacks on the United States, the issue of homeland security has become a salient point that affects all commerce in and out of the United States.[22] According to the National Strategy for Homeland Security, homeland security is officially defined as "a concerted national effort to prevent terrorist attacks within the United States, reduce America's vulnerability to terrorism, and minimize the damage and recover from attacks that do occur."[23] Many other countries, such as Canada and the United Kingdom, have responded and passed legislation that addresses the same issue.

SOURCE CODE ESCROW ACCOUNTS.

When acquiring software or the rights to use software, an escrow account might become necessary. An independent third party as an escrow agent physically stores the source code and has title to it. The escrow agent also has authority to release it under specified conditions. This arrangement can facilitate the continued use of software in the event the supplier goes out of business, runs into financial difficulties or discontinues support of the product.

PROTESTS.

Suppliers may protest if they believe they have been unfairly treated. In the private sector, the process is usually informal and involves a discussion between the supplier and buyer (and possibly other managers involved). The intent of the discussion is to explore the reasons for the supplier's protest. The process of resolution may escalate from an informal protest to a formal protest calling for an appeal process, mediation or arbitration per contract clause, or even litigation. However, a typical protest in a private organization usually is resolved through discussion and negotiation. In the public sector, the process can be more formal and may involve an administrative hearing board that listens to the supplier's complaint and decides if an appropriate remedy is required.

CLAIMS.

A *claim* refers to the right asserted by a plaintiff to payment or for an equitable remedy, such as the specific performance of a contract. (*ISM Glossary,* 2006) A claim is the opposite of a *defense,* which is a response offered by a defendant in opposition to claims made by the claimant as a reason why that claimant should not prevail.

LIMITATION OF LIABILITY.

Suppliers in general attempt to include contract language that will limit their liability for damages and loss due to warranty claims or other breaches of contract. Such statements will restrict the supply management organization's ability to recover the damages in a lawsuit. One of the most common limitations addresses the warranty claims that the supplier be permitted to repair or replace defective goods. In this case, the supply management organization is not permitted to cancel the contract and seek damages for loss.

WAIVER OF CONSEQUENTIAL DAMAGES.

To promote goodwill and to limit the potential escalation of damage disputes, contracting parties from both sides may agree to a waiver of consequential damages. Consequential damages refer to damage, loss or injury that arises not directly from a party's act (e.g., breach of contract) but from some consequence or result of that act (e.g., lost profit, lost revenue, personal inquiry or property damage).

COLLUSIVE OFFERS.

Collusion is a secret agreement to operate in a fraudulent or deceitful manner. In collusive offers, suppliers act together to "fix" their bids in a collectively advantageous manner and thus eliminate genuine competition in bidding. Federal antitrust laws are designed to prevent such collusive offers on the part of suppliers. Supply management professionals should seek the advice of counsel in cases where collusion is suspected.

SUSPENSION OF CONTRACT.

The supply management organization may suspend activities on a contract. When this occurs, the supplier must be given reasonable written notice and will need to be compensated on suspension based on the percentage of contract completion until the effective date of the suspension less any previous payments. If the suspension lasts for an extended period of time (e.g., more than 30 days), the supplier may be entitled to additional compensation for costs incurred because of the suspension.

RESERVATION OF RIGHTS.

The supply management professional when developing a contract should reserve all rights to contract performance in accordance with the stated terms and conditions. A "modifications" clause prohibits suppliers from making any changes in the contract without the consent of the buying organization. A "waiver" clause may be used to protect the purchasing organization against possible loss of contractual rights in the event the organization inadvertently fails to enforce certain rights.

ESTOPPEL.

Estoppel is a legal principle that prevents a person from asserting a position that is inconsistent with his or her prior conduct if injustice would thus result to a person who has changed position in justifiable reliance on that conduct. (*ISM Glossary,* 2006) One example of this principle might occur in agency law when a purported agent is actually an impostor. For example, a person walks into a retail store and pretends to be a sales clerk. A customer, assuming the person is a clerk, deals with the imposter and makes a purchase based on the person's representations. If the store manager has seen the unknown person pretending to be a clerk and did nothing to stop him or her, the store would be bound by the impostor's representations because the customer has relied on those representations and changed his or her position by making a purchase.

SOCIAL RESPONSIBILITY ISSUES.

Whether the purchasing organization is private or public, all organizations are part of a larger society and as a result have inalienable responsibilities to help maintain and improve the conditions of the society in which it belongs. Social responsibility is covered in greater detail in Chapter 9.

STATE OF DOMAIN/JURISDICTION.

In the United States, state of domain or jurisdiction refers to the state that has the legal authority to hear and render a decision in a particular situation. It is important to identify which court has jurisdiction before filing a lawsuit. Most contracts specify the state that has jurisdiction (generally, the state in which the contact issuer is based). Many international contracts will state which country has legal authority.

LIQUIDATED DAMAGES.

In an attempt to avoid the problems of calculating and proving damages in a lawsuit, contracting parties often will state a predetermined amount of damages, known as liquidated damages, in their agreement. Because punitive damages are not allowed in contract law cases, it is important to ensure that the liquidated damages amount is reasonable in light of the actual damages suffered.

WARRANTIES.

A warranty is a legally enforceable promise or representation as to quality or performance of goods or services made by the supplier. (*ISM Glossary,* 2006) It is a promise made by the supplier that is legally enforceable, as long as it is included in the contract. Under the law, a purchasing organization is free to bargain for broad, strong warranties or to accept a supplier's total and complete disclaimer of warranties.

REMEDIES.

Remedies relieve or correct a legal wrong. In contract terms, available remedies are money damages or an order of the court for specific performance. (*ISM Glossary,* 2006) In legal terms, *cure* refers to making the situation right and could include restoring everything back to its original state or fulfilling the contract as originally agreed. *Cover* is a remedy available to a buyer in the event of a breach of contract by the supplier. After displaying due diligence, the buyer is entitled to obtain goods in the open market and recover damages from the supplier.

6

Negotiating

Negotiations take place in all aspects of our lives. We negotiate with our spouse about when we are going to eat dinner, and we negotiate with our children about how late they are allowed to stay out. We negotiate with our coworkers about the role we play in a project, and we negotiate with our supervisor about resources. Diplomats negotiate with their counterparts about foreign policies, and organizations negotiate about contract terms.

For the purposes of supply management, negotiation is defined as an exploratory and communication process (identifying interests, walkaway alternatives and options), internally and externally, to reach a mutually satisfactory agreement. In supply management, negotiation often involves a buyer and a supplier, and each has his or her viewpoints, interests and objectives regarding all phases of a procurement transaction — including price, service, specifications, technical and quality requirements and payment terms. (*ISM Glossary,* 2006)

In particular, negotiation is an integral part of the contracting process as discussed in Chapter 5, "Contracting." Depending on the type of solicitation method used and the level of importance of the goods or services being procured, negotiation objectives and strategies from the supply management organization's perspective will vary.

Figure 6-1 provides the logical flow of negotiation, around which the rest of this chapter is organized. The process begins with negotiation objectives. Data is gathered and analyzed, alternate scenarios are discussed and the information gathered as a result is organized. Planning allows the negotiator to identify what the other party's negotiation position should be and to anticipate what the other party is likely to do. Preparatory activities allow a negotiator to realistically respond to the other party's proposals and to ascertain if the agreement negotiated is reasonable. Being a great orator or eloquent presenter is of little help when the planning and preparation is weak. In the end, the data provide strength to a negotiator's position. This chapter continues with a

Figure 6-1   Overview of Negotiation Process

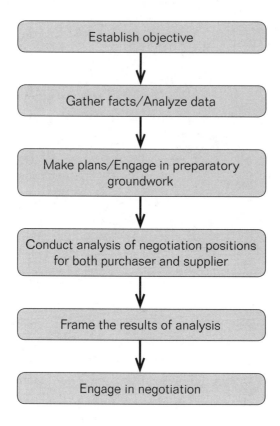

discussion of how to conduct analysis and ascertain specific target numbers and how to frame the results of analyses for negotiation. The chapter closes with a discussion of the issues involved when conducting an actual negotiation.

CHAPTER OBJECTIVES

• Discuss the underlying meaning and dynamics of fact-based negotiation.

• Appreciate the key managerial areas for setting negotiation objectives and collecting various information ranging from supply market data to cultural information.

• Consider how to engage in preparatory groundwork before the negotiation, covering such issues as site selection to planning strategies and tactics.

• Explicate the importance of gauging negotiation positions for both sides — suppliers and buyers.

• Understand how information and knowledge replaces uncertainty involved in negotiation.

• Focus on key decision points in negotiation and the ways with which to frame information to aid in making sound decisions.

• Consider the underlying issues and the process of actually conducting a negotiation.

Establishing Negotiation Objectives

Negotiation objectives vary from one setting to next; some of the most common ones will be introduced in this section. Objectives should be set with a long-term perspective. Short-term gains might jeopardize the supply management organization's long-term reputation or the fundamental relationship with a supplier. Short-term gains may be important, but ones that might cause potentially longer-term, negative effects should be avoided.

Fair and Reasonable Price

Cost control is a major consideration for all supply management professionals and generally ranks high on the list of criteria in a negotiating plan. The supply management professional, however, should not lose sight of other critical issues such as good quality, on-time delivery and stability of supply or the stable provision of a critical service. A negotiator should be careful not to drive the price so low that the supplier might lose money. The supplier should be able to meet its costs and be comfortable with the outcome. The supply management professional may have the upper hand in the negotiation at this point in time, but conditions can change, putting the supply management professional at a disadvantage.

Both Nokia and one of its major competitors were sourcing a critical part from a Japanese supplier. Nokia had a good reputation as a fair customer with this supplier, while the other competitor did not. When the part this supplier was supplying became a limited commodity, the supplier ended up shipping everything to Nokia and nothing to the other organization. The other organization, a well-known cell phone manufacturer, never recovered. Thus, it is best to seek a price that is fair and reasonable to all parties and treat each other with respect.

Timely Performance

The negotiated agreement should cover shipment of the specified product according to the production plan or delivery of the service according to the statement of work (SOW). The supplier should be advised that it will be measured against other suppliers and that a tracking system will be in place. The intent is to motivate the supplier to perform well. The supplier should be informed that late shipments and poor performance of services will not be tolerated because they can potentially cause expensive downtime and other problems. Early shipments and poor timing of services are equally undesirable. They may result in unnecessary inventory-carrying costs or, in the case of services, disruption of operations. Ideally, a just in time approach, with good quality products and services arriving just as they are needed, is the goal.

Meeting the Minimum Essential Needs of the Organization

Ultimately, the objective of a negotiation is to meet the needs of the supply management professional's organization with respect to purchased products and services. If an organization has a shortage of necessary commodities, components or services, the supply management professional's job is to secure an adequate supply from an acceptable supplier. In this case, the supply management professional is not negotiating from a position of strength. The only hope is that the volume of the order is attractive for a long-term commitment, and that the buying organization is viewed as a valued customer. The supply management professional then can assure the supplier that if the needed product or service is delivered, the supply management organization will continue to do business with the supplier even in times when supply is plentiful.

Control Over Contract Performance

Performance issues always should come first and be clearly defined in the contract. In the planning period, the supply management professional should think through the potential scenarios and list any and all issues that could cause performance problems. The supply management professional also should review the steps that could be taken to resolve each issue before problems occur. Nonetheless, stipulations must be made and spelled out in detail regarding the potential supplier's inability to perform as agreed, cancellation clauses and associated costs. The responsibilities of all parties should be made clear.

Achieving a Mutually Beneficial Agreement

One important objective in a negotiation session is to strive toward a mutually beneficial agreement. An agreement that ends in an adversarial atmosphere should be avoided at all costs, especially with a key supplier. Even in a situation where an impasse is reached and no deal is made, both parties must understand that walking away is the mutually beneficial outcome given the circumstances — in this situation, both parties agree to no agreement. A mutually satisfactory agreement between the buyer and the supplier is the best outcome, where both parties are comfortable with each other and look forward to doing business in the future. If either party is haggled to a point of embarrassment, future negotiations will be approached with caution.

All parties must be able to operate profitably under the terms of the agreement. The supply management professional and the supplier should schedule regular, frequent communication to establish and maintain a positive relationship. Each party should strive to appreciate the other's perspective. Problem-solving should focus on mutual satisfaction, rather than on a win-lose outcome.

Gathering Facts and Collecting Information

The ancient Chinese strategist Sun Tzu taught his followers to know the enemy first and then oneself when facing battle.[1] The supply management professional must learn as many facts about the supplier and its market and financial conditions as possible prior to setting a negotiation strategy as well as conducting it.

Understanding Market Forces

To understand the risk associated with a supplier's potential contract, the supply management professional needs to collect information on the supplier and its market. Pertinent areas of information include the nature of competition in the supplier's market niche (e.g., number of competing suppliers, barriers to market entry) and the specific products or services being procured (e.g., availability and readiness of substitutable products or services).

Michael E. Porter has framed such market forces in his five forces model.[2] The five forces are: (1) power of suppliers, (2) power of buyers, (3) barriers to new entrants, (4) substitutes and (5) industry rivalry. The first four forces interact and converge on the last force, industry rivalry. They are shown in Figure 6-2, adapted from Dr. Porter's earlier works.

Power of suppliers is grounded in how well and how much a supplier can control the market it is in. For instance, when a supplier provides a product or service for which there are no substitutes and the supply management professional depends on this product or service, then the supplier has power. In such a situation, the supply management organization typically tries to position itself to become more important to the supplier through long-term contracts or interlocking relationships. One typical strategy is to consolidate purchases and offer the supplier a large contract predicated on a long-term relationship.

Power of purchasers comes primarily from the buyer's ability to control prices. Generally speaking, the buyer's power is enhanced when there is low demand and high supply. Also, when the product or service purchased is undifferentiated and

Figure 6-2   Porter's Five Forces

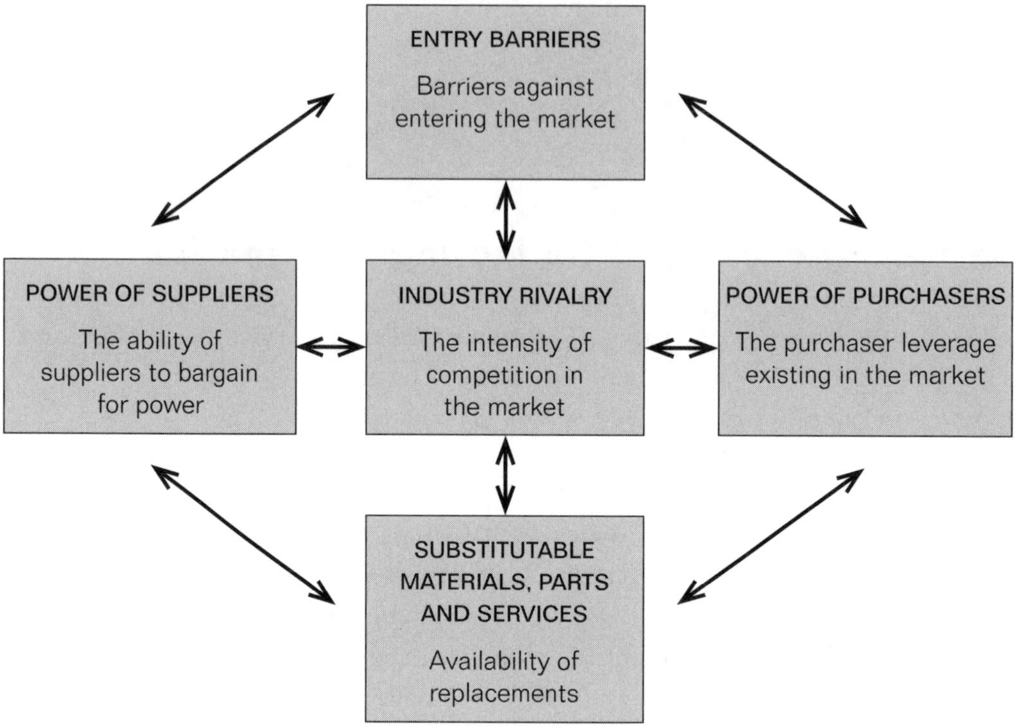

supplier switching costs are low, the buyer enjoys leverage over the supplier. In such a situation, the supply management professional would likely take an aggressive posture during a negotiation.

When the supplier's profit margin is high, the attractiveness of *market entry* by other organizations is high. At the same time, financial, technical and regulatory barriers may discourage market entry. For instance, a potential supplier might be discouraged from entering the market if the initial capital investment required is high. Entry would be made if the attractiveness overcomes the barriers. *Substitutes* also operate on two opposing forces. On the one hand, the existence of substitutable products or services offers leverage with suppliers. On the other hand, even with the availability of substitutes, the supply management professional may be discouraged from switching suppliers if the cost of doing so is too high.

Lastly, *industry rivalry* is affected by how the other four forces interact. In general, a high level of rivalry among suppliers is advantageous to the supply management organization. However, even in such a situation, if the volume of the contract is very low, the supplier may not be motivated to do business with the supply management professional. For instance, the passenger airline industry represents an extremely competitive service market with a high level of rivalry. The market is mature and saturated, and in general there is lack of differentiation among the service providers. Nonetheless, individual supply management organizations have virtually no power because the purchase is negligible from the supplier's perspective.

The supply management professional should be aware of all these forces and gather information on each prior to engaging in an actual negotiation with suppliers. Figure 6-3 summarizes the primary conditions that enhance each type of force.

Figure 6-3   Enhancing Conditions for Market Forces

MARKET FORCE	ENHANCING CONDITIONS
Power of Suppliers	There are only a few suppliers in the market. The supplier does not see the importance of selling to the industry the supply management professional belongs to. The supply management professional depends on the product or service the supplier provides. The supplier switching cost is too high. The supplier has the ability to undertake forward integration into the buyer's market.
Power of Purchasers	The supply management professional offers a large, consolidated purchase contract. The product or service the supply management professional purchases is undifferentiated and can be readily procured. The supplier switching cost is low. The supply management professional has the ability to produce in-house the product or service being purchased from the supplier. The material or parts being procured have little or no impact on the overall quality of the final product or service of the supply management professional's organization.

(continued)

Figure 6-3   continued

MARKET FORCE	ENHANCING CONDITIONS
Entry Barriers	Small numbers of organizations produce large amounts of goods or services.
	The market has highly segmented and differentiated products or services.
	Initial capital investment is very high.
	The government regulates entry.
	The market operates on a very small profit margin.
Substitutes	Long-term benefits are associated with the new, substitutable products or services.
	Switching to a substitute is low cost.
	The supply management professional has been looking for opportunities to find substitutes for strategic reasons.
Industry Rivalry	There are ample competitors.
	The industry is mature and its growth is slow.
	Little differentiation among products or services exists.
	Demand is high, but the entry barrier is low.
	There is a high cost associated with exiting.

Source: Adapted from Michael Porter, *Competitive Strategy: Creating and Sustaining Superior Performance* (New York: Free Press, 1998) and Michael Porter, "How Competitive Forces Shape Strategy," *Harvard Business Review* (March–April 1979).

Market Analysis

Porter's five forces model provides a framework for studying the market structure. The next task for the supply management professional is to analyze the market trends. The analysis now is much more specific in terms of looking at particular products or services. It becomes even more specific when breaking down the products or services into even smaller segments.

Factors Affecting Market Trends. A few key factors influence market trends. One is market fragmentation, which is closely related to the concept of industry rivalry in the five forces model. For instance, when Reynolds Metals Co. merged with

Alcoa Inc. in 2000, aluminum prices went up.[3] Such mergers by key players result in less market fragmentation. Conversely, when organizations spin off or break up, the opposite condition occurs — there is now higher fragmentation; for example, when Motorola Inc. broke up part of its semiconductor business and formed ON Semiconductor.[4] Large numbers of substitutable products can result in a more fragmented market, and a fragmented market means potentially more leverage for the buying organization. When the VCR and the DVD competed as substitutable products, a supply management professional at a large hotel chain gained additional leverage when negotiating with a VCR supplier.

Other factors must be considered, including market size and growth, technology trends, industry profitability and regulatory changes. A high-demand or expanding market would offer suppliers leverage. When a famous actor in Asia brandished a particular Samsung cell phone on a popular soap opera, the demand for that phone skyrocketed and it became difficult for cell phone retailers to carry that model. New technologies (e.g., the DVD) make old technologies (e.g., the VCR) obsolete. At least during the phase-over period of overlapping product life cycles, these products often compete as substitutable products. When an industry has a high level of profitability, the general trend is to move toward increasing competition. At the same time, suppliers in a highly profitable industry may be more willing to make price concessions. Last but not least, government regulations on safety and environmental issues can affect the market. For instance, even the federal government of the United States is keenly aware of how its policies may potentially affect the supply and distribution of energy to consumers. To protect its citizens, it has issued orders to study the impact of how the regulations affect the energy supply chain.[5]

Within the market trends, pricing tends to be of particular interest to supply management professionals. Pricing trends typically pertain to specific commodities or products within a given market. Pricing information is critical for it helps set the reference point during the negotiation. It also helps in keeping up an ongoing supplier relationship through supplier development or target pricing practices. Much of this pricing information is captured in price indexes.

Price Indexes. A price index is basically a ratio expressing the relationship between the price of a commodity at a given point in time to its price during a specified base period. This information can be used to chart changes in price levels. (*ISM Glossary,* 2006) Private organizations offer this information or a supply management organization can develop its own special indexes for specific purposes. During a negotiation, price indexes provided by the government carry weight because they come from an objective third party. The two most common price indexes in the United States provided by the government are the Producer Price Index (PPI) and the Consumer Price Index (CPI).[6] The PPI is a measurement tool compiled by the U.S. Bureau of Labor Statistics (BLS) reflecting the average change in prices charged by producers during a given time period compared to those charged in a base year. The PPI measures inflation at earlier stages of the production and marketing process than does the CPI. (*ISM Glossary,* 2006) The PPI covers about 3,000 or so commodities, including electronics, plastics, metals and hardware. By analyzing the pricing trends over a period of time, a supply management professional can compare what is shown by the PPI to the price being charged by the supplier. The CPI also is compiled by the BLS. The CPI is a monthly measure of changes in the prices of goods and services consumed by urban families and individuals. The relative importance given to individual items in the index's basket is based on periodic surveys of consumer expenditures. The CPI is computed for the nation as a whole, for each of 17 large metropolitan areas, for individual items and for commodity and service groupings. (*ISM Glossary,* 2006)

As mentioned earlier, it is possible for an organization to create its own index, for an index is really nothing more than an indicator of pricing that reflects factual information. Essentially, two components are required — a baseline measure (e.g., Nasdaq 100) and a measure of the item of interest (e.g., Qualcomm CDMA chip). The comparison of these two measures may provide a supplier price index for one particular item. This index then can be compared against another index that shows how a group of like products (e.g., chip prices across all major makers of similar products) have behaved over the same period with respect to the same baseline measure. The ultimate comparison of these two indexes will show the supply management professional the reasonableness of the price being asked by the supplier and potentially may provide grounds for price adjustments.

Key Sources of Business Data. The U.S. government is the largest single source of business data in the world, and the BLS is its principal agency that compiles data.[7] According to its mission statement, the BLS is "the principal fact-finding agency for the Federal Government in the broad field of labor economics and statistics." Its goal is to "collect, process, analyze, and disseminate essential statistical data." Its vision statement characterizes its data as being "impartial, timely, and accurate." The BLS Web site provides information on just about every product line regarding the size of the market, the number of major suppliers and general industry trends.

While the BLS is a government organization, Hoover's Inc. is a private source.[8] Its Web site provides industry trends and names the top organizations in a given industry. The coverage expands over service (e.g., real estate agencies, healthcare) and manufacturing (e.g., auto parts, fitness equipment). Hoover's offers information on trends and opportunities in the industry and can provide quarterly industry reports on financial information and industry forecasting. The database includes organizations from the Americas, Europe, Asia/Pacific, the Middle East and African regions.

Other useful information may come from published indexes appearing in *Business Week, Barron's, Purchasing* magazine and *The Wall Street Journal.*[9] In addition, industry-specific magazines such as *Electronics Weekly* and *Chemical Week,* are available.[10] One of the best-known sources for obtaining financial information on an organization or industry is Dun & Bradstreet.[11] The Securities and Exchange Commission (SEC) offers pertinent information about organizations that are required to file in the United States that can be useful when conducting trend analysis.[12] There are other sources for obtaining business data in various key countries. For instance, Indian Data offers information on trade statistics and a directory of various businesses in India, ranging from agriculture to machineries.[13] Foxter Small Business Directory is a UK online service that helps its clients locate businesses and gather business information regarding various types of products and services.[14]

Cultural Dimensions

Supply management professionals must be aware of cultural factors before engaging in negotiations with their international counterparts. A useful framework, provided by Geert Hofstede, offers four different cultural dimensions: (1) power distance, (2) uncertainty avoidance, (3) individualism versus collectivism and (4) masculinity versus femininity.[15] These dimensions are useful for understanding how various cultures hold different assumptions and value systems. Even though these dimensions were developed about 20 years ago, they still are well accepted and referenced, given cultural traits are established over a very long time and tend to remain stable over a very long time.

Power distance refers to a culture's willingness to accept inequality in power. It may occur among individuals or organizations. A culture of high power distance means people in that culture readily accept the fact that there are discrepancies in how much power one has. Low power distance means just the opposite. As shown in Figure 6-4, countries with high power distance include Mexico, India, France and Thailand. Countries with low power distance include Sweden, Costa Rica, the former West Germany and the United States.

Uncertainty avoidance considers how a culture handles ambiguity and uncertain situations. High uncertainty avoidance means that people in that culture prefer avoiding uncertainty and ambiguity and tend to support values that promote certainty and structure. Low uncertainty avoidance means that people in that culture have a high tolerance for undefined and unstructured situations. As shown in Figure 6-4, countries with high uncertainty avoidance include Japan, Costa Rica, France and

Figure 6-4   Country Comparisons on Cultural Dimensions

COUNTRY	POWER DISTANCE	UNCERTAINTY AVOIDANCE	INDIVIDUALISM AND COLLECTIVISM	MASCULINITY AND FEMININITY
Australia	7	7	2	5
Costa Rica	8*	2*	10	9
France	3	2*	4	7
India	2	9	6	6
Japan	5	1	7	1
Mexico	1	4	8	2
Sweden	10	10	3	10
Thailand	4	6	9	8
United States	6	8	1	4
(former West) Germany	8*	5	5	3

Legend: 1 = highest rank and 10 = lowest rank per each dimension.
*Countries with the same ranking (e.g., Costa Rica and [former West] Germany) had no noticeable differences.

Source: Adapted from Geert Hofstede, *Culture's Consequences, International Differences in Work-Related Values* (Thousand Oaks, CA: Sage Publications, Inc., 1997); and Geert Hofstede and Gert Jan Hofstede, *Cultures and Organizations: Software of the Mind* (New York: McGraw-Hill, 2004).

Mexico. Countries with low uncertainty avoidance include Sweden, India, the United States and Australia.

Individualism and collectivism are at two opposite ends of the same continuum. Individualism promotes self-reliance and exists in a culture whose social networks are not tightly bound together. Collectivism represents a culture whose members promote tight social connectivity and closely take care of one another. Countries with high individualism include the United States, Australia, Sweden and France. Countries with high collectivism include Costa Rica, Thailand, Mexico and Japan.

Masculinity and femininity are also at two opposite ends of the same continuum. Masculinity represents a culture that prefers characteristics such as achievement, assertiveness and control. Femininity represents a cultural preference for cooperation, group orientation and quality of life. These terms should not be considered as associated with genders but instead as reflecting cultural characteristics. Countries that value masculinity include Japan, Mexico, (former West) Germany and United States. Countries that espouse femininity include Sweden, Costa Rica, Thailand and France.

More recent studies extend Hofstede's work on cultural dimensions. One such study is the GLOBE Project, short for Global Leadership and Organizational Behavior Effectiveness. This project involved collecting information from 18,000 organizations across 62 countries and ascertained nine dimensions that explain cultural dimensions:

1. *Assertiveness:* toughness and competitiveness;

2. *Future orientation:* how much a culture values long-term planning;

3. *Gender differentiation:* differentiation of levels of gender roles;

4. *Uncertainty avoidance:* the degree of reluctance toward ambiguity and uncertainty;

5. *Power distance:* the degree to which a culture accepts power inequality;

6. *Collectivism versus individualism:* how much value is placed on tightly knit society versus individual independence and reliance;

7. *In-group collectivism:* the degree to which an individual takes pride in being a member of a group or society;

8. *Performance:* orientation to a culture that puts a premium on accomplishments and meritocracy; and

9. *Humane:* orientation to a culture that promotes fairness and caring.[16]

Figure 6-5 offers a list of sample countries that scored low or high on each of the nine dimensions. Because supply management professionals increasingly operate in an international context, it is critical they become more aware of cultural differences. In particular, when collecting and interpreting data in preparation for negotiation, it is important to keep in mind that everyone operates with some cultural biases.

Developing a Negotiation Plan

An effective supply management professional will spend an appropriate, and often significant, amount of time preparing for negotiations. When LG Electronics prepares for a negotiation with Qualcomm Inc., one of its key suppliers, the negotiation team pays ample attention on gathering market data, position analysis and even cultural

Figure 6-5   GLOBE Value Dimensions and Country Results

DIMENSION	LOW	HIGH
Assertiveness	Sweden, New Zealand, Switzerland	Germany (former East), Austria, Greece
Future Orientation	Russia, Argentina, Poland	Singapore, Switzerland, Netherlands
Gender Differentiation	Hungary, Poland, Slovenia	South Korea, Egypt, Morocco
Uncertainty Avoidance	Russia, Hungary, Bolivia	Switzerland, Sweden, Germany (former West)
Power Distance	Denmark, Netherlands, South Africa (Black population sample)	Morocco, Argentina, Thailand
Collectivism Versus Individualism	(Individualistic) Greece, Hungary, Germany (former East)	(Collectivistic) Sweden, South Korea, Japan
In-Group Collectivism	Denmark, Sweden, New Zealand	Iran, India, Morocco
Performance Orientation	Russia, Argentina, Greece	Singapore, Hong Kong, New Zealand
Humane Orientation	Germany (former West), Spain, France	Philippines, Ireland, Malaysia

Source: Robert House, Paul Hanges, Mansour Javidan, Peter Dorfman and Vipin Gupta, *Culture, Leadership, and Organizations: The GLOBE Study of 62 Societies* (Thousand Oaks, CA: Sage, 2004); Mansour Javidan and Robert House, "Cultural Acumen for Global Managers: Lessons From Project GLOBE," *Organizational Dynamics* 29(4) (2001): 289–305. Readers will note that the United States has not been included in this table; the results of the research indicated that the United States did not exhibit trends on either the high or low ends of the dimensions included in the table.

issues for LGE is based in Korea and Qualcomm is in the United States. Time should be spent reviewing the supply management organization's strengths and weaknesses, as well as those of the supplier's. By creating a list of areas to be studied, a supply management professional systematically evaluates all the issues that will have a bearing on the outcome of the negotiations.

Key Elements of the Negotiation Plan

Four key elements, when integrated, will lead to a well-prepared negotiation plan, as shown in Figure 6-6. Of the four elements shown, supplier proposal and the supply management professional's objectives cause a more immediate impact on the plan.

The first item in a negotiation plan should be an in-depth analysis of the *supplier's proposal*. The supply management organization that requested the proposal evaluates the price, delivery, specifications or the SOW if a service, terms and any deviations from the stated requirements. A thorough knowledge of the supplier's proposal can be an advantage during a negotiation, especially if the supply management professional knows the supplier's proposal better than the supplier does. Keep in mind that the supplier's proposal is usually the beginning point for negotiations, commonly referred to as *optimistic position*.

The next item in the negotiation plan should be setting objectives (*supply management's objectives*). Is the goal a lower price, higher quality, an accelerated delivery schedule or a combination of all three? In any case, a specific plan should be drawn up, and the negotiator or negotiating team should work toward the objectives. If a negotiating team is involved, the team leader, usually the supply management professional, should be selected, and all team members should be briefed on what and what not to say. Generally, team members should answer only those questions that lie within their own areas of expertise.

Supply market dynamics were discussed previously in this chapter. The *nature of products or services being procured* also was briefly discussed, but the following key aspects

---

Figure 6-6   Integrative Model of Negotiation Plan

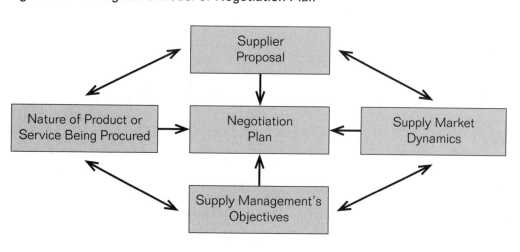

of the nature of products or services must be considered. The supply management organization needs to determine whether the nature of the product or service is differentiated or nondifferentiated and what stage of the life cycle it is in. The product or service can entail a complex or simple design with high developmental costs or low developmental costs. Lastly, the supply management organization must evaluate the risk associated with this product or service in terms of the number of potential suppliers in the market.

Negotiation Philosophies

There are many approaches to negotiating, and each depends on the nature of the market, the relative position of both the supply management professional and the supplier, and the nature of the outcome each expects from the relationship. The choice of negotiation philosophies also is affected by:

- The history of past relationships (positive or negative);
- The belief that an issue can be resolved only if someone wins and someone loses;
- The "mixed-motive" nature of most negotiations (where negotiators want their own way) but also want a continuing relationship; and
- A situation in which negotiators are accountable to someone else for their performance.

See Figure 6-7 for a summary of different styles of negotiation philosophies.

Win-Win. This philosophy is likely to be used when both parties have a high degree of concern for each other's outcomes. Examples of this include most negotiations between long-term partners and negotiations in which both the supply

Figure 6-7   Negotiation Philosophies

WIN-WIN	WIN-LOSE	LOSE-LOSE
Collaborative	Adversarial	Confrontational
Integrative	Distributive	Disinterested
Extensive interaction	Moderate interaction	Limited interaction
Long term	Medium/short term	Temporary/transient

management professional's organization and the supplier have a particular interest in doing business with the other organization.

Win-Lose. This philosophy is likely to be used when one negotiator has a high degree of concern for his or her outcome and a low degree of concern for the other's outcome. This is likely to occur if the supply management professional is in a very strong bargaining position relative to that of the supplier and the performance outcome is going to be judged by someone else. Conversely, if a negotiator has a low degree of concern for his or her own outcome but a high degree of concern for the other's outcome, the approach is likely to be accommodating or yielding. This is likely to occur if the supply management professional is in a weak bargaining position relative to that of the supplier. When both parties have a moderate concern for each other's outcomes, the philosophy is likely to be compromising — both parties may split any differences.

Lose-Lose. This philosophy is likely to be used when both negotiators have a low degree of concern for each other's outcomes. Lose-lose/confrontational negotiations are likely to occur when both parties prefer not to do business with each other but are forced into the negotiation because of circumstances beyond their control.

Preparatory Groundwork

Prior to any face-to-face negotiation with representatives from both sides, preparatory groundwork must be performed. Considerations must be given to the location, who will be on the team, what personality and cultural issues might be involved, how to deploy negotiation tactics and the alternatives involved.

The Negotiation Site

Typically, it is best to conduct negotiations at the supply management organization's location. The supply management professional will be most comfortable, will possess all the needed data, backup and support, and will be in the best position to control the negotiations. At the supply management professional's site, stress will be lower, travel fatigue will be eliminated and the supply management professional's confidence will be higher. However, negotiations at the supplier's site give the supply management professional the power to walk away.

Regardless of the site selected, wise negotiators pay close attention to security at the site. Sometimes, unethical conduct by members of the other party's negotiation team occurs. Hidden microphones, snooping and surveillance, and stealing work notes are not unheard of. Experienced negotiators are aware that they and their team members must be careful about what they discuss in public places, must pay close attention to the security of work notes, and must make sure that confidential material is secured. Concerns regarding security apply to both domestic and international negotiations.

Team Selection

In some situations, it is desirable for negotiations to be conducted by a single person, but in most cases, negotiations are best conducted by a team. A team normally is used when a product or service is complex and one person does not possess sufficient expert knowledge of all the issues. The team should consist of supply management and the other departments involved, such as engineering, quality assurance, operations, accounting and marketing. Team members should understand their individual roles, work well with other team members and support the team leader, even if they do not always agree with the team leader's opinions. Disagreements among team members never should be expressed in the presence of the supplier.

An important aspect of team negotiations is the *caucus*. The caucus is a planned or unplanned break in negotiations that gives the negotiation team an opportunity to discuss its strategy, tactics or progress before proceeding. The caucus should be used immediately when disagreement, confusion or misunderstanding occurs among members of the negotiation team. The caucus also may be used to slow down the momentum if negotiations are not going well to break up the flow or give the supplier's team an opportunity, albeit unwittingly, to start talking to each other. The caucus should be a routine part of negotiation tactics, so that calling a caucus does not provide any signals to the other party.

Collecting Relevant Information

The supply management professional needs to gather all relevant information such as the proposals and the backgrounds of the participants in the negotiation. All information that can have a bearing on the negotiations should be collected and analyzed.

A packet can be distributed to all or select members of the team that contains all or part of the following information: negotiation objectives, cost data, financial reports on suppliers, records of previous negotiations, market information, financial strength of the supplier, strengths of both parties, weaknesses of both parties, price history, quality history, specification issues, negotiation styles and personalities of those with whom the supply management professional will be negotiating and time available.

Market and Product or Service Conditions

A seller's market gives the supplier a negotiating advantage, while a buyer's market gives the negotiating advantage to the supply management professional. However, many negotiations are conducted within the context of the overall, long-term relationship between the supplier and the supply management professional. Even though short-term market conditions may give one of them an advantage, both realize that taking excessive advantage of market conditions for short-term gain may lead to long-term problems. For example, one large North American automobile manufacturer exerted tremendous pressure on its suppliers to reduce prices during the 1990s, only to find that several key suppliers later dropped the manufacturer as a customer. And a large airplane engine manufacturer found that after a series of price-cutting negotiations, its suppliers began selling parts directly to its customers, large airlines.[17]

Development of Strategies and Tactics

The detailed planning involves strategic planning, administrative planning and tactical planning. *Strategic planning* refers to the long-term goals of the supply management organization. It requires the negotiator to select suppliers that will optimize attaining the overall philosophy and objectives of the organization. Essential elements include knowledge of product-market mix, customer and environmental constraints and the basic goals of the organization concerning technology, price, policy and customer service.

Administrative planning simply refers to the logistics of getting people and information in place for the negotiations. Administrative planning already has been addressed in this chapter in the previous sections on negotiation site, collecting relevant information and market and product conditions. The goal of *tactical planning* is to obtain optimal results at the bargaining table, which involves setting goals and evaluating the strengths and weaknesses of the other party. A careful study should be made of issues, problems, agenda questions, concessions, commitments, promises, pricing, quality and delivery performance. The team leader should be selected, and negotiating tactics reviewed and discussed. Timing, ways to leverage strengths and weaknesses, delays and deadlock tactics also should be planned.

Organization Cultural Factors

As discussed previously, cross-cultural negotiations often take place between parties of different countries. When conducting cross-cultural negotiations, the ability to understand the culture of the other party is critical in reducing the number of misunderstandings that inhibit negotiations. At the same time, it should be kept in mind that different organizations also have different cultures. For instance, one organization can have a very participative culture, while the other can have a very hierarchical culture.

In that regard, the lessons from cross-cultural negotiations can be applied to negotiating with representatives from other domestic organizations. For example, a supply management professional for a local government who is purchasing computers from an organization that usually markets to commercial businesses may have to educate the supplier on the process of public-sector purchasing. Once both parties understand each other's culture, communications will improve and negotiations will proceed with fewer misunderstandings.

Analysis of Supplier's and Supply Management's Positions

A thorough study of the supplier should be made by the supply management professional or negotiating team to ensure that the supplier's position, strengths and weaknesses are understood. It may take weeks to put together all the necessary information, but the person or team who does the most homework usually will achieve the best results. Of course, the level of effort in negotiations varies with the importance of the product or service, and, obviously, it is prudent to apply the right level of effort when engaged in negotiation.

This section presents the supplier's position first, followed by supply management's. It is important to first understand the supplier's circumstances. Next are key issues that supply management controls such as timing, negotiating team composition and analyzing cost and power positions. Generally, both supply management and the supplier have alternative choices commonly known as the *best alternative to a negotiated agreement (BATNA)*. As will be discussed later, BATNA, perceived or real, has a profound impact on negotiation dynamics.

Analysis of Supplier's Position

The supply management professional must understand the following four areas of analysis regarding the supplier before engaging in a negotiation: level of supplier's desire for a contract, supplier's strategic position, supplier's financial condition and overall sources of supplier's strength.

Supplier's Desire for a Contract. An important factor to evaluate before entering into negotiations is the degree of desire that the supplier has for selling to the buying organization. The supply management professional must investigate and ascertain if market conditions might be in the supplier's favor, whether the supplier is in an industry with limited competition, or if the supplier has a patented feature, potentially making the supplier unwilling to consent to certain requirements. The reverse also may be true in supply management's favor—an adequate supply and plenty of competition may motivate the supplier to work out a reasonable contract. The supplier's desire for a contract and its perceived certainty of getting it will affect the supplier's BATNA and the supply management professional's assessment of it.

Supplier's Strategic Position. When facing a negotiating situation, the pressure is high to reduce uncertainty. Under such circumstances, what reduces uncertainty is knowing the facts and possessing relevant information. First, it is important to know the market, the supplier and the product or service. It will be helpful to gauge if the market is tight or if supply is plentiful, whether the market is likely to go up or down in the immediate and distant future, and if the supplier is a leader within the industry or a follower. It makes sense to gauge whether the supplier is positioning itself for a global expansion and for what strategic reasons. If a supplier is moving into Mexico, hoping to supply the U.S. market through the North American Free Trade Agreement (NAFTA),[18] then that could give the buying organization additional leverage points for potential collaboration or resource pooling. Questions can be raised about the supplier's technological status — whether its product or service is strong or likely to be replaced by more innovative products or services — as well as if new suppliers are entering the industry. It makes sense to investigate the supplier's financial condition by inquiring about its cash flow and other financial indicators.

Supplier's Financial Condition. The supply management professional must be able to read and interpret financial statements within the context of the supplier's industry and be able to note the changes in financial statements over time. Typically, the supply management professionals consult their accounting and financial staffs to evaluate a supplier's financial condition. Suppliers in strong financial condition may be less likely to agree to conditions that are unfavorable to them. At the same time, these suppliers bring more credibility to the negotiations regarding their ability to live up to their agreements. Contrarily, negotiations with suppliers in weak financial condition should be approached with caution. It does little good to negotiate favorable prices, delivery, and service with a supplier that may not have the financial ability to deliver as promised. Even though a developing country may show potential, when dealing with a supplier in a country that is experiencing unfavorable financial conditions, the supply management professional must closely monitor that supplier's financial condition and minimize the risks of supply interruption.

Supplier's Sources of Strength. Finally, the negotiation power of a supplier can come about in several different ways: The supplier may be the only source for a commodity or service, or it may operate in a limited competitive market where there are only one or two sources. The supplier may own a patented design or feature, or merely be the closest producer in terms of proximity from a transportation standpoint.

The supplier may offer a higher-quality product or may possess an excellent reputation for service provision, better engineering support or the best productive capacity for the supply management professional's needs. The supplier also may be the only supplier willing to deal with small volume. Additional sources of bargaining power for the supplier are superior customer service, low reject rates, comfortable payment terms and a good delivery track record whether it is for services or for products.

Analysis of the Supply Management Position

The supply management professional first must consider the skill and the authority level of the negotiator or negotiating team. Depending on the criticality of the products or services being negotiated, the right person or team must be assigned to the project. The supply management professional also needs to consider the effects of time pressures on negotiations, gauge the level of adequacy of cost/price analysis and be aware of other options.

Skill and Authority Level of the Negotiator/Negotiation Team. What makes a skilled and effective negotiator or negotiating team? In general, professional negotiators agree that planning ability, a high tolerance for ambiguity and a desire to achieve are the most important characteristics of a negotiator. Several studies have shown that the following 22 characteristics are helpful when negotiating:

1. Planning ability

2. Desire to achieve

3. Competitiveness

4. Persistence

5. Personal integrity

6. Insight

7. Analytical ability

8. Self-restraint

9. Intelligence

10. Patience/tolerance

11. Verbal clarity

12. Ability to gain respect

13. Problem-solving ability

14. Good knowledge of human nature

15. Ability to objectively consider others' ideas

16. Flexibility

17. Ability to listen

18. Tact

19. Clear, rapid ability to think

20. Decisiveness

21. High tolerance for ambiguity

22. Recognition of the importance of training and practice

Amount of Time for Negotiation. The amount of time available to negotiate an agreement invariably has an impact on its outcome. Deadlines put pressure on both the supply management organization and the supplier, but few deadlines exist that cannot be extended. In general, the party most severely affected by time constraints tends to give up negotiating strength. Contrarily, ample time for an extended negotiating session may potentially result in substantial gain. The conditions and associated alternatives for both supply management and the organization may change as the amount of time available for negotiations is increased or decreased.

Suppose a group of American and Chinese businessmen are engaged in a negotiation in Shenzhen, a major Chinese city across the bay from Hong Kong. They are negotiating to lease a large warehouse space in one of the ports off Shenzhen. The American delegates are trying to explain that they need a much larger warehouse, but the Chinese counterparts are trying to convince the Americans that the particular warehouse they are proposing could fulfill all the Americans' criteria. The Americans feel that they are being forced to take something they do not want, but they only have two days to complete the negotiation. To make the situation more complicated, the Chinese team is using a translator, even though they all speak fluent English. To avoid this type of scenario, the supply management organization should allow itself sufficient time to negotiate from a position of strength. During international negotiations, cultural differences regarding the importance of time may result in substantial disadvantages for those who do not provide sufficient time for negotiations.

Adequacy of Cost/Price Analysis. Price analysis is defined in the *ISM Glossary* (2006) as the examination of a supplier's price proposal or bid by comparison with reasonable benchmarks, without examination and evaluation of the separate elements of cost and profit making up the price. Price analysis ensures that the price to be paid is reasonable in terms of the market, the industry and the end use. An analysis of cost components can isolate and eliminate unnecessary costs. The supply management professional should collect information about manufacturing costs, direct labor, overhead, shipping expenses and administrative expenses. In cost analysis, the application of experience, knowledge and judgment to the data collected is used to project reasonable estimated contract costs. In some cases, suppliers will be unwilling to open their books on cost makeup, but with persistence, bits and pieces of information can be acquired. Quotations are other accurate and reliable ways to determine existing market prices. The supply management professional also can obtain cost/price analysis information by explicitly requesting the detailed data in the quotation. Useful estimates also may be developed based on accounting analysis, engineering analysis and industry data. A price history file is another valuable source — the frequency and percentage of increases or decreases in past periods may enable the supply management professional to project future changes.

Availability of Other Options for the Supply Management Professional. Having alternate options gives the supply management organization negotiating strength, or, as mentioned earlier in this chapter, BATNA. Alternative options exist if it is possible to purchase from other sources, if suitable alternative products are available or if the products or services can be produced in-house. Among the options listed, alternative sourcing is perhaps the least risky option to pursue. Providing alternative products or methods of service may involve extensive evaluation and engineering studies, while internal production or service provision may involve capital investment, additional labor and the development of additional in-house skills. However, of course, it is up to the supply management professional to make a careful examination to ensure compatibility and acceptability of any alternative options that the buying organization considers.

Figure 6-8   Process of Key Decision Points

BATNA	→	Supply Management Settlement Range	→	Suppler Settlement Range	→	Negotiation Zone	→	Anchor Point

Framing the Results of Analysis

Once the analyses of suppliers and its own position are completed, the supply management professional is ready to make several decisions before the negotiation as shown in Figure 6-8. These decision areas are progressive — one leads to another.

Best Alternative to a Negotiated Agreement (BATNA)

BATNA is arguably the most salient source of power for any negotiator. At one extreme, the negotiator that has no BATNA or extremely poor BATNA has little to no power. At the other extreme, the negotiator with a viable and attractive BATNA wields a great deal of power over the other party. Having other acceptable alternatives determines the level of power in the negotiation.

Therefore, a good negotiator always works hard on determining the BATNA as well as on improving it. Determining the BATNA often requires in-depth research on the part of the supply management professional because it may not be obvious at first. For example, an automaker had been using platinum for many auto parts. Platinum was expensive so the automaker's engineers worked hard to find a replacement and succeeded in using palladium for certain key parts such as catalytic converters.[19] This substitutable product to platinum gave the supply management professional the BATNA when negotiating a platinum contract. Often a new BATNA emerges as engineering continues to find new ways to make parts. The supply management professional must stay on top of engineering advancements and their viability.

Improving the BATNA may take even more effort. A major automaker was working with a supplier of the center console, the unit that sits between the driver and the passenger seat with a cup holder and a small glove compartment. This supplier was the automaker's BATNA at the time for the center console assembly, but the automaker did not like the quality of this supplier's product. Therefore, to pressure this supplier to respond to its requests, the automaker worked hard to bring another supplier on line. Once the new supplier developed the technology of making the center console, the automaker found a new BATNA and exercised much more power over the old supplier during negotiation.

Supply Management Settlement Range and Supplier Settlement Range

The supply management professional typically begins with a target price. The target price is obtained from having completed the downstream market analysis and having translated the information into product, parts or service delivery costs. The supply management professional also considers what it can pay and still sell the product or perform the service profitably or stay within budget constraints. Once the target price is established, then the acceptable range can form around the target price. The range is determined by the most optimistic price and the most pessimistic price. For the supply management professional, the most optimistic price is the most realistically desirable price below the target price, and the most pessimistic price is the most realistically undesirable price above the target price. This range often is determined by the supply management professional's knowledge of the supply market and the particular supplier's cost structure.

Needless to say, the supplier also has an acceptable range; its target price and the range defined by its most optimistic and pessimistic prices. In this case, its most optimistic price would appear above the target price and its most pessimistic price below the target price. The negotiator needs to establish a good estimate of what the supplier's settlement range is prior to engaging in negotiation. A good place to start to gauge the supplier's BATNA is by determining how badly the supplier might want the supply management organization's business and the overall value of the contract to the supplier. Setting a target price for a service is much more difficult than setting a target price for a manufactured good. In service, requirements for the deliverable vary, depending on the customer needs and other contextual factors such as when, where and how frequently the service is to take place. For instance, a training and education supplier finds that requirements for training provided for the same subject (e.g., statistical process control or negotiation-skills training) may differ depending on the customer.

Negotiation Zone

Defining and organizing the issues to identify points of similarity and difference between the buying organization and the supplier is a critical step in negotiation. The outcome of this analysis will determine how to develop strategies and tactics, select the negotiation team and devise the agenda. The supply management professional first needs to identify the area of the negotiation zone and then make plans accordingly.

Figure 6-9 shows the relationship between the ranges of prices and the zone of negotiation. Both the buying organization and the supplier develop their respective price ranges consisting of optimistic, target and pessimistic prices. Suppose a large national health-and-fitness chain is interested in purchasing a premium-brand, foam exercise mat. This mat retails for about $15 per unit, but because the contract entails a large quantity and multiyear agreement, the price is expected to be below $10 per unit.

Case A in Figure 6-9 reflects the fact that the supply management professional wants to pay less and the supplier wants more — the optimistic price of the buyer is shown as the lowest, while the optimistic price of the supplier is shown as the highest price. Also shown in Case A is no overlap between the price ranges of both parties — the pessimistic price of the buyer is lower than the pessimistic price of the supplier. When this happens, there is no negotiation zone, and this range of $0.50 is typically referred to as the negative bargaining zone. So long as both sides adhere to their settlement range, there will be no agreement. However, with re-evaluation by both parties independently, they might find a negotiation zone if and when they reconvene. How much concession one party is willing to make ultimately will depend on how strong its BATNA is. For instance, if both parties have an extremely attractive BATNA, then they are not likely to concede. On the contrary, Case B in Figure 6-9 exemplifies a situation where there is an overlap on the negotiation zone. The zone between the pessimistic price of the buyer and the pessimistic price of the supplier is the negotiation zone; in this case, the zone is between $7.00 and $8.50.

Anchor Point

A common misperception is that it is better to let the other party "show their cards first," meaning it is better for the other party to make the initial offer. However, this is not true. It is almost always better to make the initial offer, thus setting the *anchor point*. The anchor point simply means the initial offer made in the negotiation. Once an initial offer is made, the counteroffer and all subsequent offers are made around the initial one. Negotiators never really deviate that far from the initial offer except in a few extreme cases where situations change because of extreme circumstances such as a natural disaster. This is why the initial offer is called the anchor point.

One critical caveat regarding the anchor point: It must be made based on careful market research and understanding of the supplier's position. When the anchor point is cast haphazardly, it leads to a suboptimal outcome. However, when it is cast well, it sets the tone for the whole negotiation to the advantage of the negotiator. For instance, because the final outcome usually stays close to the anchor point, it is important to start the negotiation at a high point. Also, setting the anchor point puts the negotiator in the lead position.

Figure 6-9   Price Ranges and the Negotiation Zone

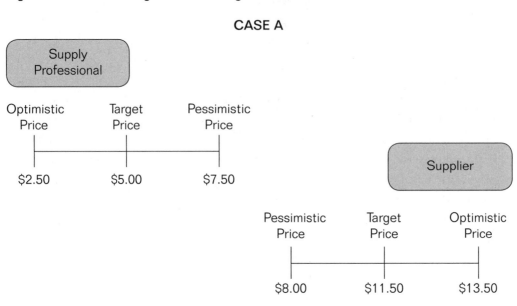

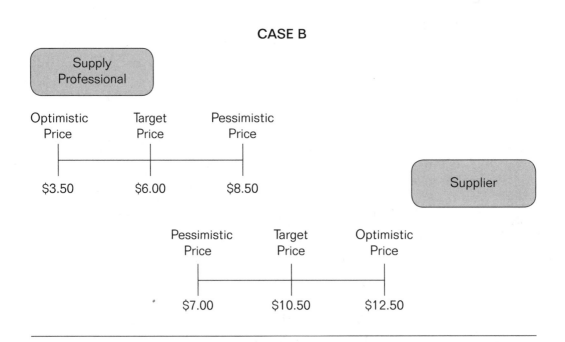

Conducting Negotiations

To conduct negotiations well, the supply management professional must be armed with pertinent facts and information. The supply management professional must be aware of certain negotiation tactics. In addition, the supplier management professional needs to understand the context within which the negotiation is being conducted, such as negotiating with a sole source or a consortium.

Documentation of Negotiations

The team must come to the negotiation prepared with the data and facts they have gathered, as presented in the previous sections. Because of problems with personnel turnover and the limitations of human memory, accurate documentation of negotiations is essential. Figure 6-10 enumerates what type of information should be documented and how it should be organized.

Negotiation Tactics

A supply management professional should keep in mind that the choice of negotiation strategies and tactics typically results from the negotiation planning process. This process includes analyzing the supplier's proposal and establishing objectives.

Figure 6-10   Areas of Documentation

KEY AREAS	DESCRIPTIONS
Subject	An overview of the negotiations, including the supplier's name and location, contract number and description of the item to be purchased.
Introductory Summary	A description of the type of contract and negotiation action involved, plus comparative figures of the supplier's proposal, the supply management professional's objectives and the negotiated results.
Particulars	A description of the product or service to be purchased and who was involved in the procurement.
Procurement Situation	A discussion of the factors in the procurement situation that affected the final decisions.
Negotiation Summary	A description of the supplier's contract pricing proposal, the supply management professional's negotiation objective and the negotiation results, tabulated in parallel form.

Selecting tactics requires planning and is determined by the direction of the negotiations — whether the negotiation philosophies are win-win, win-lose or lose-lose. Selection also depends on the relative power of the supply management professional and the supplier, and the personalities of the negotiators.

Figure 6-11 offers an overview of three types of tactics and their associated practices. Practices are framed with respect to when and how the optimistic position and target position may be revealed and reasons why. For instance, when the supply management professional is confident about reaching the agreement at the target position, he or she can disclose the optimistic position and put the supplier on notice. Then, before the impact of the supply management professional's optimistic position is realized by the other party, the target position is offered. Compared to the optimistic position, the target position looks much more attractive, so the supplier is likely to accept. However, this tactic has to be carried out carefully and has its potential pitfalls as listed in Figure 6-11.

Hardball Tactics. Figure 6-12 illustrates a few tactics that a negotiator must be aware of. This awareness is important — not necessarily to use them, but to be able to

---

Figure 6-11   Types of Tactics and Practices

TACTICS	ASSOCIATED PRACTICES
Reveal no position	The supply management professional does not want to discuss position. This strategy attempts to maneuver the supplier toward the buying organization's position by probing the supplier's proposal point by point. This strategy may work when the supplier is eager to reach agreement, when the supply management professional lacks information or when the supplier's proposal is long and complicated.
Reveal optimistic position	The supply management professional has the supplier's proposal. This approach establishes the range for negotiation on each issue. The supply management professional and the supplier then can discuss and resolve each issue.
Reveal optimistic position and then immediately offer target position	The supply management professional emphasizes the merits of being up front and the value of saving time. This strategy can backfire if the supplier refuses the offer. The supply management professional then may have to settle for something closer to the pessimistic position.

Figure 6-12   Common Hardball Tactics

TACTICS	DESCRIPTION
Best and final	This is a "take-the-offer-or-leave-the-offer" approach that counts on the other party to submit to the offered position and make concessions. It is, in essence, a method to achieve an objective quickly.
False offer	The negotiating party makes an extremely attractive offer that is impossible to implement. This type of false offer is made to entice the other party and to get its attention.
Good guy, bad guy	One person within the same negotiating team plays a "bad guy" and another person a "good guy." The other party, when harassed by the bad guy, may open up to the good guy, when, in fact, they are both on the same team.
Information planting	A piece of information is left for the other party to see in a seemingly accidental way. The other party that views this information cannot determine whether it is true, but this information may end up affecting the other party's thinking.
Red herring	During the English fox-hunting trip, a red herring was used to distract the dogs from the fox's tracks. Here, a small issue is blown into a major issue that eventually is conceded away, to keep the other party from addressing the really critical major issue.

recognize them when the other party uses them. If a decision is made to use one or more of these tactics, it is important to keep in mind that a long-term buyer–supplier relationship is built on trust and also that the other party eventually will recognize these tactics.

Additional Tactics. Figure 6–13 summarizes some additional basic negotiation tactics. This list also may serve as a checklist for the supply management professional to refer to before engaging in a negotiation. These tactics are relevant to U.S. negotiators. Those negotiating in other cultures should modify their tactics to fit their cultural situations. For instance, different cultures may have different expectations about who should speak first or implications of emotional responses. Also, the issue of body language is culturally laden. For example, folding arms in one culture may mean a sign of submission, while in another culture, it may be a sign of disagreement.

Figure 6-13   Common Negotiation Tactics

Sequence or prioritize the issues for discussion, using one of these approaches:

- Cover the major issues first, assuming that the minor issues then will fall into place,

- Cover the most troublesome issues first, assuming that the other issues then will fall into place, or

- Cover the least troublesome issues first, to get a feel for the supplier's position and to evaluate its negotiators and arrange the issues so that if one issue is settled, the rest will fall into place.

Use questions wisely. Questions should draw out information, rather than require yes or no answers, and should be phrased so they question the supplier's position without personally attacking the supplier.

Listen effectively. Rather than thinking of what your response will be, pay attention to what is being said.

Maintain initiative. Be prepared to probe for justification in areas that are unclear.

Use solid data. Be able to back up the position taken. Positions that cannot be justified hurt credibility.

Use silence. Silence often makes the other party nervous and may result in additional discussion and concessions.

Avoid emotional reactions. Emotional reactions move the negotiations from issues to personalities.

Make use of caucuses. A caucus, or recess (as discussed earlier), is an excellent way to rethink positions, interrupt the supplier's momentum or evaluate a counterproposal. Avoid backtracking when the session resumes.

Do not be afraid to say no. Do not agree unless you mean to agree.

Beware of deadlines. Before agreeing to a deadline, make sure you can live with it. It often is better to let a deadline pass than to settle for less than you can live with.

Be aware of body language. When there is a conflict between what people are saying and their body language, the body language usually is telling the truth.

Keep an open mind. Preconceived ideas block creativity that often is needed for a positive outcome.

Get it in writing. Before adjourning, get all agreements in writing and make sure the appropriate parties sign them.

Make appropriate concessions; this can produce significant gains. Concessions need not be made "one for one" or be of equal value. Your willingness, or unwillingness, to make concessions will set the tone for additional negotiations.

Use the "missing person" tactic. The missing person is the person with the final authority who is deliberately absent from the negotiations. This tactic gives the negotiator more time and provides a way out of a tight situation. However, some negotiators will not meet if someone in authority is not present. In addition, many negotiators will not make a firm offer if someone in authority is not present.

Use a target tactic. In this tactic, the supply management professional tells the supplier that he or she likes the product or service but $X is all that he or she will pay. This tactic often brings a favorable response from the supplier.

Never negotiate beyond your physical and mental endurance. The pressure of extended negotiations is physically and mentally demanding. This is especially true when the negotiator is experiencing jetlag, negotiating in unfamiliar surroundings, negotiating with suppliers from dissimilar industrial or national cultures, or is having to absorb large amounts of information. Fatigue slows thinking and clouds judgment. Scheduling shorter negotiation sessions, with adequate time for rest and exercise, and reducing the intensity of social activities should be important parts of any negotiation planning process.

Negotiating With a Sole Supplier

Negotiating with a supplier that has no or very limited competition is difficult. Several tactics are available, however, for generating competition within this arena.

These tactics deal with creating alternate choices that enable the negotiator to approach the other party with more authority. For instance, the buying organization may consider producing the item in-house. If the price is not reasonable, the buying organization may consider no longer making the product that requires the component or provide the service, or if it is still considering making the product or providing the service, looking for substitute items or processes. One or more of these potential alternate choices may be communicated to the supplier.

If the supplier is already supplying products or services to the supply management organization, the supply management professional can advise the supplier that his or her long-range interest should be in keeping the supply management professional as a customer, rather than achieving a temporary price advantage. The supply management professional can seek a win-win situation where costs, risks and savings are shared. If the supplier has high inventory levels and needs to lower them, the supply management professional can use this as leverage. If the supplier has financial problems and can use the additional business, the supply management professional can use this to his or her advantage as well.

Negotiations as a Consortium or Cooperative

A cooperative or co-op can be a for-profit or not-for-profit business. It serves its members in a single industry, such as groceries, hospitals or county governments. A consortium is a formal organization, usually comprised of private-sector, for-profit organizations. These organizations typically are noncompeting organizations from varied industries that are engaged in purchasing similar goods or services.

Similarities and Differences. Co-op members play no role in the management of the co-op's suppliers and other administrative activities. Members may recommend suppliers, but co-op management evaluates and selects suppliers. Members may order directly from the supplier, or the co-op may serve as a member's purchaser. Contrarily, members of a consortium usually are active in its management. Consortia are actively managed by commodity teams, and commodity purchases are made by lead members or by a hired third party. These commodity teams generally are comprised of supply management professionals from member organizations. The consortium usually expects its members to pay for products or services purchased on their behalf within the terms of the supplier invoice.

Even with differences in structure and operation, the purposes of consortia and co-ops are similar. Both consortia and co-ops combine the purchasing power of their members in the marketplace to achieve lower prices, better quality, reduced administrative costs, standardization, better records and greater competition. Typical criticisms that have been made against these collaborative purchasing arrangements include inferior products, longer lead times, limited item availability, increased paperwork and placing smaller suppliers at competitive disadvantages.

Antitrust violations in the United States because of restraints of trade usually are not problems for consortia if their activities represent legitimate joint purchasing within the federal antitrust safety zone.[20] If the percentage of purchases by the consortium or co-op falls below a certain percentage (e.g., in the range of 25 percent to 35 percent) of total sales in the relevant market, and if the jointly purchased products and services are less than a certain percentage (e.g., in the range of 10 percent to 25 percent of member revenues), then the co-op or consortium probably will not be challenged for antitrust violations. The antitrust division of the federal government has a business review process for evaluating whether a consortium is within this zone.[21]

Best and Final Offer

Telling the other party that this is the best and final offer as discussed in Figure 6-12, also known as the *take it or leave it price,* is a risky negotiating tactic that a supply management professional should use with caution. A supply management professional should have a BATNA ready before using this tactic, simply because the supplier can decline the offer.

Risk and Opportunity. When made, a best and final offer should be clear. Nonverbal signals should be consistent with the verbal or written offer. How the best and final offer is made can convey different meanings. The best and final offer can improve or hinder bargaining power. The manner in which it is stated can convey commitment, and can leave room for further negotiations, albeit difficult.

If a supplier presents with a best and final offer, the supply management professional from the buying organization can accept the offer, reject the offer, make a counteroffer, be noncommittal or remain silent. Being noncommittal or remaining silent may be good responses. This avoids confrontation, provides the supplier with no feedback and gives the supply management professional time to decide how to respond. As long as viable alternate choices exist, there is nothing wrong with concluding the negotiation with no resolution if a mutually satisfactory agreement cannot be reached.

Alternate Approach. An alternate approach to the best and final offer is to frame the final offer as a *close offer,* meaning close to the point where the supply management professional might place an order if the supplier agrees to the offer. For example, the supply management professional may say, "If you can do this, this, and this, we are prepared to place an order now." This approach provides the supply management professional with the option of continuing discussions if the supplier does not agree.

As discussed throughout this chapter, there are many tactics a supply management professional can use during a negotiation. Tactics are the processes and maneuvers that negotiators use to put their plans into action. As the supply management professional and his or her team prepare for the negotiation, they should keep in mind that these tactics also can be deployed by the supplier's team. As with strategies, specific tactics will vary depending on the negotiation philosophy, the relative power position of the negotiators, and the personalities of the negotiators. Effective negotiators are able to adapt their tactics to the situation and also recognize tactics used by the other party.

Summary

This chapter presents as an overview of fact-based negotiation. It begins by discussing negotiation objectives. The importance of gathering facts and information to conduct the analysis of both the supplier and supply management organization's positions is covered. Key contents of the negotiation plan and what kind of preparatory ground-work is needed is introduced. Key decision areas such as BATNA, buyer and supplier settlement ranges, negotiation zone and anchor point are discussed. Lastly, various issues surrounding the actual negotiation are covered, including key documentation requirements, negotiation tactics and negotiating with a sole supplier versus a consortium or a cooperative.

Key Points

1. Negotiation objectives should be set with a long-term perspective. Short-term tactics that may potentially have a long-term effect should be avoided.

2. A supply management professional should learn as many facts as possible about the supplier and the supplier's market and its financial conditions prior to developing and implementing a negotiation strategy.

3. Michael E. Porter's five market forces — power of suppliers, power of buyers, barriers to new entrants, substitutes and industry rivalry — offer a useful framework for supply market analysis.

4. Market fragmentation, market size and growth, technology trends, industry profitability and regulatory changes all influence market trends.

5. The two most common price indexes used in negotiations in the United States are the Producer Price Index (PPI) and the Consumer Price Index (CPI).

6. Geert Hofstede provides a useful framework that offers four different cultural dimensions — power distance, uncertainty avoidance, individualism versus collectivism, and masculinity versus femininity — that supply management professionals must be aware of before engaging in negotiations with their international counterparts.

7. Supplier proposal, buyer's objective, the nature of the product or service being procured, and supply market dynamics integrated together lead to a well-prepared negotiation plan.

8. Prior to face-to-face negotiation, considerations must be given to the location selected, who will be on the team, what personality and cultural issues might be at play, how to deploy negotiation tactics and the identification of the fallback alternatives.

9. A thorough study of the supplier should be made by the negotiator or negotiating team to ensure that the supplier's desire for a contract, strategic position, financial condition and other strengths and weaknesses are understood.

10. The supply management organization first needs to consider the skill and authority level of the negotiator or negotiating team, the effects time pressure have on negotiation, the level of adequacy of the cost/price analysis and the effect that the availability of other options can have on the negotiation.

11. Both the supply management professional and the supplier always have alternative choices, commonly known as a "best alternative to a negotiated agreement" (BATNA). The only thing that varies is how attractive or unattractive the BATNA is. Determining the BATNA often requires in-depth research on the part of the supply management professional because it may not be obvious at first.

12. Defining and organizing the issues as to similarities and differences between the supply management organization and the supplier is a critical step in negotiation. The outcome of this analysis determines the area known as the negotiation zone.

13. It is almost always better to make the initial offer first, thus setting the anchor point. The anchor point is the initial offer made in the negotiation.

14. The supply management professional must be aware of numerous negotiation tactics to either implement or identify them. The supply management professional needs to understand the context within which the negotiation is being conducted, such as negotiating with a sole source, with a consortium or with a preferred supplier.

7

Supplier Management
and Development

With increased levels of outsourcing, the topic of supplier management and development has emerged as a key managerial consideration. Honda of America Mfg. Inc. purchases more than 85 percent of its cost of manufacturing from its suppliers, and Chrysler LLC more than 70 percent. In general, suppliers account for more than 50 percent of the total goods and services, according to an Aberdeen report.[1] International sourcing and involvement with suppliers in Asia and Eastern Europe have increased, and many of these organizations come from emerging economies. How suppliers perform now has a greater impact on the buying organization's success; thus, supplier performance management has become a critical managerial issue.

About 70 percent of the organizations that responded to an Aberdeen survey noted supplier performance as the key factor that critically affects their operational success. In the service sector, suppliers often are the primary contact of customers, as in the case of call centers. Once the service operation is contracted out to a supplier, the supplier makes direct contact with the buying organization's customers. To control the service aspect of its call centers better, Dell is moving its outsourced call centers back to the United States from India.[2] Just in terms of total spend, service outsourcing is a significant spend for supply management organizations. A CAPS Research study of 128 manufacturing and service organizations reported $103.9 billion in services spend with an average service spend per participant organization of $812. This high level of service spend represented 39 percent of the total purchase spend reported.[3] Clearly, a service supplier would have a great impact on the success of the buying organization.

This chapter presents a discussion on how to select suppliers, manage suppliers and develop suppliers when their performance falls short of requirements. The chapter begins with supplier selection, followed by supplier performance appraisal, and then certification. Careful supplier selection is a prerequisite to good supplier performance. The chapter then shows readers how to develop suppliers and help them improve when falling short of expectations. Beyond developing suppliers for performance, the chapter also explores how to get product or service development ideas from suppliers through early supplier involvement and value analysis/value engineering.

CHAPTER OBJECTIVES

• Consider supplier selection criteria under the condition of changing supplier roles.

• Examine the process of supplier performance evaluation and improvement.

• Focus on the categories of supplier qualifications and in particular what to look for during site visits.

• Identify underlying managerial issues involved in supplier certifications.

• Consider the process of certification and how to categorize suppliers into varying levels of certifications.

• Reflect on the relationship between supplier development and the philosophy of continuous improvement.

• Present the process of supplier development and its associated benefits.

• Frame reverse marketing as an aggressive form of supplier development.

• Introduce supply management issues when involving suppliers in new product development.

• Make the business case for value analysis and value engineering (VA/VE) and the process of engaging in VA/VE practice.

Supplier Selection

Supplier selection is the activity the supply management organization engages in to determine which suppliers it would establish a contract with and engage in a relationship. This is by far one of the most important considerations in supply management. Supplier selection "commits resources while simultaneously impacting such activities as inventory management, production planning and control, cash flow requirements and product quality."[4] In other words, supplier selection means resource commitment; it has a direct and lasting effect on the future competitiveness of supply management professionals' organizations. Especially in recent years, with many major organizations reducing the number of suppliers they do business with, selecting the right suppliers has become an even more critical managerial consideration. According to R. Monczka, R. Trent and R. Handfield, most supply management organizations now "select suppliers much more carefully and develop close working relationships with fewer suppliers …"[5]

As mentioned previously, selecting suppliers in the service industry is even more critical than in manufacturing because service suppliers come in contact with the buying organization's customers right away. This is why leading service organizations, such as Intuit Inc. a provider of software products and services, employ an elaborate supplier selection process.[6] The process takes supply management professionals from developing a cross-functional team to preliminary supplier screening and, finally, to in-depth evaluation and qualification, all before a supplier can be selected.

New Roles and Responsibilities of Suppliers

Many major supply management organizations in various industries such as automobile, aerospace and even defense have reduced the number of suppliers they work with. For instance, Ford Motor Co. has reduced the number of its active suppliers by more than 50 percent over the past decade.[7] Other organizations, such as Honeywell and Raytheon, also have reduced their suppliers. Such downsizing of an organization's supply base has been a clear trend among large and small organizations. Simply put, it is easier and more expedient to work with a smaller number of suppliers, assuming all else remains the same. The remaining suppliers receive more — and longer-term — business. In this regard, the supplier selected by a supply management organization to become part of its supply base has become much more important than ever before. The implication is obvious: The suppliers selected become more integrated and enjoy longer-term relationships.

Naturally, remaining suppliers now have a greater share of the total value added of the final product or service. Suppliers have even expanded their capabilities by engaging in more design work. Clearly, a large percentage of control over quality, cost and delivery has been delegated to suppliers. Suppliers now have to know not only how to put things together but also how to create new products and services that the end user (i.e., the consumer) wants. For example, Chrysler LLC wants its major suppliers to understand its consumer market so they can integrate market demand into the design of their products. In this regard, the list of supplier selection criteria has been expanded beyond such traditional considerations as price, ability to meet specifications, worker turnover and others to include design capability and, more important, a supplier's ability to build long-term relationships.

Underlying Categories of Supplier Selection Criteria

Generally, "choosing the right supplier involves much more than scanning a series of price lists."[8] Selection criteria range widely from quality (e.g., internal reject rate, external reject rate, on-time service provision, etc.) to initial price offered and associated cost structure. More than 20 different criteria can exist. With the advent of information technology, a software platform such as Decision Lens (www.decisionlens.com/industries/comm_vendor.htm) can be used to manage supplier selection.

Nonetheless, it is useful to understand the underlying supplier selection categories that capture the more detailed selection criteria. Based on a survey of 156 supply management professionals, eight major categories of supplier selection criteria were developed: (1) finances, (2) consistency, (3) relationship, (4) flexibility, (5) technological capability, (6) service, (7) reliability and (8) price (see Figure 7-1).[9] These eight groups represent the major conceptual categories of supplier selection criteria.

Figure 7-1 Supplier Selection Criteria

	SELECTION CRITERIA
Finances	Financial conditions, profitability of supplier, financial records disclosure, performance awards
Consistency	Conformance quality, consistent delivery, quality philosophy, prompt response
Relationship	Long-term relationship, relationship closeness, communication openness, reputation for integrity
Flexibility	Product or service volume changes, short setup time, short delivery lead time, conflict resolution
Technological Capability	Design capability, technical capability
Service	After-sales support, sales representative's competence
Reliability	Incremental improvement, product or service reliability
Price	Low initial price

Source: Adapted from T.Y. Choi and J.L. Hartley, "An Exploration of Supplier Selection Practices Across the Supply Chain," *Journal of Operations Management* 14(4) (1996): 333-44.

Selecting Suppliers: First-Tier Suppliers
Versus Tertiary-Tier Suppliers

First-tier suppliers supply to the final assembler, while *tertiary-tier* (e.g., second-tier or third-tier) *suppliers* supply to another supplier. In the automobile industry, it appears that with the changes that have been taking place in supply chains as discussed previously, selecting suppliers for their ability to maintain a cooperative, long-term relationship is just as important for tertiary-tier suppliers as for first-tier suppliers.[10] In general, regardless of the supplier's location on the supply chain, selecting a supplier based on price alone is history.

As shown in Figure 7-1, supply management professionals view quality and delivery the same way — by consistency. Financial considerations and technological capability are more important when selecting first-tier suppliers compared to tertiary-tier ones. Overall, supply management organizations across the supply chain are looking for similar traits in their suppliers, except for the final assemblers who look for suppliers with more technological capability and more financial success. Supplier performance appraisal should build on supplier selection criteria.

Supplier Performance Appraisal

Measuring supplier performance and managing suppliers based on performance measures is critical. Poor supplier performance can cause poor customer service and production problems for the supply management organization. It also can cause product recalls, not fulfilling service delivery requirements and even safety concerns. Because of faulty tires from Firestone, the Ford Motor Co. lost $3 billion when it was forced to recall more than 13 million tires. Some experts estimate up to 250 deaths were caused by the defective tires.[11]

Evaluating Suppliers

Large organizations often do not evaluate all their suppliers. Organizations such as Raytheon or General Motors Corp. may have tens of thousands of suppliers. When asked, they generally cannot tell for sure how many suppliers they have. Bayer AG, a leading international organization in the pharmaceutical industry, goes through a separate selection process to decide which suppliers are going to be evaluated; its goal is to "evaluate 80 percent of Bayer's total procurement volume."[12] To select suppliers for evaluation, Bayer uses the following criteria: purchasing volume, strategic importance of the material or service, critical markets and suppliers, and potential for improvement.

Today, many e-business solution providers offer packages to evaluate supplier performance, keep the information at a central database, and allow ready access to the data in a variety of formats. SAP AG's R/3 offers a supplier evaluation module and associated continuous improvement tool. GlobalNetXchange (GNX) is another organization that offers an information technology (IT) package for supplier evaluation.[13] Its Web-based solution on supplier performance offers standard reports that are accessible to multiple trading partners. The supply management organization can use its key performance indicators (KPIs) and make available a supplier's performance information, along with other suppliers' performance outcomes, and benchmark information so that a supplier knows exactly where it stands.

Figure 7-2 illustrates a generic process of supplier performance evaluation and improvement. This is a high-level diagram, and the basic approach involves focusing on a collaborative solution with shared ownership. The ultimate goal of performance evaluation is to make improvements and eliminate problems at the systems level rather than merely getting around a symptom of underlying problems. Joint improvement issues are discussed later in this chapter.

Figure 7-2 Supplier Performance Management Process

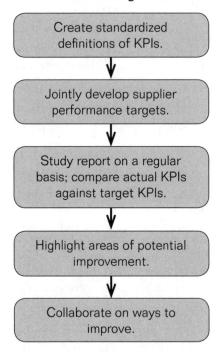

Source: Adapted from GlobalNetXchange, www.tools.p.agentrics.com/MyGenSource/sso/login.jsp.

Often before engaging a supplier in a detailed evaluation, a supply management professional may perform an overall qualification process with the supplier. To qualify a supplier, a supply management organization needs to address several major categories. Figure 7–3 lists the major categories and their underlying managerial issues and implications. When suppliers are being qualified, these categories should be evaluated in total; one category should not dominate. Also, the qualifying process must focus on the systems–level issues as well as on the infrastructure and the integration of various elements within the supplier organization.

Figure 7-3   Qualifying Categories and Their Managerial Implications

QUALIFYING CATEGORIES	MANAGEMENT ISSUES	IMPLICATIONS FOR THE BUYING ORGANIZATION
Customer Communication/ Customer Relationship Management (CRM)	How well the supplier communicates with the supply management organization; the presence of a computerized CRM system	Critical for maintaining a close working relationship and flexibility as operational and market conditions change
Supply-Chain Mapping	Whether the supplier maintains an active mapping of its supply chain; how deep in the supply chain this mapping extends	How responsive a supplier may be in terms of planning and inventory management (e.g., at which point in the supply chain it keeps the necessary inventory)
Quality Systems	Supplier's historical record on internal and external reject rates; the presence of statistical process control; use of Six Sigma and process-capability indexes; service delivery performance	Direct impact on the supply management organization's quality in terms of its product, process and service
Logistics Systems	Use of warehouses and distribution centers; presence of third-party logistics organization; source of transportation services	How well in terms of time and accuracy a supplier delivers goods and services and keeps the cost of transportation to a minimum
Financial Analysis	Supplier's financial stability measured in terms of its balance sheet, income statement, cost-control history, credit ratings, annual reports (audited), 10-K reports (if U.S. public) and other financial reports	Good indicators for supply management professionals in terms of where the supplier organization has been and where it is going

(continued)

Figure 7-3   continued

QUALIFYING CATEGORIES	MANAGEMENT ISSUES	IMPLICATIONS FOR THE BUYING ORGANIZATION
Organization and Management	How well top management leads its workers and provides stability; how many layers of management the supplier organization has	The fundamental infrastructure that affects supplier performance and the degree of opportunity to build a long-term, mutually beneficial relationship
Labor-Management Relationship	State of unionization; if unionized, its history of relationship; how management treats its workers in terms of benefits and compensation	Serious impact on worker turnover and job satisfaction; social responsibility for the supply management organization

Fundamentally, the evaluation process is data-driven, whether quantitative or qualitative. It also should entail a standardized process. For instance, ABB has a standardized performance evaluation process called the Supplier Performance Rating that consists of a data-driven approach to measure performance and offer feedback on a regular basis. ABB uses two primary KPIs, quality and delivery. Quality is defined as "percent [of] defect free lots received" and delivery as "percent of all shipped [shipments] received complete and on time, based on agreed Incoterms." These results are used for deciding future work allocation and annual awards and recognition.[14]

Once the evaluation is completed, feedback must be given. Kennametal Inc., a manufacturer of cutting tools and tooling systems, uses a form that includes four areas of measurement: product quality, on-time delivery, total cost management and payment terms (see Figure 7-4). The details of how each area is measured are shown in the scorecard. The legend on the form assists the raters in terms of how to translate their observations into numeric scores and translate terms into scores. Depending on the weights assigned to each category under a measurement area, the weighted score for each area of measurement is listed on the top line. For example, product quality is given a score of 9.3, a total of the three weighted scores from three categories. Each of four areas of measurement also is given a weight, in this case 35 percent, 30 percent, 25 percent and 10 percent. The total weighted score is given on the bottom line; in this example it is 8.4.

To intuitively feel what this score means, Kennametal uses 6.0 as the threshold point, stating that "a supplier whose score falls below 6 for two consecutive months will be required to submit a corrective action plan within 30 days." In addition, the organization makes it clear that the scores are retained and compared against the scores of other suppliers to further continuous improvement. A supplier's scores and its efforts to make improvements will be used to make future decisions regarding work allocation. The organization also encourages the suppliers to ask questions and engage in a dialogue.

Figure 7-4   Sample Scorecard from Kennametal

Your organization's performance is scored from zero to ten on four major dimensions, with weighting factors reflecting their relative importance to Kennametal, as follows:

WEIGHT	CATEGORY	RATING	SCORE
35%	PRODUCT QUALITY		9.3
	Absence of Defects	33.3%	9
	Conformance to Specs	33.3%	9
	Shipping Damage	33.3%	10
30%	ON-TIME DELIVERY (Score = percent on time, 10)	90%	9.0
25%	TOTAL COST MGMT.		7.6
	Price Reductions/Rebates	36.4%	7
	Kanban/Lean Initiatives	0%	N/A
	Consigned Inventory	14.1%	5
	Responsiveness	14.1%	10
	Lead-Time Reduction	14.1%	7
	Evaluated Receipt Settlement	0%	N/A
	Invoice Accuracy	7.1%	8
	Bar Code Shipment	0%	N/A
	Accept P-Card	7.1%	10
	No Restocking Fees	7.1%	10
10%	PAYMENT TERMS	5.0	5.0
	YOUR SCORE		8.4

QUALITY/COST SCORE KEY

Excellent 10
Very Good 9
Good 8
Average 7
Below Average . 6
Poor 5

TERMS SCORE KEY

3% 10 10
2% 10 9
1% 10 8
Net 60 . . . . 7.5
Net 45 7
Net 30 5
COD 0

Figure 7-5 lists the key evaluation factors that are instrumental in conducting an analysis of a supplier's ability to perform. The figure also includes how these factors can be probed during the performance evaluation process.

Figure 7-5   Evaluation Factors and Associated Questions

FACTORS	QUESTIONS TO ASK
Capacity/Utilization	What is the maximum production or service capacity? How much of that capacity currently is being used?
Delivery	Does the supplier have sufficient facilities to deliver the required products or services on time? What is its inventory policy? Are there any back orders?
Quality	Is there evidence of a total quality management (TQM) philosophy? What evidence does the organization show in terms of quality leadership? Quality-assurance program? What are historical internal and external reject rates?
Make-Buy Program	Overall, how much of the supplier total cost of goods sold is coming from the supplier's suppliers? How much of what is being purchased will come from those suppliers?
Cycle Time/Lead Time	What is the range of the cycle/lead times of comparable products? How would an advanced scheduling notice improve them?
Productivity	What is the supplier's present productivity? Given productivity is defined as the ratio between output and input, what is the likelihood of increasing output by keeping the same input and decreasing input by keeping the same output?
Flexibility	How able and willing is this supplier to making changes? Last-minute changes? Does the supplier's leadership have an open and flexible attitude?
References	Which organizations does the supplier list as references? What are their positions in their respective markets? Will they be willing and able to provide information on this supplier?

FACTORS	QUESTIONS TO ASK
Electronic Capabilities	Does the supplier have an enterprise resource planning (ERP) system? If so, what is it? If not, how will planning and communication take place? Can the supplier handle EDI or e-commerce transactions?
Breadth of Product Line	Does the supplier have the ability to make multiple items? Provide a variety of services? Does it have a flexible manufacturing system? If so, how well is it using the technology?

Top-Tier Suppliers Versus Second-Tier Suppliers

There is ongoing debate on how much a buying organization should be involved in measuring the performance of second-tier suppliers. Organizations such as Kennametal and Air Products Inc. segregate top-tier and second-tier suppliers and do not spend much organization resources on measuring the performance of second-tier suppliers.[15] A manager at Kennametal, referring to second-tier suppliers, said, "They're not very strategic, so we don't go through the rigor of monthly measurements for those." However, a manager from Open Ratings, a Dun & Bradstreet company, questioned the "lack of scrutiny of lower-tier suppliers." This manager commented, "You can focus your attention on what's most important, but if you don't have screws, you can't ship the product. The last thing someone running a materials organization needs is not being able to ship a product because they don't have screws."[16]

Recently, the chief procurement officer (CPO) of a major automaker visited a second-tier supplier in Phoenix, Arizona, that was supplying an electronic component to its first-tier supplier, Delphi Corp. This major automaker had been measuring the performance of what Delphi did but did not measure the performance of this second-tier supplier. However, when a quality problem reoccurred and Delphi could not respond adequately, the problem was investigated and pinpointed to this electronic parts supplier in Phoenix. All of sudden, a second-tier supplier came on the radar screen of this major automaker and the problem was deemed strategic enough to involve the CPO.

Therefore, it makes sense to start paying more attention to evaluating second-tier suppliers, and a good place to begin measuring the performance of second-tier suppliers is with ones that supply strategic parts. Honda of America does this well, and in a systematic way. Honda has approximately 400 "core" suppliers, not counting indirect materials suppliers. Many of these core suppliers are second-tier and third-tier suppliers that supply strategic parts to Honda. In the context of this particular study, about 50 percent of second-tier and higher suppliers came from Honda's core supplier list — they were chosen either directly by Honda or indirectly by the top-tier supplier who was given Honda's core supplier list. The strategic importance evolved various considerations such as cost per part, standardization, intellectual property and consistent quality. These core suppliers, regardless of their position in the supply chain of one particular subassembly (e.g., instrument panel or center console), all received a report card from Honda every month.[17]

Issues in Conducting Site Visits

The requirement to thoroughly evaluate a supplier always entails visiting the supplier facilities, whether international or domestic, or whether it's manufacturing or service-based. During site visits, the supply management professional must be aware of certain issues, such as having a clear focus and reason for conducting site visits, costs versus benefits of site visits, site inspection team composition, factors evaluated at the site and timing of visits.

A supplier visit is a great technique in terms of obtaining firsthand knowledge of the supplier's facility, work environment, logistics expertise and operational practices such as quality control, organizational layout, operator training and attitudes, as well as inventory management. Representatives from the supply management organization can gain much information on the level of technology at the supplier facility, the education and training of the workers, the general culture of the supplier organization and the working relationship between the workers and management. These visits can be costly in terms of time allocation, airfare, food and lodging, but these costs need to be weighed against potential benefits. For example, unaudited suppliers with disorganized facilities, poor inventory management, insufficient capacity and/or untrained workers eventually would lead to performance failures and negative consequences at the supply management organization's site (e.g., line downtime or high cost of recovery).

Given the cost of site visits, it is imperative the supply management organization choose its representatives well. It should have cross-functional representation consisting of individuals from supply management such as quality assurance, and also operations and engineering. The frequency of the visits depends on the level of supplier certification and in general is commensurate with the supplier's performance. As discussed later in this chapter, a supplier with a high level of certification and a proven track record of performance should not require as frequent visits as an uncertified supplier without a track record. Also, the supply management professional needs to make advance plans on the timing of the visit. Generally, the time of the visit should correspond with a slack period for the supply management professional. The supply professional may choose to visit the supplier during its busy period just to see how the system operates under stress.

During the visit, the visiting team should follow a clearly laid-out checklist of factors that need to be appraised. Because hard measures such as quality or delivery records can be obtained through documents, during the site visits it makes sense to focus on the issues of worker morale, management-worker relationships or cultural fit, such as how well the supplier's organizational culture fits with the buying organization's culture. Figure 7-6 provides a list of specific areas of evaluation.

Site visits allow an opportunity to observe and gain firsthand knowledge about the supplier. A good place to focus on is housekeeping and workplace organization. This is the most obvious aspect of facility management. When a facility is disorganized, that organization may have to deal with many wasteful practices such as time spent looking for parts and tools, hidden machine problems, duplicate work, disorganized work, etc. The team also should watch for smooth workflow. Observe the number of bottleneck operations with large work-in-process inventories sitting in front of them, and in particular pay attention to how these bottlenecks are managed.

Figure 7-6   Potential Areas of Evaluation During Site Visits

Quality of the working relationship with the supplier
Supplier's work norms and level of trust among workers
Supplier's approach to managing teams and projects
Qualification of the supplier's staff
Ease of communication with the supplier's staff, and their responsiveness and openness
Supplier's approach to the negotiations and the degree of flexibility shown
Supplier's willingness to be flexible and reach agreement
Supplier's willingness to accept and manage risk
Entrepreneurial nature of the supplier organization
Relationships between the supplier management and staff
Supplier's approach for dealing with existing customers

Source: Adapted from POISE "Evaluation Guidance." Available at www.pasa.nhs.uk/pasa/Doc.aspx?Path= %5BMN%5D%5BSP%5D/Guidance%20Documents/POISE/POISE_H_Evaluation_Guidance_V3%201_Nov04.doc.

In addition, the team should get a good sense of worker morale and worker attitude and the general culture of the organization. Worker morale is strongly influenced by upper management's treatment of its employees. Just by talking to several workers in private, the supply management professional can develop an opinion on how much those employees like or dislike working at that facility. If employees dislike the organization, high worker turnover may exist.

Supplier Certification

Supplier certification is a way to determine whether a supplier has the basic ability to meet the buying organization's needs for the goods or services that it supplies. Certification can be given to a supplier at the organizational level. Certification also can occur at a particular parts level. When a supplier receives certification at the parts level and presents it to the supply management organization, the supply management organization becomes aware of what this supplier can and cannot do before it invests time and money. Certification also gives the supply management organization an opportunity to forgo an on-site inspection.

Certification is accomplished by setting guidelines for uniform standards. For example, ISO 9000 sets standards for customer focus, involvement of people, process approach, etc. In other words, organizations with the same certification are presumed to follow the same general guidelines. One such example is ISO 14001, which addresses environmental management standards by focusing on reducing energy consumption and lowering waste generation and disposal costs. The ultimate goal of certification is to create conformance and maintain control.

Some basic factors in certification include quality, delivery, cost, technology, environmental standards, financial standards, communication capabilities and business practices and processes. The level of importance of these factors varies across industries and organizations.

Brief History of Supplier Certification

During the time of the Qin dynasty, the Great Wall was built in China. When the soldiers learned that some of the bricks had defects in them, they traced them back to the source. Apparently, there were primarily two sources for bricks: the slave camps consisting of foreign workers and the camps of their own Chinese soldiers. The workers in slave camps were less quality-conscious than China's own soldiers when making bricks. As a result, the Chinese soldiers in charge of building the Great Wall had all the bricks that came from the slave camps coded for traceability, while they did not require this code on the bricks from their own camps. The slave camps were not certified, but their own camps were. To this day, if one were to pay close attention to the bricks while walking along the Great Wall, one could tell which bricks came from the certified suppliers and which ones did not.[18]

During World War II, bomb-making factories in the United Kingdom had problems with bombs detonating while they were still in weapons factories. The Ministry of Defense placed inspectors in factories to oversee production and tried to find ways to create conformance and control, which led to the implementation of factory certification. Around the same time, the United States developed a standard for military procurement. Later, building on what the military had done, the National Aeronautics and Space Administration (NASA) put together a similar quality standard for its suppliers. The British Standard Institute (BSI) published the first UK standard for quality assurance. By 1979, it had developed BS 5750, which set the precedence for later standards. Then, the International Organization for Standardization (ISO) came into existence in 1947 and began setting management standards in 1987 with ISO 9000. With the emergence of the European Union, ISO 9000 certification has become mandatory for all suppliers wanting to do business with organizations in EU countries.[19]

Supplier Categories

To increase managerial efficiency, many supply management organizations have categorized suppliers into different groups. This type of categorization in general indicates that the supply management organization has evaluated these suppliers and has placed them in one or more than one of its categories. The supply management organization typically has a process to recognize supplier performance over a period of time. When a supplier's performance remains high over a period of time, it achieves a higher level of recognition by the supply management organization. As the supplier achieves each level, integration into the supply management organization's operation and an increased use of quality systems are accomplished. On the softer side, a higher level of trust also is generated, which often helps reduce inefficient safeguarding between the supply management organization and the supplier. Figure 7-7 contains a brief overview of these supplier categories.

Figure 7-7   Supplier Categories

CATEGORY	DESCRIPTION
Approved	Suppliers that meet the supply management organization's selection criteria and have been added to the approved list.
Preferred	Suppliers that an organization has determined meet its expectations for quality, delivery and/or price and that are able to respond to unexpected changes.
Partnered	Suppliers that have a close working relationship with the supply management organization in order to attain some advantages from each other in a positive way. A partnership in this context does not imply a legal relationship. Buyer-supplier partnerships may be of operational importance, such as a long-term, single-source relationship with an office supplier, or of strategic importance, such as a long-term, single-source relationship with a supplier of a product or service of strategic importance.
Certified	Suppliers with quality-control systems that have proved to be highly reliable, thus eliminating the need for incoming inspection.
Prequalified	Suppliers that are added to a supply management organization's approved list by passing its preliminary screening and selection criteria.
Certifiable	Suppliers that are not currently certified by the supply management organization but show strong evidence to become certified.
Disqualified	Individuals, companies or other organizations that fail to meet the standards established by a supply management organization and are barred from competing for that organization's business.
Debarred	Individuals, companies or other organizations that are suspended, usually on a temporary basis, from selling or otherwise doing business with a supply management organization.
Diverse	Suppliers that are selected to increase the diversity of a supply management organization's supply base.

An *approved supplier* has passed the necessary requirements. This may include submission of samples for testing or other steps to approve the item or service to be purchased. It also may include inspection of the supplier's manufacturing and quality systems. A *preferred supplier* provides desirable quality, delivery or prices for the supply management organization and reacts positively to unforeseen needs such as changes in order volume, specification and service requirements. These suppliers are expected to take the initiative to suggest ways to respond to these changes and meet the supply management organization's needs. They may even warn the supply management professional in advance of factors that may affect the supply management organization's operations.

A *partnered supplier* has a long-term relationship with the supply management organization. These relationships usually are marked by a large volume commitment, joint product or service development, joint production planning and ever-green contracts. Even though supply management and the supplier in this relationship may not always have a collaborative relationship (some might even be adversarial at times), they understand each other well, and their operations usually are integrated in terms of planning and processing.

A *certified supplier* is a supplier whose organizationwide quality-control system entails a large-scale quality-assurance system such as ISO 9000 or one developed by the supply management organization or industry. When certification occurs with a specific supply management organization, the quality-control systems of both supply management and the supplier are closely integrated. In this way, total costs associated with quality are reduced through the elimination of duplicate efforts and the use of statistical process control and other quality-control processes and information sources.

Prequalified suppliers are approved to do business with the supply management organization. The prequalification process entails examining such factors as financial strength, facilities, location, size, technology, labor status, management, costs, terms and references. A *certifiable supplier* is typically in one of three stages of certification: (1) in the process of becoming certified, (2) already certified by another division of the same organization or (3) certified by another organization. When a stamping organization in Cleveland, Ohio, was dropped from GM's supplier list after being certified as its Spear One supplier (Spear One is a GM supplier quality certification standard), Honda became interested in this supplier because of that certification and sent a delegate to build a relationship. This supplier was considered a certifiable supplier from Honda's perspective.

Typically, a supplier would not be disqualified until several steps have been taken to correct the underlying performance problems. *Disqualification* usually occurs as a last resort. *Debarred suppliers* are individual organizations that are suspended, usually on a temporary basis, from selling or otherwise doing business with a buying organization. *Diverse suppliers* are selected to promote diversity in a supply management organization's supply base. A supply management organization typically has a policy to maintain certain percentages of women-owned and minority-owned suppliers. Diversity is discussed in more detail in Chapter 8, "Supplier Relationship Management."

Types of Certification

There are three primary types of supplier certification: (1) international organization initiated (e.g., ISO 9000), (2) industry-specific (e.g., QS 9000) and (3) organization-specific (e.g., Boeing's supplier certification program). ISO 9000 is a quality-assurance program that places more emphasis on process and incorporates total quality-management practices in later versions. In its newest version, it applies to "organizations seeking advantage through the implementation of a quality management system; organizations seeking confidence from their suppliers that their product requirements will be satisfied; users of the products; (and) those internal or external to the organization who give advice or training on the quality management system appropriate to that organization ..."[20] QS 9000 is an application of ISO 9000 specific to the automotive industry, developed by General Motors, the Ford Motor Co. and Chrysler LLC, and launched in 1994. QS 9000 is essentially a prescribed quality-assurance system for suppliers in the automobile industry that supply parts, materials and services.

The last type of certification is organization-specific. For example, Applied Materials Inc. specializes in "nanomanufacturing technology" and sells equipment in the high-tech industry. All suppliers, new or existing, are required to perform what Applied Materials Inc. calls the F-52 ISAT self-assessment. ISAT stands for "integrated supplier assessment tool" and has five criteria: (1) standardized supplier quality assessment, (2) lean manufacturing and capacity management, (3) special process technical assessments, (4) business alignment and (5) business infrastructure. Once certification is awarded, Applied Materials makes it clear that it may conduct an on-site validation for any annual assessment. [21]

Boeing has a preferred-supplier certification program. Suppliers are evaluated on three areas: (1) advanced quality system inspection, (2) business processes and (3) performance. The benefits of being selected as a preferred supplier are selection preference and reduced inspection as well as industry recognition and additional business opportunities. There are three levels of certification: gold, silver and bronze. The scores are given on the following categories: cost, quality, product delivery, leadership, technology and support.[22]

Process of Certification

Supplier certification typically occurs at two different levels. The first is the supplier organization level; the supplier organization is certified by the supply management organization through the supplier certification process. Once the supplier is deemed capable of meeting the requirements of supply management, this supplier becomes a certified or preferred supplier (as discussed previously). A supplier is certified for both products and services; for example, the Eastman Kodak Co. certifies its suppliers when products and services consistently meet its requirements and are delivered in a timely manner.[23] The next level of certification occurs at the specific parts level. Typically, only certified suppliers become parts-certified. When the supplier and supply management engage in certifying the supplier for a specific part, both organizations already are familiar with each other and the certification process. When the specific parts are certified, the process that is reviewed and the areas of concern that are involved are much more specific and technical. Processes vary depending on the type of parts and materials, as well as on what the evaluation teams will engage in when conducting a review and how they conduct it.

Figure 7-8 shows a general process of supplier certification at the supplier organization level. First, representatives from the supply management organization and the supplier meet and agree on how to communicate with each other, review current product or service specifications, and classify desirable characteristics of the products or services. Supplier performance history also is jointly reviewed and discussed.

The next step entails a period of observation. The supplier certification team from the supply management organization observes the performance of the supplier for a period of time ranging from weeks to years. The duration of the period can be defined by the number of conforming parts and on-time units or lots based on anticipated volume, or the number of dropped calls at a call center. On occasion, for suppliers with an exceptional performance record (e.g., 100 percent conformity to all requirements to date), some supply management organizations have waived this step. In either case, it is imperative that the approach be joint and collaborative between the visiting supply management certification team and representatives from the supplier side. Without such an approach, the period of observation likely will be fraught with manipulation techniques to gain an advantage and unproductive political maneuvering, which may lead to unreliable data collection and biased observations.

Using a collaborative approach, the teams can work together to identify and solve problems. Typical problem-solving tools are available for these teams such as the Ishikawa tools that include the cause-and-effect fishbone chart, Pareto analysis, histogram and scatter diagram. There are also approaches used in the Toyota Production System (TPS), such as the five whys, kanban, andon, gemba, etc. See Figure 7-9 for a definition of these problem-solving tools.

After a period of joint performance observations and problem-solving, the teams should be ready to take actual measurements. Establishing critical quality characteristics and target values is the first thing that must be performed when actually assessing the process or products. The measurement method for each critical characteristic must be discussed, and the measurement frequency also needs to be established. Critical characteristics most significantly affect the product's *form, fit and*

Figure 7-8 Key Steps in Supplier Certification

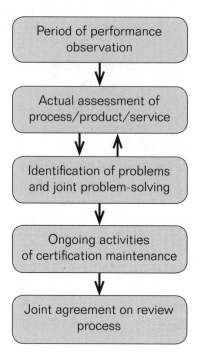

function, given the normally anticipated level of variation. Form refers to the appearance, fit refers to assembly of parts and function refers to the functionality of the part or product.

The goal of the ongoing step of the certification process is to make sure the supplier maintains the required performance level. The best way to ensure this is to emphasize continuous improvement of the process capability. The supplier needs to show evidence of an effective internal audit system. The communication flow established by the two organizations as part of step one will continue during ongoing activities to maintain certification. Once the supplier is certified, the supply management organization puts a certain level of trust in the supplier's capability. Consequently, the supplier must understand that product and service conformity and timely delivery are much more important.

Figure 7-9   Typical Problem-Solving Tools

Fishbone Chart	A cause-and-effect diagram that captures all the possible causes of a problem in a format designed to show their relationships to the problem (the effect) and to each other. The diagram resembles the skeleton of a fish.
Pareto Analysis	The process of determining the small minority of a population that accounts for the majority of a given effect. For example, in inventory management, 20 percent of the inventoried items account for 80 percent of the total dollars.
Histogram	A diagram of values measured versus the frequency with which each occurs. When a process is running normally (only common causes are present), the histogram is depicted by a bell-shaped curve.
Scatter Diagram	One of the seven tools of quality, a scatter diagram is a graph used to analyze the relationship between two variables. One variable is plotted on the x-axis and the other on the y-axis. The graph will show possible relationships between them. Regression analysis and other statistical techniques can be used to quantify that relationship.
Five Whys	The concept describes a disciplined analytical process that uses the practice of asking why a given failure occurred five times or more to get to the root cause of the problem. Each disciplined question requires a meaningful answer and analysis.
Kanban	A Japanese term meaning "signal." It is usually a printed card that contains specific information such as part name, description, or quantity, that signals a cycle of replenishment for production and materials. It is an order-release mechanism and one of the primary tools of a just in time (JIT) manufacturing system.
Andon	A tool of visual management, originating from the Japanese for "lamp." Lights are placed on machines or on production lines to indicate operation status. Common color codes are: green (normal operations), yellow (changeover or planned maintenance) and red (abnormal, machine down). Often combined with an audible signal such as music or an alarm. (see www.isixsigma.com/dictionary/Andon-585.htm)
Gemba	Japanese term that means workplace where day-to-day activities are performed. If problems occur, engineers should go to the workplace to determine why. (see www.isixsigma.com/dictionary/Gemba-858.htm)

Source: Unless noted otherwise, *ISM Glossary of Key Supply Management Terms*, 4th ed (Tempe, AZ: Institute for Supply Management™, 2006).

Supplier Development

Supplier development activities are conducted by the supply management organization to help suppliers improve the quality of the services or supplied parts and assemblies, the reliability of delivery performance and productivity leading to manufacturing cost savings. As defined in the *ISM Glossary* (2006), supplier development is a systematic effort to create and maintain a network of competent suppliers, and to improve various supplier capabilities that are necessary for the supply management organization to meet its competitive challenges. After General Motors engaged more than 2,000 suppliers in its supplier development program, a company manager stated that the gains had been "average supplier productivity improvements of more than 50 percent, lead time reductions of up to 75 percent, and inventory reductions averaging 70 percent." Honda of America, as part of its supplier development program, changed the layout of a welding process of one of its suppliers and reduced costs by more than $200,000 per year.[24] These records of accomplishments motivated many supply management organizations to engage in supplier development activities, making such activities an integral part of their supplier management strategies. Cultivating new sources of supply is discussed in Chapter 8, "Supplier Relationship Management."

Concepts of Continuous Improvement

Supplier development is based on continuous improvements that build on each other, eventually leading to a significant difference in performance. The much-heralded cost-reduction programs at Honda and Toyota, which reduced the cost of manufacturing their top-selling products, Honda Accord and Toyota Camry, by more than 25 percent during the mid-1990s, are attributed to a series of small incremental changes. For example, Honda used to attach a small capacitor to its cigarette lighter as a safety measure, but the supplier engaged in making cigarette lighters suggested that this capacitor was not necessary. Toyota's suppliers also came up with ways to cut costs and increase efficiency in how the wire harnesses were assembled. By involving suppliers in their value analysis/value engineering (VA/VE) efforts (discussed later in this chapter), Honda and Toyota made these small changes on a continuous basis. In the end, those many small changes added up to revolutionary outcomes.

Cost is an important area that requires continuous improvement. In particular, design is where about 80 percent of product and service costs are determined, and quality should be designed into products and services. Therefore, it is important to monitor design processes over time, to ensure continuous improvement techniques are applied. For example, an electronics organization had to do a $500,000 recall, only to find out later that the problem could have been corrected in the design phase for $37.

General Supplier Education and Involvement

Many large and small supply management organizations provide training for their suppliers in the areas of statistical process control (SPC), just in time (JIT) for both materials requirement planning (MRP) and kanban, enterprise resource planning (ERP), Six Sigma programs and lean operations. They also provide avenues to discuss zero-defects programs and new model launches. These training programs are offered because supplier competence in these technologies is required to create more integration with the supply management organization's operation. The goal is to help suppliers gain a comprehensive view of the supply management organization's products and service needs and how the suppliers' products and services are going to fit into the final products and services. In this regard, many organizations, such as Honda and BMW, emphasize that all their suppliers, whether top tier, second tier or third tier, are engaged in making a Honda or a BMW, because eventually all their parts will fit into the final product.

There are advantages and areas of caution when engaged in supplier training. The advantages are obvious: improvement in supplier performance, supplier's increased familiarity with the supply management organization, and establishment of an informal support network among suppliers. The areas of caution include: the supply management organization must put its promises and principles into practice and must be willing to maintain a supportive culture; otherwise, training may have no real impact on supplier performance.[25] Also, the supply management organization must ensure confidentiality of any issues that might appear and be cognizant of potential problems that might occur when competing suppliers are engaged in the same training.

In training suppliers, the concept of Toyota's "gemba" should play an important role. *Gemba* means "go, see" and in this context it entails the supply management professional visiting the supplier to see its operation as well as the supplier coming to see the supply management professional's organization. Certainly, visiting each other's facilities can help ensure a better understanding of each other's operations, resulting in opportunities for mutual improvement. In this regard, training can move beyond classroom activities and to actual events and problems that might happen on the shop floor either at the supplier's operation or at the supply management organization.

Process of Supplier Development

Figure 7-10 illustrates the overall process of supplier development.[26] This process assumes that the supply management organization is willing to commit resources to developing its suppliers. It is not effective to simply issue mandates to suppliers that they should make improvements. The process of supplier development is built on the assumption that supply management professionals are willing to get involved in the supplier's operations.

Figure 7-10   Supplier Development Process and Required Actions

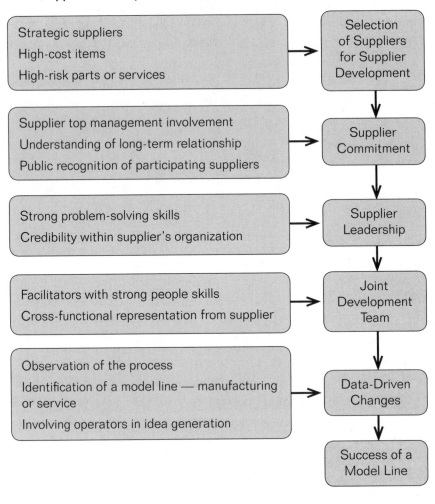

The supply management organization should segment its suppliers and start development with suppliers that deliver strategically important items. These suppliers tend to supply high-cost and high-risk items — for instance, an engine to an automaker or a microprocessor to a cell phone manufacturer. Furthermore, supplier commitment must come from the supplier's leadership team. They need to dedicate resources and be willing to celebrate and reward successes. Whatever the case may be, the supply management organization must make it clear that supplier development initiatives assist, and not replace, what they do. Also, having a commitment to a long-term relationship and expectation of relationship continuity is critical in gaining the supplier's top management commitment and participation. For example, publicly recognizing all the key suppliers that have participated or will participate in supplier development and their successes or potential successes might trigger the competitive spirit and help gain supplier commitment.

Supplier leadership for a development program normally should come from the technical personnel or middle-level management and not from top management. The changes made through the supplier development program typically occur at the core of the value-adding processes and the leader should be someone who is intimately familiar with those activities.

According to Honda, "It has got to hurt the supplier to take that person from his normal job and put him on the [development] project."[27] The leader will play a pivotal role in sustaining the development activities after the initial set of development projects with representatives from the supply management organization. Without this person championing the effort and garnering continuing support from top management, the initial enthusiasm for development activities will most likely dissipate and fall by the wayside. Therefore, top management's commitment must be translated into finding an internal leader at the supplier organization.

Reverse Marketing

While supplier development emphasizes the organization's present suppliers and their present capabilities, reverse marketing focuses on new suppliers and new capabilities. Reverse marketing is defined in the *ISM Glossary* (2006) as an aggressive approach to developing a relationship with a supplier in which supply management takes the initiative in making the proposal for the relationship and the specific business transactions. In this sense, marketing is conducted by the customer rather than by the seller, thus the term, *reverse marketing*. This requires much more direct investment by the supply management organization, requiring leadership in various aspects of financial, technical or strategic commitment.

The focus is on creating new sources and new capabilities that the supply management organization needs but presently is lacking. For instance, a bakery in Canada was caught in a cost-price squeeze in which the cost from the protein-rich "hard" flour was going up while the price of its bread was falling in the market. It needed a lower-cost supplier. The bakery first tried renegotiating with its existing suppliers but that effort failed. It then considered producing the hard flour internally but decided against it because of the associated risks. This bakery then partnered with a "soft" flour mill and agreed to help it expand its hard flour manufacturing capability. The bakery offered a long-term contract and expertise, and the soft flour mill raised the capital and lots of commitment to learn and make it work.[28]

Comparison of Supplier Development and Reverse Marketing

Figure 7-11 compares the key characteristics of reverse marketing practices to typical supplier development practices. Supplier development can occur in all types of partnerships or supplier relationships, as discussed previously, so long as supply management's commitment is minimal and the changes entail incremental improvement. However, reverse marketing requires a strategic partnership (as discussed in Chapter 8, "Supplier Relationship Management"), more direct and long-term involvement by the supply management organization, and the changes involve major shifts in the supplier organization.

Implications for Domestic and International Supplier Diversity

In the United States, many of the ideas behind reverse marketing can be applied to cultivating historically disadvantaged suppliers. Because the diversity of the market has been increasing, it makes sense to increase the diversity of a supply base. However, a supply management organization often may find that the capability of the minority-owned and women-owned suppliers, especially from economically depressed regions,

---

Figure 7-11   Comparison of Reverse Marketing and Supplier Development Practices

	REVERSE MARKETING	SUPPLIER DEVELOPMENT
Timeframe	Future	Present
Target Suppliers	Suppliers that are motivated but currently lack the capability to supply necessary parts or services	Suppliers that currently are supplying parts and services but will need to improve on quality and cost
Supply Management Commitment	Very high financial, technical and strategic leadership commitment	Moderate technical assistance
Types of Improvements	Major improvements; drastic changes	Minor improvements; incremental changes
Degree of Partnership Commitment	Strategic partnership	Any type: basic, operational, business or strategic partnership

Source: Adapted from T. Choi, "Reverse Marketing in Asia: A Korean Experience," *Business Horizon* 42(5) (1999): 34-40.

---

lag behind other suppliers in terms of quality, cost and delivery. In such cases, the strategy of reverse marketing may need to be seriously considered.

When supply management organizations begin to purchase from international suppliers in developing countries, they may be asked by the government to engage in some form of reverse marketing. The supply management organization may be mandated to maintain a certain level of local content and would have no other choice but to exercise reverse marketing. For example, when Volkswagen first moved into China, it offered some extraordinary incentives to its Chinese parts suppliers such as paying them at the European rate if the quality level met its requirements.[29] As the diversity of the supply base increases domestically and internationally, it is likely some form of reverse marketing will need to be exercised.

Creating Early Success

It is critical that the first supplier development or reverse marketing project is a success. This is in line with W. Edwards Deming's suggestion to celebrate small wins. People have a tendency to be drawn to success and it is important that workers at the supplier organization associate supplier development with success. Therefore, once the improvements are made, the success must be publicized. The joint team and the supplier leader must celebrate every small success with those involved. Getting suppliers interested in new products, services and processes early is a complimentary way to gain commitment and increase project success.

Early Supplier Involvement

Early supplier involvement (ESI) entails involving suppliers in the initial stages of the design process. Lucent Technologies, now Alcatel-Lucent, attributes its ability to reduce costs to early supplier involvement as well as early supply management involvement in new product development. Championing this effort is a group of managers called "life-cycle managers." One of the primary functions of these managers is to help members of the design team select the right supplier by informing them who the key suppliers are for a given product. One life-cycle manager says, "We get involved at the concept phase of a product and begin designing the supply chain. We help the product team discover the implications of their design ideas from a supply chain perspective." These managers are given development schedules and they bring in appropriate suppliers at appropriate times.[30]

Potential Benefits of ESI

ESI is critical because 70 percent to 80 percent of the cost of the product or service is determined during the design or specification phase. Suppliers are experts in their area, and once their ideas and capabilities are incorporated in the design phase through ESI, the supply management professional will see the benefits in the areas of faster time to market, improved functionality of the final product, improved manufacturability and quality, reduced cost and assurance of availability.

In particular, cycle-time reduction can be a tremendous benefit of ESI. By incorporating the supplier's ideas and technology rather than reinventing the wheel, the supply management professional can get new products and services to market much quicker. Also, by locating the supplier's engineers with the supply management organization's engineers, whether those engineers are responsible for service or product design, provides both organizations with the opportunity to work together to resolve problems and issues as they occur, by pooling their skills to develop better solutions. One of the earliest success stories in the United States came from Chrysler's 1995 Dodge Neon project. By involving its suppliers early on, Chrysler's Small Car Platform Team was able reduce the cycle time by about two years.[31]

Areas of Supplier Involvement

A supply management organization must consider certain managerial areas when involving suppliers in ESI — design or specification development responsibility, product or service complexity, form of specifications provided, supplier influence on specifications, timing of supplier involvement, component testing responsibility, training responsibility and supplier product or service development capability (see Figure 7-12). Each of these managerial areas is discussed in the following section.

Three options are available when considering who actually will create the design or specifications: the supply management organization, the supplier or both organizations. On the one hand, a supply management organization such as Honda has a strong preference to develop new products in-house — this approach typically is called *white box sourcing*. Honda gives its suppliers completed blueprints when sourcing. On the other hand, Chrysler has a tendency to expect its top-tier suppliers for interior subassemblies (such as center consoles or instrument panels) to understand its market and design the product. Supplier engineers are invited to design meetings during early stages to discuss the functionality of the product and are expected to come back with a technical design that meets the performance specifications — *black box sourcing*. Lastly, *gray box sourcing* refers to the supply management organization and the supplier developing the product jointly.

Figure 7-12   Characteristics of Supplier Role for Various Levels of Product or Service Complexity

ISSUE	RELATIONSHIP CHARACTERISTICS			
Supplier Role	Contractual	Consultative	Partnering	Expert
Product Complexity	Simple parts	Simple assembly	Complex assembly	Complete module
Design Responsibility	Supply	Joint	Supplier	Supplier
Specifications Provided	Complete design	Detailed specifications	Critical specifications	Concept
Supplier Influence on Specifications	None	Present capabilities	Negotiation	Collaboration
Timing of Supplier Involvement	Prototyping	Postconcept	Concept	Preconcept
Component Testing Responsibility	Minor	Moderate	Major	Complete
Supplier New Product Development Capabilities	None	Little	Moderate	High

Source: Adapted from Mitchell Fleischer and Jeffrey K. Liker, *Concurrent Engineering Effectiveness: Integrating Product Development across Organizations* (Cincinnati: Hanser Gardner Publications, 1997).

The appropriate level and timing for ESI varies with the level of product or service complexity. Some are simple parts such as fasteners and simple metal parts, and some are simple assemblies such as putting together a power supply and a computer printer. But more complex products may be involved, such as complex assembly (e.g., keyboard) and complete modules (e.g., air bags). Specifications provided to suppliers also vary and can range from providing a complete design (i.e., white box sourcing) to just a description of a concept (i.e., black box sourcing). Gray box sourcing also can range from the supply management professional providing much of the detailed specifications to only providing key descriptions for the supplier to fill in.

Often, the supplier can influence the design process only on specific issues queried by the supply management professional. However, the supplier's influence expands when the context calls for a more collaborative approach where a spontaneous exchange of ideas can take place. The timing of supplier involvement is a big issue. The supplier can be invited to participate at any point during the product or service development process. It can come in after the design or specification has been completed and during the prototyping phase. It also can get involved even before the concept phase or thereafter, such as in the postconcept phase.

Conducting component testing is another area of supplier involvement. Once the first few parts are produced, testing them for form, fit and function is a critical step in the final stage of the design process. Responsibility can range from minor to complete. Last is the broad issue of how much new product development capability a supplier should acquire and maintain; this can range from having a few design engineers with computer-aided design (CAD) capability to having a full range of engineers (e.g., design to process engineers) with more sophisticated, rapid prototyping capabilities.

Supplier Roles in Product Development

As shown in Figure 7-12, a supplier can play basically four different roles during the product and service development process: (1) contractual, (2) consultative, (3) partner and (4) expert. These roles specify varying degrees of supplier involvement. When the role is merely *contractual*, the supplier primarily responds to what the supply management organization dictates. The supply management organization provides the designs or specifications, and the supplier provides simple parts or basic services. When the role is *consultative*, the supplier's degree of involvement increases. In this case, the supply management professional brings focused design questions to the supplier who offers ideas in response. The supplier may provide simple assembly and share joint responsibility in making the design work. Once the degree of involvement expands to the *partner's level*, the supply management organization provides only the critical specifications to the supplier who then does all the design or specification work. Lastly, in the *expert's role*, the supplier is considered the full-fledged design or specification development organization for the new product or service development effort. The supplier is involved from the very beginning of the product or service development and is responsible for the complete service, system or module.

Figure 7-12 lists these roles and relates them to various areas of supplier involvement discussed previously. The descriptions that appear under each supplier role can be viewed as ideal types that offer guidance to the supply management organizations as they interact with suppliers for their design or specification involvement. For example, suppose the intent was to use suppliers in a contractual role. However, somewhere along the line, the supply management organization realizes that the level of specifications provided to the supplier is vague and at the concept level. The supply management organization then should re-evaluate how it is interfacing with the supplier. When this occurs, the supply management professional might receive complaints from the supplier about inadequate information and unreasonably high expectations. Also, if the supply management organization intended to use the supplier in an expert role, but did not involve the supplier until after the concept phase is completed, this is a lost opportunity.

Value Analysis/Value Engineering

Value analysis and value engineering (VA/VE) is one of the tools a supply management professional uses to ensure the functional usefulness of the products and services purchased — or getting the most value for the money spent. It is unwise to pay too much for something, but it is even less wise to pay too little, if customer perceived value were to suffer. VA/VE is an aid in determining whether a supply management professional is paying too much or too little for an item. The *ISM Glossary* (2006) defines value analysis as a systematic and objective evaluation of the value of a product or service, focusing on an analysis of function relative to the cost of manufacturing or providing the item or service. Value analysis provides insight into the inherent worth of the final product or service, possibly altering specification and quality requirements that could reduce costs without impairing functional suitability.

VA/VE activities should be an integral part of the supply management organization. As mentioned previously, VA/VE was the foundation of Honda and Toyota's ability to reduce the cost of manufacturing their leading products (i.e., Honda Accord and Toyota Camry) by more than 25 percent.

VA/VE and Supply Management

When a supply management professional is involved in VA/VE activities, he or she views products or services as a bundle of functions.[32] Functions are captured in product or service features that customers can observe, experience and evaluate in order to make a purchase decision. Ultimately, what is being purchased is the functions that the product or service embodies to meet the needs of the customers. Therefore, when a supply management professional makes a purchase decision, what is being procured is a set of functions that fit together to meet engineering or the customer requirements.

The supply management and engineering staffs of the buying organization typically take ownership of VA/VE projects, while in supplier organizations, engineers and marketing and supply management personnel work on them. At the interface, when these professionals get together, they may travel to facilities belonging to both organizations to observe how a design affects manufacturing and discuss the possibility for simplifying the design of a product. They may discover that the process followed for a service delivery could be modified to increase customer satisfaction. When such activities take place for new products or services, they typically are referred to as *value engineering*. If they take place for existing products or services, they are called *value analysis*.

Process of VA/VE

Following are the steps involved in the VA/VE process:

1. A Pareto analysis can be used to help select products or services as candidates for a VA/VE analysis. A Pareto analysis is defined in Figure 7-9. The potential units associated with particular functions are listed, identifying those 20 percent to 30 percent of units that contribute to most of the cost.

2. Information on those target units is collected, the situation is examined, and a detailed analysis is conducted to create feasible alternatives. At this stage, some of the cost reductions or other improvements may not be spectacular, but many small changes eventually will be significant. Each function is associated with costs, and cost tables are prepared to compare costs with suggested design changes. Basically, what-if scenarios are evaluated with these cost tables. Once analysis is conducted and creative solutions are offered, solutions must be considered more carefully and synthesized with other solutions that may have been offered earlier. For example, if a proposed solution involves eliminating one electrical component, then serious consideration should be given to how this decision may affect other areas of functionality.

3. Lastly, changes must be implemented and followed up.

Services often benefit from the questioning philosophy of value analysis/value engineering. In one case, the statement of work for janitorial services stated "vacuum all offices daily." A supplier pointed out that only high-traffic areas need to be vacuumed daily while low-traffic areas need to be vacuumed only weekly. The resulting RFP created a cost savings. Substantial savings in service purchases can be accomplished by focusing on the result of the service rather than on the details of what services must be provided.[33]

Contents of VA and VE

Conceptually, VE should be distinguished from VA. The goals of both VE and VA are the same — to maintain the functionality of a product while producing it at a reduced cost. However, as discussed previously, if VE could be considered "the art of tinkering with parts and systems during their design state to improve value,"[34] VA can be thought of as tinkering with parts and systems to improve value after the design has been crystallized. The difference lies in timing — VE typically occurs during design, while VA typically occurs during mass manufacturing.

The idea behind VA/VE is to keep the functionality of the product the same but take out the cost. VE occurs during the redesign phase of the product, while VA occurs during the continuous improvement phase after the product has been redesigned and is in production.

Parts and Modules

Use of common parts begins with standardizing those parts. The underlying goal behind this effort is to simplify the product, reduce costs and maintain the functionality of the product, an important area of VA/VE.

Modules are defined as an assembly of parts that perform a function of value to the customer. Modules are different from subassemblies for modules are used in several final products. Increased modularization reduces the overall cost of the product. To the extent that modular designs tend to require much more up-front design activities compared to conventional, nonmodular design activities, the proliferation of modularization actually will lead to a reduction of VA/VE activities.

Tight tolerances usually are associated with the robustness of the product, but they also affect the overall cost of manufacturing. Often, because design engineers are uncertain about how the tolerances eventually will stack up in the final product, they tend to overspecify the level of required tolerances. In the end, however, the market is willing to pay for robustness only to a certain extent. Therefore, it makes sense that as the design process matures, engineers and supply management professionals look for ways to decrease costs by relaxing the tolerance to a level that the market is willing to accept.

Supply management professionals are engaged in offering a service to internal users. They must be involved in all activities of managing suppliers from performance appraisal to development to early supplier involvement. More and more, supply management professionals are required to engage not only in strategic issues of managing suppliers as partners but also in technical activities such as VA/VE. With the expanding role of supply management professionals, it is imperative that they garner managerial skills as well as the required technical skills.

Summary

A supply management professional works with a group of suppliers on an ongoing basis. To ensure the continued flow of goods and services from suppliers, the supply management professional acts as the gatekeeper for all key operational issues that occur between the supply management organization and its suppliers. This chapter focuses on how a supply management professional can best manage the existing suppliers to ensure good quality, on-time delivery and competitive cost. This chapter explains what the supply management professional can do to meet those requirements.

Key Points

1. Supplier performance appraisal or evaluation is key in managing suppliers. When selecting suppliers for evaluation, the criteria of purchasing volume, strategic importance and supply market conditions may be used.

2. Do not underestimate the importance of certain second-tier suppliers to the success of the supply management organization.

3. When evaluating a supplier, many data sources are available and the information gathered from these separate sources must be corroborative. The potential data sources include performance documents, reputation as expressed by other supply management organizations and its suppliers, and observations made during site visits.

4. Supplier certification has a strong historic foundation. A supplier can be certified by a single supply management organization or by an association in a particular industry or region. Certification may apply to the whole organization or individual product or service lines.

5. Supplier development activities entail a joint process between the supply management organization and its supplier(s). This process requires the direct involvement of the supply management organization in making improvements at the supplier's organization. The underlying principle is Toyota's gemba, by which the supply management organization is urged to go and see the activities at the supplier's facility.

6. The process of supply development entails the following steps: selection of suppliers for supplier development, explicit acknowledgment of supplier commitment, requisite supplier leadership, establishment of a joint development team, implementing data-driven changes and celebration of improvements.

7. ESI should be considered in terms of the type of areas of supplier involvement (e.g., design responsibility, product or service complexity, form of specifications provided, supplier influence on specifications, timing of supplier involvement, component testing responsibility and supplier product development capability) and characteristics of the supplier role (e.g., contractual, consultative, partnering and expert).

8. Involvement of supply management throughout the new product or service development process is imperative. During the early phases, it is typically easier to pick the most obvious solution, but as the design for functions become more crystallized toward the end of the new product or service development phases, the role of VA/VE becomes more intense and the level of required effort increases.

9. VA/VE focuses on reducing the cost while keeping the same functionality of the products or services. A product or service in this regard is viewed as a bundle of functions, and VA/VE entails unbundling these functions for their role in meeting customer requirements.

10. An important area of VA/VE is to increase the use of common parts and modules or service delivery processes. Design engineers have a tendency to "overengineer" a part or a module, so it is important that the supply management professional understands the market and the supplier's capability and makes sure the overengineering is avoided to the extent feasible.

8

Supplier Relationship Management

This chapter explores building better supplier relationships for the future. Chapter 7 dealt with the present, considering how best to manage present suppliers. This chapter looks at the future and considers key managerial issues involved in building positive relationships with suppliers, increasing diversity in the supply base and taking a broader perspective to strategically managing a supply base and the supply chain.

The chapter begins by addressing how to manage the basic relationship as specified in the contract (see Chapter 5, "Contracting") for the mutual benefit of the supply management organization and the supplier. The future may hold a short-term or long-term relationship, but the relationship should be perceived by both parties as fair and equitable, a hallmark of leading organizations such as Honda Motor Co. and Toyota Motor Co.[1] Contracts spell out the mutual understanding between the supply management organization and the supplier. To build a positive relationship, the contract must be treated with care and respect, for it defines the boundaries for both parties.

After addressing the overarching issue of relationship management and building an ongoing contractual relationship with a supplier, partnerships and strategic alliances will be discussed. While not all suppliers are going to establish partnerships and strategic alliances with the supply management organization, supply management will want to forge such relationships with all of its key suppliers. In particular, when selecting new suppliers and managing the relationship for the future, diversity issues must be considered as the business environment becomes more diversified both domestically and internationally. Finally, strategic issues surrounding the total supply base management are addressed, along with a discussion of supply chain management and its implications. Figure 8-1 provides an overview of how the chapter is organized.

Figure 8-1 Supplier Relationship Management for the Future

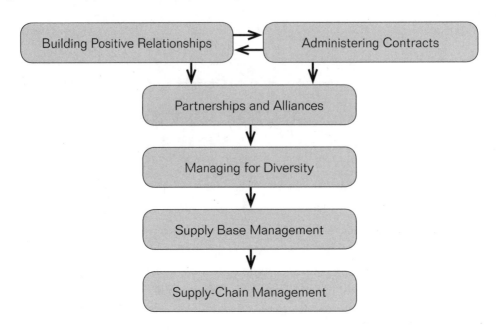

CHAPTER OBJECTIVES

• Explore the managerial issues involved in building a better supplier relationship for the future.

• Articulate the tangible and intangible benefits of a good supplier relationship.

• Consider contract administration as stipulating the context for basic relationship management.

• Examine the underlying rationale for partnership and different forms of partnership.

• Offer a special consideration to small and disadvantaged suppliers.

• Develop an overarching systems perspective of supply base management and supply-chain management.

Managing Positive Relationships

A positive relationship with suppliers provides many benefits. To reap these benefits, supply management professionals should be familiar with strategies for establishing those relationships with suppliers. Ultimately, the supply management organization may establish long-term, strategic partnerships with select suppliers.

Benefits of Good Supplier Relations

Developing goodwill between the supply management organization and suppliers has long been considered sound business policy. A good relationship facilitates good communication and can prevent many potential problems. Even if something un-expected happens (e.g., on occasion a supply management professional may need to ask a supplier to deal with a sudden surge in orders or move up a product delivery or service provision), these situations are better handled if the supply management professional maintains a cooperative business relationship with the supplier. Suppliers that are treated fairly more likely will be accommodating when dealing with rejected materials or service-related issues and other situations that may involve negotiated settlements. They also are more likely to provide technical support, inventory backup and other services. Negotiations may be shorter, terms may be simpler and disputes may be minimized.

Another more subtle yet important benefit of maintaining a good supplier relationship is that it provides a competitive advantage for the buying organization — a buying organization with good supplier relationships has a competitive advantage over other buyers. Whenever an organization has secured a resource that is hard to be duplicated by competitors, that translates into a competitive advantage.[2] A good sup-plier relationship takes time and commitment to develop; once established, it creates a competitive resource that is difficult for competitors to implement. This is in part why a leading organization such as Toyota does not mind disclosing its supply man-agement practices: even if its competitors knew how Toyota manages its suppliers, it would be very time-consuming and require intense effort on the part of its competi-tors to implement Toyota's practices.

Instilling a Culture of Good Relations

Establishing good supplier relations depends on the supply management professional's ability and willingness to foster the creation and improvement of a mutually satisfying arrangement. Several areas of management focus are needed to create a culture of good supplier relations. These management approaches require the collective effort of supply management professionals at the supply management organization and should not be left up to one or two individual supply management professionals.

A culture of good communication is where a good relationship starts; good communication facilitates the exchange of information in a complete and clear fashion. Several interorganizational contexts require this exchange of information.

The supply management professional needs to help suppliers understand the supply management organization's need, application, and use of the purchased material or service, so that the suppliers can formulate an overall concept behind the purchases. Supply management professionals must to be realistic about what is possible in terms of the product or service, as well as future business implications. In this regard, suppliers need communication regarding the scope and limitations of the product or service, the outlook for continued use and the probable quantities required, along with any special technical or commercial requirements.

Uncertainty creates risks and requires buffers, whether in inventory, extra workers or reserved capital. In most cases, suppliers are willing to live with these issues as a way of life. However, if the supply management organization does not keep its word and has a tendency to make unreasonable demands, that behavior breeds mistrust and lack of confidence, which, in turn, creates higher uncertainty for suppliers. In this type of relationship, suppliers know they have to build additional steps into their work processes and would prefer dealing with a different supply management organization if there is a choice to minimize their cost of doing business. Therefore, supply management professionals must remain true to their word and endeavor to develop a mutual confidence and trust in the statements and intents for the sake of both parties. They also need to show mutual consideration by not making unreasonable demands and by giving as much notice as possible about changes in schedules or instructions. They need to keep an open mind and be willing to waive or modify nonessential details of the agreement, if the modification does not impair quality and is to the advantage of either party.

Suppliers remember and appreciate the supply management organization taking a genuine interest in the mutual give-and-take of procurement, rather than focusing on strict contract fulfillment. This includes suggestions for cost reduction in the product or service itself and in methods of packing, shipping, usage, delivery and accounting. Maintaining good relations leads to an active desire to fulfill contractual obligations, minimizing inquiries and expediting action and ensuring prompt processing and payment of invoices.

Creating Good Relations

In addition to cultural issues such as values and norms, a supply management organization can adopt specific tactics to promote positive relationships with suppliers (see Figure 8-2).

Contract administration, including holding the supplier accountable for its performance commitments, should be conducted to preserve and enhance the supplier relationship as much as possible.

Figure 8-2 Relational Tactics and Descriptions

TACTICS	DESCRIPTIONS
Top Management Meetings and Business Reviews	For key suppliers, top management from the buying organization should meet periodically with supplier top management to discuss long-term strategies and objectives. Many leading organizations, such as Bristol-Myers Squibb, Intel or Toyota, hold such meetings. At these meetings, market trends are discussed and potential expansion plans are shared. More long-term technology issues are addressed and potential investment decisions are weighed.
Customer Focus	Everyone in the supply chain should understand that everyone serves the same final customer. This creates a common focus and is akin to how Honda tells all its parts and raw materials suppliers in its supply chain that they are engaged in manufacturing a Honda. All suppliers, regardless of where they are in the supply chain, have a common focus.
Timely Payment of Invoices	There is no better way to usher in a positive sentiment from suppliers than to pay them on time. Suppliers rely on payments from the supply management organizations to support their operations. Late payments undoubtedly create ill will and may cause financial problems affecting the supplier's ability to pay its suppliers or to perform its contract, thus unfavorably affecting the purchaser's customer service.
Periodic Supplier Surveys	Periodically solicit supplier feedback through surveys, asking questions about communications, general treatment (e.g., whether the supply management professionals are treating them with respect), accuracy of specifications, timeliness of payment and equitable application of policies and access to new opportunities.
Technology for Better Communications	Technologies can enhance two-way communications. The Internet, electronic data interchange (EDI) or enterprise resource planning (ERP) can provide excellent computer linkages. Certain Internet technologies can facilitate face-to-face communication.[3] The meetings often are critical to maintaining clear expectations and good performance.

(continued)

Figure 8-2   continued

TACTICS	DESCRIPTIONS
Supplier Training	Some supply management organizations provide their suppliers with training to help them improve quality and other processes. This is an investment in the supplier's performance, as well as an investment in the relationship. For instance, large Korean organizations, such as LG Electronics and Samsung, are known to offer training workshops for their suppliers that cover such wide-ranging topics as managerial leadership skills, problem-solving techniques and the application of computer-aided design (CAD).[4]
Assurance of Confidentiality	All cost, technology and performance information related to a supply management organization's suppliers should remain strictly confidential. Information leaked to one supplier about another often gets back to that supplier and may jeopardize the long-term relationship. Many organizations, such as Deere & Co., sign mutual confidentiality agreements with suppliers, but often suppliers choose not to enforce them because they do not want to risk losing business. However, they will remember the misconduct of the supply management organization and will be hesitant to engage in an open and trusting relationship with the supply management organization. Therefore, the supply management organization should strive to develop a reputation among its suppliers that it conducts business honorably by keeping such information in strict confidence.

Contract Administration

This section considers how to administer contracts and supplier management while building positive supplier relationships, whether long term or short term. Open and fair administration of a contract is the starting point for building such a relationship.

Contract Administration Concepts

Contract administration is the management of various facets of a contract to ensure that the contractor's total performance is in accordance with the contractual commitments and that obligations to supply management are fulfilled (*ISM Glossary*, 2006). Once fair pricing and terms and conditions for the organization are reached through effective negotiations, the focus turns to ensuring the organization receives full value for its expenditures. Contract administration involves all actions taken concerning a particular contract or purchase order after it is signed until final delivery, acceptance and closeout procedures are completed.

The U.S. government has been taking the lead in improving contract administration.[5] The Office of Federal Procurement Policy states that establishing a mutual understanding by communicating through conference or letter is the first step to good contract administration, once an award has been made. The understanding must to cover "the nature of the work, the type of contract, and the experience and commitment of the personnel involved." The policy also recommends establishing a "partnering" relationship to facilitate communication and avoid future problems. It cites construction projects as having been successful regarding contract administration through partnerships. Some key contract management concepts are discussed in the following sections.

Work Control. The concept of *work control* is necessary because contract administration needs to ensure that the supplier's performance complies with the contract and that the supplier is compensated for its work. Steps taken as part of work control include: work ordering, work completion, work inspection and acceptance, invoicing and payment. Once the work is ordered and completed, the outcome is inspected as a way of monitoring. When the work is accepted, it is invoiced and payment is issued.

For some types of contracts (e.g., indefinite delivery contracts, time and material or labor-hour contracts and cost-reimbursement contracts), the work ordering and work authorization processes are deferred until after the award. In those circumstances, ordering becomes a postaward or contract administration matter. In particular, procedures for cost reimbursement for contract work control often are considerably more complex than controls for other types of contracts (see Chapter 5, "Contracting," for more details). These procedures are used in large cost-reimbursement contracts extending over several years. Many cost-reimbursement contracts require establishing and maintaining the process of annual work plans (AWPs), work authorizations and notices to proceed (NTPs) as a means to assist in cost and schedule control. The AWP is a document that delineates the tasks to be performed in the budget year and a schedule leading to their completion. The NTP normally includes a statement of work, those key schedule milestones for task accomplishment, and the total amount of funds allotted to the tasks. On receiving the NTP, the supplier begins work and starts cost and schedule reporting for the tasks concerned.

Compliance. To assure compliance, a supply management professional must monitor supplier activities. This involves several techniques and procedures for determining if satisfactory delivery or contract completion is to occur in timely manner.

Contract performance is monitored to determine if it will be performed according to the contract requirements or if problems are developing that need to be addressed.

Even though contract compliance may primarily be the responsibility of the supply management organization, the actual day-to-day monitoring and administration may be conducted by other departments of the organization or third-party entities. For extremely complex contracts, very specialized purchases or highly technical contracts, the supply management professional may enlist the assistance of the internal customer using the product or service or a third-party administrator. The supply management professional must work closely with the end user and the third-party administrator so they understand not only the contract but also organization operating policies and procedures. The supply management organization has first-line responsibility to provide this information to these administrators, and well-established bilateral communication lines are critical. Ultimately, contract compliance involves having a clearly understood plan of action if the supplier fails to perform or the purchasing activity has a change of requirements.

Financial Responsibility. From the award of a contract to closeout, one concern for a supplier is to receive payment in a timely manner for work completed. The different types of contracts used by the supply management professional create different financial relationships between the supply management professional and the supplier. For instance, the supplier with a firm fixed-price contract has a strong incentive to perform in the most economical way, for every amount saved below the contract price is additional profit.

Under other contracts, such as labor-hour, time and materials and cost-reimbursement contracts, the supplier has little incentive to perform in the most economical way. Here, the supplier is entitled to compensation for either a fixed amount per hour or the costs incurred in doing the work, provided the expenses are not unreasonable. The work description in such contracts usually is broad because it is difficult to predict just what the supplier is required to do. This gives the supplier wide contractual authorization, which can permit the supplier to perform and charge for efforts other than those specifically desired by the supply management organization. Under such contracts, the supply management professional, or another representative at a remote location, needs to monitor and guide the supplier's efforts to prevent waste of funds and ensure the organization receives the services needed within the amount budgeted.

Approving Systems. The logic behind approving systems is to add the final control point to make sure the supplier takes financial responsibility in the cases discussed previously — labor-hour, time and materials and cost-reimbursement contracts. For instance, the U.S. federal government relies on a number of formalized programs to determine whether its major suppliers conform to law, regulation, good business practice and the federal norm. Many other governmental, quasi-governmental and institutional clients impose similar, although generally less rigid, requirements.

Obviously, no specific approval requirements exist when a firm fixed-price contract is applied. In cases of labor-hour, time and materials and cost-reimbursement contracts, however, requirements include a subcontract consent review process, supplier purchasing system review, employee compensation and other review programs. The most common of these formalized programs is the subcontract consent review process, which is explained in the subcontracts clause of most major contracts. In the case of government work, this clause requires suppliers to follow the "federal norm" in their award of subcontracts and purchase orders, and to request specific written consent to place certain larger subcontracts and purchase orders. The goal is to ensure that the supplier has made decisions for expenditures in accordance with the interest of its constituents (i.e., taxpayers) by reviewing the total system of subcontracts and purchase orders awarded by the prime supplier to its suppliers. In the private sector, this type of review can be performed by a group of delegates from the supply management organization or by an independent consulting organization specializing in external auditing.

Administrative Responsibilities. When administrating a contract, areas of responsibility for the supply management professional involve rules of purchasing, contract law, transportation, health and safety regulations and social responsibility. Most of these issues are delineated in the contract, and the supply management professional can collaborate with other experts in the supply management organization to achieve a successful closeout. However, the difficulty of administering a contract increases when a change or adjustment must be made. Changes fall into two primary areas: price adjustment clauses and administration change orders.

Generally, *price adjustment clauses* may result when changes occur in the supplier's established labor or materials costs. Adjustments are made according to the fluctuations in the supplier's established prices and with applicable labor and material cost indexes. The *administration change order* may become necessary when the terms as specified in the present contract must be modified regarding price, quantity, quality, delivery or other terms of agreement. Therefore, it is critical that the original contract define the equitable procedure for handling such changes for a proper settlement.

Contract Terms and Conditions. The supply management professional must know the terms and conditions of the contract to ensure that both parties are in compliance. Terms and conditions include information on quantity, price, delivery, shipping requirements, payment terms, quality specifications, engineering drawings and other related documents, sampling plans, conditions of acceptance, other important factors affecting acceptability of the product or service, and standard boilerplate terms and conditions. These provide legal protection to the supply management organization on matters such as contract acceptance, delivery performance, contract termination, shipment rejections, assignment and subcontracting, patent rights and payment procedures.

Documentation Requirements. Each contract has its own documentation requirements. The contract administrator is responsible for determining what they are and seeing that they are met. The documentation requirements may pertain to work orders, invoicing, work plans and performance measurements. Supplier insurance forms, bond requirements, verification of tax payments and verification of material payments by the supplier also may require necessary documentation. The procedure may be formal with written checklists or may involve handwritten notes in the contract file. The goal is to document all actions and verify all requirements.

Subcontract Plans. The supply management organization usually reserves the right to prior approval of subcontracting work planned by the supplier. On occasion, the supply management professional may have reservations about its supplier subcontracting work out and, therefore, create a contract that explicitly prohibits the supplier from subcontracting. Barring such reservation, contracts permit a supplier to subcontract as necessary to satisfactorily deliver performance requirements. Typically, the subcontractor clause is enforced in all cost-plus contracts and in fixed price with incentive contracts (see Chapter 5, "Contracting").

Contract Closeout. Contract closeout occurs when the terms of the contract are completed and both parties take actions to close out a contract. Typically, those actions include verifying that all work has been duly performed, accepted, properly invoiced and fully paid for. The supplier delivers all warranty documents. Bond agreements are terminated as appropriate. In the most complex contracts, a checklist for closeouts is recommended with the appropriate parties' signatures signifying completed work or action.

Supplier Management Concepts

Active supplier management is a vital ingredient in maintaining a long and mutually fruitful relationship with suppliers. The supply management professional must exercise professionalism toward the suppliers when the relationship involves long-term, strategic settings such as large dollar volume contracts, construction contracts, most service and maintenance contracts, and a just in time environment. A supply management professional should consider the following key areas of supplier management.

Standards of Performance. The first step in establishing a positive relationship with a supplier is by promoting a thorough understanding — by both the supply management organization and the supplier — of the standards of performance. The supply management professional should hold a conference with the prospective supplier either immediately before or after the contract is awarded to establish this understanding. The standards of performance as captured in the performance measures must be delineated in the specifications or statement of work, explicating the types of measurement methods when appropriate. The measures are regularly monitored and reviewed with the supplier while the contract is being administered.

Annual Work Plan. An annual work plan (AWP) is a document used in contract administration that provides the initial definition of tasks to be performed in the budget year and a schedule for their accomplishment (*ISM Glossary*, 2006). In the United States, the federal government has been a leader in procuring services and practices using a well-defined AWP. For instance, the U.S. Social Security Administration provides an AWP that outlines its major tasks and communicates them to its key constituents.[6] The AWP provides the initial definition of tasks to be performed in the given fiscal year and a schedule for completion. The AWP provides both funding guidance and program schedule requirements. Its writing is guided by the information given to the supplier by the supply management organization regarding the expected levels of funding, milestones based on the current master program schedule, and relevant scope information. During the AWP review, the supplier resource projections are reviewed and, on approval, tasks to be undertaken can be scheduled.

The specific elements of an AWP generally include goals and assumptions, work authorization review results, a schedule, staffing plan and cost estimate for the fiscal year. The AWP should be updated at the middle of each fiscal year. Work authorizations generally cover a variety of duties, including work breakdown structure designations for the work (see the appendix at the end of Chapter 5), information regarding the duration of the work authorization, the baseline cost estimate for the work, and references to the existing AWP and notices to proceed (NTP) to be issued subsequent to the work authorizations.

Supplier Feedback. In addition to monitoring the supplier's performance and providing feedback as presented in Chapter 7, an often overlooked aspect of successful supplier management is the solicitation of supplier feedback. Xerox Corp., for example, has been asking its suppliers to provide feedback regarding how Xerox performs as a supply management organization. The areas of supplier feedback may cover contracting, knowledge of the supply management professionals, accuracy of engineering specifications, specification of quality requirements and timeliness of payments.

Feedback may be sought through a written survey or face-to-face meetings. Surveys can reach a large group of suppliers, and face-to-face meetings can obtain contextually richer information from suppliers. Either way, the supply management organizations using supplier feedback usually find that the feedback plays a significant role in improving supplier relations, and ensuring that high-quality materials and services are received on time.

Management of Supplier. When evaluating a supplier's progress, the supply management professional focuses on actual progress toward completing the work. Data about progress may be obtained from a variety of sources: production progress conferences, field visits to the supplier's facility and periodic progress reports by the supplier.

If an organization's supply management structure is organized around the suppliers (e.g., typically smaller organizations), the same individual is likely to perform the purchasing and supplier management functions. In other organizations (e.g., typically larger and government organizations), the functions of purchasing and supplier management may be separated. In either case, there are typically two primary ways of supervising a supplier — on-site approach and remote approach. On-site management means the representative from the supply management organization or an end user is either located at the site of the project (e.g., the supplier's facility) or makes frequent visits to the site to oversee the project. For example, the supply management organization at Bank of America trains the users of supplier-provided services to monitor and report supplier performance, for the users are most knowledgeable about supplier performance on a day-to-day basis.[7] Remote management can take many forms such as analyses of the supplier's invoices for price compliance from the purchaser's accounting office, review of workflow charts from the supply management organization and teleconferencing with the supplier. Management by exception entails comparing the expected performance and actual performance of the supplier and taking remedial action when large discrepancies occur. For management by exception to be effective, the contract must delineate clearly what constitutes a large discrepancy.

Progress Reports. The supply management organization may specify the requirement for the production progress information in the RFP and resulting contract. The ensuing reports frequently show the supplier's actual and forecasted deliveries as compared to the contract schedule, potential delay factors, and status of incomplete preproduction work (i.e., design and engineering, tooling and construction of prototypes). The reports also should contain narrative sections in which the supplier explains any difficulties and the action or actions proposed or taken to overcome them.

In some instances, the supplier is required by the terms of the contract to submit a phased production or service delivery schedule for review and approval. A phased schedule shows the time required to perform the planning, designing, purchasing, tooling, facility rearrangements, component manufacture, subassembly, final assembly, testing and shipping. Production or service delivery progress reports do not replace the requirement to conduct visits to the supplier's facility or the work site on crucial contracts. The right to conduct such visits must be established in the RFP and resulting contract. On critical contracts, where the cost is justified, it may be desirable to adopt the on-site supplier management approach discussed previously.

Customer Feedback. To exercise continuous improvement, feedback must be sought from both internal and external customers. From the perspective of supply management professional, internal customers are internal users of the services or goods purchased by the contract. They represent the production department that needs to use the goods or services, the finance department that must pay the invoices, the quality-control department that might be required to inspect goods received, the warehousing department that might store and reship goods received, the marketing department that uses the service provider for creative work, and senior management officials. The areas of feedback may cover any and all aspects of the supply management process as discussed in Chapter 5: how well the needs were communicated and understood, supplier selected, price determined, orders placed and followed through, charges verified and discrepancies reconciled.

Clearly, the activities of supply management are intertwined with the activities of other departments and all together these activities affect the external customer — the customer of the supply management organization. These external customers can be consumers, large original equipment manufacturers, government agencies and other organizations that pay the invoice issued by the supply management organization. Even though supplier management typically faces upstream activities, it is important to pay close attention to how the work affects the downstream, or external, customers.

Issues of Reciprocal Relationship and Reciprocity

Structurally, a *reciprocal relationship* occurs when two organizations are buying and supplying to each other at the same time. This particular relationship arrangement in and of itself occurs frequently and is not necessarily troublesome. However, what becomes troublesome is if preference is given to a particular supplier because this supplier is also the customer. This situation typically is referred to as *reciprocity*. In other words, having a reciprocal relationship may not necessarily be a bad thing, but the practice of reciprocity may be. It may constitute a violation of U.S. antitrust laws if it tends to restrict competition or trade or is coerced. For example, two organizations may buy from and supply to each other if they need each organization's expertise for what they do. Then two organizations create a reciprocal relationship. However, if one organization intentionally ignores the negative evaluation data of the other organization hoping to obtain a new business contract from that organization, then this type of action spells reciprocity.

Clearly, reciprocity can be illegal in some countries, such as in the United States. The key factor used to determine illegality is the degree to which any reciprocal activity tends to restrict competition. It is legal to buy from customers without economic threat and without intent of restricting competition. In a questionable situation, however, the burden of proof rests with the supply management organization.

Many supply management organizations try to avoid reciprocal relationships if at all possible, because they could potentially restrict competition. The issue of potential reciprocity may lead an organization to a point where the principle of buying and selling based on competition may be compromised. A supplier that also buys as a customer may start to relax competitive efforts in technical and production areas as a result of reduced competition. The possibility of a supply management organization getting a bad reputation because of reciprocity also is something to be aware of. At the same time, the supply management professional should note that reciprocity is practiced much more widely in the international arena. International organizations, for instance, may receive government contracts on the condition that they meet local content requirements, forcing the nondomestic supplier to develop new local suppliers. This concept is explained in more depth in Chapter 10, "International Sourcing Issues." When Volkswagen first signed the joint venture agreement with the Chinese government and formed the Shanghai Automotive Industry Corporation (SAIC), it brought its own suppliers from Europe who then bought and sold parts with local Chinese suppliers to meet the local content requirement.[8]

Conflict and Dispute Resolution

Supply management professionals often are referred to as the *windows* of an organization. They are the conduits through which the internal users see external suppliers and external suppliers see the supply management organizations as users of their services or products. That is why when conflicts arise between the internal users and external

·suppliers during the course of contracts, supply management professionals often play central roles in resolving disputes.

The supply management professional's role as a negotiator extends beyond the contract negotiation and into contract administration. When the contract is negotiated, agreed on and signed, both parties do the best they can to ensure that their organizations' policies and regulations are followed, the contract terms are clearly understood, and the potential changes are anticipated and stipulated. However, unforeseen events do occur and disputes may rise between the end user and the supplier. Often, the supply management professional is the last resort for both parties to reach agreement on disputes prior to seeking legal redress.

As changes occur, it may become necessary to terminate a contract or renegotiate the terms. The supply management professional may take on the role of go-between to settle liquidated damages and lost profit claims by the supplier or the supply management organization. The supply management professional also may assist in problem resolution for the supplier's internal matters that may affect contract performance. Supply management professionals often are looked on as impartial sources that both the supplier and the buying organization can look to for fair and just resolution of conflicts. The supply management organization's position must be considered, but the supply management professional must resolve issues in an ethical, legal manner so that both parties believe a win-win solution has been reached.

Today's expanding international business environment includes trade agreements such as the North American Free Trade Agreement (NAFTA), loosely structured associations such as the Association of Southeast Asian Nations (ASEAN), and merging countries into economic units such as the European Union (EU). Thus, it is important to understand conflict resolution practices and plan for conflicts that may arise from contracts that cross international borders and cultures. Clearly, the U.S.-centric approach is unlikely to prevail when sourcing internationally. Social and business cultural differences must be accounted for, and concepts such as a preaward conference and frequent postaward follow-up become even more important to minimize the potential for conflict. Experienced supply management professionals understand that other cultures place different values on matters such as time, relationships, quality and payment due dates, and they also know how different they are and apply their knowledge in managing international suppliers.

Establishing Partnerships and Strategic Alliances

The term *partnership* is used synonymously .with *alliance* and is defined as a close relationship between a buyer and a supplier to attain some advantages from each other in a positive way. A partnership in this regard does not necessarily imply a legal one. A buyer-supplier partnership may be operational, such as a long-term, single-source relationship with an office materials supplier, or strategic, such as a long-term, single-source relationship with a supplier of a goods or service of strategic importance, for example, engines or healthcare services (*ISM Glossary*, 2006).

The systematic leveraging of supply management's resources and capabilities is important in partnership through mutually beneficial relationships with other internal and external players, to strengthen the organization's competitive advantage. Selecting suppliers as partners involves more than the usual up-front analysis; therefore, it is best to use a team approach to selecting partners. Such a team usually will involve purchasing, engineering, operations, quality control, the department impacted by the service and senior management. To sustain the partnership, both the supply management organization and the supplier must keep abreast of changing technology through periodic meetings through other forms of communication. The supply management organization must be open regarding its needs and must agree to protect the supplier from sudden changes that may leave the supplier with excess goods, materials or capacity. The supply management organization may have to perform cost/price analysis of the supplier's operations to ensure the supplier earns a fair profit and to provide a fair price for the supply management organization.

Nature of Relationship

A supplier possibly may add more value as an alliance partner than in a routine relationship. An alliance between a supply management organization and a supplying organization requires the mutual recognition and acknowledgment of a long-term relationship between both organizations. This relationship typically requires implementing ongoing joint teams and senior management involvement and support. It should lead to mutual idea generation and creative problem-solving and regularly made contact and visibility.

Information-sharing takes place on a continual basis through such programs as early supplier involvement in new product or service development and participation in concurrent engineering and project management. In the end, the partnering supplier is given an opportunity to make a contribution to the supply management organization's competitive advantage through continually improving efforts and sharing risks and rewards.

Rationale for Partnership

When partnering, the supply management professional must be able to answer the question, "What does the supplier gain by entering into a partnership with us?" In many instances, unless this question is addressed adequately, the supplier may be reluctant to enter into a long-term partnership. A few years ago, a leading supply management professional at TRW Automotive became exasperated by small suppliers resisting long-term relationships. This supply management professional thought the small suppliers should welcome receiving a long-term contract from TRW, but the suppliers really did not want to tie up their capacities for just one large organization. Large organizations such as TRW should be aware that many small suppliers hesitate to rely on one large customer and, thus, market flexibility results. Competition drives the supplier in the same way it drives the supply management organization. Therefore, it is important that benefits are clearly delineated and understood by both the supplier and the supply management organization.

Some of the potential benefits may come from the ability to reduce lead time, and increase flexibility, market responsiveness, and competitive advantage for both organizations. Also, both organizations may be able to reduce administrative costs and inventory management costs. Instead of having separate quality-assurance programs, the two organizations may be able to employ a joint, integrated quality program. The supplier and the supply management organization may gain mutually beneficial technical information from each other.

Forms of Partnerships

There are four basic types of partnership or alliance: (1) basic, (2) operational, (3) business and (4) strategic. The types vary, depending on the level of process integration or business coupling.

A *basic partnership* can be formed with any supplier. It involves treating the supplier with a basic level of trust and honest communication. It tends to be tactical and short term. An *operational partnership* is one in which the supplier performs a service or supplies a product as a matter of routine or as part of the transaction flow of business, not as an additional commitment. While there may be some joint problem-solving, there are no ongoing, cross-organizational teams. However, it is crucial that the supply management professional receive accurate information from the supplier about potential shortages, changes and prices, because the item is important to the supply management organization.

A *business partnership* is one in which the supply management organization wants the supplier to provide some unique or specialized product or service. Here, increased recognition of mutual dependence exists. The supplier may invest in additional assets (e.g., dedicated line or equipment), specialized personnel (e.g., on-site personnel) or technology (e.g., specific to the buying organization). The supply management organization will have reduced the supply base and committed volume for an extended period of time, but the benefit to the supply management organization is not strategic or core to the organization's success. Lastly, a *strategic partnership* involves goods or services that are of strategic importance to the success of the supply management organization. This type of partnership requires sharing long-term strategies, and the parties must agree on the risks and rewards of such a relationship and how these risks and rewards will be shared. Ongoing, joint cross-organizational teams and top management support, contact and visibility are the mainstays of strategic partnerships.

Developing Partnerships

Generally, four steps are involved in developing a supplier partnership: (1) initial analysis, (2) opportunity analysis, (3) recommendation and plans and (4) implementation and outcome measurements. Often, supplier partnerships naturally develop over time with existing suppliers, or are specifically sought out if the supply management organization believes such a relationship may be mutually beneficial beyond a "routine" supplier relationship. Conducting the *initial analysis* entails supplier identification and/or selection, strategy development, obtaining commitments from team leaders and key stakeholders, kickoff meetings, drafting the overall timeline for relationship development and measuring the results. The *opportunity analysis* involves the following key activities:

- A detailed analysis of the supply chain and processes;
- Identifying and validating potential benefits;
- Finalizing key opportunities of the relationship; and
- Updating the executives of both organizations.

Developing *recommendations and plans* addresses more concrete activities. In addition to creating a list of recommendations and plans, a joint business case must be made in specific terms, metrics identified and executive approval obtained. Lastly, the recommendations and plans need to be *implemented and measured*. Resources must be obtained, problem solutions provided, the process of implementation monitored and individual and team accomplishments measured and recognized.

Maintaining Partnerships

Once the partnership has been implemented, the supply management professional must focus on sustaining the relationship. As with any relationship, this requires a good deal of effort, discipline and communication. Both organizations need to be reminded of the potential benefits. Unilateral decision-making is detrimental to a partnership, so both organizations must continue to use joint planning and continuous improvement to keep the dialogue going and ideas flowing.

The partnership must be highly visible in both organizations and must receive high levels of approval. This relationship must be backed up by data on how the purported benefits are materializing. Both organizations must recognize incentives for good performance. Successes need to be celebrated jointly. However, when the partnership is not well maintained, it can break down in a very visible way. The breakdown of the partnership between Ford and Firestone is a well-publicized example.[9] Another well-recognized breakup occurred between OfficeMax and Ryder Integrated Logistics. After 21 months of a seven-year contract, OfficeMax sued Ryder Integrated Logistics for breach of contract. Soon after that, Ryder Integrated Logistics filed a countersuit and eventually received a $5.1 million settlement from OfficeMax.[10] Long-term buyer-supplier partnerships create activities at all levels of organizations and receive a lot of visibility; their demise also creates high visibility and subsequent pain felt by both organizations.

Concluding Partnerships

Both organizations may get to a point where the partnership no longer is mutually beneficial and all opportunities to revitalize the alliance have been exhausted or the business opportunity has changed. The relationship then should be modified to suit the organizations' needs. It is prudent to develop terms for the end of the partnership while the partnership is being developed.

Supplier Mentorship

Supplier mentoring provides assistance to suppliers in a wide variety of ways. It may focus on a specific issue such as training for statistical process control (SPC) or take a more generic approach by loaning an internal consultant (e.g., process engineer) to help ramp up a new line or organize workers into teams. Some organizations even have provided systems software to assist in implementing Six Sigma programs, as well as support sales and marketing efforts. One extreme form of mentoring involves lending capital to suppliers to make technology investments, for instance, in production-line automation.

Supplier mentorship often is used as a way of fulfilling corporate citizenship. Sandia Corp., an organization that develops technologies related to national security, made a strategic decision to engage in supplier mentoring to promote the economic growth of New Mexico and its surrounding areas.[11] Supplier mentorship naturally addresses women–owned and minority–owned businesses. A consulting organization such as Management Decisions Inc. (MDI), for example, offers supplier mentorship services to supply management organizations when they are interested in expanding their participation with diverse suppliers.[12] MDI lists executive mentoring, tracking and measuring diversity levels and helping to identify diverse suppliers.

Supplier Diversity

Special attention is required in selecting a diverse group of suppliers and instituting a small business and small disadvantaged supplier development program. Socially and economically disadvantaged supplier programs such as minority purchasing initiatives and women-owned business programs continue to grow in the United States and are being instituted in other countries. The impetus behind these programs includes government legislation, social responsiveness, the development of alternate sources of supply, the need to increase market share and the need to meet the demands of their customers. Organizations that have made a commitment to purchasing from minority-owned and women-owned suppliers typically have specific policies for dealing with them. In general, a minority-owned business is defined as one that is at least 51 percent owned, controlled and operated by an ethnic or racial minority-group member. A woman-owned business is defined as one that is at least 51 percent owned, controlled and operated by one or more women.

Small Business and Small Disadvantaged
Business Requirements

The legislative history of minority business development in the United States can be traced back to 1968, when the Small Business Administration (SBA) established a program to channel federal purchases to socially or economically disadvantaged owners of small businesses. In 1969, the U.S. Office of Minority Business Enterprise was established within the U.S. Department of Commerce to mobilize federal resources to aid minorities in business. In 1978, Public Law 95507 mandated that bidders for federal contracts in excess of $500,000 for goods and services and $1,000,000 for construction submit, prior to a contract award, a plan that includes percentage goals for the utilization of minority-owned businesses. In 1983, President Ronald Reagan signed Executive Order 12432, which directs all federal agencies to develop specific goal-oriented plans for expanding procurement opportunities for minority-owned businesses. The Federal Acquisition Streamlining Act (FASA), signed into law in 1994, established 5 percent governmentwide agency goals for small disadvantaged business and five percent goals for women-owned business.

A supplier is considered a small business (SB) if its size is consistent with the government size standard specified in Federal Acquisition Regulation (FAR) 19.102.[13]

Depending on the industry, the qualification for SB is based on either the number of employees or the average annual receipts. For instance, in the manufacturing, wholesale and retail sectors, a supplier with fewer than 500 employees qualifies as an SB. For agriculture, construction, transportation and services, a broad range of $0.5 million to $100 million of an organization's average annual receipts has been assigned as a qualification for receiving a small business designation.[14]

An SB is a small disadvantaged business (SDB) if at least 51 percent is owned and controlled by an individual(s) who is(are) categorized as socially and economically disadvantaged as defined by the federal government. Groups of individuals classified as socially and economically disadvantaged include such ethnic minorities as African-Americans, Hispanics, Native Americans and Asian-Americans. For an owner to receive classification for SDB, his or her net worth, excluding equity in the business and primary residence, may not exceed $750,000.

To do business with the U.S. government and be certified as an SDB, a business owner must register with the Central Contractor Registration (CCR), the primary registration database for the U.S. government.[15] Since October 1, 2003, by federal mandate, any business wishing to conduct business with the federal government under an FAR-based contract must be registered with the CCR before being awarded a contract.

The SBA certifies organizations under its 8(a) Business Development Program, the Small Disadvantaged Business (SDB) program and the Historically Underutilized Business Zone (HUBZone) program.[16] Small, women-owned, veteran-owned and service-disabled veteran-owned businesses rely largely on self-certification, but a competitor or other interested party may protest and question this self-certification. Some state governments offer favorable terms for certified SBs through bid preferences and other monetary benefits. States such as California, Ohio and Oregon provide measures to benefit SBs.[17] Additionally, some city governments offer favorable terms for SBs as well.

Managerial Issues in Developing Programs

Most supply management organizations have a small business/small disadvantaged business (SB/SDB) statement in their policy manuals. The CEO or some other top executive of the organization generally signs the policy statement. Most organizations also include separate SB/SDB procedures in their procedures manuals. Many organizations also designate minority-supplier coordinators to deal with SB/SDB businesses. According to a CAPS Research report on supplier diversity programs, more than 72 percent of the organizations surveyed followed written procedures for sourcing professionals regarding contracting with small and/or minority-owned businesses, with 71 percent setting financial goals for contracts awarded to this supplier segment. Sixty-nine percent of the organizations encouraged their top-tier suppliers to maintain supplier diversity programs, with 59 percent tracking second-tier supplier diversity spend. Overall, the study respondents indicated that their organizations' supplier diversity spend as a percentage of total supply management spend was an average of slightly more than 20 percent. Forty-four percent of the organizations employed a full-time program coordinator.[18]

Figure 8-3 provides a list of managerial issues and benefits that drive diversity programs. However, there also can be impediments. Some organizations may encounter varying degrees of hostility, as well as active or passive resistance, to SB/SDB efforts. Prejudicial attitudes can be overcome through education and training. Lack of supply management training in minority business matters itself can be considered an impediment to the SB/SDB initiatives. This can be alleviated through seminars, networking, associations, leadership and guidance from the minority supplier coordinator.

Sources of Information

The SBA has a computerized directory of SB and SDB sources. This directory, officially known as PRO-Net, contains information on more than 75,000 small, minority-owned and women-owned businesses. PRO-Net is an electronic gateway to procurement information for and about small businesses. It is a search engine for contracting officers, a marketing tool for small organizations and a link to procurement opportunities and important information. In addition, minority business directories are available. For many supply management professionals, Diversity Information Resources (DIR), formerly TRY US Resources, is the best known, as well as the most widely used, minority business directory. Business.com, the search engine for managing businesses, contains an international directory of more than 65,000 business categories. Other sources also are available, as highlighted in Figure 8-4.

Supply Base Management

To create a world-class supply base, it is important for a supply management organization to establish an integrated supply network in its supply base.[19] It needs to rationalize or optimize its supply base and ultimately engage in the proactive development of suppliers (e.g., reverse marketing as discussed in Chapter 7, "Supplier Management and Development") and engage them in integrative development. In creating a world-class supply base, it is important to consider how *supply base* is related to *supply network* and the major decisions the supply management organization needs to make to achieve integration in its supply base.

Figure 8-3   Management and Diversity Programs

MANAGERIAL ISSUES	DESCRIPTIONS
Organizational Policies	Policies typically address the following: purpose of the program, definition of an SB/SDB, scope of the program, objectives and benefits of the program, responsibility of the organization toward the SB/SDB, exceptions to the program, execution strategies and tracking methodologies, reporting procedures and the person in the organization who has the responsibility for coordinating the program.
Strategic Benefits	Establishment of an active SB/SDB initiative enhances an organization's image with the community and with its minority and female customers. It also will help organizations that are government contractors meet government requirements. If an organization is in a consumer-based business or supports such a business, image is very important to the organization and to the bottom line.
Goal Assessment	Accurate assessment of initiative goals should begin with the proper coding of the supplier base, which lists all the organization's large, small, minority-owned and women-owned suppliers. Periodic reports of all supplier activity within these categories should be generated to compare goals with actual performance and to take corrective action where goals are not being met.
Customer-Driven Requirements	Because of the demographic changes in the United States today, SB/SDB initiatives are becoming more market-driven than compliance-driven. With more than three million minority-owned businesses and nine million women-owned businesses in the United States, consumer-related businesses and those that sell to them are very conscious of the changing demographics of the consumer base and the need for inclusion of minorities and women-owned businesses in the procurement process.

Supply Network and Supply Base

Supply network is a network of supplier organizations that exist upstream to a supply management organization. It consists of suppliers that the supply management organization selects as well as suppliers that its suppliers select. The suppliers that the supply management organization selects are within the purview of the supply management

Figure 8-4 Sources of Information

NAME	DESCRIPTION
Small Business Administration (SBA)	As of January of 2004, PRO-Net was being integrated with the U.S. Department of Defense's Central Contractor Registration (CCR). If interested in conducting market research and confirming eligibility for SBA's procurement preference programs, the pertinent information can be found on the CCR Web site at www.ccr.gov/ under "Dynamic Small Business Search."
Minority-Owned Business Directories	The directory/database of Diversity Information Resources includes more than 8,500 certified minority-owned and women-owned businesses, listed by both commodity and state. It can be found at www.diversityinforesources.com/. Small business is one of the major categories within Business.com and focuses on providing assistance to start-up businesses and for implementing small business ideas. The directory of minority-owned businesses may be found under this category and works as a resource for and about minority-owned businesses. It can be found at www.business.com/directory/small_business/minority-owned_businesses/.
	Many Internet sites provide information about minority-owned businesses. One such site is called Internet Resources for Minority Business Owners at www.libsci.sc.edu/bob/class/clis748/Studentwebguides/minoritybus.htm.
	It lists a variety of different Internet sites that provide useful information for minority business owners and others interested in learning about them. The National Directory of Minority-Owned Business Organizations lists more than 37,000 minority-owned organizations. It is considered the comprehensive source for information on federally certified minority-owned and women-owned businesses and is published by Business Research Services Inc. in Washington, DC.
Women-Owned Businesses	In addition to the previously mentioned Internet sites, others focus on women-owned businesses. The National Association of Women Business Owners (NAWBO) publishes a directory that currently is available only to its members. This group states that more than 8 million women-owned businesses exist in the United States (www.nawbo.org). The Women's Business Enterprise National Council (WBENC) provides information on certified businesses through an Internet database, WBENCLink. The council states that more than 9.1 million women-owned businesses generate $3.8 trillion in sales. The WBENC list currently contains more than 1,600 certified women-owned businesses (www.womenconnect.com/wbenc).

NAME	DESCRIPTION
Minority-Owned Business Development Councils	The National Minority Supplier Development Council (NMSDC) has 38 Minority Purchasing Councils in the country. These councils are funded by more than 3,500 majority-owned concerns, including more than 150 of the top Fortune 500 organizations. They commit more than $36 billion annually to minority-owned concerns. Council membership includes more than 15,000 certified minority-owned concerns. The primary tasks of these councils are the certification of minority business suppliers; the referral of corporate purchasers to minority suppliers; support in developing, expanding or promoting corporate minority purchasing programs; dissemination of information; training and technical assistance; and maintenance of corporate and supplier directories and other publications (www.nmsdcus.org).
Local Minority/ Women Chambers of Commerce	Local minority chambers of commerce include the Asian Business Association, the Black Business Association of Los Angeles, the Miami-Dade Chamber of Commerce, the Latin Business Association, the U.S. Hispanic Chamber of Commerce and the National Black Chamber of Commerce. For contact information for these and other associations, refer to the Encyclopedia of Associations or library.dialog.com/bluesheets/html/bl0114.html.
Business Fairs	These are trade fairs. Many entities, including cities, counties, states, individual organizations, women's organizations and local minority purchasing councils conduct business fairs. There are many business fairs; one sample can be found at www.bizfair.org/.

organization and may be actively managed by the supply management organization; however, the suppliers that its suppliers select often are unknown to the supply management organization and, as far as the supply management organization is concerned, this part of the supply network typically happens without its proactive participation.[20] Often this part of a supply network is more expansive than the controlled part consisting of suppliers that the supply management organization selects.

In this regard, a supply network is "all inter-connected [suppliers] that exist upstream to a [supply management organization] in the value system," and a supply base is "a portion of the supply network that is actively managed by the [supply management organization] through contracts and purchasing of parts, materials and services."[21]

Managing a Supply Base

Figure 8-5 depicts the relationship between the supply management organization and its suppliers in the supply base as well as the relationships among the suppliers. The arrows going out from the supply management organization to its suppliers represent the direction of management influence. Suppliers often can influence the supply management organization; however, the overall leadership of managing a supply base belongs with the supply management organization. The black dots within the supply base represent the suppliers scattered throughout the supply network. The lines that connect these suppliers represent the relationships that exist between suppliers as discussed previously.

The supply management organization influences its suppliers through contracting and administering its relationships. In Figure 8-5, this influence is shown with arrows directed from the supply management organization to its suppliers. Among suppliers, buyer-supplier relationships may exist. These relationships are depicted with solid lines connecting the suppliers in Figure 8-5. In other words, some suppliers in the supply base may supply to other suppliers. A common misconception when considering a supply base is to think all suppliers in the supply base are top-tier suppliers. Many suppliers in the supply base may, in fact, be second-tier or third-tier suppliers. For instance, *directed* sourcing may take place where a supply management organization

---

Figure 8-5   The Supply Management Organization and Its Supply Base

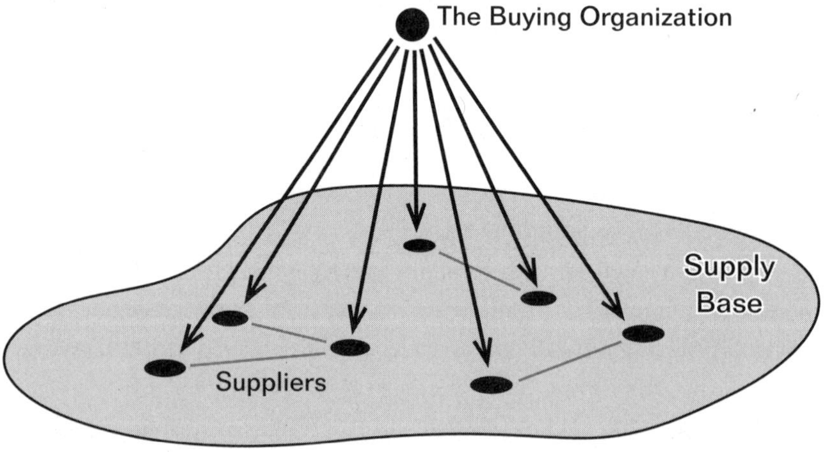

Source: Adapted from T.Y. Choi and D.R. Krause, "The Supply Base and Its Complexity: Implications for Transaction Costs, Risks, Responsiveness, and Innovation," *Journal of Operations Management* 24(5) (September 2006): 637-52.

---

tells its top-tier suppliers to obtain certain parts from another, specifically designated supplier.

In this context, three managerial considerations must be addressed when strategizing supply base management:[22] The first is the number of suppliers in the supply base, as depicted by the number of black dots within the supply base in Figure 8-5. When a supply management organization makes a decision to reduce its supply base, it is, in essence, addressing the issue of the number of suppliers it carries in its supply base. The second is the nature of relationships between suppliers. When two suppliers are connected, as shown by a solid line between them, different types of relationships may emerge: Some of them may work together well in a cooperative relationship while some may not and an adversarial relationship may develop. Finally, a supply management professional must be mindful of the cultural and operational similarities and differences among suppliers. Some suppliers may be job shops or small specialized manufacturing operations, while others may be assembly plants or continuous-flow manufacturers. Some may be supplying services such as call center operations. All these organizations are likely to have different cultural traits such as open communications or more guarded communications. At the same time, they may share similar cultural traits or operational traits such as common inventory management strategies. These three considerations — number of suppliers, interrelationships among suppliers and degree of differentiation among suppliers — are what can be controlled by the supply management organization when managing suppliers collectively.

Number of Suppliers. This aspect of supply base management often is referred to as *supply base rationalization* or *optimization*. Here, the focus is on controlling how many suppliers a supply management organization should utilize for a given product or service. The *ISM Glossary* (2006) defines supply base rationalization as determining and maintaining the appropriate number of suppliers by item/category depending on the risk and value of the item/category. Initially, rationalization often means reducing the size of the supply base. Longer term, the process focuses more on managing the size of the supply base particularly as market dynamics change. This method reduces the expenses involved in qualifying and maintaining large supplier bases. The issues of single sourcing, dual sourcing, multiple sourcing or parallel[23] sourcing apply here.

Although somewhat exceptional, in the case of *single sourcing*, there is one supplier in the supply base for the given product or service, and in the case of *dual sourcing*, there are two. Most of the situations that a typical supply management organization faces fall under either multiple sourcing or parallel sourcing. In *multiple sourcing*, a supply management organization maintains multiple suppliers in its supply base and distributes the quantity among them to maintain competition.

The accepted wisdom is that a large number of suppliers in a supply base may be good for competition but may not be good in terms of higher administrative costs. A large number also makes it difficult to establish close relationships with suppliers. Thus, many supply management organizations have rationalized their supply bases. Often, however, some organizations go too far and face the issue of then adding to the supply base.[24]

Interrelationships Among Suppliers. Sometimes, the supply management organization wants suppliers to work together, and sometimes it does not. Relationships between suppliers matter to the supply management organization.[25] In fact, it is becoming more common for suppliers to work together to develop a new product or provide a new service at the supply management organization's request.

Three types of supplier-supplier relationships have been observed: (1) competitive, (2) cooperative and (3) co-opetitive.[26] In a *competitive relationship*, suppliers are aware of each other and, in fact, may interact and even exchange information. However, they keep each other at arm's length and are fully aware that they also are competitors. A *cooperative relationship* entails suppliers working together to either manage the flow of products or services or to get involved in a joint venture. They may share production or service capacity or come together to bring a new product or service to the common market they serve. Finally, the *co-opetitive relationship* may be the most common. In this relationship, suppliers both compete and cooperate simultaneously. For instance, several suppliers might come together on an ad hoc basis at the request of the supply management organization and develop a product or service. However, in the end, they may compete against each other to provide the product or service. Figure 8-6 reviews the pros and cons of each type of supplier-supplier relationship from the supply management organization's perspective.

Differentiation of Suppliers. This aspect of supply base management probably is most overlooked and most difficult to engage in, yet perhaps represents the most promising and untapped area. Differentiation of suppliers may occur in the areas of organizational culture, operational practices, technical capabilities and geographical separation. The basic premise is that less differentiation among suppliers may lead to efficiency and supplier responsiveness but more differentiation might contribute to supplier innovation when working together on a joint project.

For example, when the suppliers share common cultural norms and values (such as continuous improvement or getting at the root cause), it becomes easier for the supply management organization to coordinate their activities. It would create inefficiencies and reduce responsiveness if one supplier operated on a push system, while the other used a pull. If suppliers were within close proximity, coordination also

Figure 8-6   Trade-Offs From the Supply Management Organization's Perspective

COMPETITIVE	Pros	Maintains leverage power; control of information exchange between suppliers
	Cons	Lack of supplier synergy; high administrative and transaction costs
COOPERATIVE	Pros	Information and knowledge sharing; capacity flexibility
	Cons	Potential for supplier collusion; forward integration by suppliers
CO-OPETITIVE	Pros	Opportunity to gain advantage of both competitive and cooperative relationships; low supplier switching cost
	Cons	Relationship uncertainty; risk of suppliers' opportunistic behaviors

Source: Adapted from T.Y. Choi, A. Wu, L. Ellram and B.R. Koka, "Supplier-Supplier Relationships and Their Implications for Buyer-Supplier Relationships," *IEEE Transactions on Engineering Management* 49(2) (May 2002): 119-30.

would become easier and less costly. However, if they are too much alike and know each other too well, homogeneity of ideas may increase. In this regard, the supply management organization has to mix in high differentiation and low differentiation depending on what the situation calls for.

When a supply management organization considers management of its supplier relationship, it typically looks at one supplier at a time in a dyadic context or just the number of suppliers (e.g., how many suppliers it has in the supply base). When managing suppliers, supplier differentiation (e.g., how similar or dissimilar suppliers are) and supplier interrelationship (e.g., what their relationships among themselves might be) need to be considered. This type of consideration takes supply management professionals beyond the simple dyadic context and forces them to manage suppliers as part of an overall system.

Supply-Chain Management and Its Implications

As discussed previously, supply chains are supply networks. The supply chain as defined in the *ISM Glossary* (2006) is a network of organizations that extend downstream to customers' customers' customers and upstream to suppliers' suppliers' suppliers. Because a supply network extends beyond the purview of the supply management organization, the supply management professional must identify different portions of the supply network the supply management organization intends to manage for strategic reasons. Therefore, *supply-chain management (SCM)* is the design and management of seamless, value-added processes across organizational boundaries to meet the real needs of the end customer. The development and integration of people and technological resources are critical to successful supply-chain integration. Supply-chain management identifies and manages specific supply chains that are critical to a supply management organization's operations. It deals with the planning and control of materials and service flows, from earliest suppliers to end users, including disposal and end-of-life issues. Supply-chain management involves cooperatively managing interorganizational relationships for the benefit of all parties involved, to maximize the efficient use of resources in achieving the supply chain's customer-service goals.

SCM allows supply management professionals to optimize their resources including inventories, capacities and transportation. Transaction mechanisms across many organizations substantially reduce expenses resulting from normal business uncertainties. Sharing accurate demand information across the chain is cited by many as critical to achieving the maximum benefits of supply-chain management.

In particular, a major advantage of supply-chain management is risk reduction. *Risk reduction* refers to the ability of the organization to lower the overall probability of risk and cost of conducting business by sharing assets and information, as well as joint planning between various members of the supply chain. For example, sharing logistics assets within the supply chain can increase an organization's flexibility. Information-sharing can reduce costs and uncertainty, by allowing supply-chain members to anticipate and plan for the actions of other members.

As more information is shared with all members of the supply chain, and opportunities for increasing both effectiveness and efficiency are sought, the supply management organization becomes a logical focal point because of its understanding of the transactions, inventories and inbound transportation, as well as its knowledge of the operations of its principal suppliers.

When a supply management organization has many suppliers that use the same raw materials and its collective supplier volume for those raw materials is greater than that of its individual suppliers, the supply management organization might contract with the second-tier supplier of raw materials on behalf of its first-tier suppliers. The supply management organization can leverage the volume to gain better service, visibility and pricing.

Supply process mapping is performed to identify the current competitive state of the supply chain. This is performed by drawing a map of lead times and inventory levels. The relationships on the maps then are analyzed to determine where cycle time, inventory improvements or service improvements are possible, relative to the best industry practices. In this regard, two variables are important: supply process length (the sum of time spent in a series of connected supply-chain processes) and supply process volume (the sum of total time spent in the supply chain).[27] Supply process length is a combination of all cycle times of value-adding activities in the supply chain and can be thought of "as a measure of the time to respond to increases in demand."[28] If demand increases and the same level of inventory is maintained in the supply chain, supply process length is exactly how long it will take the increase in demand to *pull* all the activities in the supply chain. Supply process volume is a combination of supply process length and all inventories in the queue (measured in time) at various locations in the supply chain. It can be thought of as "a measure of the time to respond to decreases in demand" and "the time needed to drain the whole supply chain at the current rate of throughput."[29]

This chapter discusses building positive relationships, administering contracts and managing for diversity. As overall strategic initiatives, the chapter addresses establishing partnerships and managing supply base and supply chains. All these considerations contribute to creating mutually beneficial relationships between the supply management professional and its suppliers.

Summary

The focus of this chapter is on how to build a better supplier relationship for the future. The chapter begins with a discussion of selecting new suppliers and considers the issues of selecting suppliers beyond the top tier. Contract management and its implications are addressed, followed by a discussion of short-term and long-term relationships. Several tactics and issues are presented on how to build a positive relationship with suppliers, including an extensive discussion on the impact of diversity and the strategy of reverse marketing. Finally, supply base management is discussed by framing the supply base as a system of suppliers that the supply management professional actively manages.

Key Points

1. The key benefit of maintaining good supplier relations is that it creates a competitive resource that is difficult to be copied by the competitors.

2. Establishing good supplier relations relies on the supply management professional's ability and willingness to foster the creation and improvement of a mutually

satisfying arrangement. It requires the collective effort of the supply management organization and should not be left to one or two individual supply management professionals.

3. When administering contracts, the supply management professional must pay attention to the details such as work control, compliance, financial and administrative responsibility, contract terms and conditions, documentation and closing out the contract on completion.

4. The annual work plan (AWP) provides the initial definition of tasks to be performed in the given fiscal year and a schedule for accomplishment. During the AWP review, the supplier resource projections are reviewed and, on approval, the tasks to be undertaken can be scheduled.

5. The four basic types of partnership or alliance include: (1) basic, (2) operational, (3) business and (4) strategic. The types vary, depending on the level of process integration or business coupling.

6. Having a reciprocal relationship may not necessarily be a bad thing, but the practice of reciprocity is. Two organizations may buy from and supply to each other in a reciprocal relationship if they depend on each other's expertise. If one organization selects the other organization as a supplier, hoping to obtain new business from that organization, reciprocity would result.

7. Supplier mentoring provides assistance to suppliers in a wide variety of ways. It may focus on a specific issue such as training for statistical process control (SPC) or take a more generic approach by loaning an internal consultant (e.g., process engineer) to help ramp up for a new line or organize workers into teams.

8. Special attention is required when selecting a diverse group of suppliers and instituting a small business and disadvantaged supplier development program. The impetus behind these programs includes government legislation, social responsiveness, the development of alternate sources of supply, the need to increase market share and the need to meet customer demands.

9. The totality of a supply network often is invisible to a supply management organization, but the portion that the supply management organization actively engages in managing is called the *supply base*. This supply base includes not only top-tier suppliers but also second-tier and third-tier suppliers when the supply management professional is engaged in directed sourcing.

10. Supply base management entails more than rationalizing the number of suppliers; it also involves managing the interrelationships among suppliers and taking advantage of their similarities and dissimilarities.

11. Supply process mapping is undertaken to identify the current competitive state of the supply chain. This is performed by drawing a map of lead times and inventory levels across a supply chain.

9

Social and Legal Responsibilities of Supply Management Professionals

Supply management professionals are agents for their organizations. To that end, they are accountable to their employer, profession, government and society for socially responsible decisions and actions. The Institute for Supply Management™ (ISM) defines social responsibility as a framework of measurable corporate policies and procedures and resulting behavior designed to benefit the workplace and, by extension, the individual, organization and community in the areas of community, diversity, environment, ethics, financial responsibility, human rights and safety. Other organizations have echoed a similar definition by calling social responsibility the "obligation to make choices and take actions that will contribute to the welfare and interests of society as well as the organization."[1] In this regard, supply management professionals must be familiar with the framework in previous ISM statements, and make choices and carry out actions to uphold the corporate and government policies and procedures for all stakeholders, including society.

The impetus behind corporate social responsibility (CSR) evolves from several sources, most notably government, nongovernment organizations (NGO), institutional investors and consumers, as shown in Figure 9-1. For instance, Greenpeace, an NGO, worked hard for the acceptance of Greenfreeze, a relatively unknown environment-friendly refrigerant, after the extreme heat wave of 2006 in the global region that stretches from Athens to Mumbai. The increasing purchasing power of consumers in rural India has led Unilever India to act more socially responsible by introducing new detergents and bacteria-fighting soap to reduce water-borne illnesses.[2] These drivers have caused many multinational organizations, such as Sony, Motorola and IBM, to adopt written policies on corporate social responsibility with specific references to

Figure 9-1   Social Responsibility and Supply-Chain Implications

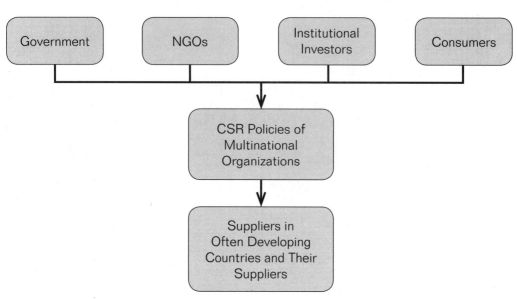

Source: Adapted from M. Bhandarkar and T. Alvarez-Rivero, "From Supply Chains to Value Chains: A Spotlight on CSR," in *Industrial Development for the 21st Century: Sustainable Development Perspectives* (New York: United Nations, 2007).

managing their suppliers and their suppliers' suppliers (i.e., whom their suppliers source from).

Recognizing the importance of CSR and its implications for supply management professionals, this chapter begins with a discussion of how ISM views social responsibility. Ethical issues and how they impact the supply management profession and ultimately individual supply management professionals then are reviewed from a legal perspective. As agents of their organizations, supply management professionals hold authority, and with this authority comes responsibility and liability. This chapter discusses what it means to be a socially responsible supply management professional and how that fits into the larger organizational context. Finally, laws and regulations are reviewed, from commercial laws to regulations governing disposal of materials. The chapter closes with a discussion of managing scrap and surplus and its impact on the environment.

CHAPTER OBJECTIVES
• Become familiar with ISM's position on various concepts related to corporate social responsibility and the supply management professional's role.

- Ascertain supply management's role in establishing ethical standards and policies and communicating them to other supply management professionals as well as internal customers and suppliers.

- Overview laws governing ethical issues and various related management areas.

- Consider issues of agency involving supply management professionals and their associated authority and liability.

- Study various roles of supply management professionals as socially responsible agents.

- Review laws and regulations applicable to supply management professionals in such areas as health, safety, environment and intellectual property.

- Study two key government organizations in the United States and their roles in overseeing trade and safety — the Department of Transportation and the Department of Homeland Security.

- Consider the supply management professional's role in managing scrap and surplus.

Institute for Supply Management™ and Social Responsibility

Institute for Supply Management™ defines social responsibility as a framework of measurable corporate policies and procedures to benefit the individual, the organization and the community in the areas of community, diversity, the environment, ethics, financial responsibility, human rights and safety.[3] A report filed by CAPS Research delineated the role of supply management professionals in the area of social responsibility as "a wide array of behaviors that broadly fall into the category of environmental management, safety, diversity, human rights and quality of life, ethics and community and philanthropic activities."[4]

The report offers a list of socially responsible activities that pertain to supply management professionals. Figure 9-2 shows key activities organized by the six categories previously mentioned.

Principles of Social Responsibility

ISM views the social responsibility of a supply management professional as first residing inside the professional's own organization and then in other organizations within the supply chain upstream and downstream from that professional's own organization. Furthermore, considerations are given for domestic issues as well as international. Implications of these principles are broad and overarching. See Figure 9-3 for an overview of the social responsibility espoused by ISM.[5]

ISM is not alone in its global quest to disseminate and implement these principles. Other global organizations also are involved, such as Business for Social Responsibility (BSR; www.bsr.org/), the World Business Council for Sustainable Development (WBCSD; www.wbcsd.ch/templates/TemplateWBCSD5/layout.asp?type=p&MenuId=MQ&doOpen=1&ClickMenu=LeftMenu) and the United Nations through its Global Compact (http://unglobalcompact.org/). BSR is a nonprofit business association that recognizes "environmental and social challenges … affect all aspects of

Figure 9-2 Supply Management Professional's Socially Responsible Activities

CATEGORY	ACTION DESCRIPTIONS
Environmental Consciousness	Ensures suppliers are engaged in environmentally sound practices: Sources from suppliers with environmentally sound practices Recycles and reuses parts and materials whenever possible Identifies and sources nonhazardous alternatives
Ethical Issues to Avoid	Avoids creating fictitious data or documentation to gain advantage over suppliers Avoids exaggerating the seriousness of problems to obtain concessions Avoids blaming suppliers for problems caused by the buying organization Avoids sharing suppliers' confidential data with other suppliers
Diversity	Sources from minority-owned and women-owned businesses Expands the list of diverse suppliers
Human Rights and Quality of Life	Ensures suppliers do not engage in business with organizations using sweatshop labor Ensures suppliers comply with child-labor laws Asks suppliers to pay a "living wage" to their workers
Safety Concerns	Ensures supplier plants operate in a safe manner by conducting audits and reviews Ensures the safe movement of incoming parts and materials
Community and Philanthropic Activities	Helps develop local suppliers Auctions off or donates gifts received from suppliers

Source: Adapted from Craig R. Carter and Marianne M. Jennings, *Purchasing's Contribution to the Socially Responsible Management of the Supply Chain* (Tempe, AZ: Center for Advanced Purchasing Studies, 2000).

Figure 9-3   Social Responsibility Principles for Supply Management Professionals

SOCIAL RESPONSIBILITY CATEGORY	PRINCIPLE OVERVIEW
Community	The principles that guide behavior in this area provide support and value to communities, including the supply management professional's own supply chain. They encourage members of a supply management professional's supply chain (i.e., suppliers and customers) to also strive to add value in their respective business communities.
Diversity	Diversity requires being proactive. The supply management professional needs to promote purchasing from socially diverse suppliers. This might involve getting proactively involved in the development of suppliers. Supply management professionals also are expected to encourage diversity within their own organizations and proactively promote diverse employment practices throughout the supply chain.
Environment	Principles regarding the environment have broad implications. Supply management professionals should encourage their own organizations and others to be proactive in examining opportunities to be environmentally responsible within their supply chains either upstream or downstream. They also should communicate the importance of environmental responsibility to their suppliers and encourage the development and inclusion of environmentally friendly practices and products throughout their organization.
Ethics	Supply management professionals must be aware of ISM's *Principles and Standards of Ethical Supply Management Conduct*. They also are expected to abide by their own organization's code of conduct.
Financial Responsibility	Supply management professionals need to practice socially responsible attitudes and behavior regarding financial matters. They need to be knowledgeable about applicable financial standards and requirements, use sound financial practices and ensure transparency in financial dealings. Furthermore, they must actively promote and practice responsible financial behavior throughout the supply chain.

(continued)

Figure 9-3   continued

SOCIAL RESPONSIBILITY CATEGORY	PRINCIPLE OVERVIEW
Human Rights	Regardless of where in the world the business takes place, people should be treated with dignity and respect. Supply management professionals need to support and respect the protection of international human rights within the organization's sphere of influence and to encourage the organization and its supply chain to avoid complicity in human or employment rights abuses.
Safety	Supply management professionals need to promote a safe environment for each employee in their own organizations and supply chains — each organization is responsible for defining what "safe" means within its organization. Supply management professionals also need to support the continuous development and training of safety practices throughout the organization and supply chain.

Source: Institute for Supply Management™, www.ism.ws/SR/

business operations — from supply chain to marketplace …" It helps companies "to achieve success in … ethical values, people, communities and the environment."[6] One organization it has helped is Novartis AG. When this pharmaceutical organization tried to implement its Corporate Citizenship Policy by ensuring all employees worldwide are receiving a living wage, BSR stepped in to help Novartis devise ways to compute the living wage levels across the world and implement a sustainable program working closely with local management.[7]

The WBCSD is another global organization dedicated "to provide business leadership as catalyst for change toward sustainable development …"[8] It is a CEO-led association with some 200 organization memberships and takes the issue of corporate social responsibility seriously through "the continuing commitment by business to behave ethically and contribute to economic development while improving the quality of life of the workforce and their families as well as of the local community and society at large."[9] The ISM principles have been articulated to lead in such global efforts to be socially responsible, especially when the activities pertain to supply management issues such as forced or involuntary labor issues in organizations in developing nations or health and safety issues as listed in Figure 9-2.

The United Nations launched its Global Compact in 2000. This initiative came from the UN Secretary General to promote 10 principles related to protecting human rights, labor rights and the environment. The Global Compact asks multinational organizations to "embrace, support and enact, within their sphere of influence, a set of core values in the areas of human rights, labor standards, the environment and anticorruption." Since its inception in 2000, the UN Global Compact has grown to include approximately 1,300 organizations.[10]

ISM Social Responsibility Prioritization Tool

ISM has developed a tool intended to help an organization prioritize its activities on stated social responsibility areas to determine gaps. The Web-based tool offers interactive means of evaluating and identifying gaps.[11] The tool consists of the following steps (illustrated in Figure 9-4):

1. Establish the organization's business priorities: a rank needs to be assigned in each key business area, where 10 is the highest ranking and 1 the lowest. Rankings

---

Figure 9-4 ISM's Tool for Prioritizing and Identifying Social Responsibility Gaps

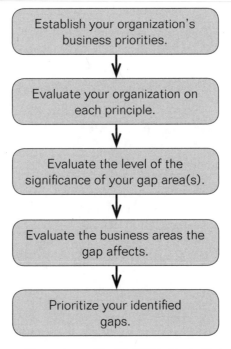

Source: Institute for Supply Management™, www.ism.ws/files/SR/SRPrioritizationTools.xls

should be based on how important each area is to the organization's overall strategic goal and market value.

2. Review the practices based on each principle: this is accomplished by detailing what the organization is doing in its current state and defining known gaps and areas of concern.

3. Determine the significance of the gap based on the size of the gap and its importance to one's industry.

4. When all the information has been collected, conclusions can be drawn. In the end, this evaluation process alerts the organization to what it needs to focus on first to improve its business practices in a socially responsible way.

This type of evaluation tool is becoming more important, given that many individual multinational organizations have implemented globally overarching social responsibility programs affecting their suppliers as well as workers employed at these suppliers. For instance, IBM follows a program on Supply Chain Social Responsibility by which the organization holds itself and its supply-chain members to high standards of social responsibility. It has published "IBM Supplier Conduct Principles," which covers a wide range of issues similar to the ones addressed in the ISM principles. For instance, IBM holds its suppliers responsible for not practicing forced or child labor and for implementing fair wages, benefits and work hours. It also holds its suppliers accountable for protecting the environment and conducting their businesses in an ethical manner. These principles have been incorporated into IBM's supplier selection processes and active compliance monitoring. From IBM's supplier's standpoint, IBM's expectations are "customer-driven requirements." If the suppliers want to win and retain IBM's business, they must meet these CSR standards.[12]

Safety Issues

The supply management professional must be aware of the policies and procedures of safety-related matters for their own organizations as well as their suppliers. Only when safety is maintained for both the buyer and the supplier, can a fruitful long-term relationship be established. Worker safety issues usually encompass the following: machine guarding, hazardous materials, personal protective equipment, ergonomics, lifting procedures, extreme temperatures and emergency procedures.

Because machines can pose operating hazards, they should be guarded in a *poka-yoke* fashion (mistake-proofing or fool-proofing) rather than simply relying on workers to be careful. There should be an explicit policy for handling hazardous materials, such as a designated storage area for chemicals. Labels should be read carefully and material safety data sheets (MSDS) should be studied. MSDS are documents that provide information about physical dangers, safety procedures and emergency response techniques related to hazardous materials contained in purchased products (*ISM Glossary*, 2006). MSDS often list personal protective equipment (PPE) to be worn when handling such materials. Typical PPEs include safety goggles, gloves and boots. MSDS and attached instructions must be posted clearly and monitored for compliance. *Ergonomics* is the science of meshing technology, the work environment and the needs of individual workers (*ISM Glossary*, 2006). Workplace ergonomics addresses how to lift heavy objects safely, assume correct postures when working and avoid extreme temperatures.

In large organizations, usually a safety department oversees these safety-related issues. The safety department typically offers training programs, publishes safety newsletters and maintains records of safety-related occurrences. The U.S. Occupational Safety and Health Administration (OSHA), discussed later in this chapter, also provides safety training materials. OSHA offers information on industry best practices if an organization is interested in benchmarking other organizations for any particular area of safety. Other organizations also provide information on safety and industry best practices, such as Occupational Hazards (www.occupationalhazards.com). Some of the required recordkeeping practices regarding safety are posting MSDS and keeping track of incidents that violate safety standards.

The European counterpart of OSHA in the United States is the European Agency for Safety and Health at Work (EASHW; http://osha.europa.eu/). This agency was created in 1996 to make Europe's workplaces "safer, healthier and more productive." The EASHW works with governments, organizations and individual workers and serves as a single reference point for occupational safety and health information. It also collects safety data and publishes new scientific research results.

Ethical Issues

The supply management organization should have written documentation to clearly communicate organizational policies and procedures to supply management professionals, internal customers and suppliers. The content of these policies and procedures manuals may address the following issues: the scope and level of supply management authority, organizational structure and responsibility, processes and procedures for dealing with suppliers, forms and document control and retention, and ethics policies that cover such issues as unacceptable sharp practices[13] such as knowingly deceiving a supplier and gift receiving. Documentation also should cover matters pertaining to federal, state, local and international laws that affect supply management as well as the actions of those within the organization. It is of utmost importance that all concerned parties understand that different organizations follow different policies and procedures and different countries abide by different laws and legal proceedings.

Developing policies and procedures can be a complex process. However, such documents facilitate communication while eliminating confusion, encouraging standardization and assisting in the training of new personnel. They also provide protection for the organization under certain circumstances. The following section discusses the laws governing ethical issues and how supply management professionals may conduct ethical supplier management. A discussion then is offered on what organizational and individual factors precede ethical behavior, followed by a case study of the Gap Inc. that illustrates the concepts discussed.

Laws Governing Ethical Issues

There are many applicable laws and regulations, as discussed later in this chapter, but laws that pertain to supply management ethics involve primarily three areas of concerns: (1) defamation, (2) disparagement and (3) bribery. *Defamation* is a publicly made, false and malicious statement, either oral or written, that injures another's character, fame or reputation (*ISM Glossary*, 2006). When these statements are made in writing, it is called libel. When made orally, it is called slander. *Disparagement*, applied to supply management, generally refers to making statements that are untrue or misleading about the quality or performance of another's goods or services in an attempt to influence others (e.g., the public) to not buy those goods or services.

Because supply management professionals hold power to affect procurement decisions, bribery often becomes an important issue. *Commercial bribery* refers to giving cash, gifts or other favors in return for business, favors or influencing the behavior of another party. Rulings on commercial bribery rest on the *doctrine of agency*, by which any breach of faith on the part of the agent, who is recognized by law as keeping a fiduciary position, is not permitted. A supply management professional generally is considered an agent of the organization, which will be discussed later in this chapter in the section on laws and regulations pertaining to social responsibility. When crossing national and cultural boundaries, however, the issue of bribery and gifting often gets blurred. For instance, China has very strict laws against taking bribes. Nonetheless, expensive gifts are exchanged quite frequently, and when these gifts are refused, the offering party may, in fact, take offense. As China becomes more open to the outside world and its communist laws and capitalist economy become integrated, many of these issues undoubtedly will be addressed.

Ethical Supply Management

Issues of ethical supply management practices can arise at any time. Supply management professionals must take great care to understand ethical matters, both generally and those specific to the organizations or industries in which they work. Most organizations have resources to address any questions or concerns related to ethical practice — the supply management professional should seek guidance from these internal resources if questions arise. Many organizations also provide explicit statements about their supply management code of ethics. Philips Electronics, an organization from the Netherlands that manufactures appliances, lighting and medical systems, published a Supply Management/Purchasing Code of Ethics.[14] The code covers a wide range of issues from acting honestly to reporting violations, and under each code are detailed descriptions of how that code translates to specific actions. For instance, under the code of "Pay suppliers in line with Philip's Rules," there are specific references about whom the recipient of the payment must be (e.g., the organization and never an individual) and how a cash payment is never allowed.

Institute for Supply Management™ updated and approved a new list of standards in 2005 that guide the ethical conduct of supply management professionals. This list also is accompanied by a detailed discussion of the intended meaning of these standards in areas of perceived impropriety, responsibilities to the employer, conflict of interest, issues of influence, confidential and proprietary information, supplier relationships, reciprocity, applicable laws, socially diverse practices, professional competence, national and international supply management conduct and responsibilities to the profession.[15] ISM states the following motto as the leading principle: "Loyalty to your organization, justice to those with whom you deal and faith in your profession."[16] The ISM standards of supply management conduct were developed from these principles (see Figure 9-5).

Dual Standards

The previously mentioned standards offer behavioral guidelines. However, areas that are not clearly defined still appear. One such area involves the *dual standard* between purchasing and sales functions.[17] The report filed by ISM's Ethical Standards Committee identified the existence of the dual standard in organizations. Buying organizations tend to view their sales professionals having lunches with their customers as being ethical and a good practice in building a partnership. However, organizations often view this same behavior with their supply management professionals as demonstrating a conflict of interest. Supply management professionals need to recognize why their organizations feel this way and address any issues involving ethics.

Figure 9-5. ISM Ethical Standards

AREAS OF STANDARD	ISM STATEMENT	EXPLANATIONS
Perceived Impropriety	"Avoid the intent and appearance of unethical or compromising practice in relationships, actions and communications."	Perceived unethical or compromising practices have the same negative consequences as actual unethical or compromising practices. For instance, even though receiving a small gift from a supplier may have no effect on a sourcing decision whatsoever, it needs to be avoided if it could potentially create a perception of impropriety by other suppliers.
Responsibilities to the Employer	"Demonstrate loyalty to the employer by diligently following the lawful instructions of the employer, using reasonable care and granted authority."	As an agent, the supply management professional must uphold the interest of the employing organization with no selfish motives for personal gain.
Conflict of Interest	"Avoid any personal business or professional activity that would create a conflict between personal interests and the interests of the employer."	Because supply management professionals are gatekeepers of large expenditures, they must avoid using their positions to promote benefits to themselves or others they have close relationships with such as family members, personal friends or close business associates.
Issues of Influence	"Avoid soliciting or accepting money, loans, credits or preferential discounts and the acceptance of gifts, entertainment, favors or services from present or potential suppliers that might influence, or appear to influence, supply management decisions."	The objectivity of sourcing decisions must be maintained. The decisions need to be guided by the law, corporate policy and the best interests of the buying organization.

(continued)

Figure 9-5 continued

AREAS OF STANDARD	ISM STATEMENT	EXPLANATIONS
Confidential and Proprietary Information	"Handle confidential or proprietary information with due care and proper consideration of ethical and legal ramifications and governmental regulations."	Supply management professionals deal with many different types of information to do their job well: price, bid or quotation, cost analysis, design, etc. Some or all of this information may be considered confidential or proprietary and should not be disclosed improperly. Even when sharing properly, it should occur only on a need-to-know basis and the recipient must be fully informed of the implication of such information.
Supplier Relationships	"Promote positive supplier relationships through courtesy and impartiality."	Just because the supplier depends on the supply management organization for contracts and the supply management professional holds the authority to influence contract decisions does not mean the supplier can be treated without respect or dignity. It is true that suppliers with partnership relationships may need to be treated preferentially, but it is also true that all other suppliers need to be extended the same courtesy and impartiality.
Reciprocity	"Avoid improper reciprocal agreements."	Reciprocal relations occur during the course of business. If these relationships affect decision-making, then reciprocity has taken place and that is improper. Reciprocity entails a sense of obligation and is both a legal and ethical issue that needs to be charted carefully and openly.
Applicable Laws	"Know and obey the letter and spirit of laws applicable to supply management."	Applicable laws are discussed in more detail later in this chapter. Supply management professionals must uncompromisingly abide by the letter and spirit of the applicable laws such as agency law, contract and commercial laws, antitrust laws, as well as international laws in countries in which they are conducting business.

(continued)

Figure 9-5   continued

AREAS OF STANDARD	ISM STATEMENT	EXPLANATIONS
Socially Diverse Practices	"Encourage support for socially diverse practices."	All suppliers, large or small, regardless of the ethnic background of the ownership, need to be given equal opportunity to compete. As discussed in Chapter 8, historically disadvantaged groups may need to be developed to promote diversity.
Professional Competence	"Develop and maintain professional competence."	The practice of agency assumes professional competence. Supply management professionals are expected to be competent and able to carry out their tasks by their employer, suppliers and society at large. They need to garner both ethical standards and technical skills.
National and International Supply Management Conduct	"Conduct supply management activities in accordance with national and international laws, customs and practices, your organization's policies and these ethical principles and standards of conduct."	In general, supply management professionals should follow the more stringent of the laws of their own country or the laws of the country in which they are conducting business. Supply management is practiced in many different ways throughout the world. Legal systems and business customs vary. Supply management professionals need to be knowledgeable about these variations, to avoid any potential conflict that may arise in a national and international context.
Responsibilities to the Profession	"Enhance the stature of the supply management profession."	The field of supply management has expanded beyond any single function such as purchasing or materials management. Members of this field need to promote each other in an ethical manner and help sustain reputations at the highest level.

When more than 90 percent of respondents to a survey of supply management professionals and their peers replied "to no extent whatsoever or to almost no extent" to the question that probed the extent to which meals, gifts and entertainment with suppliers might influence sourcing decisions, the question of dual standard came to the fore. Reconsideration might be in order regarding the appropriateness of the stringent policies against supply management professionals for engaging in informal interactions and exchanges with their suppliers. There were no clear conclusions, but it is important to note that the issue of dual standard itself is being raised. According to a sampling of comments from the survey, duality does exist and has some merit, but avoiding extremes is essential. Suppliers have reduced their budgets for entertainment and other information activities and a supply management professional "must not lose sight of this and relax as the champion of ethical behavior."[18]

Drivers and Barriers of Ethical Practices

The same ISM study articulates understanding the present ethical practices and drawing future directions for ethical behavior as goals of the survey.[19] With more than 1,200 respondents replying to the survey, it delineates factors that affect ethical practices.

According to the study, the potential barriers to ethical behavior include: pressure to perform, business priorities, differing standards across functions, no internal consequences, supplier pressures, ineffective training and regulatory compliance. The drivers of ethical behavior are listed at two different organization levels — the lower level where policies meet individual behavior and the higher level that affects the entire organization such as organization culture. At the lower level, the listed drivers include individual employee values, a people-oriented organizational culture that promotes corporate citizenship, and policies that include explicit sanctions and punishment for unethical behavior. At the higher level, the driver is listed as an organization culture that focuses on long-term strategic gains, not short-term bottom-line gains.

These results point to the need for having comprehensive and explicit ethical policies as a prerequisite. These policies must be implemented at the organizational level and embraced by everyone in the organization. It takes a concerted effort from top management to lower-level work units to instill ethical standards, but once they become part of the culture, they offer consistent and overarching behavioral guidelines for the members of the organization.

The Gap Inc. and Its Social Responsibility[20]

The Gap Inc. is one of world's largest retailers, selling such brands as Gap, Banana Republic, Old Navy and Piperlime, with more than 3,100 stores and sourcing from manufacturing plants around the world. In 2004, the organization filed its 40-page-long social responsibility report, with ethical sourcing at the center of the report. The report stated that when the suppliers did not meet Gap's requirements for labor standards, they no longer were used. The Gap Inc. stopped doing business with 136 suppliers and declined bids from more than 100 suppliers. Suppliers came from such areas as China, Africa, India and Central and South America, and violations ranged from failing to provide protective gear to physical abuse and "psychological coercion."

During the 1990s the Gap Inc. created a sophisticated internal system to monitor compliance with ethical sourcing practices. Its goal is to conduct business with suppliers that do not exhibit persistent violations of the Gap Inc.'s policies regarding wage, health and safety requirements. While the Gap Inc. implemented 100 percent monitoring of its factories over time, the public was unaware of this. For example, investors and advocacy groups such as Domini Social Investments filed a shareholder resolution for more transparency. The Gap Inc. management realized that more openness was required, and this realization led to filing the social responsibility report.

This report was exceptional in its candor: "For us to be transparent, we had to be willing to live with bad reactions to the report." The report delineates how the organization intended to take the next step by allowing an outside review team to scrutinize its own internal monitoring. It also has plans to re-evaluate its production goals that could potentially cause labor abuses such as overtime without pay. It even has plans to expand its efforts to support industry standards.

The Gap Inc. sources only from the suppliers that conform to its Code of Supplier Conduct. Supply management professionals become the focal point in this effort by working closely with the owners of manufacturing factories by approving their practices and continuing to monitor them. Supply management professionals become intimately familiar with the production processes and materials used for production and also for packaging and delivery. They act as agents of the buying organizations, enforcing their policies and educating the external constituents (e.g., suppliers).

Issues Of Agency, Authority And Liability

Agency is the legal relationship that exists between two parties by which one (the agent) is authorized to perform or transact specified business activities for the other (the principal). (*ISM Glossary*, 2006) As the supply management professional represents the organization, the supply management professional becomes the agent of its employer, who, in turn, is the principal. At the same time, when a supply management professional signs a contract with a supplier, the former acts as a representative of the principal, and the latter becomes the agent. When a supply management professional meets with a salesperson representing the supplier, they both meet as agents of their respective organizations. When a contract is signed, as legal representatives, they obligate their organizations for the buying organization to act as the principal and the supplier as an agent to perform a task.

Issues of Agency

As mentioned previously, an agent is a person or organization authorized to act for another person or organization in prescribed dealings with a third party. A *principal* is defined as a person or organization that has authorized another (the agent) to act on its behalf. For most employees, the employer is the principal. In this regard, as an agent of an organization, the supply management professional becomes the primary entity with whom suppliers will interact. For instance, when an organization contacts an import broker to facilitate international transactions, the organization becomes the buyer and the principal, and the broker becomes the supplier of service and, thus, the agent. In other words, the supplier relies on the supply management professional's statements and instructions, either in writing or orally, to engage in requested activities. From the organization's perspective, the sales representative acts as the agent of the supplier and has the authority to speak for the supplier. Sales representatives, however, often have far less authority to act on behalf of their principals than do supply management professionals.

Agent Authority

Supply management professionals generally have the authority to make final buying decisions within an organization. Often, these decisions are made by cross-functional teams that focus on issues of sourcing. In either case, the supply management professional acts as the contracting officer representing the organization to the supplier. In this situation, the supply management professional is known as the general agent and has the broadly defined authority provided by the employer, the principal. As organizations increase the level of outsourced goods and services, the supply management professional's responsibility as the representative/agent of the principal increases.

Given the large amounts of expenditures for which a supply management professional is responsible, the guidelines and instructions to the supply management professional must be clearly articulated. The levels of transferred authority from the employer to a particular supply management professional may vary depending on the need as well as that individual supply management professional's experience, education and perceived competency. Once a contract is offered and accepted, the agent-principal relationship between the supply management professional and the employer is established. The supply management professional has the right to know from the organization the specifics of the scope of authority; however, as long as the supply management professional engages in work in an ethical and faithful manner to the best of his or her ability and with the best interest of the organization, the supply management professional's obligations as an agent have been met.

Personal Liability

A supply management professional can be held personally liable if he or she engages in an activity without the authority of the employer. The supply management professional is liable for any damaging and illegal activities performed outside the scope of expressed authority, even if they were intended to benefit the employer.

The concept of agency can be captured in two dimensions: actual authority and apparent authority. *Actual authority* is imparted from the principal (employer) to the supply management professional (agent), while *apparent authority* is a type of authority created in an agency relationship when a principal permits an individual to operate in a fashion that allows third parties to believe that the individual is an authorized agent of the principal. It represents unauthorized purchasing or bypassing of the purchasing function by other functions within an organization (*ISM Glossary*, 2006). Actual authority represents what the supply management professional is authorized to do to manage supplies through such activities as contracting or supplier relationship management. Apparent authority is what the supplier *perceives* the scope of authority of someone from the buying organization to be. If the supply management professional acts within the scope of actual authority, then the supply management professional has no personal liability. However, if the supply management professional behaves outside of actual authority, then the supply management professional may be personally liable with potentially serious consequences. If the act exceeds actual authority but the supplier perceives it to be within the apparent authority, then the buying organization is still responsible for the agreement. Here, the buying organization as the principal may seek legal action against the supply management professional, the agent, for exceeding authority and misrepresenting the organization to the supplier. If, however, the act occurs outside actual authority and exceeds any perceived (apparent) authority, the buying organization is not responsible for the agreement and may be in a position to hold the supply management professional personally liable.

As an agent of his or her employer, the supply management professional is responsible for a wide array of issues from interpreting a purchase requisition to supplier selection to contracting and contract closeout, as discussed in Chapter 5, "Contracting." As every organization is embedded in a larger context of a community of organizations and society at large, the supply management professional needs to be a socially responsible agent both internally and externally.

The Supply Management Professional as a Socially Responsible Agent

Social responsibility cuts across the areas of ethical, environmental and fair supply management practices. These issues need to be woven into the fabric of an organization and individual behavior.

The Supply Management Professional as an Ethical Agent

The ISM ethical practices study emphasizes that supply management professionals are agents of their organizations and should strive to "hold themselves to high ethical standards, even if the organization is not supportive."[21] When it comes to the law, the supply management professional must stay within the actual authority previously discussed. However, when it comes to an ethical context, the supply management professional should try to exceed what the organization stipulates. One respondent of the ISM ethical study articulated that "such standards will allow you to maintain your integrity with your suppliers and in the marketplace."

The Supply Management Professional as a Gatekeeper of Confidential Information

In the ISM survey, when respondents were asked if they shared confidential information about one supplier with another supplier, about 75 percent claimed "to no extent whatsoever to almost no extent." On the one hand, it is encouraging that most respondents (75 percent) have acted responsibly by not sharing confidential information. On the other hand, what that also means is that the other 25 percent of respondents have responded in the affirmative and admitted to violating the professional ethical standards regarding confidential information.

Written comments from respondents corroborate this observation. One person stated, "What is confidential to one is not to the other ... I am continually amazed at one's ability to justify and rationalize outlandish behavior." One respondent called for allowing a different standard for the situation where there is a strategic partnership and confirmed that the organization uses "preferential consideration" when interacting with suppliers with strategic partnerships. Another respondent identified situations in which the supplier asked the supply management professional to disclose confidential information about another supplier and issued a need for better "suppliers' ethics."

This type of debate indicates that handling confidential information continues to operate in an area that is not clearly defined. In any case, it is clear that supply management professionals act as gatekeepers of confidential information and must act in the most responsible manner possible by abiding by the code of conduct as articulated by ISM and also by the organizations they serve.

The Supply Management Professional in the Larger Organization

In the agency role, a supply management professional is embedded in a larger organization's culture that affects individual behavior. Most organizations (e.g., 60 percent to 70 percent)[22] as represented in the ISM ethical practices survey are identified as driven by short-term results or quarterly fiscal results at some level (e.g., most, very or somewhat). Respondents articulated that this type of short-term orientation is, in fact, "hurting organizations ethically" and "pressure to make the numbers can lead to inappropriate decisions."

At the same time, more than half of the organizations (e.g., 57 percent) are shown as trying to ensure awareness of their organizations' codes of conduct by all employees at the level of "a great extent or very great extent." Organizations first try to select ethically oriented employees when hiring, and then instill a sense of what constitutes an ethical behavior in the employees from the time when employment begins. This type of effort clearly helps employee conduct and assists in the supply management professional's role as agent of the organization when facing external organizations.

Even in an international context, "especially when adjusting to low-cost country sourcing, business practice may seem counter to U.S. or European ethics. Through education and leadership in an organization, ethics will not be compromised and ways of working and doing business (in low-cost countries) can be carried out in an ethical manner."[23] Therefore, an organization's leadership must try to create a culture that promotes ethical decisions and actions, within which a supply management professional can operate. In other words, to the extent supply management professionals are an integral part of the larger organization, there is an internal inconsistency if top management asks individual managers to act socially responsible when there is no culture of social responsibility at the organizational level. Also, when facing another organization from a different culture, the differences in culture and how these differences may affect ethical behavior must be noted and articulated.

The Supply Management Professional as a Risk Mitigator

Supply management professionals not only need to be ethical managers but also economic agents promoting the interests of their organizations. For any risk issues that arise from supply markets or working with suppliers, the supply management professional can address them through contracts, insurance, legal protection, communication and planning. Purchase orders and contract terms and conditions always contain clauses disclaiming or limiting a supply management professional's responsibility for damages resulting from supplier violation of existing laws. Also, sound supply management practices dictate that suppliers who come onto the supply management organization's property have adequate insurance coverage for damage and personal injury to themselves and others. Furthermore, there is risk of loss disputes relating to the transfer of goods between two organizations. Typically, the supplier that is in possession of the goods bears the risk of loss, but the risk would transfer on delivery. However, as discussed in Chapter 5, "Contracting," if the supplier is in breach of a contract, then the supply management organization has the legal right to rejection and the supplier retains the risk until the situation is addressed and cured.

Managing a Socially Responsible Supplier and Supplier's Suppliers: Nokia

Nokia explicitly states that it is not engaged in sourcing raw materials but processed parts, components and subassemblies from international suppliers. This statement has significant implications to social responsibility, for Nokia may appear to be transferring the responsibility of managing natural resources to its suppliers. However, this is not the case. It means that Nokia recognizes that suppliers' activities account for "a substantial part of the life-cycle environmental impact of Nokia products."[24] Therefore, recognizing it has "complex and deep supply chains," it intends to reach beyond its top-tier suppliers to their suppliers and their suppliers' suppliers.[25] Currently, Nokia works predominantly with its first-tier suppliers educating them about Nokia's ethical and environmental policies. The plan is to have these first-tier suppliers educate their suppliers under Nokia's supervision.

Internally, Nokia continues to train its supply management professionals regarding "competence development activities on ethical and environmental issues." The basic ethics training topics include the concept of corporate social responsibility, the Nokia code of conduct, social requirements for suppliers and practical information on auditing social aspects in regular supplier assessments. The environmental training addresses environmental management, material restrictions, implications for sourcing practices and supplier requirements.[26]

Evaluation and Certification of Suppliers for Environmental Business Practices

To ensure that suppliers follow good business practices that incorporate environmental issues, formalized evaluation and certification programs are established. Some organizations, such as IBM and Novartis, require suppliers to meet specific standards in their operations. Some require suppliers to develop their own equivalent standards or obtain certification from an existing industry standard.[27]

Once a standard for environmental issues has been implemented, there are numerous ways to validate how well the suppliers comply with the requirements. First, suppliers can audit themselves using their own internal auditors. These typically have no vested interest in audit results and are removed from potential conflicts of interest. The results are written into a report and filed with the organization. Suppliers can be monitored by the supply management organization through regularly administered written surveys or other archived documents that offer evidence for compliance. In some cases, their products or services may be inspected for materials content or method of service delivery, or representatives from the supply management organization can physically go to the suppliers and audit their practices. Other evaluation methods include certification to an eco-labeling program and auditing per ISO 14010 and 14011 standards. Figure 9-6 summarizes how some organizations are evaluating their suppliers for environmental business practices.

When communicating with suppliers about the expectations of socially responsible, environmentally friendly business practices, these suppliers must understand how they will be monitored and evaluated. It is also critical that they realize the consequences for failing to comply. For instance, Federated Department Stores has implemented "a three-step process of action" that is applied to suppliers that violate the organization's Supplier Code of Conduct.[28] The punitive steps include suspending shipments until the corrective actions have taken place as well as measures to prevent such noncompliance. Punitive steps go beyond the policies of any one organization. Key laws and regulations address ethical issues surrounding supply management and failing to comply leads to punitive actions. To avoid that, a basic understanding and familiarity with key applicable laws and regulations is necessary.

Applicable Laws and Regulations

The law acts as a system of policies, rules and regulations enforced for the safety and well-being of a country and its citizens. It outlines behavior that is permitted and not permitted. In any country, laws stipulate the threshold of actions beyond which serious consequences occur for violators. For instance, consider the case of drinking and driving. There are explicit laws in the United States about the level of blood alcohol content beyond which a driver can be arrested — for instance, Washington State lists an alcohol concentration of 0.08 or higher as being illegal. To the extent that drinking impairs driving, the best option would be to avoid drinking altogether before driving; if someone does drink, there is an explicit threshold beyond which this

Figure 9-6   Evaluation of Suppliers for Environmental Practices

COMPANIES	PRODUCTS	SUPPLIER EVALUATION
Advanced Micro Devices (AMD)	Processors for computers	Suppliers are audited, categorized and prioritized according to potential risk.
Andersen Corp.	Windows and doors	Suppliers' practices are evaluated for environmental, health and safety issues.
Ashland Specialty Chemical	Chemical	Different audit protocols are used for different suppliers.
Bristol-Myers Squibb	Pharmaceutical, beauty and nutritional products	Multiple tools are used, ranging from surveys, reference checks, publicly available data and site visits.
Hewlett-Packard	Electronics	The organization met with other electronics manufacturers and developed a standardized environmental questionnaire to minimize suppliers' efforts to comply with multiple measurements.
Intel Corp.	Computer and peripheral equipment	All supplier representatives working on Intel compounds must have received mandatory safety training.
Occidental Chemical Corp.	Chemical	Suppliers are required to meet the same health, environmental and safety standards that are required of Occidental.
Quantum Corp.	Electronics	The organization worked with other electronics manufacturers to create a database of environmentally restricted substances and the resulting information is used in sourcing decisions.

Source: Adapted from Pollution Prevention Resource Center (PPRC), "Supply Chain Management for Environmental Emprovement," *Greening the Supply Chain* (2004), available from www.pprc.org/pubs/grnchain/eval.cfm.

act of drinking is not legally tolerated. In this regard, laws may be viewed as providing minimum requirements for ethical practices; for instance, legal responsibilities are considered a lower order requirement compared to ethical responsibilities.[29]

Before laws were enacted to govern business transactions, there was less uniformity of business behavior regarding how ethical a businessperson had to be in terms of being fair and open. In the United States, federal laws govern transactions between states, while state laws govern transactions within states. In the remainder of this section, various types of laws and regulations are covered that can affect the work of supply management professionals.

Common Law

The *ISM Glossary* (2006) defines the common law system as a legal system based on the English tradition of a limited body of written law, emphasizing usage and custom as the basis for case outcomes, where judges are constrained by the principle of precedent; that is, following the outcome of previous cases. Consequently, common law has become a major part of legal systems in countries around the world that have historic ties to the British Empire (e.g., India, Hong Kong, United States). As distinguished from statutory law, common law derives its authority from long-established usage and societal custom and from the judgments and decisions of courts recognizing such usage and custom. In the United States it is the system of law followed at the federal level and by all but one state.

Common law is distinguishable from civil code law (sometimes referred to as "Roman" law) systems followed in continental Europe, Mexico and South America. These code systems do not rely on custom and usage but rather on explicit codes of behavior established by the governing authority. Because of its history with France and Spain, Louisiana in the United States follows Napoleonic code (one example of a civil code system) rather than common law.

One part of common law is the law of contracts. Common law principles of contracting apply to all contracts. They may, however, be overridden by statutory provisions contained in the Uniform Commercial Code (UCC). Where the UCC does not apply, the common law of contracts provides the rules and standards for interpreting and enforcing contracts.

In the supply management arena, the common law of contracts applies primarily in cases involving real estate and services at least in the United States. It is also applicable to UCC-covered contracts to deal with issues not addressed by the UCC. In other words, the common law of contracts provides the legal foundation for all contracting.[30]

Commercial Laws

Commercial law, also known as business law, governs activities involved in business and commerce. These activities entail contracting, hiring and manufacturing and sale of consumer goods. In the United States, the federal government controls interstate commerce and the states under its authority. There have been efforts to institute a unified body of commercial law; the most successful effort has been the adoption of the Uniform Commercial Code (UCC).

Uniform Commercial Code. To make business laws more predictable and uniform and reduce differences that exist under common law from state to state, the *Uniform Commercial Code (UCC)* was introduced during the 1950s in the United States. Its different sections (referred to as "articles") address various aspects of commercial transactions, including contracting. All 50 U.S. states have adopted all or parts of the UCC in some form. UCC Article 2 and Article 2A have direct application to supply management professionals. The state of Louisiana has not adopted most of the UCC, but has its own version of UCC Article 2.

UCC Article 2 includes a variety of default provisions that take effect in case the contracting parties are silent on certain issues in relation to the sale of goods. In the case of pricing, the article stipulates that when the parties do not settle the price, the price has to be a "reasonable price at the time of delivery." Article 2A is similar to Article 2, but it addresses the leasing of goods (but not real estate) rather than their sale.

Generally, UCC Articles 2 and 2A cover the issues of warranties, risk of loss, seller's rights and obligations, and buyer's rights and obligations. Warranties ensure the buyer of a certain level of quality of goods provided by a supplier. Article 2 also includes transportation terms such as *FOB (free on board)* and *C & F (cost and freight)*. Various forms of the terms are discussed in *Effective Supply Management Performance*, Volume 2 in the ISM Professional Series. Other transportation issues such as bills of lading and freight bills are covered by UCC Article 7.

Sarbanes-Oxley Act. More recently, in 2002, the Sarbanes-Oxley Act (SOX) was enacted at the federal level in the United States to restore investor confidence after the well-documented financial collapse of major U. S. corporations. SOX mainly applies to publicly traded companies and is administered by the Securities and Exchange Commission (SEC). The goal of SOX is to promote alignment between shareholders, by the board of directors and the executive management team.

Initially, SOX focused on financial reporting and accounting issues, but it has been evolving to include supply-chain management.[31] The law addresses disclosure and documentation of business processes and evaluation of internal managerial controls related to financial reporting. The act still is evolving and, conceivably, the processes and documentation of interfacing external organizations such as suppliers may impact the work of supply management in a significant way as the interpretation and implementation of this law moves forward. Possibly over time SOX or similar state laws will extend their requirements to privately held companies, nonprofits and other business entities.

Furthermore, SOX presently applies only to U.S. registered companies. Moves are under way to instigate similar legislation in countries such as Japan and South Korea and in the European Union.

Restraint of Trade

Because supply management professionals are involved in procuring goods and services in a competitive environment, practices that ensure competition are critical in upholding the free market philosophy. As mentioned in Chapter 5, four primary laws address restraint of trade or antitrust issues in the United States: the Sherman Antitrust Act, the Clayton Act, the Robinson-Patman Act and the Federal Trade Commission Act (see Figure 9-7).

Department of Transportation and Department of Homeland Security

Two federal departments in the United States oversee trade and safety — the Department of Transportation (DOT) and the Department of Homeland Security (DHS). These governing bodies enact rules and regulations that require compliance.

The DOT was founded in 1966 by an act of the U.S. Congress. Its mission is to "serve the United States by ensuring a fast, safe, efficient, accessible and convenient transportation system that meets our vital national interests and enhances the quality of life of the American people, today and into the future."[32] The leadership comes from the Office of the Secretary, which addresses national transportation policy issues and intermodal transportation, and reaches agreements on matters related to international transportation. The DOT includes some of the most well-known organizations — the Federal Aviation Administration (FAA), the Federal Highway Administration (FHWA), the Federal Railroad Administration (FRA), the Maritime Administration (MARAD), the National Highway Traffic Safety Administration (NHTSA), the Surface Transportation Board (STB) and others.[33]

The FAA oversees the safety issues involved in manufacturing and maintenance of aircraft and other civil aviation issues. The FHWA addresses "the country's safety, economic vitality, quality of life and the environment" by coordinating highway transportation activities with states and other partners. The FRA oversees the safety and environmental impact involving rail transportation and MARAD engages in activities related to the "adequate, well-balanced" U.S. merchant marine. The NHTSA promotes "reducing deaths, injuries and economic losses resulting from motor vehicle crashes." The STB is "an independent, bipartisan, adjudicatory body organizationally housed within the DOT [and] is responsible for the economic regulation of interstate surface transportation, primarily railroads, within the United States."[34]

Figure 9-7   Laws Governing Restraint of Trade

NAME OF ACT	DESCRIPTION
Sherman Antitrust Act	This act prohibits "contracts, combinations and conspiracies" that restrain trade or free enterprise. The court examines the facts and circumstances surrounding the alleged practices and applies a "rule of reason" in determining whether those practices were in restraint of trade. The act covers group boycotts, reciprocal purchasing and consortium buying practices.
Clayton Act	This act deals with such trade practices as tying business arrangements, full-line forcing and exclusive agreements. These practices are deemed unlawful when they substantially reduce competition or create a monopolistic situation. Tying arrangements occur when the purchasing of one item is contingent on purchasing another item. Full-line forcing represents a similar situation where to purchase one or two items from a supplier, the supply management professional would have to purchase a full line of items.
Robinson-Patman Act	An amendment to the Clayton Act that focuses on anti-competitive practices where certain buying entities receive potentially discriminatory prices (e.g., lower prices) from a supplier compared to other buying entities. The act prohibits direct and indirect price discrimination where those price differences substantially reduce competition, and prohibits a supplier from paying a commission to a supply management professional and a supply management professional from accepting one. It also requires a supplier to treat all buying organizations in a consistent manner.
Federal Trade Commission Act	Responsible for the creation of the Federal Trade Commission, the FTC has the authority to determine the meaning of "restraint of trade." The FTC is charged with identifying unfair methods of competition and deceptive practices in commerce. All proposed corporate mergers undergo the FTC's test for unfair competition. The FTC shares antitrust enforcement authority with the U.S. Department of Justice.

The DHS is another key federal department that addresses safety issues related to trade and commerce. As briefly introduced in Chapter 5, the DHS "is responsible for protecting the movement of international trade across U.S. borders, maximizing the security of the international supply chain, and for engaging foreign governments and trading partners in programs designed to identify and eliminate security threats before these arrive at U.S. ports and borders." For instance, an initiative called Container Security Initiative (CSI) was created to screen high-risk containers at the source before they are put on the cargo vessel bound for the United States. Customs–Trade Partnerships Against Terrorism (C-TPAT) is a partnership to secure supply chains — as a voluntary government-business program to promote improvement of international supply chains while securing U.S. border security.[35] The DHS also manages security information and facilitates sharing it with other federal, state, local and private entities. In case of a catastrophic event such as a terrorist attack or a natural disaster, the DHS will lead and coordinate appropriate responses and engage in recovery efforts. Many large organizations have been working with the DHS to assist in its quest to accomplish these goals as well as similar organizations in other countries.

For instance, IBM offers information technology (IT) solutions to implement "security while ensuring logistical efficiency … by [providing] the framework to help safeguard against disruptive threats by fostering new levels of visibility, accountability and resiliency."[36] One example of an IT solution is Information On Demand.[37] Since the DHS established guidelines for creating fusion centers for exchanging critical information in the event that security is threatened, IBM has responded and created Information On Demand to exchange and integrate information across different entities and identify potential solutions.[38]

Health and Safety Laws

As evident in the description of the DOT and the DHS, when laws are enacted, the health and safety of citizens emerge as the critical issues. Since the 1960s, organizations have been subject to many social changes affecting the well-being of workers. In particular, as mentioned previously, the Occupational Safety and Health Act (OSHA) has dictated safety in workplaces.

Supply management professionals often are in positions to protect themselves, their organizations and internal users from possible liability by proactively managing suppliers to ensure compliance with OSHA and other similar laws. This may be accomplished by including a "compliance with the law" clause in contracts and appropriate indemnification provisions. However, this does not eliminate OSHA requirements on the part of the buying organization. OSHA serves to protect the organization in the event supplier action or inaction violates OSHA. Also, effective supplier selection, discussed in Chapter 7, will reduce exposure to risk.

Environmental Laws

The U.S. Environmental Protection Agency (EPA) was established to implement and enforce federal laws relating to clean air, clean water, waste disposal and related matters.[39] Additionally, hundreds of state, local and international laws deal with environmental issues. Thus, suppliers and supply management professionals have made changes in products, services and methods of doing business. For instance, the Earth Summit held in Rio de Janeiro, Brazil, in 1992 led to the adoption of the United Nations Framework Convention on Climate Change and the Convention on Biological Diversity.[40] An extension of this meeting, the World Summit on Sustainable Development,[41] was held in 2002 in Johannesburg, South Africa.

In recent years, environmental laws have been legislated into standards for industrial and consumer environmental emissions and into disposal of industrial and household wastes, particularly hazardous wastes. Some experts have argued that economic growth is to blame for increasing amounts of emissions and wastes and that economic growth should be curtailed. Others believe that, for economic well-being, growth must continue and that controls and incentives should be used to monitor future generations of emissions and wastes and to ensure safe disposal of those that have already been generated. Debates have continued over what amounts of emissions and wastes are safe as well as what might constitute a safe means of disposal. Other environmental concerns include land use, particularly wetlands and control of commercial operations on public lands such as national forests. Laws, regulations and other decisions to address environmental matters can affect productivity, the availability of natural and other resources and the cost to produce and procure products.

Supply management professionals engaged in materials disposal should keep track of applicable regulations. The primary law dealing with waste management and disposal is the Resource Conservation and Recovery Act of 1976 (RCRA). The EPA states that the goals of the RCRA are "to protect the public from harm caused by waste disposal; to encourage reuse, reduction and recycling; and to clean up spilled or improperly stored wastes."[42] The RCRA is designed to control the disposal of hazardous materials, particularly chemicals, in a landfill. This act created the "cradle-to-grave" control system that places responsibility for any hazardous waste on the generator. This applies even if the supply management organization's disposal contract contains indemnification clauses, warranties or guarantees. If the handler disposes of the material improperly, the owner is responsible. In disposing of materials, one of the supply management professional's most significant contributions is the proper qualification of sources. It is important to deal only with competent, reputable sources that know and follow regulations.

Intellectual Property and Trade Secrets

Federal patent, trademark and copyright laws provide protection for the owners of intellectual property or identifying information, but offer little protection for trade secrets. In fact, to apply for a patent, the trade secrets that pertain to that patent must be disclosed. Therefore, the National Conference of Commissioners on Uniform State Laws created a model law, the Uniform Trade Secrets Act (UTSA) that defines trade secrets, offers legal protection to owners of trade secrets, and offers legal remedies to owners in case of theft or misappropriation of trade secrets. To date, this U.S. law has been adopted by 42 states and the District of Columbia. In addition, the federal Industrial Espionage Act requires a minimum value of $100,000 of the secret involved and requires a higher burden of proof than does the UTSA. It also requires that the secret must involve interstate commerce, and any fines levied go to the federal government.

To avoid disclosing their own confidential information, organizations should have standard procedures in place, including the use of nondisclosure agreements (NDAs). An NDA is a freestanding agreement or contract provision restricting the disclosure of certain information, generally proprietary information, given by one party to the other in the course of contract performance and imposing liability for unauthorized disclosure. To ensure enforceability, NDAs must be signed before information is disclosed. Thus, a confidentiality provision contained within a contract may not be acceptable if confidential information has been disclosed prior to finalization of the contract. Whether covered by nondisclosure agreements or not, supply management professionals should exercise due care in the dissemination of any information related to their organizations, their supply management function or the business of their suppliers.

Management of Scrap and Surplus

As discussed previously, managing scrap and surplus has long been recognized as being both difficult and important. However, with the emerging prominence of environmental issues and the increasing cost of raw materials, it has become even more critical. As the supply of natural resources becomes depleted, management of excess material such as scrap and surplus is becoming an important cost consideration as well as an environmental one.

The effort to manage scrap and surplus materials requires a good deal of ingenuity and creativity. Supply management professionals should play a critical role in this effort, as gatekeepers of the materials that come in and out of the organization. For instance, they oversee the management of reclaimed or salvaged materials and typically are in charge of selling such materials in the market and trying to recapture value. Efficient and effective recycling — the practice of returning usable materials cast off from a process into a production stream for another use — should be the goal of supply management professionals.

Proactive Supply Management

Supply management professionals have a unique opportunity to help their organizations reduce the amount of scrap and materials their organizations produce. With supply management professionals increasingly involved in product and service design initiatives, they are able to offer recommendations regarding the sustainability of the materials and parts being used prior to production or service delivery.[43] At Herman Miller Inc., an international provider of office furniture and services, supply management learned to look at products and materials in a different way. The organization considers three key points when evaluating every product and project:

- Is this made out of a product that is harmful to the environment?

- Is it made out of recycled products?

- Is it easily dissembled and recyclable?[44]

Many organizations, both domestic and international, are working on ways to reduce their waste impact.

Disposable Materials

Scrap materials are defined as the residue from operations and off-specification production items that cannot be reworked or used for the originally intended purposes. Typically, there are three types of scrap — home scrap, prompt-industrial scrap and obsolete scrap. *Home scrap* refers to scrap that can be reused immediately upon its creation, such as trimmings from iron ingots or skimming from molten steel. *Prompt-industrial scrap* usually is generated from discrete manufacturing operations such as metal sheets after the stampings have been made out of them or trimmings from paper mills after the papers have been cut to size and packaged. This type of scrap requires prompt attention; otherwise, it can hinder the normal operations of the organization. *Obsolete scrap* refers to worn-out items such as old motors and other tools and equipment that have mechanical parts that wore out after repeated uses.

Scrap should be differentiated from spoilage and waste. Spoilage refers to items that become unusable during the course of an operation, such as food that falls on the floor in a food-manufacturing operation or manufacturing defects that cannot be reworked. Waste is slightly different from spoilage for it happens during the course of an operation but cannot be reclaimed and thus has little value. Waste refers to unusable by-products of manufacturing such as dust, smoke, paper trim or gases. Finally, obsolete goods that still are operational but have outlived their usefulness include old equipment and supplies that remain in good shape, but technology has moved on and they have become obsolete as a result. A technologically outdated 486 computer chip still functioning in an old PC is example of an obsolete scrap.

Managing Scrap and Surplus Disposal

The disposal of scrap and surplus items entails selling rather than buying. This aspect of materials management typically is the responsibility of the supply management professional. Supply management professionals generally understand the price trends of various types of materials. Because their demands are once-removed and supplies vary unexpectedly, the prices of surplus materials tend to fluctuate more than the prices of regular raw materials. In the case of low supply, the demand for surplus materials can cause the price to increase dramatically. Generally, no other individuals in an organization are more qualified to handle such issues than are supply management professionals. If the surplus is to be used internally, supply management professionals are the most knowledgeable and qualified to manage the process.

Internal Use. Typically, this is the preferred way of disposing of scrap and surplus materials. Surplus materials may be used to substitute other materials. For instance, the Ford Motor Co. once stocked up on palladium, for this surplus material can be used in place of other materials such as platinum. Obsolete goods can be reprocessed or remanufactured into useful goods. For instance, a surplus of short pipes that are otherwise obsolete can be reprocessed through welding — they can be welded together into a longer pipe that can be used for a productive purpose. Several old engines or motors can be remanufactured into one or two working engines or motors — they can be taken apart and the working parts put back together into a working whole.

There are alternate ways of reusing scrap. Home scrap can be reused as discussed previously. Prompt-industrial scrap also can be reused if the organization finds creative ways to reuse it. For example, small memo pads can be made from trimmed papers, and small parts such as washers can be stamped out of scrap skeletal sheets of metal. This type of effort might incur additional processing costs, but often the savings that result from reusing these scraps can be substantial. Some automobile companies have recycled tires into savings by using them to manufacture small rubber parts or make shock-absorbing pads that ease the fatigue of standing workers.

Return to Supplier. Surplus materials can be returned to the supplier, depending on the contractual arrangement. For instance, for nonferrous materials (e.g., copper), an agreement can be reached in advance with the suppliers of those materials that the scrap eventually would be returned to them. The material can be returned in its original form or as scrap. For precious metals or materials that are in shortage, a clause may be included in the contract for the supply management organization to return all surplus goods to the supplier.

Sell to Intermediaries. Brokers and dealers specialize in surplus materials. The advantage to individual organizations is that they often are able to consolidate surplus materials to the level of quantity that can be meaningful to potential buyers. Brokers are intermediaries that typically do not take ownership of goods, while dealers often take ownership and then engage in selling.

Economics of Surplus

The traditional acts of buying and selling focus on demand, and its economics assumes unlimited amounts of natural resources. In this scenario, advertising and marketing play important roles in creating demand, and the assumption is that the raw materials can continue to be unearthed economically. However, in the case of surplus, the economic perspective changes regarding creating demand and unearthing raw materials. Here, the supply matters more than the demand — supply in this case is already in a unique, processed state and the focus is on managing the existing supply to meet demand rather than creating demand by processing natural resources. The economics of surplus assumes natural resources are limited: The focus is on preventing the depletion of natural resources rather than on unearthing new ones.

However, locating demand often is very challenging. A prevalent mentality holds that surplus is bought rather than sold — it is more difficult to unload surplus than to find a source to buy. Also, an organization tends to stress the importance of surplus management, often acting on the premise of social responsibility rather than on short-term economic gain. Consequently, while manufacturing organizations that operate based on demand can attain high inventory turnover, surplus dealers focus more on having high levels of inventory and low inventory turnover so materials are available to fulfill demand.

A professional association in the United States that sets standards for dealing in surplus and other undifferentiated goods is the Institute of Scrap Recycling Industries, Inc. (ISRI), which focuses on scrap processing and recycling. The association provides standards for metals, paper, plastics, glass, rubber and textiles. Its primary purpose is to increase "awareness of the industry's role in conserving the future through recycling …"[45] The association was created as a result of a merger between the National Association of Recycling Industries (NARI) and the Institute of Scrap Iron and Steel (ISIS). With the advent of the Internet, online services focus on recycling, returning and remanufacturing. One such Internet service is called SSI — Material Recycling & Surplus Asset Service. SSI is a single-source provider that deals in base metals, precious metals, plastics and other miscellaneous metals for such major organizations as Motorola, Canon Inc., Ericsson and Microsoft Corp.[46]

Summary

As agents of the buying organization, supply management professionals often face the issues surrounding social responsibility. As they interact with external organizations, they contend with the ethical as well as the legal implications of their decisions. ISM has taken the lead by identifying and articulating what corporate social responsibility means for supply management professionals. ISM also offers guidelines for ethical behavior involving supply management. This chapter discusses what it means to be socially, legally and ethically responsible supply management professionals.

Key Points

1. Supply management professionals are agents of their organizations. They are responsible to their employers, profession and society for their socially responsible decisions and actions.

2. The impetus behind corporate social responsibility (CSR) comes from several sources, such as nongovernment organizations (NGO), government, institutional investors and consumers.

3. ISM views social responsibility of a supply management professional as residing first inside one's own organization and then in other organizations within the supply chain, upstream and downstream from the supply management professional's own organization.

4. Supply management departments should have written documentation to clearly communicate organizational policies and procedures to supply management professionals, internal customers, suppliers and customers.

5. Three types of law primarily govern ethics that pertain to supply management: defamation, disparagement and bribery. Defamation includes both libel and slander.

6. Standards issued by ISM, revised in 2005, to guide the supply management professional's ethical conduct cover perceived impropriety, responsibilities to the employer, conflicts of interest, issues of influence, confidential and proprietary

information, supplier relationships, reciprocity, applicable laws, socially diverse practices, professional competence, national and international supply management conduct and responsibilities to the profession.

7. The drivers of ethical behavior are listed at two different organization levels: the lower level where policies meet individual behavior and the higher level where the whole organization is affected.

8. In the context of supply management, several different agency relationships may be created. The supply management professional may represent the buying organization and become the agent of the buying organization, the principal. Likewise, a sales representative is an agent of the supplier.

9. Supply management professionals can be held personally liable if they engage in activities without the authority of their employers.

10. Laws of agency can be captured in two dimensions: actual authority and apparent authority.

11. Supply management professionals act as the gatekeepers of confidential information and must abide by the code of conduct as articulated by ISM and also by the organizations they serve.

12. The Uniform Commercial Code (UCC) includes a variety of default provisions that take effect in case the contracting parties are silent on certain issues in relation to the sale or lease of goods.

13. The goal of the Sarbanes-Oxley Act (SOX) is to promote alignment between shareholders, the board of directors and the executive management team.

14. Because supply management professionals are involved in procuring goods and services in competitive environments, practices that ensure competition are critical in upholding the free-market philosophy. Four primary laws address restraint of trade or antitrust issues: the Sherman Antitrust Act, the Clayton Act, the Robinson-Patman Act and the Federal Trade Commission Act.

15. The Environmental Protection Agency (EPA) was established to implement and enforce federal laws relating to clean air, clean water, waste disposal and related matters. Hundreds of state, local and international laws also deal with environmental issues.

16. Patent, trademark and copyright laws provide protection for the owners of intellectual property, but offer little protection for trade secrets. To apply for a patent, the trade secrets that pertain to that patent must be disclosed. The Uniform Trade Secrets Act (UTSA) defines trade secrets, offers legal protection to owners of trade secrets, and offers legal remedies to owners in case of theft or misappropriation of trade secrets.

17. Supply management professionals engaged in materials disposal should keep track of applicable regulations. The primary law in the United States that deals with disposal is the Resource Conservation and Recovery Act of 1976 (RCRA).

18. As the supply of natural resources becomes depleted, the management of excess material such as scrap and surplus is becoming an important consideration, particularly in regard to social responsibility, as well as the world economy.

19. The disposal of scrap and surplus items is the responsibility of supply management professionals, who, generally, are most familiar with the price trends of the various types of materials.

20. Internal use is the preferred way of disposing of scrap and surplus materials. Surplus materials can be returned to the supplier, depending on the arrangements, or disposed of using a broker or dealer who specializes in surplus materials.

10

INTERNATIONAL SOURCING ISSUES

Multinational organizations have increased their usage of international sourcing strategies. Domestic suppliers alone may not meet all the competitive needs of a multinational organization. International sourcing has emerged as a critical component of organizational strategy aimed at reducing costs, raising product or service quality, increasing manufacturing flexibility and improving design.

There are several reasons for the increase in international sourcing as a strategic weapon in the restructuring of an organization's operations. Almost all are directly related to gaining competitive advantage and market share by improving strategic positioning in response to a changing business environment. The principle changes in the business environment that underlie the move by multinational organizations to evolve are as follows:

- Intense global competition,

- Pressure to reduce and control operating costs,

- Need for operational flexibility,

- Need for different service outcomes for different customers,

- Shorter product/service development cycles,

- Stringent quality standards,

- Ever-changing technology,

- Free organizational resources for other purposes, and

- Produce products for emerging markets

The final chapter of this book discusses the strategic importance of supply management from an international sourcing perspective. Topics covered include

procedural and managerial issues related to international procurement, transportation/
distribution implications, differences between acquiring from international versus
domestic sources and the impact of international currency exchange rate fluctuations
on global sourcing.

CHAPTER OBJECTIVES

• Describe and explain the distinct phases of the supply management cycle for international sourcing.

• Explain how negotiating prices and terms with an international supplier poses additional challenges to the supply management professional.

• Discuss why cultural and language barriers exacerbate the difficult task of negotiating
with an international supplier.

• Explain why the costs associated with inbound movements of goods and services are
almost always higher in global sourcing compared to domestic sourcing.

• Prove that exchange rates volatility can significantly impact the price paid for imported merchandise.

International Sourcing and Procurement Issues

As with domestic sourcing, the supply management cycle for international sourcing
has six distinct phases.

1. Recognition of need,

2. Source identification,

3. Source evaluation,

4. Evaluation of quotations,

5. Subjective analysis and negotiation, and

6. Contract management.

A supply management department may deal with hundreds of sources for thousands of items. This creates a difficult administrative job for supply management personnel. International sourcing involves a series of tasks similar to domestic sourcing,

but these tasks differ in their complexity and level of detail. The principle differences are described below.

Source and Product Identification

Organizations interested in international sourcing can identify potential sources of supply in several ways. Commercial attachés, large banks, government documents, global trading organizations and national state departments are some of the sources of information that can be used by organizations engaged in global sourcing.

At LG Electronics Corp., source identification is preceded by an organizational needs analysis. This is accomplished through a survey of organizational units by the office of the director of procurement. The purpose of the survey is to identify unmet needs pertaining to a product, technology, quality and/or some service. Based on the needs assessment, a search is initiated to identify world-class suppliers.

Global marketing of products and services is creating both opportunities and challenges for the organization and the supply management function. A number of considerations go into selecting products or services suitable for cross-border sourcing. One consideration is the length of supply lines (distance of suppliers); another is the need to clearly communicate specifications, terms and conditions of the purchase contract, as well as the extent of supplier development required (including site visits). The following list of considerations typifies some of the criteria that may be used in selecting products or services for cross-border sourcing.

- Stability of design,

- Statement of work,

- Duration of anticipated association with supplier,

- Whether the product requires continuous runs,

- Completeness of engineering and other documentation,

- Desired service levels,

- Ability to provide technical/quality assistance,

- Language proficiencies,

- Ability to provide assistance for various time zones,

- Materials and tooling required, and

- Necessary visits.

In some instances, the supply management professional may be forced to use a certain international supply source. Buying from a subsidiary of one's organization is an example of being required to do business with a mandatory supplier.

Qualifying Sources

In the domestic market, an organization has legal recourse against a supplier that fails to honor contractual agreements. This same legal recourse either may not exist or be too burdensome when dealing with an international supplier. An organization's top management needs to establish the risk profile for the organization and how this risk profile then gets translated into real options for a supply management organization. For example, what is the risk–cost tradeoff for adding a second (or nth) international supplier, and how does this match up with the organization's risk profile? A good rule to follow is to reduce the risk of nonperformance by qualifying the international supplier before allowing the supplier to bid on a contract. Any good risk analysis and management strategy allows for both contingency plans and exit strategies.

Considerations important in international source qualification include experience of the supplier as an international source, financial strength of the supplier, the ease with which effective communication can be established, human resource policies of the country and supplier and implications for inventories (e.g., size or location).

Experience. A majority of the respondents participating in a study done by the authors designed to identify principles and practices of international sourcing reported that a careful evaluation of the supplier's experience and management expertise was essential to selecting a reliable international supplier. The supply management professional should ask for and check references from organizations doing business with the international supplier.[1]

Financial Strength. The financial strength of a supplier needs to be checked carefully. The potential supplier should be capable of meeting the increased expenditures necessary for equipment, marketing and additional inventory. A director of corporate procurement for a multinational organization suggests USD $10 million in sales and 100 employees as the lower limit for the size of the international supplier.[2]

Communication and Technology. It is essential to ensure that good communication lines exist. Multinational organizations should require an international supplier to designate a global representative who can ensure that communication lines are kept open. As the involvement of an organization in international sourcing increases, the need for developing information systems and technology to support source identification, supplier development and qualifications, relocation of purchased materials, logistics and inventory controls will increase.

Inventory. International sources must be willing and have the capability to maintain higher levels of inventory to compensate for longer supply lines, tight specifications and stringent delivery requirements. Issues such as warehousing capabilities and locations, as well as inventory containers that will accommodate different modes of transportation (e.g., ship to rail) must also be considered.

Longer-Term Orientation. Because of the length of time it takes to identify, develop and qualify international sources, it is important for organizations to strive for a long-term association with a supplier.

Human Resource Management Issues. Practices and issues that include labor skills, labor practices, human rights considerations and cultural differences need to be considered, addressed and continuously monitored.

Corporate Governance and Responsibility. Legal implications of international contracts, intellectual property protection and rights and brand management, including the risk of product service pirating, need to be addressed.

Analyzing Quotations from International Sources

Requests for quotation (RFQs) from international suppliers generally issued by a manufacturing division are usually routed through an international procurement office, trading agent, broker or the organization's subsidiary. The international procurement office or the trading agent handles the transmittal of the RFQs to potential suppliers. This office generally performs such liaison functions as supplier search and surveys, distribution of RFQs and transmittal of proposals from suppliers. At Honeywell International, field offices are generally staffed with engineers with considerable marketing experience. This joint engineering and marketing experience provides a better linkage between product/market (customer) needs and supplier requirements.

Proposals from suppliers in response to RFQs or RFPs[3] are sent back to the operating division for evaluation. Some cost elements that should be considered in comparing proposals from international suppliers include the following:

- Unit price,
- Supplier selection,
- Supplier management,
- Export taxes,
- Global transportation costs,
- Insurance,
- Tariffs,
- Brokerage costs,

- Letter of credit,

- Cost of money including currency conversion,

- Inland (domestic and international) freight cost,

- Risk of obsolescence,

- Cost of rejects,

- Damage in transit,

- Inventory holding costs,

- In-country transportation infrastructures,

- Language skills,

- Technical and communication support,

- Employee travel costs,

- Length of supply line,

- Political climate, and/or

- Complexity of technology or other regional infrastructure considerations.

Purchase orders are released by the individual divisions to suppliers through the organization's supply management office.

In addition, information is requested on the business practices of the supplier, including whether a letter of credit is required, the name of the bank handling the letter of credit, payment terms for open account transactions, principal customers of the international supplier, FOB point and size and scope of a supplier's operation (e.g., number of employees, annual sales volume, and market share).

The responsibility of the supply management organization is to develop requirements specifications and statements of work, specify supplier qualification criteria (done by divisional supply management professionals), perform analysis and provide negotiation assistance, place orders and coordinate with the organizations global procurement supply management office. Physical distribution and traffic supply management personnel handle shipment details, global carrier control and dealing with customs or brokers. Criteria for supplier qualification are often the same as for domestic suppliers. However, an understanding of the transportation, logistics and delivery schedules are amplified based on international scope and coverage.

Negotiating Prices and Terms

Negotiating prices and terms with an international supplier poses additional challenges to a supply management organization. Cultural and language barriers exacerbate the task of negotiating with a supplier and might require the services of an interpreter (see Chapters 5 and 6 for an in-depth discussion of country culture and negotiations). Extensive preparation is required before serious negotiations can be undertaken with an international source. This preparation includes a study of costs, supplier's management strengths, supplier's growth potential, service provision history, currency exchange rates and handling of rejected materials.[4]

Increasingly, organizations are turning to consulting organizations for cost analysis and projections for currency exchange rate projections. One consulting organization uses a computerized model that projects the cost of manufacturing a specific component in Asia by analyzing its material content, part geometry and manufacturing steps required to produce the component. The model uses data on labor, materials, energy, transportation and factory overhead costs. The organization's database can project costs for products in 16 countries. The computer model equips a supply management organization with detailed knowledge of an international supplier's components of cost, both present and future, both materials and services.[5]

Besides costs, a checklist of purchase conditions might include specific carriers and modes of transportation from the international source to the importing organization's home country, payment of transportation insurance, provisions for returning and/or replacing defective goods and the method of payment. The supply management department usually makes payment arrangements, especially when a letter of credit is involved.

Much has been written about protection of intellectual property rights (IP), human rights, sustainability and related issues. All of these might need to be addressed during the negotiation of a contract and the development of a relationship. Country specific accounting standards and practices are often different; these differences can have huge implications for an organization's tax liability. The supply management professional needs to involve corporate tax experts to help determine the best supplier.

Customs Regulations and Requirements

International sourcing negotiations between the supply management organization and supplier have to take into consideration both international and domestic customs rules and regulations. Many supply management organizations seek the assistance of a custom house broker that can provide information on commodity class descriptions that permit the most favorable duties, special tariffs,[6] and the effects, if any, of agricultural regulations and regional differences in the interpretation and/or application of customs rules and regulations. The levying of duties is also affected by international politics and the status of exporting nations as trading partners. For example, one organization clears all imports for each ordering facility at one prespecified customs point close to the ordering facility. This organization uses the services of a customs broker for clearing imported goods.

For example, VF Corp., a seller of apparel, must decide whether to bring goods for sale in Canada directly into Canada or into the U.S. for some value add then ship to Canada. This creates the possibility of duty drawback. The Duty Drawback Statute, originally passed as the Tariff Act by the U.S. Congress in 1789, entitles organizations to receive a refund of customs duties paid on imported merchandise that are subsequently exported as part of a finished product (*ISM Glossary*, 2006). The refund from filing a drawback claim translates into additional profits; however, many organizations fail to take advantage of this unique opportunity. In fact, the law allows a claimant to file a drawback on exports up to three years old, thus creating the potential for a substantial recovery amount in the first year of establishing a program.

Organizing for Global Operations

Organization strategy, structure and coordination are the overarching mechanisms used to control and coordinate the materials or services acquisition activities of an organization's international operations. Without a sound organizational infrastructure to provide for the establishment of responsibilities, reporting, coordination and effective communication, it would be difficult to integrate the efforts of those with responsibilities for international sourcing activities and decisions. Recognizing the need for a higher level of coordination and the interdependencies that exist in international operations, organizations have turned to the supply chain management concept of organizational design. Under this concept, the management of sourcing is viewed as a shared responsibility among functional groups that span the continuum of sourcing to distribution.

Developing an organizational structure that is effective in managing the complexity of international sourcing within the supply management plan requires an analysis of the internal and external factors that influence an organization's operation environment. Myriad political, economic and cultural factors external to the organization affect the organizational structure. The political environment (e.g., tax structures and legal constraints), the stability of a government and its regulatory agencies, exchange rate considerations, and cultural diversity (i.e., differences in languages, differing attitudes toward quality of life and diversity of skill levels) all pose significant operational problems for a multinational organization unaccustomed to dealing with these divergent considerations. These considerations, therefore, affect the design of an effective organizational structure.

Global factors such as management preferences and product or service characteristics also influence organizational needs. Management preferences are frequently related to centralization or decentralization of organizational responsibilities, authority and accountability. Product or service specific factors, such as the diversity of a product or service span, affect the degree of interdependence desirable between organizational subunits. For example, if the final product or service is unique to each division of a multinational organization, then the organizational interdependence is low. In contrast, if the products produced or services performed by different divisions are functionally similar, then a higher degree of organizational interdependence is desirable due to the economy of shared advanced technologies, technical expertise, and research and development costs, among other things. In sum, the degree of interdependence influences the choice of a particular organizational structure.

The Impact of Global Supply Management on Other Functions

Globalization of the marketplace, international competition and changes in the business environment have all contributed to the increase in international sourcing. The push to buy internationally is on, in both small and large organizations. International sourcing will continue to grow as a matter of corporate policy. Organizations interviewed for a study conducted by the authors all have corporate supply management offices for international sourcing and procurement established under corporate policies.[7] International supply management sourcing opportunities are changing the mix of manufacturing and service organizations (through make/buy decisions) and thereby affecting capital investment requirements and the infrastructure within organizations. For example, transportation is increasingly becoming the responsibility of the supply management function. In a 2005 ISM survey of managers and executives of Fortune 1,000 companies, 79 percent indicated transportation was part of the supply management department's responsibility.

International sourcing has had a significant effect on operations in both the manufacturing and service sectors. The reduction in the number of components and manufactured subassemblies, implementation of just in time (JIT), an increase in the quality of manufactured goods, changes in manufacturing infrastructure, use of international suppliers to provide back office and front office operations from thousands of miles away, and closer cooperation and working relationships among manufacturing, marketing and supply management personnel are direct consequences of international sourcing initiatives. Expertise in international supply management is a competitive weapon. Recognition of this has led to its growth in organizations throughout the world, a trend that is likely to continue. Supply management professionals are being called on to play a different role as organizations push toward integration of international suppliers into their manufacturing and service systems. Developing stable production plans, simpler designs, standard protocols for service delivery, process designs that ensure a smooth production or service flow, and tighter linkages with supply management and marketing is more essential for organizations than ever before.

Some unique issues arise when the decision to purchase internationally is made within the organization. Cross-functional input into the procurement process is mandatory, if potential problem areas are to be avoided. A key to effective international sourcing is selecting flexible suppliers of the highest quality. This is often difficult to assess in that data concerning suppliers and their respective quality performance is often not readily available. Organizations sourcing internationally should make frequent visits to potential sources to assess supplier capability. Because these visits may require a team assessment, resource allocation constraints become key.

Quality problems from an international supplier can have an onerous impact on production and customer service perceptions. The pipelines for goods are long, distances are great, languages and cultures are different and misunderstandings common. All parties must clearly understand quality specifications or statements of work before the supplier begins production or service delivery. Engineering, quality assurance, marketing and operations must work together to assure the highest level of supplier quality. When poor quality does occur, correcting lost customer ill-will, returns, reimbursement and replacement of the offending items can be quite complex. The bottom line is to avoid defects at all costs.

Most cross-border shipments will be made by ocean shipment and the lead-time will be several weeks. This means that the supply management organization must plan capacity and material use on a much longer time frame. Schedules must be stabilized or inventories can mount to unacceptable levels. JIT is difficult to attain with an international supplier.

Expediting an international supplier's shipments takes on a more critical role due to the expanded supply chain. The supply management professional must be on good terms with the international supplier's personnel. In fact, the quality of an international supplier's management is probably equally important as the quality of the purchased product or service during the selection decision.

During the past 20 years, international currency exchange rates have floated freely with respect to the U.S. dollar, other than the Chinese yuan. Fluctuations have been, at times, precipitous. This means that before signing a contract, the supply management professional must work closely with finance to forecast likely exchange rate movement scenarios and likely methods for moderating the impact for such fluctuations. Arbitrarily contracting for payment in U.S. dollars makes little economic sense in most cases. Supplier management must also manage and monitor currency decisions for the European Community as the EU continues to include additional member states.

Transportation and Distribution Implications in International Sourcing

The costs and complexity associated with inbound movement, such as transportation, warehousing, materials handling, packaging, documentation, in-transit inventory carrying, order processing and communications costs, are usually higher in international sourcing as compared to domestic sourcing. This is because of the potential for larger shipment distances, greater order cycles times, multiple transportation modes and complex documentation requirements that are often associated with the import process. Another category of costs that becomes relevant when an organization is purchasing in the global marketplace relates to national and economic boundaries. Shipments traverse national and economic boundaries, and certain costs are associated with overcoming political and economic trade barriers. In fact, transport-related costs are such a large factor in international trade that prices are often evaluated in terms of *landed costs*. Landed costs are a subset of the total cost of ownership (TCO), and are defined as the total accumulation of costs for an imported item, including purchase price plus freight, handling, duties, customs clearance and storage to a designated point (*ISM Glossary*, 2006).

Trade barriers result from government policies or regulations that restrict international trade. The costs or restraints include tariffs, import permit costs, import duties or licenses, export licenses, local content requirements, subsidies, import quotas, and import and transit taxes. Trade barriers are the result of a nation's governmental processes, but economic trade barriers are more often the outcome of less controllable international factors such as a nation's relative position among nations in the world money and commodity markets. Economic trade barrier costs include those costs associated with monetary exchange rate differences, as well as specialist fees for agencies that facilitate exchange between different economies (e.g., bank fees, customs-house broker charges, freight forwarder costs and import broker fees). Some governments attempt to manage or remove these trade barriers through a variety of legislative means such as duty-free zones, economic development zones and commercial advice through local attachés.

A cost analysis in international sourcing is more complex than in the domestic arena due to the additional cost categories that must be considered. For example, the supply management organization now has to decide whether to incur customs-house broker fees that may result in lower duties paid on imports because the broker has a better understanding of the tariff product classifications than the importing organization's management does. An importer may also be faced with the decision of whether to pay higher prices for a freight forwarder with lower damage rates to allow the organization to reduce packaging costs and/or the risk of an inadequate supply. The importance of logistics-related cost considerations in international sourcing is highlighted by the case of a multinational manufacturing organization with headquarters in California.

In the past, this organization obtained all of the parts required to support production at its cross-border facilities by ordering them from U.S. suppliers and shipping them to the organization's California warehouse. From the warehouse, the parts with the required documentation were sent cross-border by air express. Using this two-stage process, it took from three to five days to move a single component from its international supplier through the organization's warehouse to receiving facilities in, for example, Saudi Arabia. In addition, customs clearance at the destination country sometimes took up to a week, and the movement of parts from the airport to the international facility was also costly and time consuming.

To speed the flow of goods through the supply pipeline, the organization turned to DHL International GmbH and arranged for the air express company to provide door-to-door service from the original supplier to the cross-border facility, bypassing the organization's warehouse. In the new arrangement, the organization continues to be responsible for documentation. DHL plays a double role in the shipment process by moving parts directly from the supplying factory to the carrier's hub at Kennedy International Airport and at the same time picking up documents from California and attaching them to the freight in New York for express shipment cross-border. In the destination country, DHL handles all customs clearance and payment of duties in addition to delivering the parts to the receiving facility. By including domestic and global transit time, the system saves from one to three days of transit time.

Transportation Options

The decisions made by an organization regarding transportation are important in today's world. Decisions are vital as supply chains become longer, more complex and increasingly external to the organization. Determining the proper modality represents huge tradeoffs in time, cost and required oversight as organizations pursue low-cost country sourcing and market expansions. Sourcing and using logistics and transportation providers is not a buyer's market anymore. Better sourcing and price are obtained with longer-term arrangements that fit the provider's business and capabilities. Yet even better cost-driven pricing is obtained when working with the provider's economics and investment cycles. The supply management professional should be aware of the various market drivers, including globalization, intense competition, short product life cycles, deregulation and environmental issues. The ability to execute the transportation and logistics strategies within the global supply chain better than competitors will lead to improved relative performance.[8]

There are five modes of transportation: water, motor carrier, rail, air and pipeline. Each has unique characteristics. When considering a transportation modality, the supply management professional should assess the following factors.

- Types of goods to be transported, including size, weight, density, packaging and specific physical characteristics;

- Which mode or combination of modes will be best suited to meet the organization's needs;

- Delivery requirements, including the time needed; and

- Organizational requirements.

With the increase in international sourcing, third-party logistics providers have also increased. Many organizations will use this service as the growth of outsourcing and international sourcing continues.

Truck (Motor Carriage or Highway Transportation). Few goods are moved without highway transportation at some point. The majority of shipments are semi-finished or finished goods. They have smaller shipment sizes than rail. Truck organizations fall into two categories.

1. *Less-than-truckload (LTL),* which collect smaller shipments and consolidate them into full truckloads. There are a few large LTL carriers.

2. *Truckload (TL),* which is the amount of freight required to fill a truck by cubic or mass and is the bases for shipment for a TL rate. Usually in excess of 10,000 pounds with rates adjusted for high cube products. (*ISM Glossary,* 2006)

LTL shipments are considered fairly dependable and fast. Trucks are commonly used for shipments across borders within the European continent. In other parts of the world, trucking organizations are hired to complete ocean shipments. This mode is relatively reliable. The chance of damage is minimal and provides for flexibility. However, it is neither the fastest nor cheapest option. The supply management professional must be aware of the infrastructure and logistics issues relative to every specific country in which the organization does business.

Air Transportation. Air is the fastest form of transportation but also the most expensive. More shippers are using air due to globalization, however. Dependability and reliability are relatively high. There are additional constraints with using this mode, such as physical characteristics or dimensions of the products shipped.

Water Shipping. Water service is limited to inland waterways or the ocean. However, it provides service where rail or truck is not feasible. It is a low-cost option for transporting large quantities of product globally or over inland waterways. Water shipping is typically slow due to long transport times, slow methods of handling and unexpected delays due to weather. Also the chance of damage is greater due to more handling. At least one other mode, such as rail or truck, is generally needed to complete the freight movement to its final destination. Thus, organizations must determine the most effective combination of modes to ensure efficient freight movements. Water shipping is often supplemented by air shipping when a faster mode is needed for emergency shipments. It helps promote international trade, and demand for container ships is on the rise as well as port congestion.

Rail Transportation. The relatively large capacity of railcars has made this mode of transportation ideal for large-volume movement of low-value commodities and bulk cargo. Railroads typically haul raw materials (e.g., coal or lumber) and low-value products (e.g., food or wood products) long distances. Travel time is slow, with significant time spent on loading and unloading activities. Shipping costs are less than air or truck. However, they may offer other special services, such as guaranteed expedited service or stop-offs to load or unload. Rail service is often available at ocean ports to continue the movement of international shipments to their destination.

Pipeline. Pipelines are limited to the movement of crude oil, refined oil products and coal slurry. Movement is slow but possible 24 hours a day and dependable. Capacity is also high and the chance of damage or loss is low.

The Pros and Cons of International Sourcing

The benefits of international sourcing must be weighed against the costs of longer transportation links. Countries that are contiguous can use shipments that can be transported overland via truck or rail, but international shipments must be made by air or ship. Air transport involves relatively high freight charges, yet is the preferred method for international shipments of sensitive items such as electronic equipment and perishables. International shipping services feature lower costs for the transportation of goods, but at much slower speeds. Water transportation is typically used for large-volume purchases and the transport of raw materials.

When goods are shipped by water, in addition to the transportation charges, inventory carrying costs will increase because of the increased inventory required in the supply line due to longer lead-times. The additional inventory necessary to support an extended transportation pipeline is one of the often overlooked costs of international sourcing. For example, it may take up to five weeks for a shipment to move from an Asian supplier via sea to a buyer in the Midwest region of the United States. Continuous use of the product requires an uninterrupted flow from the supplier to the purchasing organization. Thus, there may be five separate weekly shipments at various positions en route to the destination. This five weeks' worth of inventory is costly in terms of its financial investment as well as its transportation. Pipeline inventory costs must be included in comparisons of the total landed cost of distant suppliers versus local suppliers.

The most frequently used international terms for transportation are known as the Incoterms.[9] These terms, controlled by the International Chamber of Commerce (ICC), determine: (1) who will pay the freight, (2) who will be liable for customs duties and (3) who will bear the risk of loss of the cargo. Thirteen Incoterms define the different points where responsibilities are transferred from the seller to the purchaser. The ICC recommends that "Incoterms 2000" be referred to specifically whenever the terms are used, together with a location. For example, the term *delivered at frontier (DAF)* should be accompanied by a reference to an exact place and the frontier to which delivery is to be made, such as *FCA Kuala Lumpur Incoterms 2000*. Incoterms are discussed in more detail in *Effective Supply Management Performance* from the ISM Professional Series. Some examples of terms follow.

- *EXW — EX WORKS [named place]*. Used for any mode of transport. All responsibilities, costs and risk pass to the buyer at the seller's loading dock. If the goods are damaged in the seller's factory, the seller is responsible for the damage. If the goods are damaged while being loaded onto the carrier at the seller's loading dock, the buyer is responsible.

- *FAS — FREE ALONGSIDE SHIP [named port of shipment]*. Used only for ship transport (inland waterway and seagoing). Seller must deliver the goods to the dock, next to the ship, and the seller is responsible for export customs clearance.

- *FOB — FREE ON BOARD [named port of shipment]*. Used for ship transport. Seller must load the goods onto the ship.

- *CFR — COST AND FREIGHT [named port of destination].* Used for ship transport. Same as FOB, but the seller must pay for shipping to the destination port.

- *CIF — COST, INSURANCE AND FREIGHT [named port of destination].* Used for ship transport. Same as CFR, but seller pays for insurance and names buyer as beneficiary.

In international business, however, the customer may have a good reason for wanting to control the transportation element or at least part of it. For example, a large organization by virtue of its significant supply management leverage may be able to negotiate lower freight rates than a smaller supplier. Also, an organization that makes substantial purchases in a certain geographic region might attain some economic advantage by consolidating its purchases with respect to shipment. Even an organization preferring to buy on a *near-delivered* basis may see some benefit in controlling local customs clearance. It might be advantageous for the supplier to leave local delivery from the port of importation to an inland destination to its distant customer, who is in a better position to oversee the final stages of delivery.

The options available should be carefully considered and reviewed by the supply management professional in order to minimize the total cost of an international purchase. In order to determine the cost of import transportation, the supplier should be required to quote the two prices: (1) the FOB port price, and (2) the CFR (or CIF) global port price (buyer-selected port). Once a supply management professional has received both quotes, the freight costs as quoted by the supplier can be determined. The supply management professional can then negotiate and obtain alternate costs from an ocean carrier or airline. If the supply management professional's freight costs are less than the costs implied by the supplier's quoted price, the supplier should be requested to ship FOB port using the supply management organization's designated carrier. Otherwise, the supplier's CFR quote should be accepted. Because some cross-border suppliers may attempt to make a profit on transportation costs, such a comparison is well advised.

Whether a supply management organization routinely assumes responsibility for the freight element of its international purchases is a tactical issue that is affected by the volume of international purchases the organization engages in, as well as its opportunities for consolidating inbound shipments. If a supply management organization decides to assume responsibility for the logistics involved in international sourcing, this would necessitate a closer linkage between the supply management professionals responsible for the procurement and logistics functions than is necessary for domestic operations. The supply management organization ultimately will pay the logistics costs one way or another in the total cost of doing business. The question is who can pay those charges most efficiently and economically.

Managing International Exchange Rate Risk

Many supply management professionals do not pay enough attention to the issue of exchange rates and managing the risk of exchange rate fluctuations because they incorrectly believe this is the job of the organization's finance department.[10] However, once the sourcing decision is made, many of the options available to the finance department are predetermined. The other misconception is that contracting in the supply management professional's currency solves all problems. The medium of payment for most international purchases is currency. However, as discussed later in this chapter, countertrade may be required to be used in international business transactions. The currency used for international purchases may be the purchasing organization's, the supplier's or possibly the currency of a third country. The currency selected for payment can result in higher or lower purchase costs over the life of a contract due to volatile exchange rates. This section explores international exchange rate issues in supply management and presents a framework of exchange rate management techniques available to supply management professionals who source internationally.

The Importance of Exchange Rates in Supply Management

Exchange rates impact the price paid for imported merchandise when payment is in the supplier's currency and there is a lag between the time the contract is signed and payment is made. Depending on the country of the supplier and the direction of the exchange rate movement, an organization can end up paying substantially more or less than the original contract price. For example, suppose that on January 3, 20xx a U.S. supply management professional enters into a one-year contractual agreement with a Japanese supplier that calls for equal monthly payments in yen. Furthermore, assume that the contract, when signed on January 3, specified that at the prevailing exchange rate (202.48 yen per U.S. dollar) each monthly payment would equal 20.248 million yen ($100,000). Depending on the exchange rate volatility of the yen with respect to the U.S. dollar over the duration of the contract, the total cost to the buyer could be higher or lower than the expected $100,000 per month.

The issue becomes even more complicated when two or more international suppliers from countries with different currencies are being considered for a contract. Each potential supplier's currency would fluctuate differently in relation to the U.S.

dollar. Therefore, each contract, if consummated, would ultimately cost different U.S. dollar amounts.

Responding to Currency Movements

An organization can pursue various approaches in response to volatile exchange rates. Supply management professionals making payment in an international currency may attempt to lessen the risk of an adverse price fluctuation through the use of currency futures or a risk-sharing contractual agreement. On the other hand, an organization may wish to exploit existing or expected favorable exchange rate differentials in identifying and selecting suppliers. For example, an organization in the United States might deliberately place orders with suppliers dealing in currencies that are expected to lose value against the dollar.

Certain factors involved with currency fluctuations can be recognized and tracked over time. Exchange rates move in cycles. In the past, attempts to forecast short-term exchange rates have not met with much success; however, some technically oriented forecasting services have done well in forecasting longer term directional currency movements. Longer term movements are becoming more predictable as the value of a country's currency becomes a means of fostering increased exports or decreased imports or both.

Exchange Rate Management

Research has identified a wide range of currency management approaches, leading to the construction of a conceptual framework for exchange rate management approaches. The conceptual framework for currency management strategies is principally designed for U.S. importers serving domestic markets. Organizations with both domestic and international markets have additional strategies and resources available to them, some of which are beyond the scope of this book.

The conceptual framework consists of two major strategy categories: the *macrolevel* and the *microlevel*. Macrolevel strategies affect the sourcing decision and the volume/timing of purchases; microlevel strategies are employed after both the source selection and volume/timing decisions have been made and are frequently used to protect the organization from adverse currency fluctuations. The conceptual framework for both macrolevel and microlevel exchange rate management is presented in Figure 10-1.

Macrolevel Exchange Rate Strategies

The use of exchange rate information in the supplier selection decision is important to successful global sourcing. Because of volatile exchange rate fluctuations, two equally capable suppliers from different countries that quote the same U.S. dollar equivalent

Figure 10-1   Conceptual Framework for Currency Management

Macro Strategies
1. Exchange rate information is used as an input to the source selection decision.
2. Exchange rate information is used as an input to the volume/timing of purchases decision.
Micro Strategies
1. Payment in U.S. dollars
2. Buying international currency forward
3. Buying international currency futures
4. Risk-sharing contract agreement
5. Payment in supplier currency

price at a particular point in time can end up having significantly different costs over the extended life of a requirements contract.

Supply management professionals thoroughly screen potential international suppliers using myriad complementary factors, which include quality, delivery, service, technical support, price, financial status, managerial capability and more. But, it is still rare to find books, articles and trade publications that simultaneously explain the importance of exchange rates in international sourcing and advocate their use in the supplier selection decision.

The Volume and Timing of Purchases. Historically, supply management has viewed markets as being somewhat dichotomous; that is, those markets in which the factors of supply and price could be considered reasonably stable in the short run and those markets in which the factors of supply and price fluctuate significantly in the short run. For example, products purchased in stable markets might consist of standard off-the-shelf items such as many MRO supplies purchased from domestic sources. Because the price of such materials is relatively stable over the short term, the volume and timing of purchases in order to exploit favorable price differentials is a nonissue.

In contrast, unstable markets provide the supply management professional with an opportunity to either exploit favorable price changes or avoid unfavorable price differentials through the timing of purchases. If the price of a particular item is expected to increase, the supply management professional could purchase in a larger than usual quantity and store the item in inventory until needed.

In the international marketplace, there really is no such thing as a stable marketplace. Even though an international supplier consistently quotes the same price for its products over time, the exchange rate for that supplier's currency with respect to the dollar is constantly changing. In such cases, the timing of purchases can significantly impact the material's purchase cost, final product price and, thereby, overall product competitiveness.

Microlevel Exchange Rate Strategies

Microlevel strategies can be employed after decisions regarding both the source selection and volume/timing of purchases have been made. These strategies are frequently used to protect the supply management organization from unexpected, shorter term currency fluctuations.

Payment in U.S. Dollars (Risk Avoidance). One way to avoid the risk of volatile exchange rates is for the supply management professional in the United States to pay in U.S. dollars. This strategy transfers the risk of an adverse currency fluctuation to the supplier. By specifying payment in U.S. currency, a buying organization assures itself a fixed future price in U.S. dollars whether or not the exchange rate fluctuates. Thus, the supply management professional has an organization cost for planning purposes and has precluded the occurrence of future fluctuations.

Buying International Currency Forward (Risk Avoidance). An alternative strategy is to buy *forward*, for future receipt, the needed international currency from a financial institution at a fixed exchange rate. The *ISM Glossary* defines forward buying as buying in excess of current requirements. Organizations may buy ahead as a matter of strategy or because of anticipated shortages, strikes or price increases. This practice also removes the risk of an unfavorable currency fluctuation, providing the organization with a known future price. The forward market for international exchange is a worldwide network consisting mainly of banks and brokers trading electronically. The amount of currency covered by a given contract is determined by negotiation, and quotations are for a stated number of days into the future based on an individual's needs (e.g., 30, 90 or 180 days).

In forward buying, a commission is paid to the bank handling the transaction, which is set by the *spread* between the bank's buy and sell price; this commission is not easily determined by the customer. To engage in forward buying, the organization must have a line of credit with the bank. Because the expense of individual contracting is large, the forward market is limited to very large customers dealing in international trade.

Supply Management Futures Contracts (Risk Minimization). Another hedging mechanism is to buy a *future* or contract to purchase the needed amount of international currency from one of the currency commodity exchanges. If the supply management professional's selected currency of payment goes up in value in the interim before the payment becomes due, the supply professional sells the contract for a profit and uses the profit to make up the difference when making payment. If, on the other hand, the supply management professional's selected currency falls in value, the buyer loses value when the futures contract is sold, but makes up most of the differential at the time of payment. Because realized returns on the futures contract are uncertain, hedging does not remove risk altogether but instead reduces it.

Futures contracts are traded on an organized exchange such as the Chicago Mercantile Exchange or the National Stock Exchange of India in Mumbai (the largest stock futures trading exchange in the world, followed by JSE Limited in Sandton, Gauteng, South Africa).

Although only individuals may be members of the exchange, brokers are afforded the opportunity to trade for their clients or for their own accounts. Unlike the forward market, which is limited to very large customers, the futures market is accessible to anyone needing hedge facilities. Hedging is defined in the *ISM Glossary* as a "futures" purchase or sale entered into for the purpose of balancing a sale or purchase already made, or under contract, in order to offset the effect of potential market price fluctuations. In the futures market, contracts are traded on major currencies only (e.g., euro, British pound, Canadian dollar, Swiss franc, Japanese yen, U.S. dollar and the Mexican peso) and the contract amounts and delivery or maturity dates are standardized. Maturity dates for currency futures occur on the third Wednesday of March, June, September and December. Less than 1 percent of the contracts are settled by actual delivery.

In buying currency futures, an organization does not actually make a payment equal to the value or price of the contract. Instead the organization pays its broker a hedge or trade account margin that is refunded to the organization at the time its contract is sold. This margin varies from broker to broker and also over time based on the volatility of the exchange rate. The margin amount may be posted in cash, a bank letter of credit or in short-term U.S. Treasury instruments. There is also a brokerage fee per contract that becomes due when the contract is sold.

Contractual Agreements (Risk Sharing)

One method of sharing the risk between the buyer and supplier of an adverse exchange rate movement is to use a *risk-sharing contract*. One common type of risk-sharing contract stipulates that exchange rate losses (or gains) are to be equally shared by both parties.

Thus, for example, if the buying power of the U.S. dollar decreases, the loss incurred by the purchasing organization computed with respect to the original contract price (expressed in U.S. dollars) is split in half and subtracted from the current (higher) cost of the needed quantity of international currency. If the buying power of the U.S. dollar increases, the gain experienced by the organization is divided in two and added to the current (lower) cost of the needed quantity of international currency.

Another type of risk-sharing contract employs an *exchange rate window*. The window is defined as plus or minus some percentage movement in the exchange rate. As long as the exchange rate varies within the window, no adjustments to price are made. If the exchange rate moves outside the window, the price is adjusted. The adjustment process might require renegotiation of the contract price or it might involve a risk-sharing formula (e.g., losses or gains outside of the window are equally shared by both parties).

A risk-sharing contract may be requested by the supplier when payment is in the buyer's currency. The adjusted future cost to the buyer in this situation is identical to the adjusted future cost when payment is in the supplier's currency and risk sharing is used. This encompasses risk sharing done in conjunction with payments in both the supplier's and the buyer's currencies.

An examination of practical results suggests the potential benefits of incorporating exchange rate forecast information into the decision process. For example, if a supply management professional has forecast information that strongly indicates the buying power of the U.S. dollar is going to decrease over the time horizon of interest, it would be advantageous to pay in U.S. dollars. However, if the supplier raises the U.S. dollar price to incorporate a substantial risk premium or insists in payment in its own currency, the buyer would be well advised to pay in the supplier's currency and hedge the risk using currency futures or by buying forward. On the other hand, if the buyer anticipates that the value of the U.S. dollar is likely to fluctuate minimally, that buyer might want to use risk sharing and make payments in whatever currency the supplier prefers.

The discussion presented in this chapter is intended to familiarize supply management professionals with the mechanics of macrolevel and microlevel exchange rate management techniques and demonstrate the potentially significant benefits of using exchange rate management strategies in global supply management. Exchange rate considerations are an important facet of international procurement. The astute supply management professional can save an organization a great deal of money and make that organization's products or services more competitive in the international marketplace through the wise use of exchange rate information.

International Countertrade: Linking Purchases to Markets

IBM presently sources many goods and services from coastal regions of China. In the past these regions were considered low cost, but that is no longer the case. In order to maintain a low-cost footprint, IBM will progressively move further inland over time. Unfortunately, often a supplier—whether qualified or not qualified—can be found in developing regions. In order to source from these low-cost regions, a great deal of supplier development and investment of resources is required. Part of this investment may require receiving some supplier output as repayment of investment. This requires a form of countertrade and has become common in developing countries and regions.

In simple terms, *countertrade* is any type of transaction that requires, as a condition of the original sale, that goods be bought either as a trade-balancing mechanism or as full or partial payment for the goods sold. Some form of countertrade frequently is used in international business transactions (*ISM Glossary*, 2006). The ancient business of trading a few sheep for a head of cattle has grown into a sophisticated worldwide trading activity with significant economic impact on the worldwide market. Starting with simple trading of goods and services for other goods and services, the modern concept of countertrade has evolved into a diverse set of activities that include five distinct types of trading arrangements: barter, counterpurchase, offset, compensation or buyback, and switch trading.

Barter. *Barter* is the act of exchanging one good or service for another, as distinct from trading by use of currency. Barter is also a form of countertrade sometimes used in international business (*ISM Glossary*, 2006). Barter, though seemingly the simplest trading arrangement, has become an unpopular countertrade arrangement. For example, if goods are not exchanged simultaneously, one party ends up financing the other party for a time. Barter also risks one of the parties ending up with goods that the trading partner does not want and cannot use. For these reasons and others, barter is viewed by multinationals as the most restrictive countertrade arrangement and is primarily used for one-time deals with the least creditworthy or trustworthy trading partners.

Counterpurchase. *Counterpurchase* is a form of countertrade that occurs when an organization agrees to purchase a specified volume of materials from a country in return for a sale made to that country (*ISM Glossary*, 2006). It occurs when an organization agrees to buy a certain amount of materials from a country to which a sale is made. For example, China-based organization X sells some of its products to British-based organization Y. In exchange for the sale, China-based organization X agrees to spend some set percentage of the monetary proceeds of the sale importing goods produced by international country Y. Both trading partners agree to pay for the majority of their purchases in cash and fulfill their individual sales obligations to each other over a specified time frame, usually less than five years.

Offset. *Offset* is another form of countertrade, similar to counterpurchase, in which a supplier selling to a foreign organization agrees to purchase a certain quantity of materials from the country it supplies. The primary difference is that the supplier can fulfill its obligation by purchasing from any business organization in the country it supplies. This term is primarily used in the sale of military hardware (*ISM Glossary*, 2006). Offset arrangements are most frequently performed with centrally planned economies.

Compensation or Buyback. *Compensation* or *buyback* occurs when an organization in one country builds a plant in or supplies technology, equipment, training or other services to another country and agrees to take a certain percentage of the plant's output as partial payment for the investment (*ISM Glossary*, 2006). For example, Occidental Petroleum Corp. negotiated a $20 million deal with Russia in which Occidental would build several plants there and receive ammonia over a 20-year period as partial payment.[11]

Switch Trading. *Switch trading* is the use of a specialized, third-party trading house in a countertrade arrangement, in which switch traders frequently trade countertrade credits for cash, and the trading house sells the credits to another country that needs the goods (*ISM Glossary*, 2006). For example, organization X concludes a countertrade arrangement with some country in which it agrees to take some amount of goods as partial payment. Organization X cannot really use and does not want these goods. Therefore, organization X sells to a third-party trading house at a discount the contract for these goods. The third-party trading house in turn finds another organization that can use these goods and resells the contract at a profit. These arrangements frequently substitute trade credits, spendable later, for cash. Often times, switch trading is used by organizations or countries to correct various types of trade imbalances. For example, if Hungary sells chemicals to France at a certain value, France credits Hungary's trade account for a certain amount of trade credits, which Hungary can use in the future to buy some prespecified French goods. If Hungary does not want to buy French goods, it sells these credits to a third-party trading house at a discount. The third-party trading house then searches for a country or organization that needs to buy French goods and sells the credits to this country or organization at a small profit.

Implementation of a countertrade strategy could be very confusing for the multinational organization embarking upon countertrade for the first time. Furthermore, a complicated process such as countertrade must be well managed in order to be successful. This requires an understanding of the options available to and actions required by each multinational organization as it implements countertrade arrangements.

Regulations Pertaining to Restricted Parties and Countries

Trade sanctions against a specific country are sometimes imposed in order to punish that country for some action. An embargo, a severe form of externally imposed isolation, is a blockade of all trade by one country on another. For example, the United States has had an embargo against Cuba for more than 40 years. Recently, China has been pressured to consider a trade embargo against Libya in response to the genocide in Darfur. Also, the European Union has approved a trade embargo against Iran regarding some very technical nuclear-related equipment.

Though there are usually few trade restrictions within countries, international trade is usually regulated by governmental quotas and restrictions, and often taxed by tariffs. Tariffs are usually on imports, but sometimes countries may impose export tariffs or subsidies. All of these are called trade barriers. If a government removes all trade barriers, a condition of free trade exists. A government that implements a protectionist policy establishes trade barriers.

The *fair trade movement*, also known as the *trade justice movement*, promotes the use of labor, environmental and social standards for the production of commodities, particularly those exported from emerging to developed nations. It involves the practice of providing a fair and reasonable price for goods and services produced, as well as the meeting of certain social and environmental standards during the production of those goods and/or services.

Standards may be voluntarily adhered to by importing organizations, or enforced by governments through a combination of employment and commercial law. Proposed and practiced fair trade policies vary widely, ranging from the commonly adhered to prohibition of goods made using slave labor to minimum price support schemes such as those for coffee in the 1980s. Nongovernmental organizations also play a role in promoting fair trade standards by serving as independent monitors of compliance with fair-trade labeling requirements.

Summary

Implementing an international supply management strategy can be confusing, and needs to be managed well to be successful. There is a process flow of activities that a multinational organization might use to establish an international sourcing practice. First, an organization must formally plan for sourcing internationally. Multinational organizations should establish a formal decision-making process before embarking on international sourcing by starting with a comprehensive analysis of needs. This needs analysis process should identify procurement requirements, strategies for fulfilling these requirements and their relationship to overall corporate and competitive goals. The needs analysis process should lead to the identification of commodities and components suitable for international sourcing. An assessment of material needs is best done under the direction of a corporate supply management department using a program planning and budgeting (i.e., bottom up) approach. Such an approach forecasts material needs at the plant and divisional levels and aggregates up to the corporate level. This approach offers the advantages of comprehensiveness of planning and a fuller participation in the planning process by various organizational units.

Second, it is necessary to create an international sourcing function at the organization level responsible for gathering information, such as potential suppliers and price trends, and evaluating opportunities for purchasing internationally. Because international sourcing involves long supply lines, pipeline inventories, difficult negotiation, cultural differences and communication problems, expertise in domestic supply management does not readily translate to international sourcing. For example, supply management professionals must become familiar with the electronic transfer of information abroad, customs regulations, international modes of transportation and the effect of exchange rate fluctuations on the cost of imported merchandise.

Third, a supply management organization embarking upon international sourcing should obtain cross-functional support for this effort. Because of the length of transportation supply lines associated with sourcing abroad and the resulting increased potential for supply disruptions, an organization engaged in international sourcing needs to achieve a higher level of interaction with and support from other functional areas such as manufacturing, design engineering and quality assurance. Achieving such a high level of cross-functional support is a challenge to most organizations. The following activities might prove useful, and in many cases are essential.

- Soliciting the direct involvement by top management;
- Formally integrating international sourcing within the organization's corporate strategy;

- Designing organizational structures that support the cross-functional planning approach, such as matrix or product line structures; and

- Emphasizing the value chain approach to materials management by adopting a systems view of the procurement, manufacturing, service and transportation functions.

Fourth, the manufacturing, service and supply management planning and control activities need to be precisely integrated. Such integration of planning and control systems is critical to the success of an international sourcing initiative For example, organizations engaged in just in time deliveries and manufacturing need to fine tune their inbound logistics systems to use global sources while keeping pipeline inventory levels at a minimum. Careless or inadequate planning will exacerbate problems, create excessive inventory and/or out-of-stock positions, destabilize production plans and ruin customer service levels.

Fifth, organizations engaging in international sourcing have a variety of alternatives available for organizing personnel. Which alternative is chosen depends on factors such as the level of specialized international buying knowledge available within the organization and the expected volume and frequency of international purchases. Some of those alternatives are: (1) cross-border supply management office, (2) import broker or merchant, (3) global trading organization and (4) assignment within the corporate supply management function. Each of these alternatives has advantages and disadvantages.

Sixth, the corporate supply management group should be continually evaluating the strategy and practice of buying from abroad given changing business conditions. Each organization should have a portfolio of suppliers, both domestic and international. The allocation of supply management dollars among this portfolio should be in accordance with organizational strategies aimed at cost reduction, technological leadership and quality competitiveness, and others. Careful consideration should be given to the length of supply management contracts and the degree of integration needed with the supplier's operations system.

Key Points

1. The supply management cycle for international sourcing has several distinct phases: (1) recognition of need; (2) source identification; (3) source evaluation; (4) evaluation of quotations; (5) subjective analysis and negotiation; and (6) contract management.

2. Negotiating prices and terms with an international supplier poses additional challenges to the supply management professional. Cultural and language barriers exacerbate the difficult task of negotiating with a supplier.

3. A sound organizational infrastructure is essential in order to provide for the establishment of responsibilities, reporting, coordination and effective communication.

4. The costs associated with inbound movements, such as transportation, warehousing, materials handling, packaging, documentation, in-transit inventory carrying, order processing and communications costs, are almost always higher in global sourcing compared to domestic sourcing.

5. Exchange rates volatility can impact the price paid for imported merchandise when payment is in the supplier's currency and there is a lag between the time the contract is signed and payment is made.

6. The modern concept of countertrade has evolved into a diverse set of activities that include five distinct types of trading arrangements: (1) barter, (2) counterpurchase, (3) offset, (4) buyback and (5) switch trading.

Endnotes

Chapter 1

1. Kim Langfield-Smith and Michelle R. Greenwood, "Developing Co-operative Buyer-Supplier Relationships: A Case Study of Toyota," *Journal of Management Studies* 35(3) (1998): 331–53.

2. This section is based on the following book: Joseph R. Carter, *Purchasing: Continued Improvement Through Integration* (Homewood, IL: Business One Irwin, 1993).

3. This includes the inventory control component that includes materials management, disposition/investment recovery, distribution, receiving and warehousing.

4. Lisa M. Ellram and W. Tate, "Managing and Controlling the Services Supply Chain at Intuit," *PRACTIX*, (Tempe, AZ: CAPS Research, August 2004), available at www.capsresearch.org.

5. Lisa M. Ellram, "Total Cost of Ownership: An Analysis Approach for Purchasing," *International Journal of Physical Distribution & Logistics Management* 26(5) (1995): 4–23.

6. This section is based the following research study: J. Carter, P. Carter, R. Monczka, J. Blascovich, T. Slaight and W. Markham, *Succeeding in a Dynamic World: Supply Management in the Decade Ahead* (Tempe, AZ: CAPS Research, 2007).

7. A. Agarwal, S. Narain and A. Sharma, "Green Politics," *Global Environmental Negotiations* 1(vi) (1999): 409. Also, Abigail R. Jahiel, "The Organization of Environmental Protection in China," *The China Quarterly* 156 (December 1998): 757–87.

Chapter 2

1. J.P. Womack, D.T. Jones and D. Roos, *The Machine That Changed the World* (New York: Rawson Associates, 1990).

2. An interesting view of the conventional corporate budgeting processes is provided by Michael C. Jensen in his article, "Corporate Budgeting Is Broken; Let's Fix It," *Harvard Business Review* (November 2001): 94–101.

3. Maureen Donnelly and Gary Prod, "Budget in the Right Stuff," *Purchasing Today* ® 10(2) (February 1999): 12.

4. The notation of e-RFx refers to an electronic request for x, where x is a quotation, proposal or information. The electronic communications process is used to shorten cycle time and reduce transaction costs (*ISM Glossary*, 2006).

5. Outsourcing is the use of a supplier to provide a product or service that the organization may have the ability to supplement internally. See R.M. Monczka, J.R. Carter, W.J. Markham, J.D. Blascovich, and T.H. Slaight, "Outsourcing Strategically for Sustainable Competitive Advantage" (Tempe, AZ: CAPS Research, 2005), available at www.atkearney.com/shared_res/pdf/Strat_Outsourcing_S.pdf.

6. Commodity exchanges include the Chicago Board of Trade; Chicago Mercantile Exchange; Sugar and Cocoa Exchange, New York; COMEX, Division of New York Mercantile Exchange; International Petroleum Exchange; Kansas City Board of Trade; London International Financial Futures Exchange; Minneapolis Grain Exchange; Singapore International Monetary Exchange; and the Sidney Futures Exchange, to name a few.

7. Commodity terminology includes: *Future* — A future is a contract for the purchase or sale and delivery of a commodity at some future date. *Spot price* — A spot price is the price for a commodity if it is purchased for cash on an exchange.

8. Pirkko Ostring, "A Quantitative Supplier Financial Analysis," *Inside Supply Management* ® 14(12) (December 2003): 6. This article also provides detailed information about the use of a number of financial ratios to evaluate suppliers.

9. Select the company of interest, and then select Research, Financial Results, Ratio Analysis. A wide variety of ratios are available.

10. W. Frawley, G. Piatetsky-Shapiro and C. Matheus, "Knowledge Discovery in Databases: An Overview," *AI Magazine*, (Fall 1992): 213–28.

11. D. Hand, H. Mannila, and P. Smyth, *Principles of Data Mining* (Cambridge, MA: MIT Press, 2001).

Chapter 3

1. The problems with traditional methods of overhead allocation and how these can be improved on are presented in depth in Lisa M. Ellram, "The ABCs of Fair Costing," *Purchasing Today* ® 10(3) (March 1999): 39–42, www.ism.ws/pub/ISMMag/ismarticle.cfm?ItemNumber=11361.

2. For a more in-depth explanation of ABCM, see Gary Cokins, *Activity-Based Cost Management: An Executive's Guide* (New York: John Wiley & Sons, 2001), or the classic work by Robert S. Kaplan and Robin Cooper, *Cost and Effect: Using Cost Management Systems to Drive Profitability and Performance* (Boston: Harvard Business School Press, 1997).

3. See also Ellram, "The ABCs of Fair Costing."

4. *Controlling Costs by Controlling Your Inventory*, ISM Program Handbook (April 1, 2004), www.ism.ws/education/SatSemDetail.cfm?ItemNumber=5846.

5. This point was made many decades go by quality gurus like W. Edwards Deming, Joseph M. Juran and Genichi Taguchi. Yet, many firms have not embraced the criticality of the quality imperative.

6. For a more complete description of the role of supply management in target costing, see Lisa M. Ellram, "The Execution of Target Costing in U.S.-firms: Theory Versus Practice," *Journal of Supply Chain Management* 42(2) (2006): 13–21; or M.E. Smith, L. Buddress and A.R. Raedels, "The Strategic Use of Supplier Price and Cost Analysis," ISM's 91st Annual International Supply Management Conference, www.ism.ws/eduaction/pastconfdetail.cfm?itemnumber=14522.

7. Improved cost estimating for purchased services is noted as one of the significant areas of opportunity for improvement by L.E. Ellram, W.L. Tate and C. Billington, "Services Supply Management: The Next Frontier for Improved Organizational Performance," *California Management Review* 49(4) (Spring 2007): 43–57.

8. H.J. Figgie, *The Harry Figgie Guide to Cost Reduction and Profit Improvement* (Chicago: Probus Publishing, 1988), p. 12.

9. FASB Statement No. 13, *Accounting for Leases*, www.fasb.org/project/leases.shtml.

10. Ibid.

Chapter 4

1. The sourcing decision is a modern day derivative of the traditional make-buy decision. For the sake of simplicity, the term *outsourcing* is used in this chapter as synonymous with sourcing.

2. J.R. Carter, A. Maltz, E. Maltz and T. Yan, "How Procurement Managers View Low Cost Countries and Geographies: A Perceptual Mapping Approach," *International Journal of Physical Distribution and Logistics Management* (2008).

3. J.R. Carter and R. Narasimhan, "Is Purchasing Really Strategic?" *International Journal of Purchasing and Materials Management* 32(1) (Winter 2008): 20–8.

4. Insourcing is the act of bringing inside an organization a function that has been performed outside the organization (i.e., outsourced) (*ISM Glossary*, 2006).

5. Charlet Atkinson, "Supply Chains Dependency," *Inventory Management Review* (February 1, 2006), www.inventorymanagementreview.org/2006/02/supply_chains_d.html.

6. Nanette S. Levinson and Minoru Asahi, "Cross-National Alliances and Interorganizational Learning," *Organizational Dynamics* 24(2) (Autumn 1995): 50–63.

7. Aimin Yan and Barbara Gray, "Bargaining Power, Management Control, and Performance in United States-China Joint Ventures: A Comparative Case Study," *The Academy of Management Journal* 37(6) (1994): 1478–517.

8. Carter, Maltz and Yan, "How Procurement Managers View Low Cost Countries."

9. Ibid.

10. The United Nations Convention on Contracts for the International Sale of Goods (CISG) is a treaty offering a uniform international sales law that, as of 2006, had been ratified by 70 countries that account for three-quarters of all world trade. The CISG is one of the more successful international conventions, due in no small part to its flexibility in allowing contracting states the option of taking exception to specified articles. This flexibility was instrumental in convincing sovereign states with disparate legal traditions to subscribe to an otherwise uniform code. A key point of controversy had to do with whether a contract requires a written memorial to be binding. In formerly communist countries, contracts were not valid unless written, but in most Western nations oral contracts are accepted. Western nations thus had no objection to signing, and many formerly communist nations exercised their ability to exclude those articles relating to oral contracts, enabling them to sign as well. Notably, the UK is not among the countries that have ratified the CISG, despite being a leading jurisdiction for the choice of law in international commercial contracts.

11. Andrew C. Revkin, "178 Nations Reach a Climate Accord; U.S. Only Looks On," *The New York Times* (July 24, 2001), p. A1.

Chapter 5

1. A. Flynn, "Eastman Kodak Company Worldwide Sourcing Practice," *PRACTIX* (Tempe, AZ: CAPS Research, 2005).

2. A sample of such a procedural form used by an anonymous high tech company can be found on page 89 of Robert M. Monczka, Robert J. Trent and Robert B. Handfield, *Purchasing and Supply Chain Management* (Cincinnati: South-Western College Publishers, 2005).

3. F. Hedderich, R. Giesecke and D. Ohmsen, "Identifying and Evaluating Chinese Suppliers: China Sourcing Practices of German Manufacturing Companies," *PRACTIX* (Tempe, AZ: CAPS Research, 2006).

4. See the case of the organization that procured testing equipment involving nine suppliers: Zhachui Wu and Thomas Y. Choi, "Supplier-Supplier Relationships in the Buyer-Supplier Triad: Building Theories From Eight Case Studies," *Journal of Operations Management* 24(1) (December 2005): 27–52.

5. Contract solicitation/RFP can be found at http://communitydispatch.com/Contract_Solicitation__RFP_Announcements_84/index.shtml.

6. See NILS INSource, http://insource.nils.com/gloss/GlossaryTerm.asp?tid=2147.

7. K.M. Eisenhardt, "Agency Theory: An Assessment and Review," *Academy of Management Review* 14(1) (1989): 57–74. Also see Monczka, Trent, Handfield, *Purchasing and Supply Chain Management*, p. 159.

8. See http://converge.com/.

9. There are many basic economics books that address this argument. One example is D. Salvatore, *Principles of Economics* (New York: McGraw-Hill, 2003).

10. V. Mabert and T. Schoenherr, "An Online RFQ System: A Case Study," *PRACTIX* (Tempe, AZ: CAPS Research, 2001).

11. Joseph L. Cavinato, Anna E. Flynn and Ralph G. Kauffman, *The Supply Management Handbook*, 7th ed. (New York: McGraw-Hill, 2006), pp. 647–48.

12. G.C. Bogert and D.H. Oaks, *Cases and Texts on the Law of Trusts*, (New York: Foundation Press, 1978).

13. Cavinato, Flynn and Kauffman, *The Supply Management Handbook*, pp. 649–50.

14. See www.thefreedictionary.com/general+damages/.

15. More discussion on service contracting can be found in "Purchasing Services" by L. Yelvington, in *Supply Management Handbook*, eds. J.L. Cavinato, A.F. Flynn and R.G. Kauffman (New York: McGraw-Hill, 2006).

16. B.J. Wright, "Construction Services Supply Management," in *Supply Management Handbook*, eds. Joseph L. Cavinato, Anna E. Flynn and Ralph G. Kauffman (New York: McGraw-Hill, 2006).

17. The AIA has now created a Microsoft Word-based software platform from which all forms can be downloaded. More information can be found at www.aia.org/docs_default/.

18. Some examples of SOW can be found at http://sparc.airtime.co.uk/users/wysywig/sow_mt.htm and www.intrex.net/ssp/example.htm.

19. T. Choi, J. Budny and N. Wank, "Intellectual Property Management: A Knowledge Supply Chain Perspective," *Business Horizons* 47(1) (January 2004): 37–44.

20. Ibid.

21. See www.cisg.law.pace.edu/cisg/text/treaty.html.

22. See www.davislogic.com/homeland_security.htm and www.whitehouse.gov/infocus/homeland/.

23. See www.whitehouse.gov/homeland/book/sect2.pdf.

Chapter 6

1. Sun Tzu, *Art of War* (Boston: Shambhala, 2005).

2. Adapted from Michael Porter, *Competitive Strategy: Creating and Sustaining Superior Performance* (New York: Free Press, 1998) and Michael Porter, "How Competitive Forces Shape Strategy," *Harvard Business Review* (March-April 1979).

3. See www.alcoa.com/global/en/news/news_detail.asp?newsYear=2000&pageID=17837-2001 _03_20.

4. See www.businessweek.com/bwdaily/dnflash/june2000/sw00620.htm.

5. See www.whitehouse.gov/news/releases/2001/05/20010518-6.html.

6. See www.bls.gov/ppi/ppivcpi.pdf.

7. See www.bls.gov/.

8. See www.hoovers.com/.

9. See www.businessweek.com/, www.barrons.com/, www.purchasing.com/, and www.wsj. com/.

10. See www.electronicsweekly.com/ and www.chemweek.com/.

11. See www.dnb.com/.

12. See www.sec.gov/.

13. See www.indiandata.com/.

14. See www.foxter.dk/default.aspx.

15. Geert Hofstede and Gert Jan Hofstede, *Culture and Organizations: Software of the Mind*, 2nd ed. (New York: McGraw-Hill, 2004); Geert Hofstede, "The Interaction Between National and Organizational Value Systems," *Journal of Management Studies* (22) (195): 347–57; and Geert Hofstede, "The Cultural Relativity of the Quality of Life Concept," *Academy of Management Review* (9): 389–98.

16. Robert House, Paul Hanges, Mansour Javidan, Peter Dorfman, and Vipin Gupta, *Culture, Leadership, and Organizations: The GLOBE Study of 62 Societies* (Thousand Oaks, CA: Sage, 2004) and Mansour Javidian and Robert House, "Cultural Acumen for Global Managers: Lessons from Project GLOBE," *Organizational Dynamics* 29(4): 289–305.

17. C. Rossetti and T. Choi, "On the Dark Side of Strategic Sourcing: Experiences From the Aerospace Industry, *Academy of Management Executive* 19(1) (2005): 46–61.

18. See www.tech.mit.edu/Bulletins/nafta.html and www.fas.usda.gov/itp/Policy/NAFTA/ nafta.asp.

19. See http://autorepair.about.com/cs/generalinfo/a/aa080401a.htm.

20. See www.ism.ws/pubs/InfoEdge/InfoEdgeIssue.cfm?ItemNumber=10158.

21. Ibid.

Chapter 7

1. Emily Kay, "Ways to Measure Supplier Performance," *Purchasing* (March 3, 2005).

2. Elizabeth Corcoran, "Dell Moves Outsourced Jobs Back to U.S. Shores," *Forbes.com* (April 28, 2004); www.msnbc.msn.com/id/4853511/.

3. Wendy L. Tate and Lisa M. Ellram, "Services Spend Management: Outsourcing/Offshoring Your Services Spend," *CAPS Research* (August 31, 2006): 4.

4. R. Narasimhan, "An Analytical Approach to Supplier Selection," *Journal of Purchasing and Materials Management* 19(4) (Winter 1983): 27–32.

5. Monczka, Trent and Handfield, *Purchasing and Supply Chain Management*, p. 302.

6. Ellram and Tate, "Managing and Controlling the Services Supply Chain."

7. R. Austin, "Ford Motor Company: Supply Chain Strategy," *Harvard Business School Case 699-198* (March 3, 1999).

8. See www.businesslink.gov.uk/bdotg/action/layer?topicId=1073920782&r.s=sl.

9. T.Y. Choi and J.L. Hartley, "An Exploration of Supplier Selection Practices Across the Supply Chain," *Journal of Operations Management* 14(4) (1996): 333–44.

10. Ibid.

11. Kay, "Ways to Measure Supplier Performance."

12. Bayer Business Services, *Supreme Supplier Relationship Management*, www.procurement. bayer.com/procmt/byc_cpstd_en.nsf.

13. See www.tools.p.agentrics.com/MyGenSource/sso/login.jsp.

14. The ABB Group, *Supplier performance assessment*, www.abb.com/cawp/seitp161/ e4d128636caefa9ec12569ac0032f1c2.aspx.

15. Kay, "Ways to Measure Supplier Performance."

16. Ibid.

17. T.Y. Choi and Y. Hong, "Unveiling the Structure of Supply Networks: Case Studies in Honda, Acura, and DaimlerChrysler," *Journal of Operations Management* 20(5) (September 2002): 469–93.

18. This story was collected during a trip taken by the author to China.

19. A detailed discussion of the emergence of ISO can be found in *Friendship Among Equals* by Jack Latimer (Geneva, Switzerland: International Organization for Standardization, 1997). Chapters of this book available from www.iso.org/iso/friendship_equals/. Also see www.iso.org/iso/en/ aboutiso/introduction/index.html#four.

20. See www.iso.org/iso/iso_catalogue/catalogue_tc/catalogue_detail.htm?csnumber=42180.

21. See www.appliedmaterials.com/.

22. See www.boeing.com/companyoffices/doingbiz/supplier_portal/spm_pamphlet.pdf.

23. See www.kodak.com/US/plugins/acrobat/en/corp/purchasing/EK_SQP_brochure_revised _2005.pdf.

24. J.L. Hartley and T.Y. Choi, "Supplier Development: Customers as a Catalyst of Process Change," *Business Horizon* 39(4) (July-August): 37–44.

25. Jeffrey Liker and Thomas Y. Choi, "Building Deep Supplier Relationships," *Harvard Business Review* (December 1, 2004).

26. This model is built largely based on work by the following authors: Hartley and Choi, "Supplier Development" and Daniel R. Krause, Robert B. Handfield and Thomas V. Scannell, "An Empirical Investigation of Supplier Development: Reactive and Strategic Processes," *Journal of Operations Management* 17(1) (1998): 39–58.

27. Hartley and Choi, "Supplier Development."

28. M.R. Leenders and D.L. Blenkhorn, *Reverse Marketing: The New Buyer-Supplier Relationship*, (New York: Free Press, 1988).

29. David Upton and Diane Long, "Shanghai Volkswagen," *Harvard Business School Case 696-092* (1996).

30. J. Carbone, "Lucent's Supply Chain Focus Fattens Margins," *Purchasing Magazine* (2002).

31. See www.allpar.com/neon/design.html.

32. Lisa M. Ellram and Thomas Y. Choi, *Supply Management for Value Enhancement*. (Tempe, AZ: National Association of Purchasing Management, 2000).

33. Michael A. McGinnis, "Value Analysis and Value Engineering: Basics," Workshop Presentation at ISM's 90th Annual International Supply Management Conference, May 2005.

34. L. Cappell, "Deere Sir: Former Honda Sourcing Boss Brings Ideas to New Field," *Automotive News* 28(1) (1988).

Chapter 8

1. Liker and Choi, "Building Deep Supplier Relationships."
2. This idea of socially complex and nonimitable practice being a competitive advantage has been applied to supply chain management. See M. Rungtusanatham, F. Salvador, C. Forza, and T. Choi, "Supply-Chain Linkages and Operational Perspective: A Resource-Based-View Perspective," *International Journal of Operation & Production Management* 23(9) (2003): 1084–99. The underlying idea comes from the following sources: J. Barney, "Firm Resources and Sustained Competitive Advantage," *Journal of Management* 17(1) (1991): 99–120 and B. Wernerfelt, "A Resource-Based View of the Firm," *Strategic Management Journal* 5(1984): 171–80.
3. See www.adobe.com/products/breeze/index.html.
4. T. Choi, "Reverse Marketing in Asia: A Korean Experience," *Business Horizons* (September-October, 1999): 34–40.
5. See www.acquisition.gov/bestpractices/bestpcont.html.
6. See http://oig.hhs.gov/publications/docs/workplan/2008/Work_Plan_FY_2008.pdf.
7. Lisa Ellram and Wendy Tate, "Bank of America: Services Purchasing and Outsourcing," *PRACTIX* (Tempe, AZ: CAPS Research, 2006).
8. Upton and Long, "Shanghai Volkswagen."
9. John Greenwald, "Inside the Ford/Firestone Fight," Time (May 29, 2001).
10. See http://findarticles.com/p/articles/mi_m0EIN/is_2000_Oct_31/ai_66573722.
11. See www.sandia.gov/supplier/.
12. See www.mdicareers.com/itstaffing/diversity.htm.
13. The following Web site has small business size standard matched to standard industrial classification (SIC) codes: www.sba.gov/regulations/siccodes/.
14. Hokey Min, Mark E. Nissan and Michael A. McGinnis, "Gaining Competitive Advantages Through a Supplier Diversity Program," *PRACTIX* (Tempe, AZ: CAPS Research, December 1999).
15. The registration process can be found in the CCR Handbook at www.ccr.gov/handbook.aspx.
16. See www.dhhs.gov/osdbu/faqs/.
17. Detailed benefits of SB certification for CA can be found at www.pd.dgs.ca.gov/smbus/sbcert.htm.
18. *Focus On…Supplier Diversity Programs 2007*, (Tempe, AZ: CAPS Research, November 2007).
19. D.R. Krause and R.B. Handfield, *Focus Study: Developing a World-Class Supply Base*. (Tempe, AZ: Center for Advanced Purchasing Studies, 1999).
20. T.Y. Choi, , K.J. Dooley and M. Rungtusanatham, "Supply Networks and Complex Adaptive Systems: Control Versus Emergence," *Journal of Operations Management*, 19 (2001): 351–66.
21. T.Y. Choi and D.R. Krause, "The Supply Base and Its Complexity: Implications for Transaction Costs, Risks, Responsiveness, and Innovation," *Journal of Operations Management*, 24 (2006): 637–52.

22. The three managerial issues introduced here are discussed in Choi and Krause (2006) as key elements to consider when managing a supply base as a system. It also corresponds with the three variables in the NK model explained by Kauffman; see Stuart A. Kauffman, *The Origins of Order: Self-Organization and Selection in Evolution* (New York: Oxford University Press, 1993) and Stuart A. Kauffman, *At Home in the Universe: The Search for the Laws of Self-Organization and Complexity* (New York: Oxford University Press, 1996).

23. J. Richardson, "Parallel Sourcing and Supplier Performance in the Japanese Automobile Industry," *Strategic Management Journal* 14(5) (1993): 339–50.

24. Krause and Handfield, *Developing a World-Class Supply Base.*

25. Thomas Y. Choi, A. Wu, Lisa Ellram, and B.R. Koka, "Supplier-Supplier Relationships and Their Implications for Buyer-Supplier Relationships," *IEEE Transactions on Engineering Management*, 49(2) (May 2002): 119–30; Wu and Choi, "Supplier-Supplier Relationships in the Buyer-Supplier Triad."

26. Ibid.

27. Charles Scott and Roy Westbrook, "New Strategic Tools for Supply Chain Management," *International Journal of Physical Distribution & Logistics Management* 21(1) (1991): 23–33.

28. Ibid.

29. Ibid.

Chapter 9

1. Richard L. Daft, *Management* (Mason, OH: South-Western College Publishing, 2007) See also E.W. Szwajkowski, "The Myths and Realities of Research on Organizational Misconduct," in *Research in Corporate Social Responsibility*, ed. J.E. Post (Greenwich, CT: JAI Press, 1986).

2. M. Bhandarkar and T. Alvarez-Rivero, "From Supply Chains to Value Chains: A Spotlight on CSR," in *Industrial Development for the 21st Century: Sustainable Development Perspectives*, United Nations Department of Economic and Social Affairs (New York: United Nations, 2007).

3. See www.ism.ws/SR/content.cfm?ItemNumber=4767&navItemNumber=5503.

4. C.R. Carter and M.M. Jennings, *Purchasing's Contribution to the Socially Responsible Management of the Supply Chain* (Tempe, AZ: Center for Advanced Purchasing Studies, 2000).

5. See www.ism.ws/SR/content.cfm?ItemNumber=4767&navItemNumber=5503.

6. See www.bsr.org/.

7. Ibid.

8. See www.wbcsd.ch/templates/TemplateWBCSD5/layout.asp?type=p&MenuId=MQ&doOpen=1&ClickMenu=LeftMenu.

9. Ibid.

10. See http://web.amnesty.org/pages/ec-globalcompact9principles-eng/.

11. See www.ism.ws/files/SR/SRPrioritizationTool.xls.

12. See www-03.ibm.com/procurement/proweb.nsf/ContentDocsByTitle/United+States~Supply+chain+social+responsibility.

13. The *ISM Glossary* (2006) defines sharp practice as an indirect misrepresentation, unscrupulous shrewdness, deceit or trickery, just short of actual fraud. Such actions are usually designed for short-term gain, but typically act to the detriment of good long-term supplier relations based on honesty, truth and respect.

14. See www.philips.com/About/Investor/businessprinciples/index.page/.

15. The details of these issues are discussed at www.ism.ws/tools/content.cfm?ItemNumber=4740.

16. Institute for Supply Management™, *Ethics & Social Responsibility*, www.ism.ws/tools/content.cfm?ItemNumber=4740&navItemNumber=15959.

17. J. Baranowski, "Ethical Practices, Drivers & Barriers: Supply Professionals and Their Peers Weigh In," a presentation made based on a survey of supply management professionals and their peers on behalf of the ISM Ethical Standards Committee (May 8, 2006).

18. Ibid.

19. Ibid.

20. Cheryl Dahle, "Gap's New Look: The See-Through," *Fast Company* 86 (September 2004): 69, www.gapinc.com/public/SocialResponsibility/socialres.shtml.

21. Baranowski, "Ethical Practices, Drivers & Barriers."

22. Ibid.

23. Ibid.

24. See www.nokia.com/A4230065/.

25. See www.nokia.com/NOKIA_COM_1/Corporate_Responsibility/CR_Report_2005/pdfs/nokia_cr_report_2005.pdf.

26. Ibid.

27. "Supply Chain Management for Environmental Improvement," in *Greening the Supply Chain*, Pollution Prevention Resource Center (PPRC) (2004), www.pprc.org/pubs/grnchain/eval.cfm.

28. D.E. Boyd, R.E. Spekman and P. Werhane, "Corporate Social Responsibility and Global Supply Chain Management: A Normative Perspective," *Darden Graduate School of Business Working Paper Series*, Paper No. 04-05 (2004).

29. Craig. R. Carter, "Purchasing Social Responsibility—What Is It and Where Should We Be Headed?" in *Supply Management Handbook*, eds. Joseph L. Cavinato, Anna E. Flynn, and Ralph G. Kauffman (New York: McGraw-Hill, 2006), pp. 393–407.

30. Helen Pohlig, *Legal Aspects of Supply Management*, (Tempe, AZ: Institute for Supply Management™, 2008).

31. M. Barratt, M. Savidge and R. Barratt, "Sarbanes-Oxley: Overall Good Intentions but Is It Good for Your Supply Chain?" *Supply Chain Management Review* (November 2006): 34–40.

32. See www.dot.gov/mission.htm.

33. See www.dot.gov/summary.htm.

34. See www.dot.gov/mission.htm.

35. See www.dhs.gov/xcommtrad/.

36. See www-03.ibm.com/industries/government/doc/jsp/indseg/all/f/index.jsp?P_SolutionArea=25546909&desc=yes.

37. See www-03.ibm.com/industries/government/doc/content/resource/thought/1610011109.html?g_type=pspot.

38. See www-03.ibm.com/industries/government/doc/jsp/indseg/all/f/index.jsp?P_SolutionArea=25546909&desc=yes.

39. See www.epa.gov/.

40. See http://en.wikipedia.org/wiki/International_environmental_law.

41. See http://en.wikipedia.org/wiki/World_Summit_on_Sustainable_Development.

42. See www.epa.gov/.

43. John Yuva, "Earn More From Dispositioned Assets," *Inside Supply Management* ® 18(8) (2007): 21–3.

44. Mary Siegfried, "Sourcing for Sustainability," *Inside Supply Management* ® 18(3) (2007): 26–7.

45. See www.isri.org/am/Template.cfm?Section=Home1.

46. See www.recycle.net/trade/r09936.html.

Chapter 10

1. J.R. Carter, R. Narasimhan and S.K. Vickery, "International Sourcing for Manufacturing Operations, Research Monograph No. 3, Operations Management Association," (1988); available through Naman and Schneider Associates Group, Waco, Texas.

2. Ibid.

3. A request for proposal (RFP) is an invitation for suppliers, through a bidding process, to submit a proposal on a specific product or service. An RFP typically involves more than the price. The RFQ is used where discussions are not required with bidders (mainly when the specifications of a product or service are already known), and price is the main or only factor in selecting the successful bidder. RFQ may also be used as a step prior to going to a full-blown RFP to determine general price ranges.

4. R. Narasimhan and J.R. Carter, "Organization, Communication and Co-ordination of International Sourcing," *International Marketing Review* 7(2) (1990): 6–20.

5. J.R. Carter, T. Slaight and J. Blascovich, "The Future of Supply Management: Technology, Collaboration, Supply Chain Design," *Supply Chain Management Review* 11(7) (2007): 44–50.

6. A list or system of duties imposed by a government on "selected" imported or exported goods. For example, governments frequently place additional "special tariffs" on certain categories of agricultural goods.

7. J.R. Carter and R. Narasimhan, "Purchasing in the International Marketplace: Principles, Practices, and Implications for Operations," *Journal of Purchasing and Materials Management* 26(3) (Summer 1990): 2–11.

8. J. Cavinato and R. Strang, "Logistics and Supply Megatrends–2007," presented at ISM's Annual International Supply Management Conference, Las Vegas, NV (May 2007).

9. International Chamber of Commerce (October 2007), www.iccwbo.org/incoterms.

10. J.R. Carter and S.K. Vickery, "Managing Volatile Exchange Rates in International Purchasing," *Journal of Purchasing and Materials Management* 24(4) (Winter 1988): 13–20 and J.R. Carter and S.K. Vickery, "Currency Exchange Rates: Their Impact on Global Sourcing," *The Journal of Purchasing and Materials Management* 25(3) (Fall 1989): 19–25.

11. J.R. Carter and J. Gagne, "The Do's and Don'ts of International Countertrade," *Sloan Management Review* 29(3) (Spring 1988): 31–38.

References

Chapter 1

Cavinato, J.L., A.E. Flynn and R.G. Kauffman (Eds.). *The Supply Management Handbook*, 7th ed., McGraw-Hill, New York, 2006.

Carter, J., P. Carter, R. Monczka, J. Blascovich, T. Slaight and W. Markham. *Succeeding in a Dynamic World: Supply Management in the Decade Ahead*, CAPS Research, Tempe, AZ, 2007.

Flynn, A., M.L. Harding, C.S. Lallatin, H.M. Pohlig and S.R. Sturzl (Eds.). *ISM Glossary of Key Supply Management Terms*, 4th ed., Institute for Supply Management™, Tempe, AZ, 2006.

Leenders, M.R., H.E. Fearon, A.E. Flynn, and P.F. Johnson. *Purchasing and Supply Management*, McGraw-Hill/Irwin, New York, 2006.

Chapter 2

Leenders, M.R., P.F. Johnson, A.E. Flynn and H.E. Fearon. *Purchasing and Supply Management*, McGraw-Hill/Irwin, New York, 2006.

Monczka, R.M., W.J. Markham, J.R. Carter, J.D. Blascovich and T.H. Slaight. *Outsourcing Strategically for Sustainable Competitive Advantage*, Joint Research Project of CAPS Research and A.T. Kearney, Tempe, AZ, 2005.

Ostring, P. "A Quantitative Supplier Financial Analysis," *Inside Supply Management*®, (14:12), December 2003, p. 6.

Chapter 3

Cokins, G. *Activity-Based Cost Management: An Executive's Guide*, John Wiley & Sons, New York, 2001.

Ellram, L.E., W.L. Tate and C. Billington. "Services Supply Management: The Next Frontier for Improved Organizational Performance," *California Management Review*, (49:4), Spring 2007, pp. 43–57.

Ellram, L.M. "The ABCs of Fair Costing," *Purchasing Today*®, (10:3), March 1999, pp. 39–42.

Ellram, L.M. "The Execution of Target Costing in U.S.-firms: Theory Versus Practice," *Journal of Supply Chain Management*, (42:2), 2006, pp. 13–21.

Flynn, A., M.L. Harding, C.S. Lallatin, H.M. Pohlig and S.R. Sturzl (Eds.). *ISM Glossary of Key Supply Management Terms*, 4th ed., Institute for Supply Management™, Tempe, AZ, 2006.

Kaplan, R.S., and R. Cooper. *Cost and Effect: Using Cost Management Systems to Drive Profitability and Performance*, Harvard Business School Press, Boston, 1997.

Smith, M.E., L. Buddress and A.R. Raedels. *The Strategic Use of Supplier Price and Cost Analysis*, ISM's 91st Annual International Supply Management Conference, 2006.

Chapter 4

Flynn, A., M.L. Harding, C.S. Lallatin, H.M. Pohlig and S.R. Sturzl (Eds.). *ISM Glossary of Key Supply Management Terms*, 4th ed., Institute for Supply Management™, Tempe, AZ, 2006.

Chapter 5

Allen, S., and A. Chandrashekar. "Outsourcing Services: The Contract Is Just the Beginning." *Business Horizons*, (43:2), 2000, pp. 25–34.

Bragg, S.M. *Outsourcing: A Guide to Selecting the Correct Business Unit, Negotiating the Contract, Maintaining Control of the Process*, John Wiley & Sons, New York, 1998.

Cavinato, J.L., A.E. Flynn and R.G. Kauffman (Eds.). *The Supply Management Handbook*, 7th ed., McGraw-Hill, New York, 2006.

Cox, A., and I. Thompson. *Contracting for Business Success*, Thomas Telford, London, 1998.

Degraeve, Z., and F. Roodhooft. "Improving the Efficiency of the Purchasing Process Using Total Cost of Ownership Information: The Case of Heating Electrodes at Cockerill Sambre S.A.," *European Journal of Operational Research*, (112:1), 1999, pp. 42–53.

Domberger, S. *The Contracting Organization: A Strategic Guide to Outsourcing*, Oxford University Press, Oxford, 1998.

Emiliani, M. "Business-to-Business Online Auctions: Key Issues for Purchasing Process Involvement," *Supply Chain Management*, (5:4), 2000, pp. 176–186.

Flynn, A., M.L. Harding, C.S. Lallatin, H.M. Pohlig and S.R. Sturzl (Eds.). *ISM Glossary of Key Supply Management Terms*, 4th ed., Institute for Supply Management™, Tempe, AZ, 2006.

Jackson, J.H., and D. Sciglimpaglia. "Toward a Role Model of the Organizational Purchasing Process," *Journal of Purchasing and Materials Management,* (10), 1974, pp. 68.

Mabert, V.A., and T. Schoenherr. "An Online RFQ System: A Case Study," *PRACTIX*, CAPS Research, Tempe, AZ, 2001.

Mabert, V.A., and T. Schoenherr. "Evolution of Online Auctions in B2B E-Procurement," *PRACTIX*, CAPS Research, Tempe, AZ, 2001.

Meier, R.L., M.R. Williams and R.B. Singley. "The Strategic Role of Reverse Auctions in the Quotation and Selection Process," *PRACTIX*, CAPS Research, Tempe, AZ, 2002.

Nishiguchi, T. *Strategic Industrial Sourcing: The Japanese Advantage.* Oxford University Press, New York, 1994.

Perry, J.H., and C.A. Perkins. "Operationalizing Quality Considerations in the Purchasing Process," *International Journal of Purchasing and Materials Management*, (28:1), 1992, pp. 10.

Ruzicka, M. "Invoiceless Procurement: Streamlining the Receiving and Billing Processes," *PRACTIX*, CAPS Research Tempe, AZ, 2000.

Smeltzer, L., and M. Ruzicka. "Electronic Reverse Auctions: Integrating the Tool With the Strategic-Sourcing Process," *PRACTIX*, CAPS Research, Tempe, AZ, 2000.

Chapter 6

Bulow, J.I., and P. Klemperer. "Auctions Versus Negotiations," *American Economic Review*, (86), 1996, pp. 180–194.

Kaufmann, L., and C.R. Carter. "Deciding on the Mode of Negotiation: To Auction or Not to Auction Electronically," *The Journal of Supply Chain Management*, (40:2), 2004, pp. 15–26.

Lewicki, R.J., and J.A. Litterer. *Negotiation*, Richard D. Irwin, Homewood, IL, 1985.

Metty, T., R. Harlan, Q. Samelson, T. Moore, T. Morris, R. Sorensen, A. Schneur, O. Raskina, R. Schneur, J. Kanner, K. Potts and J. Robbins. "Reinventing the Supplier Negotiation Process at Motorola," *Interfaces*, (35:1), 2005, pp. 7–23.

Pruitt, D.G. *Negotiation Behavior*, Academic Press, New York, 1981.

Raiffa, H. *The Art and Science of Negotiation*, Harvard University Press, Cambridge, 1982.

Raiffa, H., J. Richardson and D. Metcalfe. *Negotiation Analysis: The Science and Art of Collaborative Decision Making*, Harvard University Press, Cambridge, 2003.

Reyes-Moro, A., J.A. Rodríguez-Aguilar, M. López-Sánchez, J. Cerquides and D. Gutierrez-Magallanes. "Embedding Decision Support in E-sourcing Tools: Quotes, a Case Study," *Group Decision and Negotiation Journal*, (12:4), 2003, pp. 347–355.

Rubin, J.Z., and B.R. Brown. *The Social Psychology of Bargaining and Negotiation*, Academic Press, New York, 1975.

Smeltzer, L.R., J. Manship and C.L. Rossetti. "An Analysis of the Integration of Strategic Sourcing and Negotiation Planning," *The Journal of Supply Chain Management*, (39:4), 2003, pp. 16–25.

Weber, C.A., J.R. Current and A. Desai. "Non-Cooperative Negotiation Strategies for Vendor Selection," *European Journal of Operational Research*, (108:1), 1998, pp. 208–223.

Chapter 7

Carter, P.L., J.R. Carter, R.M. Monczka, T.H. Slaight and A.J. Swan. "The Future of Purchasing and Supply: A Ten-Year Forecast," *Journal of Supply Chain Management*, (36:1), 2000, pp. 14–26.

Flynn, A., M.L. Harding, C.S. Lallatin, H.M. Pohlig, and S.R. Sturzl (Eds.). *ISM Glossary of Key Supply Management Terms*, 4th ed., Institute for Supply Management™, Tempe, AZ, 2006.

Handfield, R.B., D.R. Krause, T.V. Scannell and R.M. Monczka. "Avoid the Pitfalls in Supplier Development," *Sloan Management Review*, (41:2), 2000, pp. 37–49.

Hartley, J.L., and T.Y. Choi. "Supplier Development: Customers as a Catalyst of Process Change," *Business Horizons*, July-August 1996, pp. 37–44.

Krause, D.R., and L.M. Ellram. "Critical Elements of Supplier Development: The Buying-Firm Perspective," *European Journal of Purchasing and Materials Management*, (3:1), 1997, pp. 21–31.

Krause, D.R., and L.M. Ellram. "Success Factors in Supplier Development," *International Journal of Physical Distribution and Logistics Management*, (27:1), 1997, pp. 39–52.

Krause, D.R., R. Handfield and T.V. Scannell. "An Empirical Investigation of Supplier Development: Reactive and Strategic Processes," *Journal of Operations Management*, (17:1), 1998, 39–58.

Monczka, R., R. Trent and R. Handfield. *Purchasing and Supply Chain Management*, 2nd ed., South-Western, Cincinnati, OH, 2002.

Patterson, J.L., and K.M. Amann. "Strategic Sourcing: A Systematic Approach to Supplier Evaluation, Selection, and Development," *PRACTIX*, CAPS Research, Tempe, AZ, 2000.

Pearson, J.N., and L.M., Ellram. "Supplier Selection and Evaluation in Small Versus Large Electronics Firms," *Journal of Small Business Management*, (33:4), 1995, pp. 53–65.

Stuart, I., and D. McCutcheon. "The Manager's Guide to Supply Chain Management," *Business Horizons*, (43:2), 2000, pp. 35–44.

Trent, R.J., and R.M. Monczka. "Achieving Excellence in Global Sourcing," *MIT Sloan Management Review*, (47:1), 2005, pp. 24–32.

Verma, R., and M.E. Pullman. "An Analysis of the Supplier Selection Process," *International Journal of Management Science*, (26:6), 1998, pp. 739–750.

Chapter 8

Brennan, R., and P.W. Turnbull. "Adaptive Behavior in Buyer-Supplier Relationships," *Industrial Marketing Management*, (28:5), 1999, pp. 481–495.

Dwyer, F.R., P.H. Schurr and S. Oh. "Developing Buyer-Seller Relationships," *Journal of Marketing*, (51), April 1987, pp. 11–27.

Dyer, J.H., D.S. Cho and W. Chu. "Strategic Supplier Segmentation: The Next 'Best Practice' in Supply Chain Management," *California Management Review*, (40:2), 1998, pp. 57–77.

Handfield, R.B., G.L. Ragatz, K.J. Petersen and R.M. Monczka. "Involving Suppliers in New Product Development," *California Management Review*, (42:1), 1999, pp. 59–82.

Heide, J.B. "Interorganizational Governance in Marketing Channels," *Journal of Marketing*, (58), January 1994, pp. 71–85.

Heide, J.B., and G. John. "Alliances in Industrial Purchasing: The Determinants of Joint Action in Buyer-Supplier Relationships," *Journal of Marketing Research*, (27:1), 1990, pp. 24–36.

Heide, J.B., and R.L. Stump. "Performance Implications of Buyer-Supplier Relationships in Industrial Markets: A Transaction Cost Explanation," *Journal of Business Research*, (32:1), 1995, pp. 57–66.

Helper, S. "How Much Has Really Changed Between U.S. Automakers and Their Suppliers?" *Sloan Management Review*, (32:4), 1991, pp. 15–28.

Kanter, R.M. "Collaborative Advantage: The Art of Alliances," *Harvard Business Review*, (72:4), 1994, pp. 96–108.

Leenders, M.R., and D.L. Blenkhorn. *Reverse Marketing: The New Buyer-Supplier Relationship*, Free Press, New York, 1988.

Liker, J.K., and T.Y. Choi. "Building Deep Supplier Relationships," *Harvard Business Review*, (82:12), 2004, pp. 104–113.

Lyons, T.F., A.R. Krachenberg and W. Henke, Jr. "Mixed Motive Marriages: What's Next for Buyer-Supplier Relations?" *Sloan Management Review*, (31:3), 1990, pp. 29–36.

Ogden, J.A., and M.W. McCarter. "Better Buyer-Supplier Relationships Through Supply Base Reduction and Supplier Performance Measurement," *PRACTIX*, CAPS Research, Tempe, AZ, 2004.

Chapter 9

Carter, C.R. *Ethical Issues in Global Buyer-Supplier Relationships*, CAPS Research Focus Studies, Tempe, AZ, 1998.

Carter, C.R. "Ethical Issues in International Buyer-Supplier Relationships: A Dyadic Examination," *Journal of Operations Management*, (8:2), 2000, pp. 191–208.

Carter, C.R. "Purchasing and Social Responsibility: A Replication and Extension," *The Journal of Supply Chain Management*, (40:4), 2004, pp. 4–16.

Carter, C.R., and J.R. Carter. "Interorganizational Determinants of Environmental Purchasing: Initial Evidence From the Consumer Products Industries," *Decision Sciences*, (29:3), 1998, pp. 659–684.

Carter, C.R., and M. Dresner. "Environmental Purchasing for Indirect Materials," *PRACTIX*, CAPS Research, Tempe, AZ, 1999.

Carter, C.R., and M.M. Jennings. *Purchasing's Contribution to the Socially Responsible Management of the Supply Chain*, CAPS Research Focus Studies, Tempe, AZ, 2000.

Carter, C.R., R. Kale and C.M. Grimm. "Environmental Purchasing and Firm Performance: An Empirical Investigation," *Transportation Research Part E: Logistics and Transportation Review*, (36:3), 2000, pp. 219–228.

Chrisman, J.J., and A.B. Carroll. "Corporate Responsibility—Reconciling Economic and Social Goals," *Sloan Management Review*, (25:2), 1984, pp. 59–65.

Drumwright, M.E. "Socially Responsible Organizational Buying: Environmental Concern as a Noneconomic Buying Criterion," *Journal of Marketing*, (58), July 1994, pp. 1–19.

Gattiker, T. "Environmental Management: Purchasing's Cross-Functional Role," *PRACTIX*, CAPS Research, Tempe, AZ, 2006.

Mintzberg, H., R. Simons and K. Basu. "Beyond Selfishness," *Sloan Management Review*, (44:1), 2002, p. 67.

Narasimhan, R. *Environmental Supply Chain Management*, CAPS Research Focus Studies, Tempe, AZ, 1998.

Philip, K., and N. Lee. *Corporate Social Responsibility: Doing the Most Good for Your Company and Your Cause*, John Wiley & Sons, New York, 2004.

Rondinelli, D.A., and T. London. "How Corporations and Environmental Groups Cooperate: Assessing Cross-Sector Alliances and Collaborations," *Academy of Management Executive*, (17:1), 2003. pp. 61–76.

Vogel, D. *The Market for Virtue: The Potential and Limits of Corporate Social Responsibility*, Brookings Institution Press, Washington, DC, 2005.

Waddock, S., and N. Smith. "Corporate Responsibility Audits: Doing Well by Doing Good," *Sloan Management Review*, (41:2), 2000, pp. 75–83.

Chapter 10

Cavinato, J., and R. Strang. *Logistics and Supply Megatrends–2007*, presented at ISM's Annual International Supply Management Conference, Las Vegas, NV, May 2007.

Czinkota, M.R., I.A. Ronkainen and M.H. Moffett. *International Business*, 7th ed. South-Western Publishing, Mason, OH, 2005.

Index